LAROUSSE
SPANISH
VERBS

21, RUE DU MONTPARNASSE 75283 PARIS CEDEX 06

Concept

Gabrielle Lloret Linares

Publishing manager

Janice McNeillie

Translation and adaptation

Sinda López

Data management

Monika Al Mourabit, Aurélie Prissette

Data conversion and typesetting

Anna Bardon, Fabrice Jansen

© 2007, Larousse

21, rue du Montparnasse F-75283 Paris Cedex 06

www. larousse-bilingues.com

ISBN 978-2-0354-2142-5

Sales: Houghton Mifflin Company, Boston

CONTENTS

CONTENTS

INTRODUCTION

People learning Spanish come up against two major difficulties which need to be tackled before they can begin to communicate. They need to possess a certain amount of vocabulary and master the grammar, of which verbs form an essential part.

The conjugation of Spanish verbs is considered difficult because there are so many irregular verbs. In order to begin to learn them, it is essential to group them in types rather than just in an alphabetical listing. This is what we aim to do in *Larousse Spanish verbs* by presenting tables of irregular verbs in a logical and systematic manner which can serve as models. The verb tables, as well as showing all forms of the verb, highlight all irregular forms so that these are obvious to the eye and can be more easily learnt. As an additional aid, each table is preceded by a box giving a grammatical summary of the irregularities and any exceptions.

This approach of full verb tables plus grammatical summary helps you to gain an understanding of how certain verbs conjugate so that you can learn the rules and apply them to verbs which belong to the same group, without worrying about having to learn each one individually.

In order to be able to do this, you will need to be familiar with certain basic grammatical terms that are used in the Verb table section and the Grammar summary. The Glossary at the front of the book provides these terms together with their definitions so that you can consult them whenever you need to.

Each definition is accompanied by examples which help to clarify the term.

The sections of the book

1. Verb tables

The choice of a model verb is based on the criteria that it should be in current use (except the few cases of defective verbs which are not often used but which have a peculiar conjugation worth noting) as well as be representative enough of the verbs which follow the same conjugation. The characteristics or rules shared by a group of verbs which conjugate the same are listed in the summary box preceding each verb table.

The verb forms are not preceded by the subject personal pronouns yo, tú, él, etc., but rather by their grammatical label of 1st person singular, 2nd person singular, etc. The reason for this lies in the fact that Spanish verbs already contain the information relating to person in the conjugated ending. This is one of the main characteristics of the Spanish verb which differs from English and is explained more fully at the very beginning of the Grammar summary.

■ Classification principles

All Spanish verbs, both regular and irregular, are divided into three groups which are easily identifiable by their infinitive ending.

First group: stem + ar: amar, soñar, estar...

Second group: stem + er: temer, hacer, poder...

Third group: stem + ir: partir, pedir, decir...

Three different stems can be used to form the simple tenses.

- The stem of the verb, without the infinitive ending, is used to form the present indicative, the present subjunctive, the imperative, the imperfect indicative, the gerund and the past participle.
- The whole of the infinitive form is used to form the future indicative and the conditional.
- The 3rd person plural of the preterit drops the final syllable to provide us with the third stem which is used to form the imperfect and the future subjunctive.

So, the term 'irregular verb' will be used to denote all stem-changing verbs that involve one or more vowel or consonant changes.

The classification of the model verb tables is based on two principles.

■ First classification principle

An irregular stem must not be confused with a simple spelling change.

This type of spelling change merely exists to preserve the sound and is not classified as an irregularity. Spelling changes apply equally to regular and irregular verbs.

For example, in order to keep the sound of the last consonant of the stem, many verbs undergo a spelling change. Apart from this small change, these verbs are perfectly regular.

In addition, an irregular verb can combine an irregular stem with standard spelling changes. The thing that makes it count as irregular though is the fact that it has an irregular stem. Verbs which share the same irregularity are grouped in a way that makes it easier to distinguish between what is a true irregularity and what is just a standard

Ending	Model verb	Spelling change
-car	sacar (13)	c › qu before e
-cer	vencer (14)	c › z before a, o
-cir	zurcir (15)	c › z before a, o
-zar	cazar (16)	z › c before e
-ger	proteger (17)	g › j before a, o
-gir	dirigir (18)	g › j before a, o
-gar	llegar (19)	g › gu before e
-guir	distinguir (20)	gu › g before a, o
-quir	delinquir (21)	qu › c before a, o

spelling change, which all helps when trying to learn irregular verbs.

Example: the verb trocar (29) is irregular because the vowel of the stem changes to a diphthong, ue, in some moods, tenses and persons. In addition, the stem contains the [k] sound which in Spanish is written with a c when it precedes a and o, but which changes to qu before e and i. This verb, therefore, undergoes a spelling change when the ending begins with e or i. This spelling change is only a consequence of the irregularity of the verb.

■ Second classification principle

The most irregular verbs, that is those with several stem changes, are the ones that are most frequently used in day-to-day Spanish conversation and it is therefore essential to learn them from the start. These are the basic verbs: ser, estar, haber, tener, poder, poner, ir, saber... These are the auxiliary verbs or verbs which are used in that role to express things such as existence and belonging, as well as the modal verbs which express ideas such as possibility, permission or intention.

The way we have classified the model verbs follows an incremental pattern starting with the least irregular and working up to those which have the most irregularities, including four defective verbs at the end. It seems logical that these highly irregular verbs, which have many irregularities in common – especially the sixteen verbs which have a strong preterit – should be placed at the

end. Their position at the end of the verb tables reflects their degree of irregularity and should be viewed as an indication of their difficulty and prominence in the Spanish language.

■ General classification

The verb tables have been classified as follows:

1. Three prefectly regular verbs representing each of the three groups.

2. Regular verbs with a consonant or vowel change in the stem.

3. Irregular verbs in order of increasing irregularity. These verbs may also undergo standard spelling changes.

4. Defective verbs.

2. Grammar summary

The Spanish verb system also needs an organized grammar and this is provided in the form of systematic, easy-access sections in the Grammar summary. This summary deals with the formation of simple and compound tenses as well as the role of the verb in relation to other parts of speech such as personal pronouns, object pronouns, adverbial phrases and prepositions.

There were two main objectives in deciding how to present this summary so that it complements the verb tables:

- to provide a coherent view of the verb system. Each subject is presented systematically under the standardized headings of 'Formation' (for example, of a mood like the subjunctive) and 'Usage' (showing how the subjunctive is used in Spanish).

- to try and draw out any comparisons and differences between the way Spanish and English verbs function.

3. Dictionary of verb structures

This dictionary builds on the points described in the Grammar summary, in particular the topics towards the end which show the importance of the verb + preposition structures so prevalent in Spanish. The dictionary includes many of the verbs which are followed by a preposition and gives examples and translations.

4. Index

The Index of verbs includes over 9,500 Spanish verbs each followed by a number which refers them to the relevant model. The crossreferencing system is kept simple as the number after the verb links you directly to the verb table number at the top of each page, thus bringing together these two sections of the book.

Larousse Spanish verbs, as well as offering an innovative and efficient classification of verbs, provides a complete picture of the Spanish verb, which makes learning them so much easier.

The structure and presentation of the book guarantee the user a systematic explanation of the Spanish verb system as well as providing easily-accessible answers to any specific queries.

Verb number given in the index for verbs following this conjugation.

Summary box about the verb table. Irregularities of verb conjugation shown.

TROCAR

29

Irregular verb

The o of the *stem** becomes ue in the present indicative, the present subjunctive, and in the imperative.
Compare tr**ue**cas (the *stress** falls on the vowel of the stem) and troc**a**ron (where the stress falls on the vowel of the *ending**).

In addition to this, the c becomes qu in the preterit (1st p. sing.), the present subjunctive, and the imperative.
■ *Diphthong** o › ue
■ Spelling c › qu before e

Characteristics or rules shared by a group of verbs which conjugate the same.

	Impersonal
	Simple forms
Infinitive	trocar
Gerund	trocando
Past participle	trocado

Personal moods

	Indicative		Subjunctive	
	Simple forms	Compound forms	Simple forms	Compound forms
	Present	**Perfect**	**Present**	**Past**
1st p. sing.	trueco	he trocado	trueque	haya trocado
2nd p. sing.	truecas	has trocado	trueques	hayas trocado
3rd p. sing.	trueca			haya trocado
1st p. plur.	trocamos			hayamos trocado
2nd p. plur.	trocáis			hayáis trocado
3rd p. plur.	truecan			hayan trocado
	Imperfect	**Past perfect**	**Imperfect**	**Past perfect**
1st p. sing.	trocaba	había trocado	trocara	hubiera trocado
	trocabas	habías trocado	trocaras	hubieras trocado
	trocaba	había trocado	trocara	hubiera trocado
	trocábamos	habíamos trocado	trocáramos	hubiéramos trocado
	trocabais	habíais trocado	trocarais	hubierais trocado
3rd p. plur.	trocaban	habían trocado	trocaran	hubieran trocado
	Preterit	**Past anterior**		
1st p. sing.	troqué	hube trocado	trocase	hubiese trocado
2nd p. sing.	trocaste	hubiste trocado	trocases	
3rd p. sing.	trocó	hubo trocado	trocase	
	trocamos	hubimos trocado	trocásemos	
	trocasteis	hubisteis trocado	trocaseis	
	trocaron	hubieron trocado	trocasen	
	Future	**Future perfect**	**Future**	**Future perfect**
1st p. sing.	trocaré	habré trocado	trocare	hubiere trocado
2nd p. sing.	trocarás	habrás trocado	trocares	hubieres trocado
3rd p. sing.	trocará	habrá trocado	trocare	hubiere trocado
1st p. plur.	trocaremos	habremos trocado	trocáremos	hubiéremos trocado
2nd p. plur.	trocaréis	habréis trocado	trocareis	hubiereis trocado
3rd p. plur.	trocarán	habrán trocado	trocaren	hubieren trocado
	Present conditional	**Conditional perfect**		
1st p. sing.	trocaría	habría trocado		
2nd p. sing.	trocarías	habrías trocado		
3rd p. sing.	trocaría	habría trocado		
1st p. plur.	trocaríamos	habríamos trocado		
2nd p. plur.	trocaríais	habríais trocado		
3rd p. plur.	trocarían	habrían trocado		

Irregular stem shown.

Conjugations split into simple and compound forms.

Two forms of the conjugation of the subjunctive given.

Spelling changes shown.

Imperative

Present	Forms using the subjunctive stem
trueca (tú)	trueque (él, ella, usted)
trocad (vosotros)	troquemos (nosotros)
	truequen (ellos, ellas, ustedes)

45

9

GLOSSARY

■ Tonic accent or stress

Basically, the purpose of the tonic accent is to show which vowel or syllable should be stressed. The accent is expressed as a rise in pitch. This is a dynamic accent, and is referred to as 'stress.'

- In words ending in a vowel, n or s, the stress falls on the penultimate syllable.

In manzana (*apple*), the stress falls on the 2nd syllable, za. This means it is stressed more than the other two.

In comía (*he/she ate*), the accent shows the i vowel is stressed and creates a *hiatus*.

- In words ending in a consonant (except n or s), the stress falls on the last syllable: cantar (*to sing*), Madrid, pastel (*cake*)...

In pájaro (*bird*), the stress, which falls on the first syllable, is shown by a written accent. The accent is used to mark irregular cases. Otherwise, according to the general rule, the stress should fall on the last syllable but one which here would be ja.

■ Aspect

The unfolding action described by the form of the verb – the beginning, duration and end – is called 'aspect.' Each event is described by the tense of the verb (present, past, future).

Pablo comía.
Pablo was eating.

Pablo había comido.
Pablo had eaten.

The difference between these two examples isn't to do with the tense (as both are in the past) but rather the aspect, i.e. the description of whether an action is taking place, **Pablo comía**, or whether it's already finished, **había comido**.

■ Auxiliary

An 'auxiliary' is a verb used to form compound tenses and the *passive voice*.

- In Spanish, compound tenses are formed with the auxiliary haber.

He dormido.
I slept.

- The passive voice is formed with two auxiliaries, ser and estar.

La puerta es cerrada por el profesor.
The door is closed by the teacher.

El rey está acompañado por la reina.
The king is accompanied by the queen.

■ Ending

The ending of a word (noun, pronoun, article, adjective, verb) gives you the grammatical information. Together with the *stem* (which contains the sense), it constitutes an inflected form. (See *Inflection*.)

Libros (*books*).

In libros, os indicates the gender (masculine) and the number (plural).

In a verb, the ending shows the *mood*, the tense and the person.

Canto (*I sing*).

In this verb, the ending o shows the mood (indicative), the tense (present) and the person (1st person singular).

■ Diphthong

A diphthong is a compound vowel (two consequent vowels) which changes in tone as it is sounded. It constitutes a single syllable. There are two types.

- The diphthong which starts with a closed vowel and ends in an open vowel.

Empiezo.
I start.

With ie, we start with the *yod*, or closed semivowel [j], and end in the open vowel [e].

- The diphthong which starts with the most open vowel, [a], and ends with the yod.

Hay.
There is.

With ay, we start with [a], the open vowel, and end with the yod.

■ Enclisis

Enclisis is the technical term given to tagging a word onto

the end of another word. Adding a pronoun onto the end of a verb, for example, is a common case in point. The unit constitutes a single word with the stress applying to only one syllable. The most common cases in Spanish relate to the infinitive, the gerund and the imperative.

Estaba escribiéndole.
I was writing to him.

The enclitic pronoun le is added onto the gerund escribiendo.

Inflection

An inflection consists in joining the *stem* of a word, the part which carries the meaning, and an *ending* which contains the grammatical information.
In a noun, the ending shows its function in the sentence.
In a verb, the ending provides information on the mood, the tense, the person. This is one of the ways in which Spanish differs from English.

Escribo.
I write.

In the Spanish, the single verbal form contains the whole information.

Hiatus

When two vowels appear together, there are two possible ways of pronouncing them: either as a hiatus, or a *diphthong*.
- If each vowel forms a separate syllable, it is a hiatus.

Escribía: es/cri/bí/a
He was writing.

- If two vowels joined together form a syllable (compound syllable), this is called a diphthong.

Puedo: pue/do
I can.

Impersonal

'Impersonal' can refer to a *mood* or a verb, and generally, to anything that does not have a person as the subject.
Verbal forms which are not attributable to a person such as the infinitive, the gerund and the past participle, are classified as impersonal.

concluir
to conclude
Llueve.
It is raining.

Romance languages

Romance languages are a related group of languages which have a common origin in spoken Latin but have evolved differently. This family includes French, Spanish, Portuguese, Italian, Rumanian, Catalan, Galician, Provençal...

Speaker

The speaker is the person who is trying to communicate something be it orally, in writing or through gestures. In the verb system, the reference point is always the speaker.

Cantabais.
You were singing.

I, the speaker, speaking from my point of view in the present, am saying that you were singing.

Verbal phrase

A phrase is a group of words formed by at least a noun (nominal phrase), a verb (verbal phrase) or an adverb (adverbial phrase). Usage is what makes these known as 'fixed expressions.'
ser de
to be from, to be made of
Verb + preposition de
haber que
to need, must
Verb + relative pronoun que

Mood

The position adopted by the *speaker* of the action being described is known as 'mood.'
When forming a verb, choosing the mood is the first stage before the *aspect*, the *voice*, the tense and the person.

Es verdad que has venido.
It is true that you have come.

No me gusta que hayas venido.
I am not happy that you have come.

In the two statements above, it isn't the action that is different. In both cases 'he/she has come.' The difference is held in the position adopted by the speaker.

In the 1st example, he states a fact without implying anything or including his own opinion. This is the indicative mood.

In the 2nd example, he takes up a position (no me gusta or me gusta). This is the subjunctive mood.

■ Impersonal mood

The *impersonal* mood applies to verb forms which do not take a personal subject and which do not show who the speaker is via the inflection. These are: the infinitive, the gerund (or present participle) and the past participle.

In English, an impersonal verb always takes the impersonal pronoun 'it': *It is raining./It rained.*

In Spanish, impersonal verbs are conjugated in the third-person singular which gives the tense. The impersonal subject is assumed in the meaning of the verb: Llueve./Llovió.

■ Preposition

A preposition serves to link two parts of a sentence. Without prepositions, many words would not be able to be linked directly. The choice of preposition clarifies the relationship between the two parts of the sentence. (See p. 130-131.)

El reloj de mi hermana.
My sister's watch.

De here serves to link two nouns: el reloj and mi hermana.

Voy a París.
I am going to Paris.

A here links the verb and the proper noun (which acts as an adverbial phrase).

Se lo diré a mi hermana.
I'll tell my sister.

A here links the verb and the noun phrase (the indirect object of the verb).

■ Main clause

A simple sentence contains only one clause.
A complex sentence contains at least two clauses.

The main clause is a basic sentence containing a subject and a verb. It can stand alone. A *subordinate clause* is dependent on the main clause.

Es improbable.
A simple sentence which stands alone. (subject + verb).

It is unlikely.

Es improbable que lo haya hecho.
Main clause (which could stand alone) compared to the subordinate clause (which couldn't).

It is unlikely that he has done it.

■ Subordinate clause

A subordinate clause is always dependent on the *main clause*. Subordinate clauses can never stand alone.

Es improbable que lo haya hecho.
Subordinate clause dependent on the main clause.

It is unlikely that he has done it.

Que lo haya hecho is not a standalone sentence.

■ Stem

The stem is the part which contains the meaning of a word.

To form a verb, you take the stem and add an *inflected ending* which gives the grammatical information.

Together they form a conjugated verb.

Verbs can be conjugated from several stems.

Canto *I sing*
From the stem cant, the present indicative, the present subjunctive, and the preterit are formed.

Cantaré *I will sing*
From the stem cantar (the infinitive), the future and the future conditional are formed.

Cantaron *They sang*
From the stem canta, the imperfect subjunctive (which has two possible forms ra and se) and the future subjunctive are formed.

The more irregular a verb is, the greater the range of stems used to conjugate it.

poder → pued, pod, pud, podr

■ Direct/indirect object

An 'object' is a word or clause which is dependent on a verb in a sentence. Verbs can have a direct object (where no *preposition* is necessary) or an indirect object (with a preposition).

Hoy pienso terminar.
I'm going to finish today.

Hoy quiero terminar.
I want to finish today.

The object, terminar, is the object of the verb quiero. It is a direct complement of the verb as there is no preposition. This is known as a 'direct object.'

Pienso en las vacaciones.
I'm thinking about my vacation.

Las vacaciones is the object of the verb pienso.
The object here is introduced by the preposition en. This is known as an 'indirect object.'

■ Active voice

A verb can have an 'active voice' or a 'passive voice.' The form depends on the relationship between the verb, the subject and the object. When the subject of the verb is the person or thing performing the action, or in other words is the agent of the verb, the verb is an 'active verb' or is in the 'active voice.'

Marta come la manzana.
Present tense
Marta eats the apple.

Marta ha comido la manzana.
Present perfect tense
Marta ate the apple.

Marta is the subject of the verb and the agent of the action come.
This action relates to the object, la manzana, which is the 'patient' or the noun affected by the action of the verb.

■ Passive voice

When the subject of the verb is affected by the action, or the action is done to it, the verb is in the 'passive voice.'

La puerta es cerrada por Marta.
The door is closed by Marta.

La puerta is the subject of the verb es cerrada.
Here, the subject is affected by an action performed by the agent of the verb, Marta.

■ Yod

When the vowel /i/ forms part of a *diphthong*, it can be pronounced in two ways. This is referred to as a 'yod' or 'semivowel' or 'semiconsonant.'
- When it is the first letter of the diphthong, it functions as a semiconsonant: **empiezo** (*I start*).
- When it is the second letter of the diphthong, it functions as a semivowel: **hay** (*there is*).

Verb

tables

CLASSIFICATION OF MODEL VERBS

A M A R

Regular verb

Regular verbs have a *stem** which doesn't change, and to which inflected *endings** are added: am**an**, am**ábamos**, am**aron**, am**éis**...

In the indicative, the future simple and the present conditional are formed from the infinitive. In the subjunctive, the imperfect and the future are formed from the 3rd person plural of the indicative preterit. (See p. 124.)

■ 1st type

Impersonal mood		
	Simple forms	Compound forms
Infinitive	amar	haber amado
Gerund	amando	habiendo amado
Past participle	amado	

Personal moods			
	Indicative		**Subjunctive**
	Simple forms	Compound forms	Simple forms	Compound forms

	Indicative Simple forms	**Indicative** Compound forms	**Subjunctive** Simple forms	**Subjunctive** Compound forms
	Present	**Perfect**	**Present**	**Past**
1st p. sing.	amo	he amado	ame	haya amado
2nd p. sing.	amas	has amado	ames	hayas amado
3rd p. sing.	ama	ha amado	ame	haya amado
1st p. plur.	amamos	hemos amado	amemos	hayamos amado
2nd p. plur.	amáis	habéis amado	améis	hayáis amado
3rd p. plur.	aman	han amado	amen	hayan amado
	Imperfect	**Past perfect**	**Imperfect**	**Past perfect**
1st p. sing.	amaba	había amado	amara	hubiera amado
2nd p. sing.	amabas	habías amado	amaras	hubieras amado
3rd p. sing.	amaba	había amado	amara	hubiera amado
1st p. plur.	amábamos	habíamos amado	amáramos	hubiéramos amado
2nd p. plur.	amabais	habíais amado	amarais	hubierais amado
3rd p. plur.	amaban	habían amado	amaran	hubieran amado
	Preterit	**Past anterior**		
1st p. sing.	amé	hube amado	amase	hubiese amado
2nd p. sing.	amaste	hubiste amado	amases	hubieses amado
3rd p. sing.	amó	hubo amado	amase	hubiese amado
1st p. plur.	amamos	hubimos amado	amásemos	hubiésemos amado
2nd p. plur.	amasteis	hubisteis amado	amaseis	hubieseis amado
3rd p. plur.	amaron	hubieron amado	amasen	hubiesen amado
	Future	**Future perfect**	**Future**	**Future perfect**
1st p. sing.	amaré	habré amado	amare	hubiere amado
2nd p. sing.	amarás	habrás amado	amares	hubieres amado
3rd p. sing.	amará	habrá amado	amare	hubiere amado
1st p. plur.	amaremos	habremos amado	amáremos	hubiéremos amado
2nd p. plur.	amaréis	habréis amado	amareis	hubiereis amado
3rd p. plur.	amarán	habrán amado	amaren	hubieren amado
	Present conditional	**Conditional perfect**		
1st p. sing.	amaría	habría amado		
2nd p. sing.	amarías	habrías amado		
3rd p. sing.	amaría	habría amado		
1st p. plur.	amaríamos	habríamos amado		
2nd p. plur.	amaríais	habríais amado		
3rd p. plur.	amarían	habrían amado		

Imperative	
Present	**Forms using the subjunctive stem**
ama (tú)	ame (él, ella, usted)
amad (vosotros)	amemos (nosotros)
	amen (ellos, ellas, ustedes)

TEMER

Regular verb

For each simple form of the verb (temo, temía, temí...) there is a corresponding compound form, which is always formed with the verb haber: he temido, había temido, hube temido...
Spanish verbs inflect and it is the *ending** which supplies the information on form, making it unnecessary to use subject personal pronouns as required with English verbs. (See p. 102.)

■ 2nd type

Impersonal mood

	Simple forms	Compound forms
Infinitive	temer	haber temido
Gerund	temiendo	habiendo temido
Past participle	temido	

Personal moods

	Indicative		Subjunctive	
	Simple forms	Compound forms	Simple forms	Compound forms
	Present	**Perfect**	**Present**	**Past**
1st p. sing.	temo	he temido	tema	haya temido
2nd p. sing.	temes	has temido	temas	hayas temido
3rd p. sing.	teme	ha temido	tema	haya temido
1st p. plur.	tememos	hemos temido	temamos	hayamos temido
2nd p. plur.	teméis	habéis temido	temáis	hayáis temido
3rd p. plur.	temen	han temido	teman	hayan temido
	Imperfect	**Past perfect**	**Imperfect**	**Past perfect**
1st p. sing.	temía	había temido	temiera	hubiera temido
2nd p. sing.	temías	habías temido	temieras	hubieras temido
3rd p. sing.	temía	había temido	temiera	hubiera temido
1st p. plur.	temíamos	habíamos temido	temiéramos	hubiéramos temido
2nd p. plur.	temíais	habíais temido	temierais	hubierais temido
3rd p. plur.	temían	habían temido	temieran	hubieran temido
	Preterit	**Past anterior**		
1st p. sing.	temí	hube temido	temiese	hubiese temido
2nd p. sing.	temiste	hubiste temido	temieses	hubieses temido
3rd p. sing.	temió	hubo temido	temiese	hubiese temido
1st p. plur.	temimos	hubimos temido	temiésemos	hubiésemos temido
2nd p. plur.	temisteis	hubisteis temido	temieseis	hubieseis temido
3rd p. plur.	temieron	hubieron temido	temiesen	hubiesen temido
	Future	**Future perfect**	**Future**	**Future perfect**
1st p. sing.	temeré	habré temido	temiere	hubiere temido
2nd p. sing.	temerás	habrás temido	temieres	hubieres temido
3rd p. sing.	temerá	habrá temido	temiere	hubiere temido
1st p. plur.	temeremos	habremos temido	temiéremos	hubiéremos temido
2nd p. plur.	temeréis	habréis temido	temiereis	hubiereis temido
3rd p. plur.	temerán	habrán temido	temieren	hubieren temido
	Present conditional	**Conditional perfect**		
1st p. sing.	temería	habría temido		
2nd p. sing.	temerías	habrías temido		
3rd p. sing.	temería	habría temido		
1st p. plur.	temeríamos	habríamos temido		
2nd p. plur.	temeríais	habríais temido		
3rd p. plur.	temerían	habrían temido		

Imperative

Present	Forms using the subjunctive stem
teme (tú)	tema (él, ella, usted)
temed (vosotros)	temamos (nosotros)
	teman (ellos, ellas, ustedes)

PARTIR

Regular verb

The conjugations of the 2nd and 3rd types of regular verb are very similar. The only forms that differ are: the infinitive, the 1st and 2nd person plural of the present indicative and the 2nd person plural of the imperative.

■ 3rd type

Impersonal mood		
	Simple forms	Compound forms
Infinitive	partir	haber partido
Gerund	partiendo	habiendo partido
Past participle	partido	

Personal moods				
	Indicative		**Subjunctive**	
	Simple forms	Compound forms	Simple forms	Compound forms
	Present	**Perfect**	**Present**	**Past**
1st p. sing.	parto	he partido	parta	haya partido
2nd p. sing.	partes	has partido	partas	hayas partido
3rd p. sing.	parte	ha partido	parta	haya partido
1st p. plur.	partimos	hemos partido	partamos	hayamos partido
2nd p. plur.	partís	habéis partido	partáis	hayáis partido
3rd p. plur.	parten	han partido	partan	hayan partido
	Imperfect	**Past perfect**	**Imperfect**	**Past perfect**
1st p. sing.	partía	había partido	partiera	hubiera
2nd p. sing.	partías	habías partido	partieras	hubieras
3rd p. sing.	partía	había partido	partiera	hubiera
1st p. plur.	partíamos	habíamos partido	partiéramos	hubiéramos
2nd p. plur.	partíais	habíais partido	partierais	hubierais
3rd p. plur.	partían	habían partido	partieran	hubieran
	Preterit	**Past anterior**		
1st p. sing.	partí	hube partido	partiese	hubiese partido
2nd p. sing.	partiste	hubiste partido	partieses	hubieses partido
3rd p. sing.	partió	hubo partido	partiese	hubiese partido
1st p. plur.	partimos	hubimos partido	partiésemos	hubiésemos partido
2nd p. plur.	partisteis	hubisteis partido	partieseis	hubieseis partido
3rd p. plur.	partieron	hubieron partido	partiesen	hubiesen partido
	Future	**Future perfect**	**Future**	**Future perfect**
1st p. sing.	partiré	habré partido	partiere	hubiere partido
2nd p. sing.	partirás	habrás partido	partieres	hubieres partido
3rd p. sing.	partirá	habrá partido	partiere	hubiere partido
1st p. plur.	partiremos	habremos partido	partiéremos	hubiéremos partido
2nd p. plur.	partiréis	habréis partido	partiereis	hubiereis partido
3rd p. plur.	partirán	habrán partido	partieren	hubieren partido
	Present conditional	**Conditional perfect**		
1st p. sing.	partiría	habría partido		
2nd p. sing.	partirías	habrías partido		
3rd p. sing.	partiría	habría partido		
1st p. plur.	partiríamos	habríamos partido		
2nd p. plur.	partiríais	habríais partido		
3rd p. plur.	partirían	habrían partido		

Imperative	
Present	**Forms using the subjunctive stem**
parte (tú)	parta (él, ella, usted)
partid (vosotros)	partamos (nosotros)
	partan (ellos, ellas, ustedes)

AISLAR

Regular verb

Since the *stress** falls on the i of the stem, the *hiatus** aí is created in the following forms: the present indicative and subjunctive (1st, 2nd and 3rd person singular and 3rd person plural), and the imperative (2nd and 3rd person singular and 3rd person plural). In those cases, there is a written accent on the í.
■ Spelling ai › aí

Impersonal mood		
	Simple forms	Compound forms
Infinitive	aislar	haber aislado
Gerund	aislando	habiendo aislado
Past participle	aislado	

Personal moods				
	Indicative		**Subjunctive**	
	Simple forms	Compound forms	Simple forms	Compound forms
	Present	**Perfect**	**Present**	**Past**
1st p. sing.	**aís**lo	he aislado	**aís**le	haya aislado
2nd p. sing.	**aís**las	has aislado	**aís**les	hayas aislado
3rd p. sing.	**aís**la	ha aislado	**aís**le	haya aislado
1st p. plur.	aislamos	hemos aislado	aislemos	hayamos aislado
2nd p. plur.	aisláis	habéis aislado	aisléis	hayáis aislado
3rd p. plur.	**aís**lan	han aislado	**aís**len	hayan aislado
	Imperfect	**Past perfect**	**Imperfect**	**Past perfect**
1st p. sing.	aislaba	había aislado	aislara	hubiera aislado
2nd p. sing.	aislabas	habías aislado	aislaras	hubieras aislado
3rd p. sing.	aislaba	había aislado	aislara	hubiera aislado
1st p. plur.	aislábamos	habíamos aislado	aisláramos	hubiéramos aislado
2nd p. plur.	aislabais	habíais aislado	aislarais	hubierais aislado
3rd p. plur.	aislaban	habían aislado	aislaran	hubieran aislado
	Preterit	**Past anterior**		
1st p. sing.	aislé	hube aislado	aislase	hubiese aislado
2nd p. sing.	aislaste	hubiste aislado	aislases	hubieses aislado
3rd p. sing.	aisló	hubo aislado	aislase	hubiese aislado
1st p. plur.	aislamos	hubimos aislado	aislásemos	hubiésemos aislado
2nd p. plur.	aislasteis	hubisteis aislado	aislaseis	hubieseis aislado
3rd p. plur.	aislaron	hubieron aislado	aislasen	hubiesen aislado
	Future	**Future perfect**	**Future**	**Future perfect**
1st p. sing.	aislaré	habré aislado	aislare	hubiere aislado
2nd p. sing.	aislarás	habrás aislado	aislares	hubieres aislado
3rd p. sing.	aislará	habrá aislado	aislare	hubiere aislado
1st p. plur.	aislaremos	habremos aislado	aisláremos	hubiéremos aislado
2nd p. plur.	aislaréis	habréis aislado	aislareis	hubiereis aislado
3rd p. plur.	aislarán	habrán aislado	aislaren	hubieren aislado
	Present conditional	**Conditional perfect**		
1st p. sing.	aislaría	habría aislado		
2nd p. sing.	aislarías	habrías aislado		
3rd p. sing.	aislaría	habría aislado		
1st p. plur.	aislaríamos	habríamos aislado		
2nd p. plur.	aislaríais	habríais aislado		
3rd p. plur.	aislarían	habrían aislado		

Imperative	
Present	**Forms using the subjunctive stem**
aísla (tú)	**aís**le (él, ella, usted)
aislad (vosotros)	aislemos (nosotros)
	aíslen (ellos, ellas, ustedes)

AULLAR

Regular verb

Since the *stress** falls on the u of the stem, the *hiatus** aú is created in the following forms: the present indicative and subjunctive (1st, 2nd, 3rd person singular and 3rd person plural), and the imperative (2nd, 3rd person singular and 3rd person plural). In those cases, there is a written accent on the ú.
- Spelling au › aú

Impersonal mood		
	Simple forms	**Compound forms**
Infinitive	aullar	haber aullado
Gerund	aullando	habiendo aullado
Past participle	aullado	

Personal moods				
	Indicative		**Subjunctive**	
	Simple forms	**Compound forms**	**Simple forms**	**Compound forms**
	Present	**Perfect**	**Present**	**Past**
1st p. sing.	**aú**llo	he aullado	**aú**lle	haya aullado
2nd p. sing.	**aú**llas	has aullado	**aú**lles	hayas aullado
3rd p. sing.	**aú**lla	ha aullado	**aú**lle	haya aullado
1st p. plur.	aullamos	hemos aullado	aullemos	hayamos aullado
2nd p. plur.	aulláis	habéis aullado	aulléis	hayáis aullado
3rd p. plur.	**aú**llan	han aullado	**aú**llen	hayan aullado
	Imperfect	**Past perfect**	**Imperfect**	**Past perfect**
1st p. sing.	aullaba	había aullado	aullara	hubiera aullado
2nd p. sing.	aullabas	habías aullado	aullaras	hubieras aullado
3rd p. sing.	aullaba	había aullado	aullara	hubiera aullado
1st p. plur.	aullábamos	habíamos aullado	aulláramos	hubiéramos aullado
2nd p. plur.	aullabais	habíais aullado	aullarais	hubierais aullado
3rd p. plur.	aullaban	habían aullado	aullaran	hubieran aullado
	Preterit	**Past anterior**		
1st p. sing.	aullé	hube aullado	aullase	hubiese aullado
2nd p. sing.	aullaste	hubiste aullado	aullases	hubieses aullado
3rd p. sing.	aulló	hubo aullado	aullase	hubiese aullado
1st p. plur.	aullamos	hubimos aullado	aullásemos	hubiésemos aullado
2nd p. plur.	aullasteis	hubisteis aullado	aullaseis	hubieseis aullado
3rd p. plur.	aullaron	hubieron aullado	aullasen	hubiesen aullado
	Future	**Future perfect**	**Future**	**Future perfect**
1st p. sing.	aullaré	habré aullado	aullare	hubiere aullado
2nd p. sing.	aullarás	habrás aullado	aullares	hubieres aullado
3rd p. sing.	aullará	habrá aullado	aullare	hubiere aullado
1st p. plur.	aullaremos	habremos aullado	aulláremos	hubiéremos aullado
2nd p. plur.	aullaréis	habréis aullado	aullareis	hubiereis aullado
3rd p. plur.	aullarán	habrán aullado	aullaren	hubieren aullado
	Present conditional	**Conditional perfect**		
1st p. sing.	aullaría	habría aullado		
2nd p. sing.	aullarías	habrías aullado		
3rd p. sing.	aullaría	habría aullado		
1st p. plur.	aullaríamos	habríamos aullado		
2nd p. plur.	aullaríais	habríais aullado		
3rd p. plur.	aullarían	habrían aullado		

Imperative	
Present	**Forms using the subjunctive stem**
aúlla (tú)	**aú**lle (él, ella, usted)
aullad (vosotros)	aullemos (nosotros)
	aúllen (ellos, ellas, ustedes)

AHINCAR

Regular verb

Since the *stress** falls on the i of the *stem**, the *hiatus** aí is created in the following forms: the present indicative, the present subjunctive, and the imperative.
To keep the [k] sound before the e, c becomes qu in the preterit, in all forms of the present subjunctive and in the imperative.
■ Spelling ahi › ahí and c › qu before e

Impersonal mood		
	Simple forms	Compound forms
Infinitive	ahincar	haber ahincado
Gerund	ahincando	habiendo ahincado
Past participle	ahincado	

Personal moods				
	Indicative		Subjunctive	
	Simple forms	Compound forms	Simple forms	Compound forms
	Present	**Perfect**	**Present**	**Past**
1st p. sing.	**ahí**nco	he ahincado	**ahí**nque	haya ahincado
2nd p. sing.	**ahí**ncas	has ahincado	**ahí**nques	hayas ahincado
3rd p. sing.	**ahí**nca	ha ahincado	**ahí**nque	haya ahincado
1st p. plur.	ahincamos	hemos ahincado	ahin**que**mos	hayamos ahincado
2nd p. plur.	ahincáis	habéis ahincado	ahin**qué**is	hayáis ahincado
3rd p. plur.	**ahí**ncan	han ahincado	**ahí**nquen	hayan ahincado
	Imperfect	**Past perfect**	**Imperfect**	**Past perfect**
1st p. sing.	ahincaba	había ahincado	ahincara	hubiera ahincado
2nd p. sing.	ahincabas	habías ahincado	ahincaras	hubieras ahincado
3rd p. sing.	ahincaba	había ahincado	ahincara	hubiera ahincado
1st p. plur.	ahincábamos	habíamos ahincado	ahincáramos	hubiéramos ahincado
2nd p. plur.	ahincabais	habíais ahincado	ahincarais	hubierais ahincado
3rd p. plur.	ahincaban	habían ahincado	ahincaran	hubieran ahincado
	Preterit	**Past anterior**		
1st p. sing.	ahin**qué**	hube ahincado	ahincase	hubiese ahincado
2nd p. sing.	ahincaste	hubiste ahincado	ahincases	hubieses ahincado
3rd p. sing.	ahincó	hubo ahincado	ahincase	hubiese ahincado
1st p. plur.	ahincamos	hubimos ahincado	ahincásemos	hubiésemos ahincado
2nd p. plur.	ahincasteis	hubisteis ahincado	ahincaseis	hubieseis ahincado
3rd p. plur.	ahincaron	hubieron ahincado	ahincasen	hubiesen ahincado
	Future	**Future perfect**	**Future**	**Future perfect**
1st p. sing.	ahincaré	habré ahincado	ahincare	hubiere ahincado
2nd p. sing.	ahincarás	habrás ahincado	ahincares	hubieres ahincado
3rd p. sing.	ahincará	habrá ahincado	ahincare	hubiere ahincado
1st p. plur.	ahincaremos	habremos ahincado	ahincáremos	hubiéremos ahincado
2nd p. plur.	ahincaréis	habréis ahincado	ahincareis	hubiereis ahincado
3rd p. plur.	ahincarán	habrán ahincado	ahincaren	hubieren ahincado
	Present conditional	**Conditional perfect**		
1st p. sing.	ahincaría	habría ahincado		
2nd p. sing.	ahincarías	habrías ahincado		
3rd p. sing.	ahincaría	habría ahincado		
1st p. plur.	ahincaríamos	habríamos ahincado		
2nd p. plur.	ahincaríais	habríais ahincado		
3rd p. plur.	ahincarían	habrían ahincado		

Imperative	
Present	**Forms using the subjunctive stem**
ahínca (tú)	**ahí**nque (él, ella, usted)
ahincad (vosotros)	ahin**que**mos (nosotros)
	ahínquen (ellos, ellas, ustedes)

GUIAR

Regular verb

The *stress** falls on the i of the *stem** which forms a *hiatus** with the vowel of the *ending**. This applies to the present indicative, the present subjunctive, and the imperative.
- Spelling i › í

Impersonal mood		
	Simple forms	Compound forms
Infinitive	guiar	haber guiado
Gerund	guiando	habiendo guiado
Past participle	guiado	

Personal moods			
	Indicative		**Subjunctive**

	Simple forms	Compound forms	Simple forms	Compound forms
	Present	**Perfect**	**Present**	**Past**
1st p. sing.	guío	he guiado	guíe	haya guiado
2nd p. sing.	guías	has guiado	guíes	hayas guiado
3rd p. sing.	guía	ha guiado	guíe	haya guiado
1st p. plur.	guiamos	hemos guiado	guiemos	hayamos guiado
2nd p. plur.	guiais	habéis guiado	guieis	hayáis guiado
3rd p. plur.	guían	han guiado	guíen	hayan guiado
	Imperfect	**Past perfect**	**Imperfect**	**Past perfect**
1st p. sing.	guiaba	había guiado	guiara	hubiera guiado
2nd p. sing.	guiabas	habías guiado	guiaras	hubieras guiado
3rd p. sing.	guiaba	había guiado	guiara	hubiera guiado
1st p. plur.	guiábamos	habíamos guiado	guiáramos	hubiéramos guiado
2nd p. plur.	guiabais	habíais guiado	guiarais	hubierais guiado
3rd p. plur.	guiaban	habían guiado	guiaran	hubieran guiado
	Preterit	**Past anterior**		
1st p. sing.	guie	hube guiado	guiase	hubiese guiado
2nd p. sing.	guiaste	hubiste guiado	guiases	hubieses guiado
3rd p. sing.	guio	hubo guiado	guiase	hubiese guiado
1st p. plur.	guiamos	hubimos guiado	guiásemos	hubiésemos guiado
2nd p. plur.	guiasteis	hubisteis guiado	guiaseis	hubieseis guiado
3rd p. plur.	guiaron	hubieron guiado	guiasen	hubiesen guiado
	Future	**Future perfect**	**Future**	**Future perfect**
1st p. sing.	guiaré	habré guiado	guiare	hubiere guiado
2nd p. sing.	guiarás	habrás guiado	guiares	hubieres guiado
3rd p. sing.	guiará	habrá guiado	guiare	hubiere guiado
1st p. plur.	guiaremos	habremos guiado	guiáremos	hubiéremos guiado
2nd p. plur.	guiaréis	habréis guiado	guiareis	hubiereis guiado
3rd p. plur.	guiarán	habrán guiado	guiaren	hubieren guiado
	Present conditional	**Conditional perfect**		
1st p. sing.	guiaría	habría guiado		
2nd p. sing.	guiarías	habrías guiado		
3rd p. sing.	guiaría	habría guiado		
1st p. plur.	guiaríamos	habríamos guiado		
2nd p. plur.	guiaríais	habríais guiado		
3rd p. plur.	guiarían	habrían guiado		

Imperative	
Present	**Forms using the subjunctive stem**
guía (tú)	guíe (él, ella, usted)
guiad (vosotros)	guiemos (nosotros)
	guíen (ellos, ellas, ustedes)

CAMBIAR
Regular verb

The i of the *stem** always forms a *diphthong** with the vowel of the *ending**. Compare: cambio
and guío.
- Spelling i = i

Impersonal mood		
	Simple forms	Compound forms
Infinitive	cambiar	haber cambiado
Gerund	cambiando	habiendo cambiado
Past participle	cambiado	

Personal moods				
	Indicative		**Subjunctive**	
	Simple forms	Compound forms	Simple forms	Compound forms
	Present	**Perfect**	**Present**	**Past**
1st p. sing.	cambio	he cambiado	cambie	haya cambiado
2nd p. sing.	cambias	has cambiado	cambies	hayas cambiado
3rd p. sing.	cambia	ha cambiado	cambie	haya cambiado
1st p. plur.	cambiamos	hemos cambiado	cambiemos	hayamos cambiado
2nd p. plur.	cambiáis	habéis cambiado	cambiéis	hayáis cambiado
3rd p. plur.	cambian	han cambiado	cambien	hayan cambiado
	Imperfect	**Past perfect**	**Imperfect**	**Past perfect**
1st p. sing.	cambiaba	había cambiado	cambiara	hubiera cambiado
2nd p. sing.	cambiabas	habías cambiado	cambiaras	hubieras cambiado
3rd p. sing.	cambiaba	había cambiado	cambiara	hubiera cambiado
1st p. plur.	cambiábamos	habíamos cambiado	cambiáramos	hubiéramos cambiado
2nd p. plur.	cambiabais	habíais cambiado	cambiarais	hubierais cambiado
3rd p. plur.	cambiaban	habían cambiado	cambiaran	hubieran cambiado
	Preterit	**Past anterior**		
1st p. sing.	cambié	hube cambiado	cambiase	hubiese cambiado
2nd p. sing.	cambiaste	hubiste cambiado	cambiases	hubieses cambiado
3rd p. sing.	cambió	hubo cambiado	cambiase	hubiese cambiado
1st p. plur.	cambiamos	hubimos cambiado	cambiásemos	hubiésemos cambiado
2nd p. plur.	cambiasteis	hubisteis cambiado	cambiaseis	hubieseis cambiado
3rd p. plur.	cambiaron	hubieron cambiado	cambiasen	hubiesen cambiado
	Future	**Future perfect**	**Future**	**Future perfect**
1st p. sing.	cambiaré	habré cambiado	cambiare	hubiere cambiado
2nd p. sing.	cambiarás	habrás cambiado	cambiares	hubieres cambiado
3rd p. sing.	cambiará	habrá cambiado	cambiare	hubiere cambiado
1st p. plur.	cambiaremos	habremos cambiado	cambiáremos	hubiéremos cambiado
2nd p. plur.	cambiaréis	habréis cambiado	cambiareis	hubiereis cambiado
3rd p. plur.	cambiarán	habrán cambiado	cambiaren	hubieren cambiado
	Present conditional	**Conditional perfect**		
1st p. sing.	cambiaría	habría cambiado		
2nd p. sing.	cambiarías	habrías cambiado		
3rd p. sing.	cambiaría	habría cambiado		
1st p. plur.	cambiaríamos	habríamos cambiado		
2nd p. plur.	cambiaríais	habríais cambiado		
3rd p. plur.	cambiarían	habrían cambiado		

Imperative	
Present	**Forms using the subjunctive stem**
cambia (tú)	cambie (él, ella, usted)
cambiad (vosotros)	cambiemos (nosotros)
	cambien (ellos, ellas, ustedes)

ACTUAR

Regular verb

As the *stress** falls on the u of the *stem**, the *hiatus** úa is created in the following forms: the present indicative, the present subjunctive, and the imperative.
- Spelling ua › úa, ue › úe, uo › úo

Impersonal mood		
	Simple forms	Compound forms
Infinitive	actuar	haber actuado
Gerund	actuando	habiendo actuado
Past participle	actuado	

Personal moods				
	Indicative		**Subjunctive**	
	Simple forms	Compound forms	Simple forms	Compound forms
	Present	**Perfect**	**Present**	**Past**
1st p. sing.	act**úo**	he actuado	act**úe**	haya actuado
2nd p. sing.	act**úas**	has actuado	act**úes**	hayas actuado
3rd p. sing.	act**úa**	ha actuado	act**úe**	haya actuado
1st p. plur.	actuamos	hemos actuado	actuemos	hayamos actuado
2nd p. plur.	actuáis	habéis actuado	actuéis	hayáis actuado
3rd p. plur.	act**úan**	han actuado	act**úen**	hayan actuado
	Imperfect	**Past perfect**	**Imperfect**	**Past perfect**
1st p. sing.	actuaba	había actuado	actuara	hubiera actuado
2nd p. sing.	actuabas	habías actuado	actuaras	hubieras actuado
3rd p. sing.	actuaba	había actuado	actuara	hubiera actuado
1st p. plur.	actuábamos	habíamos actuado	actuáramos	hubiéramos actuado
2nd p. plur.	actuabais	habíais actuado	actuarais	hubierais actuado
3rd p. plur.	actuaban	habían actuado	actuaran	hubieran actuado
	Preterit	**Past anterior**		
1st p. sing.	actué	hube actuado	actuase	hubiese actuado
2nd p. sing.	actuaste	hubiste actuado	actuases	hubieses actuado
3rd p. sing.	actuó	hubo actuado	actuase	hubiese actuado
1st p. plur.	actuamos	hubimos actuado	actuásemos	hubiésemos actuado
2nd p. plur.	actuasteis	hubisteis actuado	actuaseis	hubieseis actuado
3rd p. plur.	actuaron	hubieron actuado	actuasen	hubiesen actuado
	Future	**Future perfect**	**Future**	**Future perfect**
1st p. sing.	actuaré	habré actuado	actuare	hubiere actuado
2nd p. sing.	actuarás	habrás actuado	actuares	hubieres actuado
3rd p. sing.	actuará	habrá actuado	actuare	hubiere actuado
1st p. plur.	actuaremos	habremos actuado	actuáremos	hubiéremos actuado
2nd p. plur.	actuaréis	habréis actuado	actuareis	hubiereis actuado
3rd p. plur.	actuarán	habrán actuado	actuaren	hubieren actuado
	Present conditional	**Conditional perfect**		
1st p. sing.	actuaría	habría actuado		
2nd p. sing.	actuarías	habrías actuado		
3rd p. sing.	actuaría	habría actuado		
1st p. plur.	actuaríamos	habríamos actuado		
2nd p. plur.	actuaríais	habríais actuado		
3rd p. plur.	actuarían	habrían actuado		

Imperative	
Present	**Forms using the subjunctive stem**
act**úa** (tú)	act**úe** (él, ella, usted)
actuad (vosotros)	actuemos (nosotros)
	act**úen** (ellos, ellas, ustedes)

ADECUAR

Regular verb

Verbs ending in cuar keep the *diphthong** and do not have a written accent (except in the alternative forms shown below).
The following verbs also follow this model: anticuarse, apropincuarse, evacuar, licuar.
■ Spelling u = u

Impersonal mood		
	Simple forms	Compound forms
Infinitive	adecuar	haber adecuado
Gerund	adecuando	habiendo adecuado
Past participle	adecuado	

Personal moods			
Indicative		**Subjunctive**	
Simple forms	Compound forms	Simple forms	Compound forms
Present	**Perfect**	**Present**	**Past**
1st p. sing. adecuo o adec**úo**	he adecuado	adecue o adec**úe**	haya adecuado
2nd p. sing. adecuas o adec**úas**	has adecuado	adecues o adec**úes**	hayas adecuado
3rd p. sing. adecua o adec**úa**	ha adecuado	adecue o adec**úe**	haya adecuado
1st p. plur. adecuamos	hemos adecuado	adecuemos	hayamos adecuado
2nd p. plur. adecuáis	habéis adecuado	adecuéis	hayáis adecuado
3rd p. plur. adecuan o adec**úan**	han adecuado	adecuen o adec**úen**	hayan adecuado
Imperfect	**Past perfect**	**Imperfect**	**Past perfect**
1st p. sing. adecuaba	había adecuado	adecuara	hubiera adecuado
2nd p. sing. adecuabas	habías adecuado	adecuaras	hubieras adecuado
3rd p. sing. adecuaba	había adecuado	adecuara	hubiera adecuado
1st p. plur. adecuábamos	habíamos adecuado	adecuáramos	hubiéramos adecuado
2nd p. plur. adecuabais	habíais adecuado	adecuarais	hubierais adecuado
3rd p. plur. adecuaban	habían adecuado	adecuaran	hubieran adecuado
Preterit	**Past anterior**		
1st p. sing. adecué	hube adecuado	adecuase	hubiese adecuado
2nd p. sing. adecuaste	hubiste adecuado	adecuases	hubieses adecuado
3rd p. sing. adecuó	hubo adecuado	adecuase	hubiese adecuado
1st p. plur. adecuamos	hubimos adecuado	adecuásemos	hubiésemos adecuado
2nd p. plur. adecuasteis	hubisteis adecuado	adecuaseis	hubieseis adecuado
3rd p. plur. adecuaron	hubieron adecuado	adecuasen	hubiesen adecuado
Future	**Future perfect**	**Future**	**Future perfect**
1st p. sing. adecuaré	habré adecuado	adecuare	hubiere adecuado
2nd p. sing. adecuarás	habrás adecuado	adecuares	hubieres adecuado
3rd p. sing. adecuará	habrá adecuado	adecuare	hubiere adecuado
1st p. plur. adecuaremos	habremos adecuado	adecuáremos	hubiéremos adecuado
2nd p. plur. adecuaréis	habréis adecuado	adecuareis	hubiereis adecuado
3rd p. plur. adecuarán	habrán adecuado	adecuaren	hubieren adecuado
Present conditional	**Conditional perfect**		
1st p. sing. adecuaría	habría adecuado		
2nd p. sing. adecuarías	habrías adecuado		
3rd p. sing. adecuaría	habría adecuado		
1st p. plur. adecuaríamos	habríamos adecuado		
2nd p. plur. adecuaríais	habríais adecuado		
3rd p. plur. adecuarían	habrían adecuado		

Imperative	
Present	**Forms using the subjunctive stem**
adecua (tú)	adecue (él, ella, usted)
adecuad (vosotros)	adecuemos (nosotros)
	adecuen (ellos, ellas, ustedes)

Regular verb

The u of the *stem** always forms a *diphthong** with the vowel of the *ending**.
Compare actúo/averiguo.
To keep the [gw] sound before the e, the u needs to add a diaeresis in the preterit, the present subjunctive, and the imperative.
■ Spelling u = u and g › gü

Impersonal mood		
	Simple forms	Compound forms
Infinitive	averiguar	haber averiguado
Gerund	averiguando	habiendo averiguado
Past participle	averiguado	

Personal moods				
	Indicative		Subjunctive	
	Simple forms	Compound forms	Simple forms	Compound forms
	Present	**Perfect**	**Present**	**Past**
1st p. sing.	averiguo	he averiguado	averi**gü**e	haya averiguado
2nd p. sing.	averiguas	has averiguado	averi**gü**es	hayas averiguado
3rd p. sing.	averigua	ha averiguado	averi**gü**e	haya averiguado
1st p. plur.	averiguamos	hemos averiguado	averi**gü**emos	hayamos averiguado
2nd p. plur.	averiguáis	habéis averiguado	averi**gü**éis	hayáis averiguado
3rd p. plur.	averiguan	han averiguado	averi**gü**en	hayan averiguado
	Imperfect	**Past perfect**	**Imperfect**	**Past perfect**
1st p. sing.	averiguaba	había averiguado	averiguara	hubiera averiguado
2nd p. sing.	averiguabas	habías averiguado	averiguaras	hubieras averiguado
3rd p. sing.	averiguaba	había averiguado	averiguara	hubiera averiguado
1st p. plur.	averiguábamos	habíamos averiguado	averiguáramos	hubiéramos averiguado
2nd p. plur.	averiguabais	habíais averiguado	averiguarais	hubierais averiguado
3rd p. plur.	averiguaban	habían averiguado	averiguaran	hubieran averiguado
	Preterit	**Past anterior**		
1st p. sing.	averi**gü**é	hube averiguado	averiguase	hubiese averiguado
2nd p. sing.	averiguaste	hubiste averiguado	averiguases	hubieses averiguado
3rd p. sing.	averiguó	hubo averiguado	averiguase	hubiese averiguado
1st p. plur.	averiguamos	hubimos averiguado	averiguásemos	hubiésemos averiguado
2nd p. plur.	averiguasteis	hubisteis averiguado	averiguaseis	hubieseis averiguado
3rd p. plur.	averiguaron	hubieron averiguado	averiguasen	hubiesen averiguado
	Future	**Future perfect**	**Future**	**Future perfect**
1st p. sing.	averiguaré	habré averiguado	averiguare	hubiere averiguado
2nd p. sing.	averiguarás	habrás averiguado	averiguares	hubieres averiguado
3rd p. sing.	averiguará	habrá averiguado	averiguare	hubiere averiguado
1st p. plur.	averiguaremos	habremos averiguado	averiguáremos	hubiéremos averiguado
2nd p. plur.	averiguaréis	habréis averiguado	averiguareis	hubiereis averiguado
3rd p. plur.	averiguarán	habrán averiguado	averiguaren	hubieren averiguado
	Present conditional	**Conditional perfect**		
1st p. sing.	averiguaría	habría averiguado		
2nd p. sing.	averiguarías	habrías averiguado		
3rd p. sing.	averiguaría	habría averiguado		
1st p. plur.	averiguaríamos	habríamos averiguado		
2nd p. plur.	averiguaríais	habríais averiguado		
3rd p. plur.	averiguarían	habrían averiguado		

Imperative	
Present	**Forms using the subjunctive stem**
averigua (tú)	averi**gü**e (él, ella, usted)
averiguad (vosotros)	averi**gü**emos (nosotros)
	averi**gü**en (ellos, ellas, ustedes)

LEER

Regular verb

When the i is unaccented it becomes a *yod** when it appears between two vowels.
Compare leí/leyó.
The appearance of the yod in the gerund (or present participle), the preterit, the imperfect subjunctive and the future, replacing the i of the *endings** (**iendo, ió, ieron, iera, iere**) constitutes a change in spelling.

- Spelling i › y before e, o

Impersonal mood		
	Simple forms	**Compound forms**
Infinitive	leer	haber leído
Gerund	leyendo	habiendo leído
Past participle	leído	

Personal moods				
	Indicative		**Subjunctive**	
	Simple forms	Compound forms	Simple forms	Compound forms
	Present	**Perfect**	**Present**	**Past**
1st p. sing.	leo	he leído	lea	haya leído
2nd p. sing.	lees	has leído	leas	hayas leído
3rd p. sing.	lee	ha leído	lea	haya leído
1st p. plur.	leemos	hemos leído	leamos	hayamos leído
2nd p. plur.	leéis	habéis leído	leáis	hayáis leído
3rd p. plur.	leen	han leído	lean	hayan leído
	Imperfect	**Past perfect**	**Imperfect**	**Past perfect**
1st p. sing.	leía	había leído	leyera	hubiera leído
2nd p. sing.	leías	habías leído	leyeras	hubieras leído
3rd p. sing.	leía	había leído	leyera	hubiera leído
1st p. plur.	leíamos	habíamos leído	leyéramos	hubiéramos leído
2nd p. plur.	leíais	habíais leído	leyerais	hubierais leído
3rd p. plur.	leían	habían leído	leyeran	hubieran leído
	Preterit	**Past anterior**		
1st p. sing.	leí	hube leído	leyese	hubiese leído
2nd p. sing.	leíste	hubiste leído	leyeses	hubieses leído
3rd p. sing.	leyó	hubo leído	leyese	hubiese leído
1st p. plur.	leímos	hubimos leído	leyésemos	hubiésemos leído
2nd p. plur.	leísteis	hubisteis leído	leyeseis	hubieseis leído
3rd p. plur.	leyeron	hubieron leído	leyesen	hubiesen leído
	Future	**Future perfect**	**Future**	**Future perfect**
1st p. sing.	leeré	habré leído	leyere	hubiere leído
2nd p. sing.	leerás	habrás leído	leyeres	hubieres leído
3rd p. sing.	leerá	habrá leído	leyere	hubiere leído
1st p. plur.	leeremos	habremos leído	leyéremos	hubiéremos leído
2nd p. plur.	leeréis	habréis leído	leyereis	hubiereis leído
3rd p. plur.	leerán	habrán leído	leyeren	hubieren leído
	Present conditional	**Conditional perfect**		
1st p. sing.	leería	habría leído		
2nd p. sing.	leerías	habrías leído		
3rd p. sing.	leería	habría leído		
1st p. plur.	leeríamos	habríamos leído		
2nd p. plur.	leeríais	habríais leído		
3rd p. plur.	leerían	habrían leído		

Imperative	
Present	**Forms using the subjunctive stem**
lee (tú)	lea (él, ella, usted)
leed (vosotros)	leamos (nosotros)
	lean (ellos, ellas, ustedes)

S A C A R

Regular verb

Verbs ending in car, change the c to qu before e in the preterit (1st p. sing.), the present subjunctive (in all forms), and the imperative forms which use the subjunctive stem.
This spelling change applies to all regular and irregular verbs ending in car. (See trocar.)

■ Spelling c › qu before e

Impersonal mood		
	Simple forms	Compound forms
Infinitive	sacar	haber sacado
Gerund	sacando	habiendo sacado
Past participle	sacado	

Personal moods				
	Indicative		Subjunctive	
	Simple forms	Compound forms	Simple forms	Compound forms
	Present	**Perfect**	**Present**	**Past**
1st p. sing.	saco	he sacado	saque	haya sacado
2nd p. sing.	sacas	has sacado	saques	hayas sacado
3rd p. sing.	saca	ha sacado	saque	haya sacado
1st p. plur.	sacamos	hemos sacado	saquemos	hayamos sacado
2nd p. plur.	sacáis	habéis sacado	saquéis	hayáis sacado
3rd p. plur.	sacan	han sacado	saquen	hayan sacado
	Imperfect	**Past perfect**	**Imperfect**	**Past perfect**
1st p. sing.	sacaba	había sacado	sacara	hubiera sacado
2nd p. sing.	sacabas	habías sacado	sacaras	hubieras sacado
3rd p. sing.	sacaba	había sacado	sacara	hubiera sacado
1st p. plur.	sacábamos	habíamos sacado	sacáramos	hubiéramos sacado
2nd p. plur.	sacabais	habíais sacado	sacarais	hubierais sacado
3rd p. plur.	sacaban	habían sacado	sacaran	hubieran sacado
	Preterit	**Past anterior**		
1st p. sing.	saqué	hube sacado	sacase	hubiese sacado
2nd p. sing.	sacaste	hubiste sacado	sacases	hubieses sacado
3rd p. sing.	sacó	hubo sacado	sacase	hubiese sacado
1st p. plur.	sacamos	hubimos sacado	sacásemos	hubiésemos sacado
2nd p. plur.	sacasteis	hubisteis sacado	sacaseis	hubieseis sacado
3rd p. plur.	sacaron	hubieron sacado	sacasen	hubiesen sacado
	Future	**Future perfect**	**Future**	**Future perfect**
1st p. sing.	sacaré	habré sacado	sacare	hubiere sacado
2nd p. sing.	sacarás	habrás sacado	sacares	hubieres sacado
3rd p. sing.	sacará	habrá sacado	sacare	hubiere sacado
1st p. plur.	sacaremos	habremos sacado	sacáremos	hubiéremos sacado
2nd p. plur.	sacaréis	habréis sacado	sacareis	hubiereis sacado
3rd p. plur.	sacarán	habrán sacado	sacaren	hubieren sacado
	Present conditional	**Conditional perfect**		
1st p. sing.	sacaría	habría sacado		
2nd p. sing.	sacarías	habrías sacado		
3rd p. sing.	sacaría	habría sacado		
1st p. plur.	sacaríamos	habríamos sacado		
2nd p. plur.	sacaríais	habríais sacado		
3rd p. plur.	sacarían	habrían sacado		

Imperative

Present	Forms using the subjunctive stem
saca (tú)	saque (él, ella, usted)
sacad (vosotros)	saquemos (nosotros)
	saquen (ellos, ellas, ustedes)

VENCER

Regular verb

Verbs ending in a consonant + cer and some other verbs ending in cer, change the c to a z before a and o in the present indicative, the present subjunctive, and the imperative.
Note: cocer, escocer, mecer and recocer follow this model rather than parecer (> zc).

■ Spelling c > z before a, o

Impersonal mood

	Simple forms	Compound forms
Infinitive	vencer	haber vencido
Gerund	venciendo	habiendo vencido
Past participle	vencido	

Personal moods

	Indicative		Subjunctive	
	Simple forms	Compound forms	Simple forms	Compound forms
	Present	**Perfect**	**Present**	**Past**
1st p. sing.	ven**zo**	he vencido	ven**za**	haya vencido
2nd p. sing.	vences	has vencido	ven**zas**	hayas vencido
3rd p. sing.	vence	ha vencido	ven**za**	haya vencido
1st p. plur.	vencemos	hemos vencido	ven**zamos**	hayamos vencido
2nd p. plur.	vencéis	habéis vencido	ven**záis**	hayáis vencido
3rd p. plur.	vencen	han vencido	ven**zan**	hayan vencido
	Imperfect	**Past perfect**	**Imperfect**	**Past perfect**
1st p. sing.	vencía	había vencido	venciera	hubiera vencido
2nd p. sing.	vencías	habías vencido	vencieras	hubieras vencido
3rd p. sing.	vencía	había vencido	venciera	hubiera vencido
1st p. plur.	vencíamos	habíamos vencido	venciéramos	hubiéramos vencido
2nd p. plur.	vencíais	habíais vencido	vencierais	hubierais vencido
3rd p. plur.	vencían	habían vencido	vencieran	hubieran vencido
	Preterit	**Past anterior**		
1st p. sing.	vencí	hube vencido	venciese	hubiese vencido
2nd p. sing.	venciste	hubiste vencido	vencieses	hubieses vencido
3rd p. sing.	venció	hubo vencido	venciese	hubiese vencido
1st p. plur.	vencimos	hubimos vencido	venciésemos	hubiésemos vencido
2nd p. plur.	vencisteis	hubisteis vencido	vencieseis	hubieseis vencido
3rd p. plur.	vencieron	hubieron vencido	venciesen	hubiesen vencido
	Future	**Future perfect**	**Future**	**Future perfect**
1st p. sing.	venceré	habré vencido	venciere	hubiere vencido
2nd p. sing.	vencerás	habrás vencido	vencieres	hubieres vencido
3rd p. sing.	vencerá	habrá vencido	venciere	hubiere vencido
1st p. plur.	venceremos	habremos vencido	venciéremos	hubiéremos vencido
2nd p. plur.	venceréis	habréis vencido	venciereis	hubiereis vencido
3rd p. plur.	vencerán	habrán vencido	vencieren	hubieren vencido
	Present conditional	**Conditional perfect**		
1st p. sing.	vencería	habría vencido		
2nd p. sing.	vencerías	habrías vencido		
3rd p. sing.	vencería	habría vencido		
1st p. plur.	venceríamos	habríamos vencido		
2nd p. plur.	venceríais	habríais vencido		
3rd p. plur.	vencerían	habrían vencido		

Imperative

Present	Forms using the subjunctive stem
vence (tú)	ven**za** (él, ella, usted)
venced (vosotros)	ven**zamos** (nosotros)
	ven**zan** (ellos, ellas, ustedes)

ZURCIR

Regular verb

Verbs ending in a consonant + cir change the c to a z before a and o in the present indicative, the present subjunctive, and the imperative.

Verbs which follow this model are therefore regular, as opposed to irregular verbs ending in cir, which follow lucir (> zc).

■ Spelling c > z before a, o

Impersonal mood

	Simple forms	Compound forms
Infinitive	zurcir	haber zurcido
Gerund	zurciendo	habiendo zurcido
Past participle	zurcido	

Personal moods

	Indicative		Subjunctive	
	Simple forms	Compound forms	Simple forms	Compound forms
	Present	**Perfect**	**Present**	**Past**
1st p. sing.	zurzo	he zurcido	zurza	haya zurcido
2nd p. sing.	zurces	has zurcido	zurzas	hayas zurcido
3rd p. sing.	zurce	ha zurcido	zurza	haya zurcido
1st p. plur.	zurcimos	hemos zurcido	zurzamos	hayamos zurcido
2nd p. plur.	zurcís	habéis zurcido	zurzáis	hayáis zurcido
3rd p. plur.	zurcen	han zurcido	zurzan	hayan zurcido
	Imperfect	**Past perfect**	**Imperfect**	**Past perfect**
1st p. sing.	zurcía	había zurcido	zurciera	hubiera zurcido
2nd p. sing.	zurcías	habías zurcido	zurcieras	hubieras zurcido
3rd p. sing.	zurcía	había zurcido	zurciera	hubiera zurcido
1st p. plur.	zurcíamos	habíamos zurcido	zurciéramos	hubiéramos zurcido
2nd p. plur.	zurcíais	habíais zurcido	zurcierais	hubierais zurcido
3rd p. plur.	zurcían	habían zurcido	zurcieran	hubieran zurcido
	Preterit	**Past anterior**		
1st p. sing.	zurcí	hube zurcido	zurciese	hubiese zurcido
2nd p. sing.	zurciste	hubiste zurcido	zurcieses	hubieses zurcido
3rd p. sing.	zurció	hubo zurcido	zurciese	hubiese zurcido
1st p. plur.	zurcimos	hubimos zurcido	zurciésemos	hubiésemos zurcido
2nd p. plur.	zurcisteis	hubisteis zurcido	zurcieseis	hubieseis zurcido
3rd p. plur.	zurcieron	hubieron zurcido	zurciesen	hubiesen zurcido
	Future	**Future perfect**	**Future**	**Future perfect**
1st p. sing.	zurciré	habré zurcido	zurciere	hubiere zurcido
2nd p. sing.	zurcirás	habrás zurcido	zurcieres	hubieres zurcido
3rd p. sing.	zurcirá	habrá zurcido	zurciere	hubiere zurcido
1st p. plur.	zurciremos	habremos zurcido	zurciéremos	hubiéremos zurcido
2nd p. plur.	zurciréis	habréis zurcido	zurciereis	hubiereis zurcido
3rd p. plur.	zurcirán	habrán zurcido	zurcieren	hubieren zurcido
	Present conditional	**Conditional perfect**		
1st p. sing.	zurciría	habría zurcido		
2nd p. sing.	zurcirías	habrías zurcido		
3rd p. sing.	zurciría	habría zurcido		
1st p. plur.	zurciríamos	habríamos zurcido		
2nd p. plur.	zurciríais	habríais zurcido		
3rd p. plur.	zurcirían	habrían zurcido		

Imperative

Present	Forms using the subjunctive stem
zurce (tú)	zurza (él, ella, usted)
zurcid (vosotros)	zurzamos (nosotros)
	zurzan (ellos, ellas, ustedes)

CAZAR

Verbs ending in zar, change the z to a c before e in the preterit, the present subjunctive, and the imperative.

This spelling change applies to all regular and irregular verbs ending in zar. (See avergonzar and forzar.)

■ Spelling z › c before e

Impersonal mood

	Simple forms	Compound forms
Infinitive	cazar	haber cazado
Gerund	cazando	habiendo cazado
Past participle	cazado	

Personal moods

	Indicative		Subjunctive	
	Simple forms	Compound forms	Simple forms	Compound forms
	Present	**Perfect**	**Present**	**Past**
1st p. sing.	cazo	he cazado	cace	haya cazado
2nd p. sing.	cazas	has cazado	caces	hayas cazado
3rd p. sing.	caza	ha cazado	cace	haya cazado
1st p. plur.	cazamos	hemos cazado	cacemos	hayamos cazado
2nd p. plur.	cazáis	habéis cazado	cacéis	hayáis cazado
3rd p. plur.	cazan	han cazado	cacen	hayan cazado
	Imperfect	**Past perfect**	**Imperfect**	**Past perfect**
1st p. sing.	cazaba	había cazado	cazara	hubiera cazado
2nd p. sing.	cazabas	habías cazado	cazaras	hubieras cazado
3rd p. sing.	cazaba	había cazado	cazara	hubiera cazado
1st p. plur.	cazábamos	habíamos cazado	cazáramos	hubiéramos cazado
2nd p. plur.	cazabais	habíais cazado	cazarais	hubierais cazado
3rd p. plur.	cazaban	habían cazado	cazaran	hubieran cazado
	Preterit	**Past anterior**		
1st p. sing.	cacé	hube cazado	cazase	hubiese cazado
2nd p. sing.	cazaste	hubiste cazado	cazases	hubieses cazado
3rd p. sing.	cazó	hubo cazado	cazase	hubiese cazado
1st p. plur.	cazamos	hubimos cazado	cazásemos	hubiésemos cazado
2nd p. plur.	cazasteis	hubisteis cazado	cazaseis	hubieseis cazado
3rd p. plur.	cazaron	hubieron cazado	cazasen	hubiesen cazado
	Future	**Future perfect**	**Future**	**Future perfect**
1st p. sing.	cazaré	habré cazado	cazare	hubiere cazado
2nd p. sing.	cazarás	habrás cazado	cazares	hubieres cazado
3rd p. sing.	cazará	habrá cazado	cazare	hubiere cazado
1st p. plur.	cazaremos	habremos cazado	cazáremos	hubiéremos cazado
2nd p. plur.	cazaréis	habréis cazado	cazareis	hubiereis cazado
3rd p. plur.	cazarán	habrán cazado	cazaren	hubieren cazado
	Present conditional	**Conditional perfect**		
1st p. sing.	cazaría	habría cazado		
2nd p. sing.	cazarías	habrías cazado		
3rd p. sing.	cazaría	habría cazado		
1st p. plur.	cazaríamos	habríamos cazado		
2nd p. plur.	cazaríais	habríais cazado		
3rd p. plur.	cazarían	habrían cazado		

Imperative

Present	Forms using the subjunctive stem
caza (tú)	cace (él, ella, usted)
cazad (vosotros)	cacemos (nosotros)
	cacen (ellos, ellas, ustedes)

PROTEGER

Regular verb

Verbs ending in ger change the g to a j (jota) before a and o (otherwise the pronunciation would be [go], [ga]). This change affects the present indicative, the present subjunctive, and the imperative.

■ Spelling g › j before a, o

Impersonal mood		
	Simple forms	Compound forms
Infinitive	proteger	haber protegido
Gerund	protegiendo	habiendo protegido
Past participle	protegido	

Personal moods				
	Indicative		Subjunctive	
	Simple forms	Compound forms	Simple forms	Compound forms
	Present	**Perfect**	**Present**	**Past**
1st p. sing.	prote**jo**	he protegido	prote**ja**	haya protegido
2nd p. sing.	proteges	has protegido	prote**jas**	hayas protegido
3rd p. sing.	protege	ha protegido	prote**ja**	haya protegido
1st p. plur.	protegemos	hemos protegido	prote**jamos**	hayamos protegido
2nd p. plur.	protegéis	habéis protegido	prote**jáis**	hayáis protegido
3rd p. plur.	protegen	han protegido	prote**jan**	hayan protegido
	Imperfect	**Past perfect**	**Imperfect**	**Past perfect**
1st p. sing.	protegía	había protegido	protegiera	hubiera protegido
2nd p. sing.	protegías	habías protegido	protegieras	hubieras protegido
3rd p. sing.	protegía	había protegido	protegiera	hubiera protegido
1st p. plur.	protegíamos	habíamos protegido	protegiéramos	hubiéramos protegido
2nd p. plur.	protegíais	habíais protegido	protegierais	hubierais protegido
3rd p. plur.	protegían	habían protegido	protegieran	hubieran protegido
	Preterit	**Past anterior**		
1st p. sing.	protegí	hube protegido	protegiese	hubiese protegido
2nd p. sing.	protegiste	hubiste protegido	protegieses	hubieses protegido
3rd p. sing.	protegió	hubo protegido	protegiese	hubiese protegido
1st p. plur.	protegimos	hubimos protegido	protegiésemos	hubiésemos protegido
2nd p. plur.	protegisteis	hubisteis protegido	protegieseis	hubieseis protegido
3rd p. plur.	protegieron	hubieron protegido	protegiesen	hubiesen protegido
	Future	**Future perfect**	**Future**	**Future perfect**
1st p. sing.	protegeré	habré protegido	protegiere	hubiere protegido
2nd p. sing.	protegerás	habrás protegido	protegieres	hubieres protegido
3rd p. sing.	protegerá	habrá protegido	protegiere	hubiere protegido
1st p. plur.	protegeremos	habremos protegido	protegiéremos	hubiéremos protegido
2nd p. plur.	protegeréis	habréis protegido	protegiereis	hubiereis protegido
3rd p. plur.	protegerán	habrán protegido	protegieren	hubieren protegido
	Present conditional	**Conditional perfect**		
1st p. sing.	protegería	habría protegido		
2nd p. sing.	protegerías	habrías protegido		
3rd p. sing.	protegería	habría protegido		
1st p. plur.	protegeríamos	habríamos protegido		
2nd p. plur.	protegeríais	habríais protegido		
3rd p. plur.	protegerían	habrían protegido		

Imperative	
Present	**Forms using the subjunctive stem**
protege (tú)	prote**ja** (él, ella, usted)
proteged (vosotros)	prote**jamos** (nosotros)
	prote**jan** (ellos, ellas, ustedes)

DIRIGIR

Regular verb

Verbs ending in gir change the g to a j (jota) before a and o (otherwise the pronunciation would be [go], [ga]). This change affects the present indicative, the present subjunctive, and the imperative.

■ Spelling g › j before a, o

Impersonal mood		
	Simple forms	Compound forms
Infinitive	dirigir	haber dirigido
Gerund	dirigiendo	habiendo dirigido
Past participle	dirigido	

Personal moods				
	Indicative		**Subjunctive**	
	Simple forms	Compound forms	Simple forms	Compound forms
	Present	**Perfect**	**Present**	**Past**
1st p. sing.	dirijo	he dirigido	dirija	haya dirigido
2nd p. sing.	diriges	has dirigido	dirijas	hayas dirigido
3rd p. sing.	dirige	ha dirigido	dirija	haya dirigido
1st p. plur.	dirigimos	hemos dirigido	dirijamos	hayamos dirigido
2nd p. plur.	dirigís	habéis dirigido	dirijáis	hayáis dirigido
3rd p. plur.	dirigen	han dirigido	dirijan	hayan dirigido
	Imperfect	**Past perfect**	**Imperfect**	**Past perfect**
1st p. sing.	dirigía	había dirigido	dirigiera	hubiera dirigido
2nd p. sing.	dirigías	habías dirigido	dirigieras	hubieras dirigido
3rd p. sing.	dirigía	había dirigido	dirigiera	hubiera dirigido
1st p. plur.	dirigíamos	habíamos dirigido	dirigiéramos	hubiéramos dirigido
2nd p. plur.	dirigíais	habíais dirigido	dirigierais	hubierais dirigido
3rd p. plur.	dirigían	habían dirigido	dirigieran	hubieran dirigido
	Preterit	**Past anterior**		
1st p. sing.	dirigí	hube dirigido	dirigiese	hubiese dirigido
2nd p. sing.	dirigiste	hubiste dirigido	dirigieses	hubieses dirigido
3rd p. sing.	dirigió	hubo dirigido	dirigiese	hubiese dirigido
1st p. plur.	dirigimos	hubimos dirigido	dirigiésemos	hubiésemos dirigido
2nd p. plur.	dirigisteis	hubisteis dirigido	dirigieseis	hubieseis dirigido
3rd p. plur.	dirigieron	hubieron dirigido	dirigiesen	hubiesen dirigido
	Future	**Future perfect**	**Future**	**Future perfect**
1st p. sing.	dirigiré	habré dirigido	dirigiere	hubiere dirigido
2nd p. sing.	dirigirás	habrás dirigido	dirigieres	hubieres dirigido
3rd p. sing.	dirigirá	habrá dirigido	dirigiere	hubiere dirigido
1st p. plur.	dirigiremos	habremos dirigido	dirigiéremos	hubiéremos dirigido
2nd p. plur.	dirigiréis	habréis dirigido	dirigiereis	hubiereis dirigido
3rd p. plur.	dirigirán	habrán dirigido	dirigieren	hubieren dirigido
	Present conditional	**Conditional perfect**		
1st p. sing.	dirigiría	habría dirigido		
2nd p. sing.	dirigirías	habrías dirigido		
3rd p. sing.	dirigiría	habría dirigido		
1st p. plur.	dirigiríamos	habríamos dirigido		
2nd p. plur.	dirigiríais	habríais dirigido		
3rd p. plur.	dirigirían	habrían dirigido		

Imperative	
Present	**Forms using the subjunctive stem**
dirige (tú)	dirija (él, ella, usted)
dirigid (vosotros)	dirijamos (nosotros)
	dirijan (ellos, ellas, ustedes)

LLEGAR

Regular verb

In verbs ending in gar, the g is followed by a u before e in the preterit, the present subjunctive, and the imperative.
This spelling change applies to all regular and irregular verbs. (See negar, colgar and jugar.)
■ Spelling g › gu before e

Impersonal mood		
	Simple forms	Compound forms
Infinitive	llegar	haber llegado
Gerund	llegando	habiendo llegado
Past participle	llegado	

Personal moods				
	Indicative		**Subjunctive**	
	Simple forms	Compound forms	Simple forms	Compound forms
	Present	**Perfect**	**Present**	**Past**
1st p. sing.	llego	he llegado	lle**gue**	haya llegado
2nd p. sing.	llegas	has llegado	lle**gue**s	hayas llegado
3rd p. sing.	llega	ha llegado	lle**gue**	haya llegado
1st p. plur.	llegamos	hemos llegado	lle**gue**mos	hayamos llegado
2nd p. plur.	llegáis	habéis llegado	lle**gué**is	hayáis llegado
3rd p. plur.	llegan	han llegado	lle**gue**n	hayan llegado
	Imperfect	**Past perfect**	**Imperfect**	**Past perfect**
1st p. sing.	llegaba	había llegado	llegara	hubiera llegado
2nd p. sing.	llegabas	habías llegado	llegaras	hubieras llegado
3rd p. sing.	llegaba	había llegado	llegara	hubiera llegado
1st p. plur.	llegábamos	habíamos llegado	llegáramos	hubiéramos llegado
2nd p. plur.	llegabais	habíais llegado	llegarais	hubierais llegado
3rd p. plur.	llegaban	habían llegado	llegaran	hubieran llegado
	Preterit	**Past anterior**		
1st p. sing.	lle**gué**	hube llegado	llegase	hubiese llegado
2nd p. sing.	llegaste	hubiste llegado	llegases	hubieses llegado
3rd p. sing.	llegó	hubo llegado	llegase	hubiese llegado
1st p. plur.	llegamos	hubimos llegado	llegásemos	hubiésemos llegado
2nd p. plur.	llegasteis	hubisteis llegado	llegaseis	hubieseis llegado
3rd p. plur.	llegaron	hubieron llegado	llegasen	hubiesen llegado
	Future	**Future perfect**	**Future**	**Future perfect**
1st p. sing.	llegaré	habré llegado	llegare	hubiere llegado
2nd p. sing.	llegarás	habrás llegado	llegares	hubieres llegado
3rd p. sing.	llegará	habrá llegado	llegare	hubiere llegado
1st p. plur.	llegaremos	habremos llegado	llegáremos	hubiéremos llegado
2nd p. plur.	llegaréis	habréis llegado	llegareis	hubiereis llegado
3rd p. plur.	llegarán	habrán llegado	llegaren	hubieren llegado
	Present conditional	**Conditional perfect**		
1st p. sing.	llegaría	habría llegado		
2nd p. sing.	llegarías	habrías llegado		
3rd p. sing.	llegaría	habría llegado		
1st p. plur.	llegaríamos	habríamos llegado		
2nd p. plur.	llegaríais	habríais llegado		
3rd p. plur.	llegarían	habrían llegado		

Imperative	
Present	**Forms using the subjunctive stem**
llega (tú)	lle**gue** (él, ella, usted)
llegad (vosotros)	lle**gue**mos (nosotros)
	lle**gue**n (ellos, ellas, ustedes)

DISTINGUIR

Regular verb

In verbs ending in guir, the u is dropped before a and o in the present indicative, the present subjunctive, and the imperative.

This spelling change applies to regular verbs (extinguir, subdistinguir) as well as seguir and all the derivatives which follow that model.

■ Spelling gu › g before a, o

Impersonal mood		
	Simple forms	Compound forms
Infinitive	distinguir	haber distinguido
Gerund	distinguiendo	habiendo distinguido
Past participle	distinguido	

Personal moods			
Indicative		**Subjunctive**	
Simple forms	Compound forms	Simple forms	Compound forms
Present	**Perfect**	**Present**	**Past**
1st p. sing. distin**go**	he distinguido	distin**ga**	haya distinguido
2nd p. sing. distingues	has distinguido	distin**gas**	hayas distinguido
3rd p. sing. distingue	ha distinguido	distin**ga**	haya distinguido
1st p. plur. distinguimos	hemos distinguido	distin**gamos**	hayamos distinguido
2nd p. plur. distinguís	habéis distinguido	distin**gáis**	hayáis distinguido
3rd p. plur. distinguen	han distinguido	distin**gan**	hayan distinguido
Imperfect	**Past perfect**	**Imperfect**	**Past perfect**
1st p. sing. distinguía	había distinguido	distinguiera	hubiera distinguido
2nd p. sing. distinguías	habías distinguido	distinguieras	hubieras distinguido
3rd p. sing. distinguía	había distinguido	distinguiera	hubiera distinguido
1st p. plur. distinguíamos	habíamos distinguido	distinguiéramos	hubiéramos distinguido
2nd p. plur. distinguíais	habíais distinguido	distinguierais	hubierais distinguido
3rd p. plur. distinguían	habían distinguido	distinguieran	hubieran distinguido
Preterit	**Past anterior**		
1st p. sing. distinguí	hube distinguido	distinguiese	hubiese distinguido
2nd p. sing. distinguiste	hubiste distinguido	distinguieses	hubieses distinguido
3rd p. sing. distinguió	hubo distinguido	distinguiese	hubiese distinguido
1st p. plur. distinguimos	hubimos distinguido	distinguiésemos	hubiésemos distinguido
2nd p. plur. distinguisteis	hubisteis distinguido	distinguieseis	hubieseis distinguido
3rd p. plur. distinguieron	hubieron distinguido	distinguiesen	hubiesen distinguido
Future	**Future perfect**	**Future**	**Future perfect**
1st p. sing. distinguiré	habré distinguido	distinguiere	hubiere distinguido
2nd p. sing. distinguirás	habrás distinguido	distinguieres	hubieres distinguido
3rd p. sing. distinguirá	habrá distinguido	distinguiere	hubiere distinguido
1st p. plur. distinguiremos	habremos distinguido	distinguiéremos	hubiéremos distinguido
2nd p. plur. distinguiréis	habréis distinguido	distinguiereis	hubiereis distinguido
3rd p. plur. distinguirán	habrán distinguido	distinguieren	hubieren distinguido
Present conditional	**Conditional perfect**		
1st p. sing. distinguiría	habría distinguido		
2nd p. sing. distinguirías	habrías distinguido		

Imperative	
Present	**Forms using the subjunctive stem**
distingue (tú)	distin**ga** (él, ella, usted)
distinguid (vosotros)	distin**gamos** (nosotros)
	distin**gan** (ellos, ellas, ustedes)

3rd p. sing. distinguiría	habría distinguido
1st p. plur. distinguiríamos	habríamos distinguido
2nd p. plur. distinguiríais	habríais distinguido
3rd p. plur. distinguirían	habrían distinguido

DELINQUIR

Regular verb

Verbs ending in quir, change the qu to a c before a and o in the present indicative, the present subjunctive, and the forms of the imperative which use the subjunctive stem.
This spelling change also applies to the verb derrelinquir.

■ Spelling qu › c before a, o

Impersonal mood		
	Simple forms	Compound forms
Infinitive	delinquir	haber delinquido
Gerund	delinquiendo	habiendo delinquido
Past participle	delinquido	

Personal moods			
Indicative		**Subjunctive**	
Simple forms	Compound forms	Simple forms	Compound forms

	Present	**Perfect**	**Present**	**Past**
1st p. sing.	delin**co**	he delinquido	delin**ca**	haya delinquido
2nd p. sing.	delinques	has delinquido	delin**cas**	hayas delinquido
3rd p. sing.	delinque	ha delinquido	delin**ca**	haya delinquido
1st p. plur.	delinquimos	hemos delinquido	delin**camos**	hayamos delinquido
2nd p. plur.	delinquís	habéis delinquido	delin**cáis**	hayáis delinquido
3rd p. plur.	delinquen	han delinquido	delin**can**	hayan delinquido
	Imperfect	**Past perfect**	**Imperfect**	**Past perfect**
1st p. sing.	delinquía	había delinquido	delinquiera	hubiera delinquido
2nd p. sing.	delinquías	habías delinquido	delinquieras	hubieras delinquido
3rd p. sing.	delinquía	había delinquido	delinquiera	hubiera delinquido
1st p. plur.	delinquíamos	habíamos delinquido	delinquiéramos	hubiéramos delinquido
2nd p. plur.	delinquíais	habíais delinquido	delinquierais	hubierais delinquido
3rd p. plur.	delinquían	habían delinquido	delinquieran	hubieran delinquido
	Preterit	**Past anterior**		
1st p. sing.	delinquí	hube delinquido	delinquiese	hubiese delinquido
2nd p. sing.	delinquiste	hubiste delinquido	delinquieses	hubieses delinquido
3rd p. sing.	delinquió	hubo delinquido	delinquiese	hubiese delinquido
1st p. plur.	delinquimos	hubimos delinquido	delinquiésemos	hubiésemos delinquido
2nd p. plur.	delinquisteis	hubisteis delinquido	delinquieseis	hubieseis delinquido
3rd p. plur.	delinquieron	hubieron delinquido	delinquiesen	hubiesen delinquido
	Future	**Future perfect**	**Future**	**Future perfect**
1st p. sing.	delinquiré	habré delinquido	delinquiere	hubiere delinquido
2nd p. sing.	delinquirás	habrás delinquido	delinquieres	hubieres delinquido
3rd p. sing.	delinquirá	habrá delinquido	delinquiere	hubiere delinquido
1st p. plur.	delinquiremos	habremos delinquido	delinquiéremos	hubiéremos delinquido
2nd p. plur.	delinquiréis	habréis delinquido	delinquiereis	hubiereis delinquido
3rd p. plur.	delinquirán	habrán delinquido	delinquieren	hubieren delinquido
	Present conditional	**Conditional perfect**		
1st p. sing.	delinquiría	habría delinquido		
2nd p. sing.	delinquirías	habrías delinquido		
3rd p. sing.	delinquiría	habría delinquido		
1st p. plur.	delinquiríamos	habríamos delinquido		
2nd p. plur.	delinquiríais	habríais delinquido		
3rd p. plur.	delinquirían	habrían delinquido		

Imperative	
Present	**Forms using the subjunctive stem**
delinque (tú)	delin**ca** (él, ella, usted)
delinquid (vosotros)	delin**camos** (nosotros)
	delin**can** (ellos, ellas, ustedes)

ACERTAR

Irregular verb

The e of the *stem** changes to the *diphthong** ie in the present indicative, the present subjunctive, and the imperative.

Compare: ac**ie**rto (the *stress** falls on the vowel in the stem)/acert**amos** (the stress falls on the vowel in the *ending**).

■ Diphthong e › ie

Impersonal mood

	Simple forms	Compound forms
Infinitive	acertar	haber acertado
Gerund	acertando	habiendo acertado
Past participle	acertado	

Personal moods

	Indicative		Subjunctive	
	Simple forms	Compound forms	Simple forms	Compound forms
	Present	**Perfect**	**Present**	**Past**
1st p. sing.	acierto	he acertado	acierte	haya acertado
2nd p. sing.	aciertas	has acertado	aciertes	hayas acertado
3rd p. sing.	acierta	ha acertado	acierte	haya acertado
1st p. plur.	acertamos	hemos acertado	acertemos	hayamos acertado
2nd p. plur.	acertáis	habéis acertado	acertéis	hayáis acertado
3rd p. plur.	aciertan	han acertado	acierten	hayan acertado
	Imperfect	**Past perfect**	**Imperfect**	**Past perfect**
1st p. sing.	acertaba	había acertado	acertara	hubiera acertado
2nd p. sing.	acertabas	habías acertado	acertaras	hubieras acertado
3rd p. sing.	acertaba	había acertado	acertara	hubiera acertado
1st p. plur.	acertábamos	habíamos acertado	acertáramos	hubiéramos acertado
2nd p. plur.	acertabais	habíais acertado	acertarais	hubierais acertado
3rd p. plur.	acertaban	habían acertado	acertaran	hubieran acertado
	Preterit	**Past anterior**		
1st p. sing.	acerté	hube acertado	acertase	hubiese acertado
2nd p. sing.	acertaste	hubiste acertado	acertases	hubieses acertado
3rd p. sing.	acertó	hubo acertado	acertase	hubiese acertado
1st p. plur.	acertamos	hubimos acertado	acertásemos	hubiésemos acertado
2nd p. plur.	acertasteis	hubisteis acertado	acertaseis	hubieseis acertado
3rd p. plur.	acertaron	hubieron acertado	acertasen	hubiesen acertado
	Future	**Future perfect**	**Future**	**Future perfect**
1st p. sing.	acertaré	habré acertado	acertare	hubiere acertado
2nd p. sing.	acertarás	habrás acertado	acertares	hubieres acertado
3rd p. sing.	acertará	habrá acertado	acertare	hubiere acertado
1st p. plur.	acertaremos	habremos acertado	acertáremos	hubiéremos acertado
2nd p. plur.	acertaréis	habréis acertado	acertareis	hubiereis acertado
3rd p. plur.	acertarán	habrán acertado	acertaren	hubieren acertado
	Present conditional	**Conditional perfect**		
1st p. sing.	acertaría	habría acertado		
2nd p. sing.	acertarías	habrías acertado		
3rd p. sing.	acertaría	habría acertado		
1st p. plur.	acertaríamos	habríamos acertado		
2nd p. plur.	acertaríais	habríais acertado		
3rd p. plur.	acertarían	habrían acertado		

Imperative

Present	Forms using the subjunctive stem
acierta (tú)	acierte (él, ella, usted)
acertad (vosotros)	acertemos (nosotros)
	acierten (ellos, ellas, ustedes)

Irregular verb

The e of the *stem** changes to the *diphthong** ie in the present indicative, the present subjunctive, and in the imperative where it carries the stress.

As with all verbs ending in zar (see cazar), the z changes to c before e in the preterit, the present subjunctive, and the imperative.

■ Diphthong e › ie
■ Spelling change z › c before e

Impersonal mood		
	Simple forms	Compound forms
Infinitive	comenzar	haber comenzado
Gerund	comenzando	habiendo comenzado
Past participle	comenzado	

Personal moods			
Indicative		**Subjunctive**	
Simple forms	Compound forms	Simple forms	Compound forms

	Present	**Perfect**	**Present**	**Past**
1st p. sing.	comienzo	he comenzado	comience	haya comenzado
2nd p. sing.	comienzas	has comenzado	comiences	hayas comenzado
3rd p. sing.	comienza	ha comenzado	comience	haya comenzado
1st p. plur.	comenzamos	hemos comenzado	comencemos	hayamos comenzado
2nd p. plur.	comenzáis	habéis comenzado	comencéis	hayáis comenzado
3rd p. plur.	comienzan	han comenzado	comiencen	hayan comenzado
	Imperfect	**Past perfect**	**Imperfect**	**Past perfect**
1st p. sing.	comenzaba	había comenzado	comenzara	hubiera comenzado
2nd p. sing.	comenzabas	habías comenzado	comenzaras	hubieras comenzado
3rd p. sing.	comenzaba	había comenzado	comenzara	hubiera comenzado
1st p. plur.	comenzábamos	habíamos comenzado	comenzáramos	hubiéramos comenzado
2nd p. plur.	comenzabais	habíais comenzado	comenzarais	hubierais comenzado
3rd p. plur.	comenzaban	habían comenzado	comenzaran	hubieran comenzado
	Preterit	**Past anterior**		
1st p. sing.	comencé	hube comenzado	comenzase	hubiese comenzado
2nd p. sing.	comenzaste	hubiste comenzado	comenzases	hubieses comenzado
3rd p. sing.	comenzó	hubo comenzado	comenzase	hubiese comenzado
1st p. plur.	comenzamos	hubimos comenzado	comenzásemos	hubiésemos comenzado
2nd p. plur.	comenzasteis	hubisteis comenzado	comenzaseis	hubieseis comenzado
3rd p. plur.	comenzaron	hubieron comenzado	comenzasen	hubiesen comenzado
	Future	**Future perfect**	**Future**	**Future perfect**
1st p. sing.	comenzaré	habré comenzado	comenzare	hubiere comenzado
2nd p. sing.	comenzarás	habrás comenzado	comenzares	hubieres comenzado
3rd p. sing.	comenzará	habrá comenzado	comenzare	hubiere comenzado
1st p. plur.	comenzaremos	habremos comenzado	comenzáremos	hubiéremos comenzado
2nd p. plur.	comenzaréis	habréis comenzado	comenzareis	hubiereis comenzado
3rd p. plur.	comenzarán	habrán comenzado	comenzaren	hubieren comenzado
	Present conditional	**Conditional perfect**		
1st p. sing.	comenzaría	habría comenzado		
2nd p. sing.	comenzarías	habrías comenzado		
3rd p. sing.	comenzaría	habría comenzado		
1st p. plur.	comenzaríamos	habríamos comenzado		
2nd p. plur.	comenzaríais	habríais comenzado		
3rd p. plur.	comenzarían	habrían comenzado		

Imperative	
Present	**Forms using the subjunctive stem**
comienza (tú)	comience (él, ella, usted)
comenzad (vosotros)	comencemos (nosotros)
	comiencen (ellos, ellas, ustedes)

NEGAR

Irregular verb

The e of the *stem** changes to the *diphthong** ie in the present indicative, the present subjunctive, and in the imperative where it carries the stress.

As with all verbs ending in gar (see llegar), the g is followed by u before an e in the preterit, the present subjunctive, and the imperative.

- Diphthong e › ie
- Spelling g › gu before e

Impersonal mood		
	Simple forms	Compound forms
Infinitive	negar	haber negado
Gerund	negando	habiendo negado
Past participle	negado	

Personal moods				
	Indicative		**Subjunctive**	
	Simple forms	Compound forms	Simple forms	Compound forms
	Present	**Perfect**	**Present**	**Past**
1st p. sing.	niego	he negado	niegue	haya negado
2nd p. sing.	niegas	has negado	niegues	hayas negado
3rd p. sing.	niega	ha negado	niegue	haya negado
1st p. plur.	negamos	hemos negado	neguemos	hayamos negado
2nd p. plur.	negáis	habéis negado	neguéis	hayáis negado
3rd p. plur.	niegan	han negado	nieguen	hayan negado
	Imperfect	**Past perfect**	**Imperfect**	**Past perfect**
1st p. sing.	negaba	había negado	negara	hubiera negado
2nd p. sing.	negabas	habías negado	negaras	hubieras negado
3rd p. sing.	negaba	había negado	negara	hubiera negado
1st p. plur.	negábamos	habíamos negado	negáramos	hubiéramos negado
2nd p. plur.	negabais	habíais negado	negarais	hubierais negado
3rd p. plur.	negaban	habían negado	negaran	hubieran negado
	Preterit	**Past anterior**		
1st p. sing.	negué	hube negado	negase	hubiese negado
2nd p. sing.	negaste	hubiste negado	negases	hubieses negado
3rd p. sing.	negó	hubo negado	negase	hubiese negado
1st p. plur.	negamos	hubimos negado	negásemos	hubiésemos negado
2nd p. plur.	negasteis	hubisteis negado	negaseis	hubieseis negado
3rd p. plur.	negaron	hubieron negado	negasen	hubiesen negado
	Future	**Future perfect**	**Future**	**Future perfect**
1st p. sing.	negaré	habré negado	negare	hubiere negado
2nd p. sing.	negarás	habrás negado	negares	hubieres negado
3rd p. sing.	negará	habrá negado	negare	hubiere negado
1st p. plur.	negaremos	habremos negado	negáremos	hubiéremos negado
2nd p. plur.	negaréis	habréis negado	negareis	hubiereis negado
3rd p. plur.	negarán	habrán negado	negaren	hubieren negado
	Present conditional	**Conditional perfect**		
1st p. sing.	negaría	habría negado		
2nd p. sing.	negarías	habrías negado		
3rd p. sing.	negaría	habría negado		
1st p. plur.	negaríamos	habríamos negado		
2nd p. plur.	negaríais	habríais negado		
3rd p. plur.	negarían	habrían negado		

Imperative	
Present	**Forms using the subjunctive stem**
niega (tú)	niegue (él, ella, usted)
negad (vosotros)	neguemos (nosotros)
	nieguen (ellos, ellas, ustedes)

E R R A R

Irregular verb

The e of the *stem** changes to the *diphthong** ie in the present indicative and the present subjunctive where it carries the *stress**.

When the i forms a diphthong with another vowel, it becomes a y (*yod**), as in yerro.

This irregularity applies only to this verb.

■ Diphthong e › ye

	Impersonal mood	
	Simple forms	Compound forms
Infinitive	errar	haber errado
Gerund	errando	habiendo errado
Past participle	errado	

Personal moods

	Indicative		Subjunctive	
	Simple forms	Compound forms	Simple forms	Compound forms
	Present	**Perfect**	**Present**	**Past**
1st p. sing.	**yerro** o erro	he errado	**yerre** o erre	haya errado
2nd p. sing.	**yerras** o erras	has errado	**yerres** o erres	hayas errado
3rd p. sing.	**yerra** o erra	ha errado	**yerre** o erre	haya errado
1st p. plur.	erramos	hemos errado	erremos	hayamos errado
2nd p. plur.	erráis	habéis errado	erréis	hayáis errado
3rd p. plur.	**yerran** o erran	han errado	**yerren** o erren	hayan errado
	Imperfect	**Past perfect**	**Imperfect**	**Past perfect**
1st p. sing.	erraba	había errado	errara	hubiera errado
2nd p. sing.	errabas	habías errado	erraras	hubieras errado
3rd p. sing.	erraba	había errado	errara	hubiera errado
1st p. plur.	errábamos	habíamos errado	erráramos	hubiéramos errado
2nd p. plur.	errabais	habíais errado	errarais	hubierais errado
3rd p. plur.	erraban	habían errado	erraran	hubieran errado
	Preterit	**Past anterior**		
1st p. sing.	erré	hube errado	errase	hubiese errado
2nd p. sing.	erraste	hubiste errado	errases	hubieses errado
3rd p. sing.	erró	hubo errado	errase	hubiese errado
1st p. plur.	erramos	hubimos errado	errásemos	hubiésemos errado
2nd p. plur.	errasteis	hubisteis errado	erraseis	hubieseis errado
3rd p. plur.	erraron	hubieron errado	errasen	hubiesen errado
	Future	**Future perfect**	**Future**	**Future perfect**
1st p. sing.	erraré	habré errado	errare	hubiere errado
2nd p. sing.	errarás	habrás errado	errares	hubieres errado
3rd p. sing.	errará	habrá errado	errare	hubiere errado
1st p. plur.	erraremos	habremos errado	erráremos	hubiéremos errado
2nd p. plur.	erraréis	habréis errado	errareis	hubiereis errado
3rd p. plur.	errarán	habrán errado	erraren	hubieren errado
	Present conditional	**Conditional perfect**		
1st p. sing.	erraría	habría errado		
2nd p. sing.	errarías	habrías errado		
3rd p. sing.	erraría	habría errado		
1st p. plur.	erraríamos	habríamos errado		
2nd p. plur.	erraríais	habríais errado		
3rd p. plur.	errarían	habrían errado		

Imperative

Present	Forms using the subjunctive stem
yerra o erra (tú)	**yerre** o erre (él, ella, usted)
errad (vosotros)	erremos (nosotros)
	yerren o erren (ellos, ellas, ustedes)

TENDER

Irregular verb

The e of the *stem** which takes on the *stress** becomes ie in the present indicative, the present subjunctive, and the imperative. Compare: ti**e**nda/tend**a**mos.

■ *Diphthong** e › ie

Impersonal mood		
	Simple forms	Compound forms
Infinitive	tender	haber tendido
Gerund	tendiendo	habiendo tendido
Past participle	tendido	

Personal moods				
	Indicative		**Subjunctive**	
	Simple forms	Compound forms	Simple forms	Compound forms
	Present	**Perfect**	**Present**	**Past**
1st p. sing.	tiendo	he tendido	tienda	haya tendido
2nd p. sing.	tiendes	has tendido	tiendas	hayas tendido
3rd p. sing.	tiende	ha tendido	tienda	haya tendido
1st p. plur.	tendemos	hemos tendido	tendamos	hayamos tendido
2nd p. plur.	tendéis	habéis tendido	tendáis	hayáis tendido
3rd p. plur.	tienden	han tendido	tiendan	hayan tendido
	Imperfect	**Past perfect**	**Imperfect**	**Past perfect**
1st p. sing.	tendía	había tendido	tendiera	hubiera tendido
2nd p. sing.	tendías	habías tendido	tendieras	hubieras tendido
3rd p. sing.	tendía	había tendido	tendiera	hubiera tendido
1st p. plur.	tendíamos	habíamos tendido	tendiéramos	hubiéramos tendido
2nd p. plur.	tendíais	habíais tendido	tendierais	hubierais tendido
3rd p. plur.	tendían	habían tendido	tendieran	hubieran tendido
	Preterit	**Past anterior**		
1st p. sing.	tendí	hube tendido	tendiese	hubiese tendido
2nd p. sing.	tendiste	hubiste tendido	tendieses	hubieses tendido
3rd p. sing.	tendió	hubo tendido	tendiese	hubiese tendido
1st p. plur.	tendimos	hubimos tendido	tendiésemos	hubiésemos tendido
2nd p. plur.	tendisteis	hubisteis tendido	tendieseis	hubieseis tendido
3rd p. plur.	tendieron	hubieron tendido	tendiesen	hubiesen tendido
	Future	**Future perfect**	**Future**	**Future perfect**
1st p. sing.	tenderé	habré tendido	tendiere	hubiere tendido
2nd p. sing.	tenderás	habrás tendido	tendieres	hubieres tendido
3rd p. sing.	tenderá	habrá tendido	tendiere	hubiere tendido
1st p. plur.	tenderemos	habremos tendido	tendiéremos	hubiéremos tendido
2nd p. plur.	tenderéis	habréis tendido	tendiereis	hubiereis tendido
3rd p. plur.	tenderán	habrán tendido	tendieren	hubieren tendido
	Present conditional	**Conditional perfect**		
1st p. sing.	tendería	habría tendido		
2nd p. sing.	tenderías	habrías tendido	**Imperative**	
3rd p. sing.	tendería	habría tendido	**Present**	**Forms using the subjunctive stem**
1st p. plur.	tenderíamos	habríamos tendido	tiende (tú)	tienda (él, ella, usted)
2nd p. plur.	tenderíais	habríais tendido	tended (vosotros)	tendamos (nosotros)
3rd p. plur.	tenderían	habrían tendido		tiendan (ellos, ellas, ustedes)

Irregular verb

The e of the *stem** takes on the *stress** and becomes ie in the present indicative, the present subjunctive, and the imperative. Compare: disc**ie**rno/discern**imos**.

■ *Diphthong** e › ie

Impersonal mood		
	Simple forms	Compound forms
Infinitive	discernir	haber discernido
Gerund	discerniendo	habiendo discernido
Past participle	discernido	

Personal moods

	Indicative		Subjunctive	
	Simple forms	Compound forms	Simple forms	Compound forms
	Present	**Perfect**	**Present**	**Past**
1st p. sing.	discierno	he discernido	discierna	haya discernido
2nd p. sing.	disciernes	has discernido	disciernas	hayas discernido
3rd p. sing.	discierne	ha discernido	discierna	haya discernido
1st p. plur.	discernimos	hemos discernido	discernamos	hayamos discernido
2nd p. plur.	discernís	habéis discernido	discernáis	hayáis discernido
3rd p. plur.	disciernen	han discernido	disciernan	hayan discernido
	Imperfect	**Past perfect**	**Imperfect**	**Past perfect**
1st p. sing.	discernía	había discernido	discerniera	hubiera discernido
2nd p. sing.	discernías	habías discernido	discernieras	hubieras discernido
3rd p. sing.	discernía	había discernido	discerniera	hubiera discernido
1st p. plur.	discerníamos	habíamos discernido	discerniéramos	hubiéramos discernido
2nd p. plur.	discerníais	habíais discernido	discernierais	hubierais discernido
3rd p. plur.	discernían	habían discernido	discernieran	hubieran discernido
	Preterit	**Past anterior**		
1st p. sing.	discerní	hube discernido	discerniese	hubiese discernido
2nd p. sing.	discerniste	hubiste discernido	discernieses	hubieses discernido
3rd p. sing.	discernió	hubo discernido	discerniese	hubiese discernido
1st p. plur.	discernimos	hubimos discernido	discerniésemos	hubiésemos discernido
2nd p. plur.	discernisteis	hubisteis discernido	discernieseis	hubieseis discernido
3rd p. plur.	discernieron	hubieron discernido	discerniesen	hubiesen discernido
	Future	**Future perfect**	**Future**	**Future perfect**
1st p. sing.	discerniré	habré discernido	discerniere	hubiere discernido
2nd p. sing.	discernirás	habrás discernido	discernieres	hubieres discernido
3rd p. sing.	discernirá	habrá discernido	discerniere	hubiere discernido
1st p. plur.	discerniremos	habremos discernido	discerniéremos	hubiéremos discernido
2nd p. plur.	discerniréis	habréis discernido	discerniereis	hubiereis discernido
3rd p. plur.	discernirán	habrán discernido	discernieren	hubieren discernido
	Present conditional	**Conditional perfect**		
1st p. sing.	discerniría	habría discernido		
2nd p. sing.	discernirías	habrías discernido		
3rd p. sing.	discerniría	habría discernido		
1st p. plur.	discerniríamos	habríamos discernido		
2nd p. plur.	discerniríais	habríais discernido		
3rd p. plur.	discernirían	habrían discernido		

Imperative

Present	Forms using the subjunctive stem
discierne (tú)	discierna (él, ella, usted)
discernid (vosotros)	discernamos (nosotros)
	disciernan (ellos, ellas, ustedes)

SONAR

Irregular verb

Because of the *stress**, the o of the *stem** becomes ue in the present indicative, the present subjunctive, and the imperative. Compare: s**ue**nes/son**e**mos.

■ *Diphthong** o › ue

Impersonal mood		
	Simple forms	Compound forms
Infinitive	sonar	haber sonado
Gerund	sonando	habiendo sonado
Past participle	sonado	

Personal moods			
Indicative		Subjunctive	
Simple forms	Compound forms	Simple forms	Compound forms
Present	**Perfect**	**Present**	**Past**
1st p. sing. sueno	he sonado	suene	haya sonado
2nd p. sing. suenas	has sonado	suenes	hayas sonado
3rd p. sing. suena	ha sonado	suene	haya sonado
1st p. plur. sonamos	hemos sonado	sonemos	hayamos sonado
2nd p. plur. sonáis	habéis sonado	sonéis	hayáis sonado
3rd p. plur. suenan	han sonado	suenen	hayan sonado
Imperfect	**Past perfect**	**Imperfect**	**Past perfect**
1st p. sing. sonaba	había sonado	sonara	hubiera sonado
2nd p. sing. sonabas	habías sonado	sonaras	hubieras sonado
3rd p. sing. sonaba	había sonado	sonara	hubiera sonado
1st p. plur. sonábamos	habíamos sonado	sonáramos	hubiéramos sonado
2nd p. plur. sonabais	habíais sonado	sonarais	hubierais sonado
3rd p. plur. sonaban	habían sonado	sonaran	hubieran sonado
Preterit	**Past anterior**		
1st p. sing. soné	hube sonado	sonase	hubiese sonado
2nd p. sing. sonaste	hubiste sonado	sonases	hubieses sonado
3rd p. sing. sonó	hubo sonado	sonase	hubiese sonado
1st p. plur. sonamos	hubimos sonado	sonásemos	hubiésemos sonado
2nd p. plur. sonasteis	hubisteis sonado	sonaseis	hubieseis sonado
3rd p. plur. sonaron	hubieron sonado	sonasen	hubiesen sonado
Future	**Future perfect**	**Future**	**Future perfect**
1st p. sing. sonaré	habré sonado	sonare	hubiere sonado
2nd p. sing. sonarás	habrás sonado	sonares	hubieres sonado
3rd p. sing. sonará	habrá sonado	sonare	hubiere sonado
1st p. plur. sonaremos	habremos sonado	sonáremos	hubiéremos sonado
2nd p. plur. sonaréis	habréis sonado	sonareis	hubiereis sonado
3rd p. plur. sonarán	habrán sonado	sonaren	hubieren sonado
Present conditional	**Conditional perfect**		
1st p. sing. sonaría	habría sonado		

Imperative	
Present	**Forms using the subjunctive stem**
suena (tú)	suene (él, ella, usted)
sonad (vosotros)	sonemos (nosotros)
	suenen (ellos, ellas, ustedes)

Remaining present conditional / conditional perfect forms:

2nd p. sing. sonarías	habrías sonado	
3rd p. sing. sonaría	habría sonado	
1st p. plur. sonaríamos	habríamos sonado	
2nd p. plur. sonaríais	habríais sonado	
3rd p. plur. sonarían	habrían sonado	

TROCAR

Irregular verb

The o of the *stem** becomes ue in the present indicative, the present subjunctive, and in the imperative.

Compare tru**e**cas (the *stress** falls on the vowel of the stem) and troc**aron** (where the stress falls on the vowel of the *ending**).

In addition to this, the c becomes qu in the preterit (1st p. sing.), the present subjunctive, and the imperative.

■ *Diphthong** o › ue
■ Spelling c › qu before e

Impersonal mood

	Simple forms	Compound forms
Infinitive	trocar	haber trocado
Gerund	trocando	habiendo trocado
Past participle	trocado	

Personal moods

	Indicative			Subjunctive	
	Simple forms	Compound forms		Simple forms	Compound forms
	Present	**Perfect**		**Present**	**Past**
1st p. sing.	**trueco**	he trocado		**trueque**	haya trocado
2nd p. sing.	**truecas**	has trocado		**trueques**	hayas trocado
3rd p. sing.	**trueca**	ha trocado		**trueque**	haya trocado
1st p. plur.	trocamos	hemos trocado		tro**que**mos	hayamos trocado
2nd p. plur.	trocáis	habéis trocado		tro**qué**is	hayáis trocado
3rd p. plur.	**truecan**	han trocado		**trueque**n	hayan trocado
	Imperfect	**Past perfect**		**Imperfect**	**Past perfect**
1st p. sing.	trocaba	había trocado		trocara	hubiera trocado
2nd p. sing.	trocabas	habías trocado		trocaras	hubieras trocado
3rd p. sing.	trocaba	había trocado		trocara	hubiera trocado
1st p. plur.	trocábamos	habíamos trocado		trocáramos	hubiéramos trocado
2nd p. plur.	trocabais	habíais trocado		trocarais	hubierais trocado
3rd p. plur.	trocaban	habían trocado		trocaran	hubieran trocado
	Preterit	**Past anterior**			
1st p. sing.	tro**qué**	hube trocado		trocase	hubiese trocado
2nd p. sing.	trocaste	hubiste trocado		trocases	hubieses trocado
3rd p. sing.	trocó	hubo trocado		trocase	hubiese trocado
1st p. plur.	trocamos	hubimos trocado		trocásemos	hubiésemos trocado
2nd p. plur.	trocasteis	hubisteis trocado		trocaseis	hubieseis trocado
3rd p. plur.	trocaron	hubieron trocado		trocasen	hubiesen trocado
	Future	**Future perfect**		**Future**	**Future perfect**
1st p. sing.	trocaré	habré trocado		trocare	hubiere trocado
2nd p. sing.	trocarás	habrás trocado		trocares	hubieres trocado
3rd p. sing.	trocará	habrá trocado		trocare	hubiere trocado
1st p. plur.	trocaremos	habremos trocado		trocáremos	hubiéremos trocado
2nd p. plur.	trocaréis	habréis trocado		trocareis	hubiereis trocado
3rd p. plur.	trocarán	habrán trocado		trocaren	hubieren trocado
	Present conditional	**Conditional perfect**			
1st p. sing.	trocaría	habría trocado			
2nd p. sing.	trocarías	habrías trocado			
3rd p. sing.	trocaría	habría trocado			
1st p. plur.	trocaríamos	habríamos trocado			
2nd p. plur.	trocaríais	habríais trocado			
3rd p. plur.	trocarían	habrían trocado			

Imperative

Present	Forms using the subjunctive stem
trueca (tú)	**trueque** (él, ella, usted)
trocad (vosotros)	tro**que**mos (nosotros)
	truequen (ellos, ellas, ustedes)

COLGAR

Irregular verb

The *stress** causes the o of the *stem** to become ue in the indicative, the present subjunctive, and the imperative. Compare: cuelgan/colgaran.

As with all verbs ending in gar (see llegar), the g is followed by u before an e in the preterit, the subjunctive, and the imperative.

- *Diphthong** o › ue
- Spelling g › gu before e

Impersonal mood		
	Simple forms	Compound forms
Infinitive	colgar	haber colgado
Gerund	colgando	habiendo colgado
Past participle	colgado	

Personal moods				
	Indicative		**Subjunctive**	
	Simple forms	Compound forms	Simple forms	Compound forms
	Present	**Perfect**	**Present**	**Past**
1st p. sing.	cuelgo	he colgado	cuelgue	haya colgado
2nd p. sing.	cuelgas	has colgado	cuelgues	hayas colgado
3rd p. sing.	cuelga	ha colgado	cuelgue	haya colgado
1st p. plur.	colgamos	hemos colgado	colguemos	hayamos colgado
2nd p. plur.	colgáis	habéis colgado	colguéis	hayáis colgado
3rd p. plur.	cuelgan	han colgado	cuelguen	hayan colgado
	Imperfect	**Past perfect**	**Imperfect**	**Past perfect**
1st p. sing.	colgaba	había colgado	colgara	hubiera colgado
2nd p. sing.	colgabas	habías colgado	colgaras	hubieras colgado
3rd p. sing.	colgaba	había colgado	colgara	hubiera colgado
1st p. plur.	colgábamos	habíamos colgado	colgáramos	hubiéramos colgado
2nd p. plur.	colgabais	habíais colgado	colgarais	hubierais colgado
3rd p. plur.	colgaban	habían colgado	colgaran	hubieran colgado
	Preterit	**Past anterior**		
1st p. sing.	colgué	hube colgado	colgase	hubiese colgado
2nd p. sing.	colgaste	hubiste colgado	colgases	hubieses colgado
3rd p. sing.	colgó	hubo colgado	colgase	hubiese colgado
1st p. plur.	colgamos	hubimos colgado	colgásemos	hubiésemos colgado
2nd p. plur.	colgasteis	hubisteis colgado	colgaseis	hubieseis colgado
3rd p. plur.	colgaron	hubieron colgado	colgasen	hubiesen colgado
	Future	**Future perfect**	**Future**	**Future perfect**
1st p. sing.	colgaré	habré colgado	colgare	hubiere colgado
2nd p. sing.	colgarás	habrás colgado	colgares	hubieres colgado
3rd p. sing.	colgará	habrá colgado	colgare	hubiere colgado
1st p. plur.	colgaremos	habremos colgado	colgáremos	hubiéremos colgado
2nd p. plur.	colgaréis	habréis colgado	colgareis	hubiereis colgado
3rd p. plur.	colgarán	habrán colgado	colgaren	hubieren colgado
	Present conditional	**Conditional perfect**		
1st p. sing.	colgaría	habría colgado		
2nd p. sing.	colgarías	habrías colgado		
3rd p. sing.	colgaría	habría colgado		
1st p. plur.	colgaríamos	habríamos colgado		
2nd p. plur.	colgaríais	habríais colgado		
3rd p. plur.	colgarían	habrían colgado		

Imperative	
Present	**Forms using the subjunctive stem**
cuelga (tú)	cuelgue (él, ella, usted)
colgad (vosotros)	colguemos (nosotros)
	cuelguen (ellos, ellas, ustedes)

Irregular verb

Because of the *stress**, the o of the *stem** becomes üe in the present indicative, the present subjunctive, and the imperative. Compare: ag**üe**ro/agor**a**remos.
Other verbs which follow this conjugation: degollar.

■ *Diphthong** o › üe
■ Spelling g › gü before e

Impersonal mood		
	Simple forms	Compound forms
Infinitive	agorar	haber agorado
Gerund	agorando	habiendo agorado
Past participle	agorado	

Personal moods			
Indicative		Subjunctive	
Simple forms	Compound forms	Simple forms	Compound forms
Present	**Perfect**	**Present**	**Past**
1st p. sing. ag**üe**ro	he agorado	ag**üe**re	haya agorado
2nd p. sing. ag**üe**ras	has agorado	ag**üe**res	hayas agorado
3rd p. sing. ag**üe**ra	ha agorado	ag**üe**re	haya agorado
1st p. plur. agoramos	hemos agorado	agoremos	hayamos agorado
2nd p. plur. agoráis	habéis agorado	agoréis	hayáis agorado
3rd p. plur. ag**üe**ran	han agorado	ag**üe**ren	hayan agorado
Imperfect	**Past perfect**	**Imperfect**	**Past perfect**
1st p. sing. agoraba	había agorado	agorara	hubiera agorado
2nd p. sing. agorabas	habías agorado	agoraras	hubieras agorado
3rd p. sing. agoraba	había agorado	agorara	hubiera agorado
1st p. plur. agorábamos	habíamos agorado	agoráramos	hubiéramos agorado
2nd p. plur. agorabais	habíais agorado	agorarais	hubierais agorado
3rd p. plur. agoraban	habían agorado	agoraran	hubieran agorado
Preterit	**Past anterior**		
1st p. sing. agoré	hube agorado	agorase	hubiese agorado
2nd p. sing. agoraste	hubiste agorado	agorases	hubieses agorado
3rd p. sing. agoró	hubo agorado	agorase	hubiese agorado
1st p. plur. agoramos	hubimos agorado	agorásemos	hubiésemos agorado
2nd p. plur. agorasteis	hubisteis agorado	agoraseis	hubieseis agorado
3rd p. plur. agoraron	hubieron agorado	agorasen	hubiesen agorado
Future	**Future perfect**	**Future**	**Future perfect**
1st p. sing. agoraré	habré agorado	agorare	hubiere agorado
2nd p. sing. agorarás	habrás agorado	agorares	hubieres agorado
3rd p. sing. agorará	habrá agorado	agorare	hubiere agorado
1st p. plur. agoraremos	habremos agorado	agoráremos	hubiéremos agorado
2nd p. plur. agoraréis	habréis agorado	agorareis	hubiereis agorado
3rd p. plur. agorarán	habrán agorado	agoraren	hubieren agorado
Present conditional	**Conditional perfect**		
1st p. sing. agoraría	habría agorado		
2nd p. sing. agorarías	habrías agorado		

Imperative	
Present	**Forms using the subjunctive stem**
ag**üe**ra (tú)	ag**üe**re (él, ella, usted)
agorad (vosotros)	agoremos (nosotros)
	ag**üe**ren (ellos, ellas, ustedes)

3rd p. sing. agoraría	habría agorado
1st p. plur. agoraríamos	habríamos agorado
2nd p. plur. agoraríais	habríais agorado
3rd p. plur. agorarían	habrían agorado

AVERGONZAR

Irregular verb

The o of the *stem** becomes ue in the present indicative, the present subjunctive, and the imperative.

In order to keep the same pronunciation of the *diphthong** [gw], a diaeresis is added to the ü. In addition to this, the z becomes c before e

in the preterit, the present subjunctive, and the imperative. (See cazar.)

■ Diphthong o › üe
■ Spelling g › gü before e and z › c before e

Impersonal mood		
	Simple forms	Compound forms
Infinitive	avergonzar	haber avergonzado
Gerund	avergonzando	habiendo avergonzado
Past participle	avergonzado	

Personal moods				
	Indicative		**Subjunctive**	
	Simple forms	Compound forms	Simple forms	Compound forms
	Present	**Perfect**	**Present**	**Past**
1st p. sing.	**avergüenz**o	he avergonzado	**avergüenc**e	haya avergonzado
2nd p. sing.	**avergüenz**as	has avergonzado	**avergüenc**es	hayas avergonzado
3rd p. sing.	**avergüenz**a	ha avergonzado	**avergüenc**e	haya avergonzado
1st p. plur.	avergonzamos	hemos avergonzado	avergon**c**emos	hayamos avergonzado
2nd p. plur.	avergonzáis	habéis avergonzado	avergon**c**éis	hayáis avergonzado
3rd p. plur.	**avergüenz**an	han avergonzado	**avergüenc**en	hayan avergonzado
	Imperfect	**Past perfect**	**Imperfect**	**Past perfect**
1st p. sing.	avergonzaba	había avergonzado	avergonzara	hubiera avergonzado
2nd p. sing.	avergonzabas	habías avergonzado	avergonzaras	hubieras avergonzado
3rd p. sing.	avergonzaba	había avergonzado	avergonzara	hubiera avergonzado
1st p. plur.	avergonzábamos	habíamos avergonzado	avergonzáramos	hubiéramos avergonzado
2nd p. plur.	avergonzabais	habíais avergonzado	avergonzarais	hubierais avergonzado
3rd p. plur.	avergonzaban	habían avergonzado	avergonzaran	hubieran avergonzado
	Preterit	**Past anterior**		
1st p. sing.	avergon**cé**	hube avergonzado	avergonzase	hubiese avergonzado
2nd p. sing.	avergonzaste	hubiste avergonzado	avergonzases	hubieses avergonzado
3rd p. sing.	avergonzó	hubo avergonzado	avergonzase	hubiese avergonzado
1st p. plur.	avergonzamos	hubimos avergonzado	avergonzásemos	hubiésemos avergonzado
2nd p. plur.	avergonzasteis	hubisteis avergonzado	avergonzaseis	hubieseis avergonzado
3rd p. plur.	avergonzaron	hubieron avergonzado	avergonzasen	hubiesen avergonzado
	Future	**Future perfect**	**Future**	**Future perfect**
1st p. sing.	avergonzaré	habré avergonzado	avergonzare	hubiere avergonzado
2nd p. sing.	avergonzarás	habrás avergonzado	avergonzares	hubieres avergonzado
3rd p. sing.	avergonzará	habrá avergonzado	avergonzare	hubiere avergonzado
1st p. plur.	avergonzaremos	habremos avergonzado	avergonzáremos	hubiéremos avergonzado
2nd p. plur.	avergonzaréis	habréis avergonzado	avergonzareis	hubiereis avergonzado
3rd p. plur.	avergonzarán	habrán avergonzado	avergonzaren	hubieren avergonzado
	Present conditional	**Conditional perfect**		
1st p. sing.	avergonzaría	habría avergonzado		
2nd p. sing.	avergonzarías	habrías avergonzado		
3rd p. sing.	avergonzaría	habría avergonzado		
1st p. plur.	avergonzaríamos	habríamos avergonzado		
2nd p. plur.	avergonzaríais	habríais avergonzado		
3rd p. plur.	avergonzarían	habrían avergonzado		

Imperative	
Present	**Forms using the subjunctive stem**
avergüenza (tú)	**avergüenc**e (él, ella, usted)
avergonzad (vosotros)	avergon**c**emos (nosotros)
	avergüencen (ellos, ellas, ustedes)

FORZAR

Irregular verb

The o of the *stem** becomes ue in the present indicative, the present subjunctive, and in the imperative.
Compare: f**ue**rzo/forzaré.
As with all verbs ending in zar, the z becomes c before e in the preterit, the present subjunctive,

and the imperative. (See cazar.)
- *Diphthong** o › ue
- Spelling z › c before e

Impersonal mood

	Simple forms	Compound forms
Infinitive	forzar	haber forzado
Gerund	forzando	habiendo forzado
Past participle	forzado	

Personal moods

	Indicative		Subjunctive	
	Simple forms	Compound forms	Simple forms	Compound forms
	Present	**Perfect**	**Present**	**Past**
1st p. sing.	**fuerz**o	he forzado	**fuerce**	haya forzado
2nd p. sing.	**fuerz**as	has forzado	**fuerce**s	hayas forzado
3rd p. sing.	**fuerz**a	ha forzado	**fuerce**	haya forzado
1st p. plur.	forzamos	hemos forzado	for**ce**mos	hayamos forzado
2nd p. plur.	forzáis	habéis forzado	for**cé**is	hayáis forzado
3rd p. plur.	**fuerz**an	han forzado	**fuerce**n	hayan forzado
	Imperfect	**Past perfect**	**Imperfect**	**Past perfect**
1st p. sing.	forzaba	había forzado	forzara	hubiera forzado
2nd p. sing.	forzabas	habías forzado	forzaras	hubieras forzado
3rd p. sing.	forzaba	había forzado	forzara	hubiera forzado
1st p. plur.	forzábamos	habíamos forzado	forzáramos	hubiéramos forzado
2nd p. plur.	forzabais	habíais forzado	forzarais	hubierais forzado
3rd p. plur.	forzaban	habían forzado	forzaran	hubieran forzado
	Preterit	**Past anterior**		
1st p. sing.	for**cé**	hube forzado	forzase	hubiese forzado
2nd p. sing.	forzaste	hubiste forzado	forzases	hubieses forzado
3rd p. sing.	forzó	hubo forzado	forzase	hubiese forzado
1st p. plur.	forzamos	hubimos forzado	forzásemos	hubiésemos forzado
2nd p. plur.	forzasteis	hubisteis forzado	forzaseis	hubieseis forzado
3rd p. plur.	forzaron	hubieron forzado	forzasen	hubiesen forzado
	Future	**Future perfect**	**Future**	**Future perfect**
1st p. sing.	forzaré	habré forzado	forzare	hubiere forzado
2nd p. sing.	forzarás	habrás forzado	forzares	hubieres forzado
3rd p. sing.	forzará	habrá forzado	forzare	hubiere forzado
1st p. plur.	forzaremos	habremos forzado	forzáremos	hubiéremos forzado
2nd p. plur.	forzaréis	habréis forzado	forzareis	hubiereis forzado
3rd p. plur.	forzarán	habrán forzado	forzaren	hubieren forzado
	Present conditional	**Conditional perfect**		
1st p. sing.	forzaría	habría forzado		
2nd p. sing.	forzarías	habrías forzado		
3rd p. sing.	forzaría	habría forzado		
1st p. plur.	forzaríamos	habríamos forzado		
2nd p. plur.	forzaríais	habríais forzado		
3rd p. plur.	forzarían	habrían forzado		

Imperative

Present	**Forms using the subjunctive stem**
fuerza (tú)	**fuerce** (él, ella, usted)
forzad (vosotros)	for**ce**mos (nosotros)
	fuercen (ellos, ellas, ustedes)

JUGAR

Irregular verb

As the *stress** falls on the vowel of the *stem**, the u becomes ue in the present indicative, the present subjunctive, and the imperative.
To keep the [ga] sound before the e, a u is inserted after the g in the preterit and the present subjunctive.

Note: conjugar and enjugar do not have the diphthong.
- *Diphthong** u (o) › ue
- Spelling g › gu before e

Impersonal mood		
	Simple forms	Compound forms
Infinitive	jugar	haber jugado
Gerund	jugando	habiendo jugado
Past participle	jugado	

Personal moods				
	Indicative		Subjunctive	
	Simple forms	Compound forms	Simple forms	Compound forms
	Present	**Perfect**	**Present**	**Past**
1st p. sing.	juego	he jugado	juegue	haya jugado
2nd p. sing.	juegas	has jugado	juegues	hayas jugado
3rd p. sing.	juega	ha jugado	juegue	haya jugado
1st p. plur.	jugamos	hemos jugado	juguemos	hayamos jugado
2nd p. plur.	jugáis	habéis jugado	juguéis	hayáis jugado
3rd p. plur.	juegan	han jugado	jueguen	hayan jugado
	Imperfect	**Past perfect**	**Imperfect**	**Past perfect**
1st p. sing.	jugaba	había jugado	jugara	hubiera jugado
2nd p. sing.	jugabas	habías jugado	jugaras	hubieras jugado
3rd p. sing.	jugaba	había jugado	jugara	hubiera jugado
1st p. plur.	jugábamos	habíamos jugado	jugáramos	hubiéramos jugado
2nd p. plur.	jugabais	habíais jugado	jugarais	hubierais jugado
3rd p. plur.	jugaban	habían jugado	jugaran	hubieran jugado
	Preterit	**Past anterior**		
1st p. sing.	jugué	hube jugado	jugase	hubiese jugado
2nd p. sing.	jugaste	hubiste jugado	jugases	hubieses jugado
3rd p. sing.	jugó	hubo jugado	jugase	hubiese jugado
1st p. plur.	jugamos	hubimos jugado	jugásemos	hubiésemos jugado
2nd p. plur.	jugasteis	hubisteis jugado	jugaseis	hubieseis jugado
3rd p. plur.	jugaron	hubieron jugado	jugasen	hubiesen jugado
	Future	**Future perfect**	**Future**	**Future perfect**
1st p. sing.	jugaré	habré jugado	jugare	hubiere jugado
2nd p. sing.	jugarás	habrás jugado	jugares	hubieres jugado
3rd p. sing.	jugará	habrá jugado	jugare	hubiere jugado
1st p. plur.	jugaremos	habremos jugado	jugáremos	hubiéremos jugado
2nd p. plur.	jugaréis	habréis jugado	jugareis	hubiereis jugado
3rd p. plur.	jugarán	habrán jugado	jugaren	hubieren jugado
	Present conditional	**Conditional perfect**		
1st p. sing.	jugaría	habría jugado		
2nd p. sing.	jugarías	habrías jugado		
3rd p. sing.	jugaría	habría jugado		
1st p. plur.	jugaríamos	habríamos jugado		
2nd p. plur.	jugaríais	habríais jugado		
3rd p. plur.	jugarían	habrían jugado		

Imperative	
Present	**Forms using the subjunctive stem**
juega (tú)	juegue (él, ella, usted)
jugad (vosotros)	juguemos (nosotros)
	jueguen (ellos, ellas, ustedes)

MOVER

Irregular verb

Because of the *stress**, the o of the *stem** becomes ue in the present indicative, the present subjunctive, and the imperative. Compare m**ue**va/mov**amos**.

■ *Diphthong** o › ue

Impersonal mood

	Simple forms	Compound forms
Infinitive	mover	haber movido
Gerund	moviendo	habiendo movido
Past participle	movido	

Personal moods

	Indicative		Subjunctive	
	Simple forms	Compound forms	Simple forms	Compound forms
	Present	**Perfect**	**Present**	**Past**
1st p. sing.	**muev**o	he movido	**muev**a	haya movido
2nd p. sing.	**muev**es	has movido	**muev**as	hayas movido
3rd p. sing.	**muev**e	ha movido	**muev**a	haya movido
1st p. plur.	movemos	hemos movido	movamos	hayamos movido
2nd p. plur.	movéis	habéis movido	mováis	hayáis movido
3rd p. plur.	**muev**en	han movido	**muev**an	hayan movido
	Imperfect	**Past perfect**	**Imperfect**	**Past perfect**
1st p. sing.	movía	había movido	moviera	hubiera movido
2nd p. sing.	movías	habías movido	movieras	hubieras movido
3rd p. sing.	movía	había movido	moviera	hubiera movido
1st p. plur.	movíamos	habíamos movido	moviéramos	hubiéramos movido
2nd p. plur.	movíais	habíais movido	movierais	hubierais movido
3rd p. plur.	movían	habían movido	movieran	hubieran movido
	Preterit	**Past anterior**		
1st p. sing.	moví	hube movido	moviese	hubiese movido
2nd p. sing.	moviste	hubiste movido	movieses	hubieses movido
3rd p. sing.	movió	hubo movido	moviese	hubiese movido
1st p. plur.	movimos	hubimos movido	moviésemos	hubiésemos movido
2nd p. plur.	movisteis	hubisteis movido	movieseis	hubieseis movido
3rd p. plur.	movieron	hubieron movido	moviesen	hubiesen movido
	Future	**Future perfect**	**Future**	**Future perfect**
1st p. sing.	moveré	habré movido	moviere	hubiere movido
2nd p. sing.	moverás	habrás movido	movieres	hubieres movido
3rd p. sing.	moverá	habrá movido	moviere	hubiere movido
1st p. plur.	moveremos	habremos movido	moviéremos	hubiéremos movido
2nd p. plur.	moveréis	habréis movido	moviereis	hubiereis movido
3rd p. plur.	moverán	habrán movido	movieren	hubieren movido
	Present conditional	**Conditional perfect**		
1st p. sing.	movería	habría movido		
2nd p. sing.	moverías	habrías movido		
3rd p. sing.	movería	habría movido		
1st p. plur.	moveríamos	habríamos movido		
2nd p. plur.	moveríais	habríais movido		
3rd p. plur.	moverían	habrían movido		

Imperative

Present	Forms using the subjunctive stem
mueve (tú)	**muev**a (él, ella, usted)
moved (vosotros)	movamos (nosotros)
	muevan (ellos, ellas, ustedes)

COCER

Irregular verb

The o of the *stem** becomes ue in the present indicative, the present subjunctive, and the imperative.

To keep the c sound before the e or the i (ceta), the c changes to z when the *ending** starts with an a or an o. (See vencer.)

■ *Diphthong** o › ue
■ Spelling c › z before a, o

Impersonal mood		
	Simple forms	Compound forms
Infinitive	cocer	haber cocido
Gerund	cociendo	habiendo cocido
Past participle	cocido	

Personal moods			
Indicative		**Subjunctive**	
Simple forms	Compound forms	Simple forms	Compound forms

	Indicative Simple forms	**Indicative** Compound forms	**Subjunctive** Simple forms	**Subjunctive** Compound forms
	Present	**Perfect**	**Present**	**Past**
1st p. sing.	cuezo	he cocido	cueza	haya cocido
2nd p. sing.	cueces	has cocido	cuezas	hayas cocido
3rd p. sing.	cuece	ha cocido	cueza	haya cocido
1st p. plur.	cocemos	hemos cocido	cozamos	hayamos cocido
2nd p. plur.	cocéis	habéis cocido	cozáis	hayáis cocido
3rd p. plur.	cuecen	han cocido	cuezan	hayan cocido
	Imperfect	**Past perfect**	**Imperfect**	**Past perfect**
1st p. sing.	cocía	había cocido	cociera	hubiera cocido
2nd p. sing.	cocías	habías cocido	cocieras	hubieras cocido
3rd p. sing.	cocía	había cocido	cociera	hubiera cocido
1st p. plur.	cocíamos	habíamos cocido	cociéramos	hubiéramos cocido
2nd p. plur.	cocíais	habíais cocido	cocierais	hubierais cocido
3rd p. plur.	cocían	habían cocido	cocieran	hubieran cocido
	Preterit	**Past anterior**		
1st p. sing.	cocí	hube cocido	cociese	hubiese cocido
2nd p. sing.	cociste	hubiste cocido	cocieses	hubieses cocido
3rd p. sing.	coció	hubo cocido	cociese	hubiese cocido
1st p. plur.	cocimos	hubimos cocido	cociésemos	hubiésemos cocido
2nd p. plur.	cocisteis	hubisteis cocido	cocieseis	hubieseis cocido
3rd p. plur.	cocieron	hubieron cocido	cociesen	hubiesen cocido
	Future	**Future perfect**	**Future**	**Future perfect**
1st p. sing.	coceré	habré cocido	cociere	hubiere cocido
2nd p. sing.	cocerás	habrás cocido	cocieres	hubieres cocido
3rd p. sing.	cocerá	habrá cocido	cociere	hubiere cocido
1st p. plur.	coceremos	habremos cocido	cociéremos	hubiéremos cocido
2nd p. plur.	coceréis	habréis cocido	cociereis	hubiereis cocido
3rd p. plur.	cocerán	habrán cocido	cocieren	hubieren cocido
	Present conditional	**Conditional perfect**		
1st p. sing.	cocería	habría cocido		
2nd p. sing.	cocerías	habrías cocido		
3rd p. sing.	cocería	habría cocido		
1st p. plur.	coceríamos	habríamos cocido		
2nd p. plur.	coceríais	habríais cocido		
3rd p. plur.	cocerían	habrían cocido		

Imperative	
Present	**Forms using the subjunctive stem**
cuece (tú)	cueza (él, ella, usted)
coced (vosotros)	cozamos (nosotros)
	cuezan (ellos, ellas, ustedes)

OLER

Irregular verb

The o of the *stem** becomes ue in the present indicative, the present subjunctive, and the imperative.
Compare: h**ue**la/ol**a**mos.
A particular feature of this verb is that it precedes the *diphthong** with a silent h.

- Diphthong o › ue
- Spelling h before ue

Impersonal mood		
	Simple forms	Compound forms
Infinitive	oler	haber olido
Gerund	oliendo	habiendo olido
Past participle	olido	

Personal moods				
	Indicative		Subjunctive	
	Simple forms	Compound forms	Simple forms	Compound forms
	Present	**Perfect**	**Present**	**Past**
1st p. sing.	**huelo**	he olido	**huela**	haya olido
2nd p. sing.	**hueles**	has olido	**huelas**	hayas olido
3rd p. sing.	**huele**	ha olido	**huela**	haya olido
1st p. plur.	olemos	hemos olido	olamos	hayamos olido
2nd p. plur.	oléis	habéis olido	oláis	hayáis olido
3rd p. plur.	**huelen**	han olido	**huelan**	hayan olido
	Imperfect	**Past perfect**	**Imperfect**	**Past perfect**
1st p. sing.	olía	había olido	oliera	hubiera olido
2nd p. sing.	olías	habías olido	olieras	hubieras olido
3rd p. sing.	olía	había olido	oliera	hubiera olido
1st p. plur.	olíamos	habíamos olido	oliéramos	hubiéramos olido
2nd p. plur.	olíais	habíais olido	olierais	hubierais olido
3rd p. plur.	olían	habían olido	olieran	hubieran olido
	Preterit	**Past anterior**		
1st p. sing.	olí	hube olido	oliese	hubiese olido
2nd p. sing.	oliste	hubiste olido	olieses	hubieses olido
3rd p. sing.	olió	hubo olido	oliese	hubiese olido
1st p. plur.	olimos	hubimos olido	oliésemos	hubiésemos olido
2nd p. plur.	olisteis	hubisteis olido	olieseis	hubieseis olido
3rd p. plur.	olieron	hubieron olido	oliesen	hubiesen olido
	Future	**Future perfect**	**Future**	**Future perfect**
1st p. sing.	oleré	habré olido	oliere	hubiere olido
2nd p. sing.	olerás	habrás olido	olieres	hubieres olido
3rd p. sing.	olerá	habrá olido	oliere	hubiere olido
1st p. plur.	oleremos	habremos olido	oliéremos	hubiéremos olido
2nd p. plur.	oleréis	habréis olido	oliereis	hubiereis olido
3rd p. plur.	olerán	habrán olido	olieren	hubieren olido
	Present conditional	**Conditional perfect**		
1st p. sing.	olería	habría olido		
2nd p. sing.	olerías	habrías olido		
3rd p. sing.	olería	habría olido		
1st p. plur.	oleríamos	habríamos olido		
2nd p. plur.	oleríais	habríais olido		
3rd p. plur.	olerían	habrían olido		

Imperative	
Present	**Forms using the subjunctive stem**
huele (tú)	**huela** (él, ella, usted)
oled (vosotros)	olamos (nosotros)
	huelan (ellos, ellas, ustedes)

A D Q U I R I R

Because of the *stress**, the i of the *stem** becomes ie in the present indicative, the present subjunctive, and the imperative.
Compare: adqu**ie**ren/adquir**imos**.
■ *Diphthong** i › ie

Impersonal mood		
	Simple forms	**Compound forms**
Infinitive	adquirir	haber adquirido
Gerund	adquiriendo	habiendo adquirido
Past participle	adquirido	

Personal moods			
Indicative		**Subjunctive**	
Simple forms	**Compound forms**	**Simple forms**	**Compound forms**
Present	**Perfect**	**Present**	**Past**
1st p. sing. adquiero	he adquirido	adquiera	haya adquirido
2nd p. sing. adquieres	has adquirido	adquieras	hayas adquirido
3rd p. sing. adquiere	ha adquirido	adquiera	haya adquirido
1st p. plur. adquirimos	hemos adquirido	adquiramos	hayamos adquirido
2nd p. plur. adquirís	habéis adquirido	adquiráis	hayáis adquirido
3rd p. plur. adquieren	han adquirido	adquieran	hayan adquirido
Imperfect	**Past perfect**	**Imperfect**	**Past perfect**
1st p. sing. adquiría	había adquirido	adquiriera	hubiera adquirido
2nd p. sing. adquirías	habías adquirido	adquirieras	hubieras adquirido
3rd p. sing. adquiría	había adquirido	adquiriera	hubiera adquirido
1st p. plur. adquiríamos	habíamos adquirido	adquiriéramos	hubiéramos adquirido
2nd p. plur. adquiríais	habíais adquirido	adquirierais	hubierais adquirido
3rd p. plur. adquirían	habían adquirido	adquirieran	hubieran adquirido
Preterit	**Past anterior**		
1st p. sing. adquirí	hube adquirido	adquiriese	hubiese adquirido
2nd p. sing. adquiriste	hubiste adquirido	adquirieses	hubieses adquirido
3rd p. sing. adquirió	hubo adquirido	adquiriese	hubiese adquirido
1st p. plur. adquirimos	hubimos adquirido	adquiriésemos	hubiésemos adquirido
2nd p. plur. adquiristeis	hubisteis adquirido	adquirieseis	hubieseis adquirido
3rd p. plur. adquirieron	hubieron adquirido	adquiriesen	hubiesen adquirido
Future	**Future perfect**	**Future**	**Future perfect**
1st p. sing. adquiriré	habré adquirido	adquiriere	hubiere adquirido
2nd p. sing. adquirirás	habrás adquirido	adquirieres	hubieres adquirido
3rd p. sing. adquirirá	habrá adquirido	adquiriere	hubiere adquirido
1st p. plur. adquiriremos	habremos adquirido	adquiriéremos	hubiéremos adquirido
2nd p. plur. adquiriréis	habréis adquirido	adquiriereis	hubiereis adquirido
3rd p. plur. adquirirán	habrán adquirido	adquirieren	hubieren adquirido
Present conditional	**Conditional perfect**		
1st p. sing. adquiriría	habría adquirido		
2nd p. sing. adquirirías	habrías adquirido		
3rd p. sing. adquiriría	habría adquirido		
1st p. plur. adquiriríamos	habríamos adquirido		
2nd p. plur. adquiriríais	habríais adquirido		
3rd p. plur. adquirirían	habrían adquirido		

Imperative	
Present	**Forms using the subjunctive stem**
adquiere (tú)	adquiera (él, ella, usted)
adquirid (vosotros)	adquiramos (nosotros)
	adquieran (ellos, ellas, ustedes)

Irregular verb

In a large number of verbs, the last e of the *stem** becomes i in the gerund, the present indicative, the preterit, and in all simple forms of the subjunctive and all forms of the imperative, apart from the 2nd person plural, pedid.

■ Vowel change in the stem e › i

Impersonal mood		
	Simple forms	Compound forms
Infinitive	pedir	haber pedido
Gerund	pidiendo	habiendo pedido
Past participle	pedido	

Personal moods				
	Indicative		Subjunctive	
	Simple forms	Compound forms	Simple forms	Compound forms
	Present	**Perfect**	**Present**	**Past**
1st p. sing.	pido	he pedido	pida	haya pedido
2nd p. sing.	pides	has pedido	pidas	hayas pedido
3rd p. sing.	pide	ha pedido	pida	haya pedido
1st p. plur.	pedimos	hemos pedido	pidamos	hayamos pedido
2nd p. plur.	pedís	habéis pedido	pidáis	hayáis pedido
3rd p. plur.	piden	han pedido	pidan	hayan pedido
	Imperfect	**Past perfect**	**Imperfect**	**Past perfect**
1st p. sing.	pedía	había pedido	pidiera	hubiera pedido
2nd p. sing.	pedías	habías pedido	pidieras	hubieras pedido
3rd p. sing.	pedía	había pedido	pidiera	hubiera pedido
1st p. plur.	pedíamos	habíamos pedido	pidiéramos	hubiéramos pedido
2nd p. plur.	pedíais	habíais pedido	pidierais	hubierais pedido
3rd p. plur.	pedían	habían pedido	pidieran	hubieran pedido
	Preterit	**Past anterior**		
1st p. sing.	pedí	hube pedido	pidiese	hubiese pedido
2nd p. sing.	pediste	hubiste pedido	pidieses	hubieses pedido
3rd p. sing.	pidió	hubo pedido	pidiese	hubiese pedido
1st p. plur.	pedimos	hubimos pedido	pidiésemos	hubiésemos pedido
2nd p. plur.	pedisteis	hubisteis pedido	pidieseis	hubieseis pedido
3rd p. plur.	pidieron	hubieron pedido	pidiesen	hubiesen pedido
	Future	**Future perfect**	**Future**	**Future perfect**
1st p. sing.	pediré	habré pedido	pidiere	hubiere pedido
2nd p. sing.	pedirás	habrás pedido	pidieres	hubieres pedido
3rd p. sing.	pedirá	habrá pedido	pidiere	hubiere pedido
1st p. plur.	pediremos	habremos pedido	pidiéremos	hubiéremos pedido
2nd p. plur.	pediréis	habréis pedido	pidiereis	hubiereis pedido
3rd p. plur.	pedirán	habrán pedido	pidieren	hubieren pedido
	Present conditional	**Conditional perfect**		
1st p. sing.	pediría	habría pedido		
2nd p. sing.	pedirías	habrías pedido		
3rd p. sing.	pediría	habría pedido		
1st p. plur.	pediríamos	habríamos pedido		
2nd p. plur.	pediríais	habríais pedido		
3rd p. plur.	pedirían	habrían pedido		

Imperative	
Present	**Forms using the subjunctive stem**
pide (tú)	pida (él, ella, usted)
pedid (vosotros)	pidamos (nosotros)
	pidan (ellos, ellas, ustedes)

REGIR

Irregular verb

The last e of the *stem** becomes i in the gerund, the present indicative, the preterit, and in all simple forms of the subjunctive and all forms of the imperative, apart from the 2nd person plural, regid.
As with all verbs ending in gir, the g changes to j (jota) before an a and an o. (See dirigir.)
- Vowel change in the stem e › i
- Spelling g › j before a, o

Impersonal mood		
	Simple forms	Compound forms
Infinitive	regir	haber regido
Gerund	rigiendo	habiendo regido
Past participle	regido	

Personal moods				
	Indicative		**Subjunctive**	
	Simple forms	Compound forms	Simple forms	Compound forms
	Present	**Perfect**	**Present**	**Past**
1st p. sing.	**rijo**	he regido	**rija**	haya regido
2nd p. sing.	**riges**	has regido	**rijas**	hayas regido
3rd p. sing.	**rige**	ha regido	**rija**	haya regido
1st p. plur.	regimos	hemos regido	**rijamos**	hayamos regido
2nd p. plur.	regís	habéis regido	**rijáis**	hayáis regido
3rd p. plur.	**rigen**	han regido	**rijan**	hayan regido
	Imperfect	**Past perfect**	**Imperfect**	**Past perfect**
1st p. sing.	regía	había regido	**rigiera**	hubiera regido
2nd p. sing.	regías	habías regido	**rigieras**	hubieras regido
3rd p. sing.	regía	había regido	**rigiera**	hubiera regido
1st p. plur.	regíamos	habíamos regido	**rigiéramos**	hubiéramos regido
2nd p. plur.	regíais	habíais regido	**rigierais**	hubierais regido
3rd p. plur.	regían	habían regido	**rigieran**	hubieran regido
	Preterit	**Past anterior**		
1st p. sing.	regí	hube regido	**rigiese**	hubiese regido
2nd p. sing.	registe	hubiste regido	**rigieses**	hubieses regido
3rd p. sing.	**rigió**	hubo regido	**rigiese**	hubiese regido
1st p. plur.	regimos	hubimos regido	**rigiésemos**	hubiésemos regido
2nd p. plur.	registeis	hubisteis regido	**rigieseis**	hubieseis regido
3rd p. plur.	**rigieron**	hubieron regido	**rigiesen**	hubiesen regido
	Future	**Future perfect**	**Future**	**Future perfect**
1st p. sing.	regiré	habré regido	**rigiere**	hubiere regido
2nd p. sing.	regirás	habrás regido	**rigieres**	hubieres regido
3rd p. sing.	regirá	habrá regido	**rigiere**	hubiere regido
1st p. plur.	regiremos	habremos regido	**rigiéremos**	hubiéremos regido
2nd p. plur.	regiréis	habréis regido	**rigiereis**	hubiereis regido
3rd p. plur.	regirán	habrán regido	**rigieren**	hubieren regido
	Present conditional	**Conditional perfect**		
1st p. sing.	regiría	habría regido		
2nd p. sing.	regirías	habrías regido		
3rd p. sing.	regiría	habría regido		
1st p. plur.	regiríamos	habríamos regido		
2nd p. plur.	regiríais	habríais regido		
3rd p. plur.	regirían	habrían regido		

Imperative	
Present	**Forms using the subjunctive stem**
rige (tú)	**rija** (él, ella, usted)
regid (vosotros)	**rijamos** (nosotros)
	rijan (ellos, ellas, ustedes)

SEGUIR

Irregular verb

The last e of the *stem** changes to i in the gerund, the present indicative, the preterit, and in all simple forms of the subjunctive and all forms of the imperative, apart from the 2nd person plural (seguid). As with all verbs ending in guir, the u is dropped before an a and an o.

- Vowel change in the stem e › i
- Spelling gu › g before a, o

Impersonal mood		
	Simple forms	Compound forms
finitive	seguir	haber seguido
erund	siguiendo	habiendo seguido
st participle	seguido	

Personal moods				
	Indicative		Subjunctive	
	Simple forms	Compound forms	Simple forms	Compound forms
	Present	**Perfect**	**Present**	**Past**
t p. sing.	sigo	he seguido	siga	haya seguido
nd p. sing.	sigues	has seguido	sigas	hayas seguido
d p. sing.	sigue	ha seguido	siga	haya seguido
t p. plur.	seguimos	hemos seguido	sigamos	hayamos seguido
nd p. plur.	seguís	habéis seguido	sigáis	hayáis seguido
d p. plur.	siguen	han seguido	sigan	hayan seguido
	Imperfect	**Past perfect**	**Imperfect**	**Past perfect**
t p. sing.	seguía	había seguido	siguiera	hubiera seguido
nd p. sing.	seguías	habías seguido	siguieras	hubieras seguido
d p. sing.	seguía	había seguido	siguiera	hubiera seguido
t p. plur.	seguíamos	habíamos seguido	siguiéramos	hubiéramos seguido
nd p. plur.	seguíais	habíais seguido	siguierais	hubierais seguido
d p. plur.	seguían	habían seguido	siguieran	hubieran seguido
	Preterit	**Past anterior**		
t p. sing.	seguí	hube seguido	siguiese	hubiese seguido
nd p. sing.	seguiste	hubiste seguido	siguieses	hubieses seguido
d p. sing.	siguió	hubo seguido	siguiese	hubiese seguido
t p. plur.	seguimos	hubimos seguido	siguiésemos	hubiésemos seguido
nd p. plur.	seguisteis	hubisteis seguido	siguieseis	hubieseis seguido
d p. plur.	siguieron	hubieron seguido	siguiesen	hubiesen seguido
	Future	**Future perfect**	**Future**	**Future perfect**
t p. sing.	seguiré	habré seguido	siguiere	hubiere seguido
nd p. sing.	seguirás	habrás seguido	siguieres	hubieres seguido
rd p. sing.	seguirá	habrá seguido	siguiere	hubiere seguido
t p. plur.	seguiremos	habremos seguido	siguiéremos	hubiéremos seguido
nd p. plur.	seguiréis	habréis seguido	siguiereis	hubiereis seguido
rd p. plur.	seguirán	habrán seguido	siguieren	hubieren seguido
	Present conditional	**Conditional perfect**		
t p. sing.	seguiría	habría seguido		
nd p. sing.	seguirías	habrías seguido		
d p. sing.	seguiría	habría seguido		
t p. plur.	seguiríamos	habríamos seguido		
nd p. plur.	seguiríais	habríais seguido		
d p. plur.	seguirían	habrían seguido		

Imperative	
Present	**Forms using the subjunctive stem**
sigue (tú)	siga (él, ella, usted)
seguid (vosotros)	sigamos (nosotros)
	sigan (ellos, ellas, ustedes)

REÍR

Irregular verb

The e of the *stem** becomes an i in the gerund, the present indicative, the preterit, and in all simple forms of the subjunctive and the imperative, apart from the 2nd person plural reíd. The i of the *diphthong** io or ie is dropped in the preterit (rió), in the subjunctive (riera), and in the gerund (riendo). The written accent (reído) marks the *hiatus**.
- Vowel change in the stem e › i
- Vowel suppression in the stem ii › i

Impersonal mood		
	Simple forms	Compound forms
Infinitive	reír	haber reído
Gerund	riendo	habiendo reído
Past participle	reído	

Personal moods

	Indicative			Subjunctive	
	Simple forms	Compound forms		Simple forms	Compound forms
	Present	**Perfect**		**Present**	**Past**
1st p. sing.	río	he reído		ría	haya reído
2nd p. sing.	ríes	has reído		rías	hayas reído
3rd p. sing.	ríe	ha reído		ría	haya reído
1st p. plur.	reímos	hemos reído		riamos	hayamos reído
2nd p. plur.	reís	habéis reído		riais	hayáis reído
3rd p. plur.	ríen	han reído		rían	hayan reído
	Imperfect	**Past perfect**		**Imperfect**	**Past perfect**
1st p. sing.	reía	había reído		riera	hubiera reído
2nd p. sing.	reías	habías reído		rieras	hubieras reído
3rd p. sing.	reía	había reído		riera	hubiera reído
1st p. plur.	reíamos	habíamos reído		riéramos	hubiéramos reído
2nd p. plur.	reíais	habíais reído		rierais	hubierais reído
3rd p. plur.	reían	habían reído		rieran	hubieran reído
	Preterit	**Past anterior**			
1st p. sing.	reí	hube reído		riese	hubiese reído
2nd p. sing.	reíste	hubiste reído		rieses	hubieses reído
3rd p. sing.	rió	hubo reído		riese	hubiese reído
1st p. plur.	reímos	hubimos reído		riésemos	hubiésemos reído
2nd p. plur.	reísteis	hubisteis reído		rieseis	hubieseis reído
3rd p. plur.	rieron	hubieron reído		riesen	hubiesen reído
	Future	**Future perfect**		**Future**	**Future perfect**
1st p. sing.	reiré	habré reído		riere	hubiere reído
2nd p. sing.	reirás	habrás reído		rieres	hubieres reído
3rd p. sing.	reirá	habrá reído		riere	hubiere reído
1st p. plur.	reiremos	habremos reído		riéremos	hubiéremos reído
2nd p. plur.	reiréis	habréis reído		riereis	hubiereis reído
3rd p. plur.	reirán	habrán reído		rieren	hubieren reído
	Present conditional	**Conditional perfect**			
1st p. sing.	reiría	habría reído			
2nd p. sing.	reirías	habrías reído			
3rd p. sing.	reiría	habría reído			
1st p. plur.	reiríamos	habríamos reído			
2nd p. plur.	reiríais	habríais reído			
3rd p. plur.	reirían	habrían reído			

Imperative	
Present	**Forms using the subjunctive stem**
ríe (tú)	ría (él, ella, usted)
reíd (vosotros)	riamos (nosotros)
	rían (ellos, ellas, ustedes)

PUDRIR / PODRIR

Irregular verb

Pudrir is the preferred form of the old verb podrir. All the forms of the verb use the u of the *stem**
apart from the the past participle (podrido). The old form can still sometimes be used as an alternative in the following cases: the infinitive (pudrir/podrir), the 1st person singular of the preterit
(pudrí/podrí), and the 1st person singular of the simple future (pudriré/podriré).
■ Vowel change in the stem o › u

Impersonal mood		
	Simple forms	Compound forms
Infinitive	pudrir/podrir	haber podrido
Gerund	pudriendo	habiendo podrido
Past participle	podrido	

Personal moods				
	Indicative		Subjunctive	
	Simple forms	Compound forms	Simple forms	Compound forms
	Present	**Perfect**	**Present**	**Past**
1st p. sing.	pudro	he podrido	pudra	haya podrido
2nd p. sing.	pudres	has podrido	pudras	hayas podrido
3rd p. sing.	pudre	ha podrido	pudra	haya podrido
1st p. plur.	pudrimos	hemos podrido	pudramos	hayamos podrido
2nd p. plur.	pudrís	habéis podrido	pudráis	hayáis podrido
3rd p. plur.	pudren	han podrido	pudran	hayan podrido
	Imperfect	**Past perfect**	**Imperfect**	**Past perfect**
1st p. sing.	pudría	había podrido	pudriera	hubiera podrido
2nd p. sing.	pudrías	habías podrido	pudrieras	hubieras podrido
3rd p. sing.	pudría	había podrido	pudriera	hubiera podrido
1st p. plur.	pudríamos	habíamos podrido	pudriéramos	hubiéramos podrido
2nd p. plur.	pudríais	habíais podrido	pudrierais	hubierais podrido
3rd p. plur.	pudrían	habían podrido	pudrieran	hubieran podrido
	Preterit	**Past anterior**		
1st p. sing.	pudrí/podrí	hube podrido	pudriese	hubiese podrido
2nd p. sing.	pudriste	hubiste podrido	pudrieses	hubieses podrido
3rd p. sing.	pudrió	hubo podrido	pudriese	hubiese podrido
1st p. plur.	pudrimos	hubimos podrido	pudriésemos	hubiésemos podrido
2nd p. plur.	pudristeis	hubisteis podrido	pudrieseis	hubieseis podrido
3rd p. plur.	pudrieron	hubieron podrido	pudriesen	hubiesen podrido
	Future	**Future perfect**	**Future**	**Future perfect**
1st p. sing.	pudriré/podriré	habré podrido	pudriere	hubiere podrido
2nd p. sing.	pudrirás	habrás podrido	pudrieres	hubieres podrido
3rd p. sing.	pudrirá	habrá podrido	pudriere	hubiere podrido
1st p. plur.	pudriremos	habremos podrido	pudriéremos	hubiéremos podrido
2nd p. plur.	pudriréis	habréis podrido	pudriereis	hubiereis podrido
3rd p. plur.	pudrirán	habrán podrido	pudrieren	hubieren podrido
	Present conditional	**Conditional perfect**		
1st p. sing.	pudriría	habría podrido		
2nd p. sing.	pudrirías	habrías podrido		
3rd p. sing.	pudriría	habría podrido		
1st p. plur.	pudriríamos	habríamos podrido		
2nd p. plur.	pudriríais	habríais podrido		
3rd p. plur.	pudrirían	habrían podrido		

Imperative	
Present	**Forms using the subjunctive stem**
pudre (tú)	pudra (él, ella, usted)
pudrid (vosotros)	pudramos (nosotros)
	pudran (ellos, ellas, ustedes)

NACER

Irregular verb

The final consonant of the *stem** is preceded by a z in the 1st person singular of the present indicative, the present subjunctive, and in the imperative.

■ Consonant change in the stem c › zc before a, o

Impersonal mood		
	Simple forms	Compound forms
Infinitive	nacer	haber nacido
Gerund	naciendo	habiendo nacido
Past participle	nacido	

Personal moods			
Indicative		**Subjunctive**	
Simple forms	Compound forms	Simple forms	Compound forms
Present	**Perfect**	**Present**	**Past**
1st p. sing. **nazco**	he nacido	**nazca**	haya nacido
2nd p. sing. naces	has nacido	**nazca**s	hayas nacido
3rd p. sing. nace	ha nacido	**nazca**	haya nacido
1st p. plur. nacemos	hemos nacido	**nazca**mos	hayamos nacido
2nd p. plur. nacéis	habéis nacido	**nazcá**is	hayáis nacido
3rd p. plur. nacen	han nacido	**nazca**n	hayan nacido
Imperfect	**Past perfect**	**Imperfect**	**Past perfect**
1st p. sing. nacía	había nacido	naciera	hubiera nacido
2nd p. sing. nacías	habías nacido	nacieras	hubieras nacido
3rd p. sing. nacía	había nacido	naciera	hubiera nacido
1st p. plur. nacíamos	habíamos nacido	naciéramos	hubiéramos nacido
2nd p. plur. nacíais	habíais nacido	nacierais	hubierais nacido
3rd p. plur. nacían	habían nacido	nacieran	hubieran nacido
Preterit	**Past anterior**		
1st p. sing. nací	hube nacido	naciese	hubiese nacido
2nd p. sing. naciste	hubiste nacido	nacieses	hubieses nacido
3rd p. sing. nació	hubo nacido	naciese	hubiese nacido
1st p. plur. nacimos	hubimos nacido	naciésemos	hubiésemos nacido
2nd p. plur. nacisteis	hubisteis nacido	nacieseis	hubieseis nacido
3rd p. plur. nacieron	hubieron nacido	naciesen	hubiesen nacido
Future	**Future perfect**	**Future**	**Future perfect**
1st p. sing. naceré	habré nacido	naciere	hubiere nacido
2nd p. sing. nacerás	habrás nacido	nacieres	hubieres nacido
3rd p. sing. nacerá	habrá nacido	naciere	hubiere nacido
1st p. plur. naceremos	habremos nacido	naciéremos	hubiéremos nacido
2nd p. plur. naceréis	habréis nacido	naciereis	hubiereis nacido
3rd p. plur. nacerán	habrán nacido	nacieren	hubieren nacido
Present conditional	**Conditional perfect**		

		Imperative	
1st p. sing. nacería	habría nacido	**Present**	**Forms using the subjunctive ster**
2nd p. sing. nacerías	habrías nacido	nace (tú)	**nazca** (él, ella, usted)
3rd p. sing. nacería	habría nacido	naced (vosotros)	**nazca**mos (nosotros)
1st p. plur. naceríamos	habríamos nacido		**nazca**n (ellos, ellas, ustedes)
2nd p. plur. naceríais	habríais nacido		
3rd p. plur. nacerían	habrían nacido		

PARECER

Irregular verb

The irregularity applies to the present indicative, the present subjunctive, and the imperative. The most important group of irregular verbs (over 200 verbs) in current use follow this model. Note: mecer and remecer have a regular conjugation with a spelling change.

■ Consonant change in the stem c › zc before a, o

Impersonal mood		
	Simple forms	Compound forms
Infinitive	parecer	haber parecido
Gerund	pareciendo	habiendo parecido
Past participle	parecido	

Personal moods				
	Indicative		**Subjunctive**	
	Simple forms	Compound forms	Simple forms	Compound forms
	Present	**Perfect**	**Present**	**Past**
1st p. sing.	parezco	he parecido	parezca	haya parecido
2nd p. sing.	pareces	has parecido	parezcas	hayas parecido
3rd p. sing.	parece	ha parecido	parezca	haya parecido
1st p. plur.	parecemos	hemos parecido	parezcamos	hayamos parecido
2nd p. plur.	parecéis	habéis parecido	parezcáis	hayáis parecido
3rd p. plur.	parecen	han parecido	parezcan	hayan parecido
	Imperfect	**Past perfect**	**Imperfect**	**Past perfect**
1st p. sing.	parecía	había parecido	pareciera	hubiera parecido
2nd p. sing.	parecías	habías parecido	parecieras	hubieras parecido
3rd p. sing.	parecía	había parecido	pareciera	hubiera parecido
1st p. plur.	parecíamos	habíamos parecido	pareciéramos	hubiéramos parecido
2nd p. plur.	parecíais	habíais parecido	parecierais	hubierais parecido
3rd p. plur.	parecían	habían parecido	parecieran	hubieran parecido
	Preterit	**Past anterior**		
1st p. sing.	parecí	hube parecido	pareciese	hubiese parecido
2nd p. sing.	pareciste	hubiste parecido	parecieses	hubieses parecido
3rd p. sing.	pareció	hubo parecido	pareciese	hubiese parecido
1st p. plur.	parecimos	hubimos parecido	pareciésemos	hubiésemos parecido
2nd p. plur.	parecisteis	hubisteis parecido	parecieseis	hubieseis parecido
3rd p. plur.	parecieron	hubieron parecido	pareciesen	hubiesen parecido
	Future	**Future perfect**	**Future**	**Future perfect**
1st p. sing.	pareceré	habré parecido	pareciere	hubiere parecido
2nd p. sing.	parecerás	habrás parecido	parecieres	hubieres parecido
3rd p. sing.	parecerá	habrá parecido	pareciere	hubiere parecido
1st p. plur.	pareceremos	habremos parecido	pareciéremos	hubiéremos parecido
2nd p. plur.	pareceréis	habréis parecido	pareciereis	hubiereis parecido
3rd p. plur.	parecerán	habrán parecido	parecieren	hubieren parecido
	Present conditional	**Conditional perfect**		
1st p. sing.	parecería	habría parecido		
2nd p. sing.	parecerías	habrías parecido		
3rd p. sing.	parecería	habría parecido		
1st p. plur.	pareceríamos	habríamos parecido		
2nd p. plur.	pareceríais	habríais parecido		
3rd p. plur.	parecerían	habrían parecido		

Imperative	
Present	**Forms using the subjunctive stem**
parece (tú)	parezca (él, ella, usted)
pareced (vosotros)	parezcamos (nosotros)
	parezcan (ellos, ellas, ustedes)

CONOCER

Irregular verb

The final consonant of the *stem** is preceded by a z in the present indicative, the present subjunctive, and the imperative.

Note: cocer, escocer, recocer, retorcer, torcer follow a different irregular pattern. (See cocer.)

■ Consonant change in the stem c › zc before a, o

Impersonal mood		
	Simple forms	Compound forms
Infinitive	conocer	haber conocido
Gerund	conociendo	habiendo conocido
Past participle	conocido	

Personal moods			
Indicative		**Subjunctive**	
Simple forms	Compound forms	Simple forms	Compound forms
Present	**Perfect**	**Present**	**Past**
1st p. sing. conozco	he conocido	conozca	haya conocido
2nd p. sing. conoces	has conocido	conozcas	hayas conocido
3rd p. sing. conoce	ha conocido	conozca	haya conocido
1st p. plur. conocemos	hemos conocido	conozcamos	hayamos conocido
2nd p. plur. conocéis	habéis conocido	conozcáis	hayáis conocido
3rd p. plur. conocen	han conocido	conozcan	hayan conocido
Imperfect	**Past perfect**	**Imperfect**	**Past perfect**
1st p. sing. conocía	había conocido	conociera	hubiera conocido
2nd p. sing. conocías	habías conocido	conocieras	hubieras conocido
3rd p. sing. conocía	había conocido	conociera	hubiera conocido
1st p. plur. conocíamos	habíamos conocido	conociéramos	hubiéramos conocido
2nd p. plur. conocíais	habíais conocido	conocierais	hubierais conocido
3rd p. plur. conocían	habían conocido	conocieran	hubieran conocido
Preterit	**Past anterior**		
1st p. sing. conocí	hube conocido	conociese	hubiese conocido
2nd p. sing. conociste	hubiste conocido	conocieses	hubieses conocido
3rd p. sing. conoció	hubo conocido	conociese	hubiese conocido
1st p. plur. conocimos	hubimos conocido	conociésemos	hubiésemos conocido
2nd p. plur. conocisteis	hubisteis conocido	conocieseis	hubieseis conocido
3rd p. plur. conocieron	hubieron conocido	conociesen	hubiesen conocido
Future	**Future perfect**	**Future**	**Future perfect**
1st p. sing. conoceré	habré conocido	conociere	hubiere conocido
2nd p. sing. conocerás	habrás conocido	conocieres	hubieres conocido
3rd p. sing. conocerá	habrá conocido	conociere	hubiere conocido
1st p. plur. conoceremos	habremos conocido	conociéremos	hubiéremos conocido
2nd p. plur. conoceréis	habréis conocido	conociereis	hubiereis conocido
3rd p. plur. conocerán	habrán conocido	conocieren	hubieren conocido
Present conditional	**Conditional perfect**		
1st p. sing. conocería	habría conocido		
2nd p. sing. conocerías	habrías conocido		
3rd p. sing. conocería	habría conocido		
1st p. plur. conoceríamos	habríamos conocido		
2nd p. plur. conoceríais	habríais conocido		
3rd p. plur. conocerían	habrían conocido		

Imperative	
Present	**Forms using the subjunctive stem**
conoce (tú)	conozca (él, ella, usted)
conoced (vosotros)	conozcamos (nosotros)
	conozcan (ellos, ellas, ustedes)

LUCIR

Irregular verb

The irregularity applies to the stem in the present indicative, the present subjunctive, and in the imperative.

Note: desfruncir, desuncir, esparcir, estarcir, fruncir, resarcir, uncir **are regular verbs with a spelling change** c › z (zurcir).

■ Consonant change in the stem c › zc before a, o

Impersonal mood		
	Simple forms	Compound forms
Infinitive	lucir	haber lucido
Gerund	luciendo	habiendo lucido
Past participle	lucido	

Personal moods				
	Indicative		**Subjunctive**	
	Simple forms	Compound forms	Simple forms	Compound forms
	Present	**Perfect**	**Present**	**Past**
1st p. sing.	luzco	he lucido	luzca	haya lucido
2nd p. sing.	luces	has lucido	luzcas	hayas lucido
3rd p. sing.	luce	ha lucido	luzca	haya lucido
1st p. plur.	lucimos	hemos lucido	luzcamos	hayamos lucido
2nd p. plur.	lucís	habéis lucido	luzcáis	hayáis lucido
3rd p. plur.	lucen	han lucido	luzcan	hayan lucido
	Imperfect	**Past perfect**	**Imperfect**	**Past perfect**
1st p. sing.	lucía	había lucido	luciera	hubiera lucido
2nd p. sing.	lucías	habías lucido	lucieras	hubieras lucido
3rd p. sing.	lucía	había lucido	luciera	hubiera lucido
1st p. plur.	lucíamos	habíamos lucido	luciéramos	hubiéramos lucido
2nd p. plur.	lucíais	habíais lucido	lucierais	hubierais lucido
3rd p. plur.	lucían	habían lucido	lucieran	hubieran lucido
	Preterit	**Past anterior**		
1st p. sing.	lucí	hube lucido	luciese	hubiese lucido
2nd p. sing.	luciste	hubiste lucido	lucieses	hubieses lucido
3rd p. sing.	lució	hubo lucido	luciese	hubiese lucido
1st p. plur.	lucimos	hubimos lucido	luciésemos	hubiésemos lucido
2nd p. plur.	lucisteis	hubisteis lucido	lucieseis	hubieseis lucido
3rd p. plur.	lucieron	hubieron lucido	luciesen	hubiesen lucido
	Future	**Future perfect**	**Future**	**Future perfect**
1st p. sing.	luciré	habré lucido	luciere	hubiere lucido
2nd p. sing.	lucirás	habrás lucido	lucieres	hubieres lucido
3rd p. sing.	lucirá	habrá lucido	luciere	hubiere lucido
1st p. plur.	luciremos	habremos lucido	luciéremos	hubiéremos lucido
2nd p. plur.	luciréis	habréis lucido	luciereis	hubiereis lucido
3rd p. plur.	lucirán	habrán lucido	lucieren	hubieren lucido
	Present conditional	**Conditional perfect**		
1st p. sing.	luciría	habría lucido		
2nd p. sing.	lucirías	habrías lucido		
3rd p. sing.	luciría	habría lucido		
1st p. plur.	luciríamos	habríamos lucido		
2nd p. plur.	luciríais	habríais lucido		
3rd p. plur.	lucirían	habrían lucido		

Imperative	
Present	**Forms using the subjunctive stem**
luce (tú)	luzca (él, ella, usted)
lucid (vosotros)	luzcamos (nosotros)
	luzcan (ellos, ellas, ustedes)

YACER

Irregular verb

The *stem** changes in the 1st person singular of the present indicative, the simple forms of the present subjunctive and in the imperative.
The only other verb that conjugates like this is subyacer.

■ Consonant change in the stem c › zc or c › zg or c › g before a, o

Impersonal mood		
	Simple forms	Compound forms
Infinitive	yacer	haber yacido
Gerund	yaciendo	habiendo yacido
Past participle	yacido	

Personal moods			
Indicative		**Subjunctive**	
Simple forms	Compound forms	Simple forms	Compound forms

	Indicative Simple	Compound	Subjunctive Simple	Compound
	Present	**Perfect**	**Present**	**Past**
1st p. sing.	yazco, yazgo o yago	he yacido	yazca, yazga o yaga	haya yacido
2nd p. sing.	yaces	has yacido	yazcas, yazgas o yagas	hayas yacido
3rd p. sing.	yace	ha yacido	yazca, yazga o yaga	haya yacido
1st p. plur.	yacemos	hemos yacido	yazcamos, yazgamos o yagamos	hayamos yacido
2nd p. plur.	yacéis	habéis yacido	yazcáis, yazgáis o yagáis	hayáis yacido
3rd p. plur.	yacen	han yacido	yazcan, yazgan o yagan	hayan yacido
	Imperfect	**Past perfect**	**Imperfect**	**Past perfect**
1st p. sing.	yacía	había yacido	yaciera	hubiera yacido
2nd p. sing.	yacías	habías yacido	yacieras	hubieras yacido
3rd p. sing.	yacía	había yacido	yaciera	hubiera yacido
1st p. plur.	yacíamos	habíamos yacido	yaciéramos	hubiéramos yacido
2nd p. plur.	yacíais	habíais yacido	yacierais	hubierais yacido
3rd p. plur.	yacían	habían yacido	yacieran	hubieran yacido
	Preterit	**Past anterior**		
1st p. sing.	yací	hube yacido	yaciese	hubiese yacido
2nd p. sing.	yaciste	hubiste yacido	yacieses	hubieses yacido
3rd p. sing.	yació	hubo yacido	yaciese	hubiese yacido
1st p. plur.	yacimos	hubimos yacido	yaciésemos	hubiésemos yacido
2nd p. plur.	yacisteis	hubisteis yacido	yaciesen	hubieseis yacido
3rd p. plur.	yacieron	hubieron yacido	yacieseis	hubiesen yacido
	Future	**Future perfect**	**Future**	**Future perfect**
1st p. sing.	yaceré	habré yacido	yaciere	hubiere yacido
2nd p. sing.	yacerás	habrás yacido	yacieres	hubieres yacido
3rd p. sing.	yacerá	habrá yacido	yaciere	hubiere yacido
1st p. plur.	yaceremos	habremos yacido	yaciéremos	hubiéremos yacido
2nd p. plur.	yaceréis	habréis yacido	yaciereis	hubiereis yacido
3rd p. plur.	yacerán	habrán yacido	yacieren	hubieren yacido
	Present conditional	**Conditional perfect**		
1st p. sing.	yacería	habría yacido		
2nd p. sing.	yacerías	habrías yacido		
3rd p. sing.	yacería	habría yacido		
1st p. plur.	yaceríamos	habríamos yacido		
2nd p. plur.	yaceríais	habríais yacido		
3rd p. plur.	yacerían	habrían yacido		

Imperative	
Present	**Forms using the subjunctive stem**
yace o yaz (tú)	yazca, yazga o yaga (él, ella, usted)
yaced (vosotros)	yazcamos, yazgamos o yagamos (nosotros)
	yazcan, yazgan o yagan (ellos, ellas, ustedes)

R A E R

Irregular verb

The *stem** adds ig or changes to the *yod** in the present indicative, the present subjunctive, and in the imperative.

The i without an accent becomes a yod when it is between two vowels. Compare raí/rayó.

The yod which replaces the i in the *endings** (iendo, ió, ieron, iera) marks the syllable break (see leer, p. 28).

- Stem + ig or stem + yod
- Spelling i > y before a, e, o

Impersonal mood		
	Simple forms	Compound forms
Infinitive	raer	haber raído
Gerund	rayendo	habiendo raído
Past participle	raído	

Personal moods

	Indicative		Subjunctive	
	Simple forms	Compound forms	Simple forms	Compound forms
	Present	**Perfect**	**Present**	**Past**
1st p. sing.	rao, **raigo** o ra**yo**	he raído	raa, **raiga** o ra**ya**	haya raído
2nd p. sing.	raes	has raído	raas, **raigas** o ra**yas**	hayas raído
3rd p. sing.	rae	ha raído	raa, **raiga** o ra**ya**	haya raído
1st p. plur.	raemos	hemos raído	raamos, **raigamos** o ra**ya**mos	hayamos raído
2nd p. plur.	raéis	habéis raído	raáis, **raigáis** o ra**yáis**	hayáis raído
3rd p. plur.	raen	han raído	raan, **raigan** o ra**yan**	hayan raído
	Imperfect	**Past perfect**	**Imperfect**	**Past perfect**
1st p. sing.	raía	había raído	rayera	hubiera raído
2nd p. sing.	raías	habías raído	rayeras	hubieras raído
3rd p. sing.	raía	había raído	rayera	hubiera raído
1st p. plur.	raíamos	habíamos raído	rayéramos	hubiéramos raído
2nd p. plur.	raíais	habíais raído	rayerais	hubierais raído
3rd p. plur.	raían	habían raído	rayeran	hubieran raído
	Preterit	**Past anterior**		
1st p. sing.	raí	hube raído	rayese	hubiese raído
2nd p. sing.	raíste	hubiste raído	rayeses	hubieses raído
3rd p. sing.	ra**yó**	hubo raído	rayese	hubiese raído
1st p. plur.	raímos	hubimos raído	rayésemos	hubiésemos raído
2nd p. plur.	raísteis	hubisteis raído	rayeseis	hubieseis raído
3rd p. plur.	ra**ye**ron	hubieron raído	rayesen	hubiesen raído
	Future	**Future perfect**	**Future**	**Future perfect**
1st p. sing.	raeré	habré raído	rayere	hubiere raído
2nd p. sing.	raerás	habrás raído	rayeres	hubieres raído
3rd p. sing.	raerá	habrá raído	rayere	hubiere raído
1st p. plur.	raeremos	habremos raído	rayéremos	hubiéremos raído
2nd p. plur.	raeréis	habréis raído	rayereis	hubiereis raído
3rd p. plur.	raerán	habrán raído	rayeren	hubieren raído
	Present conditional	**Conditional perfect**		
1st p. sing.	raería	habría raído		
2nd p. sing.	raerías	habrías raído		
3rd p. sing.	raería	habría raído		
1st p. plur.	raeríamos	habríamos raído		
2nd p. plur.	raeríais	habríais raído		
3rd p. plur.	raerían	habrían raído		

Imperative

Present	Forms using the subjunctive stem
rae (tú)	raa, **raiga**, ra**ya** (él, ella, usted)
raed (vosotros)	raamos, **raig**amos, ra**ya**mos (nosotros)
	raan, **raig**an, ra**ya**n (ellos, ellas, ustedes)

R O E R

Irregular verb

The *stem** adds ig or changes to the *yod** in the present indicative, the present subjunctive, and in the imperative.

The i without an accent becomes a yod when it is between two vowels. Compare: roí/royó. The yod replacing the i in the *endings** (**iendo, ió, ieron, iera**) marks the syllable break (see leer, p. 28).

- Stem + ig and stem + y
- Spelling i › y before a, e, o

Impersonal mood

	Simple forms	Compound forms
Infinitive	roer	haber roído
Gerund	ro**y**endo	habiendo roído
Past participle	roído	

Personal moods

	Indicative		Subjunctive	
	Simple forms	Compound forms	Simple forms	Compound forms
	Present	**Perfect**	**Present**	**Past**
1st p. sing.	roo, **roigo** o ro**yo**	he roído	roa, **roiga** o ro**ya**	haya roído
2nd p. sing.	roes	has roído	roas, **roiga**s o ro**ya**s	hayas roído
3rd p. sing.	roe	ha roído	roa, **roiga** o ro**ya**	haya roído
1st p. plur.	roemos	hemos roído	roamos, **roiga**mos o ro**ya**mos	hayamos roído
2nd p. plur.	roéis	habéis roído	roáis, **roigá**is o ro**yá**is	hayáis roído
3rd p. plur.	roen	han roído	roan, **roiga**n o ro**ya**n	hayan roído
	Imperfect	**Past perfect**	**Imperfect**	**Past perfect**
1st p. sing.	roía	había roído	ro**ye**ra	hubiera roído
2nd p. sing.	roías	habías roído	ro**ye**ras	hubieras roído
3rd p. sing.	roía	había roído	ro**ye**ra	hubiera roído
1st p. plur.	roíamos	habíamos roído	ro**yé**ramos	hubiéramos roído
2nd p. plur.	roíais	habíais roído	ro**ye**rais	hubierais roído
3rd p. plur.	roían	habían roído	ro**ye**ran	hubieran roído
	Preterit	**Past anterior**		
1st p. sing.	roí	hube roído	ro**ye**se	hubiese roído
2nd p. sing.	roíste	hubiste roído	ro**ye**ses	hubieses roído
3rd p. sing.	ro**yó**	hubo roído	ro**ye**se	hubiese roído
1st p. plur.	roímos	hubimos roído	ro**yé**semos	hubiésemos roído
2nd p. plur.	roísteis	hubisteis roído	ro**ye**seis	hubieseis roído
3rd p. plur.	ro**ye**ron	hubieron roído	ro**ye**sen	hubiesen roído
	Future	**Future perfect**	**Future**	**Future perfect**
1st p. sing.	roeré	habré roído	ro**ye**re	hubiere roído
2nd p. sing.	roerás	habrás roído	ro**ye**res	hubieres roído
3rd p. sing.	roerá	habrá roído	ro**ye**re	hubiere roído
1st p. plur.	roeremos	habremos roído	ro**yé**remos	hubiéremos roído
2nd p. plur.	roeréis	habréis roído	ro**ye**reis	hubiereis roído
3rd p. plur.	roerán	habrán roído	ro**ye**ren	hubieren roído
	Present conditional	**Conditional perfect**		
1st p. sing.	roería	habría roído		
2nd p. sing.	roerías	habrías roído		
3rd p. sing.	roería	habría roído		
1st p. plur.	roeríamos	habríamos roído		
2nd p. plur.	roeríais	habríais roído		
3rd p. plur.	roerían	habrían roído		

Imperative

Present	**Forms using the subjunctive stem**
roe (tú)	roa, **roiga** o ro**ya** (él, ella, usted)
roed (vosotros)	roamos, **roiga**mos o ro**ya**mos (nosotros)
	roan, **roiga**n o ro**ya**n (ellos, ellas, ustedes)

ASIR

Irregular verb

A g is added to the *stem** in the 1st person singular of the present indicative, the present subjunctive, and in the imperative.

The irregular forms of the verbs asir and desasir are not often used.

■ Stem + g before a, o

Impersonal mood		
	Simple forms	Compound forms
Infinitive	asir	haber asido
Gerund	asiendo	habiendo asido
Past participle	asido	

Personal moods				
	Indicative		**Subjunctive**	
	Simple forms	Compound forms	Simple forms	Compound forms
	Present	**Perfect**	**Present**	**Past**
1st p. sing.	as**g**o	he asido	as**g**a	haya asido
2nd p. sing.	ases	has asido	as**g**as	hayas asido
3rd p. sing.	ase	ha asido	as**g**a	haya asido
1st p. plur.	asimos	hemos asido	as**g**amos	hayamos asido
2nd p. plur.	asís	habéis asido	as**g**áis	hayáis asido
3rd p. plur.	asen	han asido	as**g**an	hayan asido
	Imperfect	**Past perfect**	**Imperfect**	**Past perfect**
1st p. sing.	asía	había asido	asiera	hubiera asido
2nd p. sing.	asías	habías asido	asieras	hubieras asido
3rd p. sing.	asía	había asido	asiera	hubiera asido
1st p. plur.	asíamos	habíamos asido	asiéramos	hubiéramos asido
2nd p. plur.	asíais	habíais asido	asierais	hubierais asido
3rd p. plur.	asían	habían asido	asieran	hubieran asido
	Preterit	**Past anterior**		
1st p. sing.	así	hube asido	asiese	hubiese asido
2nd p. sing.	asiste	hubiste asido	asieses	hubieses asido
3rd p. sing.	asió	hubo asido	asiese	hubiese asido
1st p. plur.	asimos	hubimos asido	asiésemos	hubiésemos asido
2nd p. plur.	asisteis	hubisteis asido	asieseis	hubieseis asido
3rd p. plur.	asieron	hubieron asido	asiesen	hubiesen asido
	Future	**Future perfect**	**Future**	**Future perfect**
1st p. sing.	asiré	habré asido	asiere	hubiere asido
2nd p. sing.	asirás	habrás asido	asieres	hubieres asido
3rd p. sing.	asirá	habrá asido	asiere	hubiere asido
1st p. plur.	asiremos	habremos asido	asiéremos	hubiéremos asido
2nd p. plur.	asiréis	habréis asido	asiereis	hubiereis asido
3rd p. plur.	asirán	habrán asido	asieren	hubieren asido
	Present conditional	**Conditional perfect**		
1st p. sing.	asiría	habría asido		
2nd p. sing.	asirías	habrías asido		
3rd p. sing.	asiría	habría asido		
1st p. plur.	asiríamos	habríamos asido		
2nd p. plur.	asiríais	habríais asido		
3rd p. plur.	asirían	habrían asido		

Imperative	
Present	**Forms using the subjunctive stem**
ase (tú)	as**g**a (él, ella, usted)
asid (vosotros)	as**g**amos (nosotros)
	as**g**an (ellos, ellas, ustedes)

HUIR

Irregular verb

The *yod** appears in the present indicative, the present subjunctive, and in the imperative (huye). The yod which replaces the i of the *endings** in the gerund, the preterit, the imperfect and future subjunctive, and the imperative, marks the syllable break (huyó).
- *Stem** + y before a, e, o
- Spelling i › y before a, e, o

Impersonal mood		
	Simple forms	Compound forms
Infinitive	huir	haber huido
Gerund	huyendo	habiendo huido
Past participle	huido	

Personal moods			
Indicative		**Subjunctive**	
Simple forms	Compound forms	Simple forms	Compound forms
Present	**Perfect**	**Present**	**Past**
1st p. sing. **huyo**	he huido	**huya**	haya huido
2nd p. sing. **huyes**	has huido	**huyas**	hayas huido
3rd p. sing. **huye**	ha huido	**huya**	haya huido
1st p. plur. huimos	hemos huido	**huyamos**	hayamos huido
2nd p. plur. huís	habéis huido	**huyáis**	hayáis huido
3rd p. plur. **huyen**	han huido	**huyan**	hayan huido
Imperfect	**Past perfect**	**Imperfect**	**Past perfect**
1st p. sing. huía	había huido	huyera	hubiera huido
2nd p. sing. huías	habías huido	huyeras	hubieras huido
3rd p. sing. huía	había huido	huyera	hubiera huido
1st p. plur. huíamos	habíamos huido	huyéramos	hubiéramos huido
2nd p. plur. huíais	habíais huido	huyerais	hubierais huido
3rd p. plur. huían	habían huido	huyeran	hubieran huido
Preterit	**Past anterior**		
1st p. sing. huí	hube huido	huyese	hubiese huido
2nd p. sing. huiste	hubiste huido	huyeses	hubieses huido
3rd p. sing. huyó	hubo huido	huyese	hubiese huido
1st p. plur. huimos	hubimos huido	huyésemos	hubiésemos huido
2nd p. plur. huisteis	hubisteis huido	huyeseis	hubieseis huido
3rd p. plur. huyeron	hubieron huido	huyesen	hubiesen huido
Future	**Future perfect**	**Future**	**Future perfect**
1st p. sing. huiré	habré huido	huyere	hubiere huido
2nd p. sing. huirás	habrás huido	huyeres	hubieres huido
3rd p. sing. huirá	habrá huido	huyere	hubiere huido
1st p. plur. huiremos	habremos huido	huyéremos	hubiéremos huido
2nd p. plur. huiréis	habréis huido	huyereis	hubiereis huido
3rd p. plur. huirán	habrán huido	huyeren	hubieren huido
Present conditional	**Conditional perfect**		

		Imperative	
1st p. sing. huiría	habría huido	**Present**	**Forms using the subjunctive ste**
2nd p. sing. huirías	habrías huido	**huye** (tú)	**huya** (él, ella, usted)
3rd p. sing. huiría	habría huido	huid (vosotros)	**huyamos** (nosotros)
1st p. plur. huiríamos	habríamos huido		**huyan** (ellos, ellas, ustedes)
2nd p. plur. huiríais	habríais huido		
3rd p. plur. huirían	habrían huido		

ARGÜIR

Irregular verb

The *yod** appears in the present indicative, the present subjunctive, and the imperative (arguy**e**).
The yod which replaces the i in the *endings** (i**endo**, i**ó**, i**eron**, i**era**), is a spelling change which allows for a syllable break (arguy**ó**).

■ Consonant change in the *stem** u › y before **a, e, o**
■ Spelling gü › gu before y

Impersonal mood		
	Simple forms	Compound forms
Infinitive	argüir	haber argüido
Gerund	arguyendo	habiendo argüido
Past participle	argüido	

Personal moods				
Indicative			**Subjunctive**	
	Simple forms	Compound forms	Simple forms	Compound forms
	Present	**Perfect**	**Present**	**Past**
1st p. sing.	arguyo	he argüido	arguya	haya argüido
2nd p. sing.	arguyes	has argüido	arguyas	hayas argüido
3rd p. sing.	arguye	ha argüido	arguya	haya argüido
1st p. plur.	argüimos	hemos argüido	arguyamos	hayamos argüido
2nd p. plur.	argüís	habéis argüido	arguyáis	hayáis argüido
3rd p. plur.	arguyen	han argüido	arguyan	hayan argüido
	Imperfect	**Past perfect**	**Imperfect**	**Past perfect**
1st p. sing.	argüía	había argüido	arguyera	hubiera argüido
2nd p. sing.	argüías	habías argüido	arguyeras	hubieras argüido
3rd p. sing.	argüía	había argüido	arguyera	hubiera argüido
1st p. plur.	argüíamos	habíamos argüido	arguyéramos	hubiéramos argüido
2nd p. plur.	argüíais	habíais argüido	arguyerais	hubierais argüido
3rd p. plur.	argüían	habían argüido	arguyeran	hubieran argüido
	Preterit	**Past anterior**		
1st p. sing.	argüí	hube argüido	arguyese	hubiese argüido
2nd p. sing.	argüiste	hubiste argüido	arguyeses	hubieses argüido
3rd p. sing.	arguyó	hubo argüido	arguyese	hubiese argüido
1st p. plur.	argüimos	hubimos argüido	arguyésemos	hubiésemos argüido
2nd p. plur.	argüisteis	hubisteis argüido	arguyeseis	hubieseis argüido
3rd p. plur.	arguyeron	hubieron argüido	arguyesen	hubiesen argüido
	Future	**Future perfect**	**Future**	**Future perfect**
1st p. sing.	argüiré	habré argüido	arguyere	hubiere argüido
2nd p. sing.	argüirás	habrás argüido	arguyeres	hubieres argüido
3rd p. sing.	argüirá	habrá argüido	arguyere	hubiere argüido
1st p. plur.	argüiremos	habremos argüido	arguyéremos	hubiéremos argüido
2nd p. plur.	argüiréis	habréis argüido	arguyereis	hubiereis argüido
3rd p. plur.	argüirán	habrán argüido	arguyeren	hubieren argüido
	Present conditional	**Conditional perfect**		
1st p. sing.	argüiría	habría argüido		
2nd p. sing.	argüirías	habrías argüido		
3rd p. sing.	argüiría	habría argüido		
1st p. plur.	argüiríamos	habríamos argüido		
2nd p. plur.	argüiríais	habríais argüido		
3rd p. plur.	argüirían	habrían argüido		

Imperative	
Present	**Forms using the subjunctive stem**
arguye (tú)	arguya (él, ella, usted)
argüid (vosotros)	arguyamos (nosotros)
	arguyan (ellos, ellas, ustedes)

A N D A R

Irregular verb

The *stem** of this verb changes in the preterit and becomes anduv. This stem is also used for all the forms of the imperfect subjunctive and the future subjunctive. It belongs to the set of sixteen strong preterits currently in use in modern Spanish. (See p. 118.)

■ Strong preterit: stem + uv

Impersonal mood

	Simple forms	Compound forms
Infinitive	andar	haber andado
Gerund	andando	habiendo andado
Past participle	andado	

Personal moods

	Indicative		Subjunctive	
	Simple forms	Compound forms	Simple forms	Compound forms
	Present	**Perfect**	**Present**	**Past**
1st p. sing.	ando	he andado	ande	haya andado
2nd p. sing.	andas	has andado	andes	hayas andado
3rd p. sing.	anda	ha andado	ande	haya andado
1st p. plur.	andamos	hemos andado	andemos	hayamos andado
2nd p. plur.	andáis	habéis andado	andéis	hayáis andado
3rd p. plur.	andan	han andado	anden	hayan andado
	Imperfect	**Past perfect**	**Imperfect**	**Past perfect**
1st p. sing.	andaba	había andado	anduviera	hubiera andado
2nd p. sing.	andabas	habías andado	anduvieras	hubieras andado
3rd p. sing.	andaba	había andado	anduviera	hubiera andado
1st p. plur.	andábamos	habíamos andado	anduviéramos	hubiéramos andado
2nd p. plur.	andabais	habíais andado	anduvierais	hubierais andado
3rd p. plur.	andaban	habían andado	anduvieran	hubieran andado
	Preterit	**Past anterior**		
1st p. sing.	anduve	hube andado	anduviese	hubiese andado
2nd p. sing.	anduviste	hubiste andado	anduvieses	hubieses andado
3rd p. sing.	anduvo	hubo andado	anduviese	hubiese andado
1st p. plur.	anduvimos	hubimos andado	anduviésemos	hubiésemos andado
2nd p. plur.	anduvisteis	hubisteis andado	anduvieseis	hubieseis andado
3rd p. plur.	anduvieron	hubieron andado	anduviesen	hubiesen andado
	Future	**Future perfect**	**Future**	**Future perfect**
1st p. sing.	andaré	habré andado	anduviere	hubiere andado
2nd p. sing.	andarás	habrás andado	anduvieres	hubieres andado
3rd p. sing.	andará	habrá andado	anduviere	hubiere andado
1st p. plur.	andaremos	habremos andado	anduviéremos	hubiéremos andado
2nd p. plur.	andaréis	habréis andado	anduviereis	hubiereis andado
3rd p. plur.	andarán	habrán andado	anduvieren	hubieren andado
	Present conditional	**Conditional perfect**		
1st p. sing.	andaría	habría andado		
2nd p. sing.	andarías	habrías andado		
3rd p. sing.	andaría	habría andado		
1st p. plur.	andaríamos	habríamos andado		
2nd p. plur.	andaríais	habríais andado		
3rd p. plur.	andarían	habrían andado		

Imperative

Present	Forms using the subjunctive stem
anda (tú)	ande (él, ella, usted)
andad (vosotros)	andemos (nosotros)
	anden (ellos, ellas, ustedes)

S E N T I R

Irregular verb

The *diphthong* e › ie occurs in the present indicative, the present subjunctive and in the imperative.

The vowel change from e › i occurs in the simple forms of the gerund, the preterit, the present subjunctive, the imperfect subjunctive, and the future.

- Diphthong e › ie
- Vowel change in the *stem* e › i

Impersonal mood		
	Simple forms	Compound forms
Infinitive	sentir	haber sentido
Gerund	sintiendo	habiendo sentido
Past participle	sentido	

Personal moods			
Indicative		**Subjunctive**	
Simple forms	Compound forms	Simple forms	Compound forms

	Indicative Simple	Indicative Compound	Subjunctive Simple	Subjunctive Compound
	Present	**Perfect**	**Present**	**Past**
1st p. sing.	siento	he sentido	sienta	haya sentido
2nd p. sing.	sientes	has sentido	sientas	hayas sentido
3rd p. sing.	siente	ha sentido	sienta	haya sentido
1st p. plur.	sentimos	hemos sentido	sintamos	hayamos sentido
2nd p. plur.	sentís	habéis sentido	sintáis	hayáis sentido
3rd p. plur.	sienten	han sentido	sientan	hayan sentido
	Imperfect	**Past perfect**	**Imperfect**	**Past perfect**
1st p. sing.	sentía	había sentido	sintiera	hubiera sentido
2nd p. sing.	sentías	habías sentido	sintieras	hubieras sentido
3rd p. sing.	sentía	había sentido	sintiera	hubiera sentido
1st p. plur.	sentíamos	habíamos sentido	sintiéramos	hubiéramos sentido
2nd p. plur.	sentíais	habíais sentido	sintierais	hubierais sentido
3rd p. plur.	sentían	habían sentido	sintieran	hubieran sentido
	Preterit	**Past anterior**		
1st p. sing.	sentí	hube sentido	sintiese	hubiese sentido
2nd p. sing.	sentiste	hubiste sentido	sintieses	hubieses sentido
3rd p. sing.	sintió	hubo sentido	sintiese	hubiese sentido
1st p. plur.	sentimos	hubimos sentido	sintiésemos	hubiésemos sentido
2nd p. plur.	sentisteis	hubisteis sentido	sintieseis	hubieseis sentido
3rd p. plur.	sintieron	hubieron sentido	sintiesen	hubiesen sentido
	Future	**Future perfect**	**Future**	**Future perfect**
1st p. sing.	sentiré	habré sentido	sintiere	hubiere sentido
2nd p. sing.	sentirás	habrás sentido	sintieres	hubieres sentido
3rd p. sing.	sentirá	habrá sentido	sintiere	hubiere sentido
1st p. plur.	sentiremos	habremos sentido	sintiéremos	hubiéremos sentido
2nd p. plur.	sentiréis	habréis sentido	sintiereis	hubiereis sentido
3rd p. plur.	sentirán	habrán sentido	sintieren	hubieren sentido
	Present conditional	**Conditional perfect**		
1st p. sing.	sentiría	habría sentido		
2nd p. sing.	sentirías	habrías sentido		
3rd p. sing.	sentiría	habría sentido		
1st p. plur.	sentiríamos	habríamos sentido		
2nd p. plur.	sentiríais	habríais sentido		
3rd p. plur.	sentirían	habrían sentido		

Imperative	
Present	**Forms using the subjunctive stem**
siente (tú)	sienta (él, ella, usted)
sentid (vosotros)	sintamos (nosotros)
	sientan (ellos, ellas, ustedes)

ERGUIR

Irregular verb

The *diphthong* e › ye occurs in the present indicative, the present subjunctive, and in the imperative.

The vowel change e › i applies to the same forms in the gerund, the preterit, and the imperfect and future subjunctive.

- Diphthong e › ye
- Vowel change in the *stem* e › i
- Spelling gu › g before a, o

Impersonal mood

	Simple forms	Compound forms
Infinitive	erguir	haber erguido
Gerund	irguiendo	habiendo erguido
Past participle	erguido	

Personal moods

	Indicative		Subjunctive	
	Simple forms	Compound forms	Simple forms	Compound forms
	Present	**Perfect**	**Present**	**Past**
1st p. sing.	irgo o yergo	he erguido	irga o yerga	haya erguido
2nd p. sing.	irgues o yergues	has erguido	irgas o yergas	hayas erguido
3rd p. sing.	irgue o yergue	ha erguido	irga o yerga	haya erguido
1st p. plur.	erguimos	hemos erguido	irgamos	hayamos erguido
2nd p. plur.	erguís	habéis erguido	irgáis	hayáis erguido
3rd p. plur.	irguen o yerguen	han erguido	irgan o yergan	hayan erguido
	Imperfect	**Past perfect**	**Imperfect**	**Past perfect**
1st p. sing.	erguía	había erguido	irguiera	hubiera erguido
2nd p. sing.	erguías	habías erguido	irguieras	hubieras erguido
3rd p. sing.	erguía	había erguido	irguiera	hubiera erguido
1st p. plur.	erguíamos	habíamos erguido	irguiéramos	hubiéramos erguido
2nd p. plur.	erguíais	habíais erguido	irguierais	hubierais erguido
3rd p. plur.	erguían	habían erguido	irguieran	hubieran erguido
	Preterit	**Past anterior**		
1st p. sing.	erguí	hube erguido	irguiese	hubiese erguido
2nd p. sing.	erguiste	hubiste erguido	irguieses	hubieses erguido
3rd p. sing.	irguió	hubo erguido	irguiese	hubiese erguido
1st p. plur.	erguimos	hubimos erguido	irguiésemos	hubiésemos erguido
2nd p. plur.	erguisteis	hubisteis erguido	irguieseis	hubieseis erguido
3rd p. plur.	irguieron	hubieron erguido	irguiesen	hubiesen erguido
	Future	**Future perfect**	**Future**	**Future perfect**
1st p. sing.	erguiré	habré erguido	irguiere	hubiere erguido
2nd p. sing.	erguirás	habrás erguido	irguieres	hubieres erguido
3rd p. sing.	erguirá	habrá erguido	irguiere	hubiere erguido
1st p. plur.	erguiremos	habremos erguido	irguiéremos	hubiéremos erguido
2nd p. plur.	erguiréis	habréis erguido	irguiereis	hubiereis erguido
3rd p. plur.	erguirán	habrán erguido	irguieren	hubieren erguido
	Present conditional	**Conditional perfect**		
1st p. sing.	erguiría	habría erguido		
2nd p. sing.	erguirías	habrías erguido		
3rd p. sing.	erguiría	habría erguido		
1st p. plur.	erguiríamos	habríamos erguido		
2nd p. plur.	erguiríais	habríais erguido		
3rd p. plur.	erguirían	habrían erguido		

Imperative

Present	Forms using the subjunctive stem
irgue o yergue (tú)	irga o yerga (él, ella, usted)
erguid (vosotros)	irgamos (nosotros)
	irgan o yergan (ellos, ellas, ustedes)

· D O R M I R

Irregular verb

The *diphthong** occurs in the present indicative, the present subjunctive, and in the imperative. In addition to this irregularity, there is a vowel change in the gerund, the preterit, the present subjunctive, and in the simple forms of the imperfect and future subjunctive.

- Diphthong o › ue
- Vowel change in the *stem** o › u

Impersonal mood		
	Simple forms	Compound forms
Infinitive	dormir	haber dormido
Gerund	**durm**iendo	habiendo dormido
Past participle	dormido	

Personal moods			
Indicative		Subjunctive	
Simple forms	Compound forms	Simple forms	Compound forms

	Present	**Perfect**	**Present**	**Past**
1st p. sing.	**duerm**o	he dormido	**duerm**a	haya dormido
2nd p. sing.	**duerm**es	has dormido	**duerm**as	hayas dormido
3rd p. sing.	**duerm**e	ha dormido	**duerm**a	haya dormido
1st p. plur.	dormimos	hemos dormido	**durm**amos	hayamos dormido
2nd p. plur.	dormís	habéis dormido	**durm**áis	hayáis dormido
3rd p. plur.	**duerm**en	han dormido	**duerm**an	hayan dormido

	Imperfect	**Past perfect**	**Imperfect**	**Past perfect**
1st p. sing.	dormía	había dormido	**durm**iera	hubiera dormido
2nd p. sing.	dormías	habías dormido	**durm**ieras	hubieras dormido
3rd p. sing.	dormía	había dormido	**durm**iera	hubiera dormido
1st p. plur.	dormíamos	habíamos dormido	**durm**iéramos	hubiéramos dormido
2nd p. plur.	dormíais	habíais dormido	**durm**ierais	hubierais dormido
3rd p. plur.	dormían	habían dormido	**durm**ieran	hubieran dormido

	Preterit	**Past anterior**		
1st p. sing.	dormí	hube dormido	**durm**iese	hubiese dormido
2nd p. sing.	dormiste	hubiste dormido	**durm**ieses	hubieses dormido
3rd p. sing.	**durm**ió	hubo dormido	**durm**iese	hubiese dormido
1st p. plur.	dormimos	hubimos dormido	**durm**iésemos	hubiésemos dormido
2nd p. plur.	dormisteis	hubisteis dormido	**durm**ieseis	hubieseis dormido
3rd p. plur.	**durm**ieron	hubieron dormido	**durm**iesen	hubiesen dormido

	Future	**Future perfect**	**Future**	**Future perfect**
1st p. sing.	dormiré	habré dormido	**durm**iere	hubiere dormido
2nd p. sing.	dormirás	habrás dormido	**durm**ieres	hubieres dormido
3rd p. sing.	dormirá	habrá dormido	**durm**iere	hubiere dormido
1st p. plur.	dormiremos	habremos dormido	**durm**iéremos	hubiéremos dormido
2nd p. plur.	dormiréis	habréis dormido	**durm**iereis	hubiereis dormido
3rd p. plur.	dormirán	habrán dormido	**durm**ieren	hubieren dormido

	Present conditional	**Conditional perfect**	
1st p. sing.	dormiría	habría dormido	
2nd p. sing.	dormirías	habrías dormido	
3rd p. sing.	dormiría	habría dormido	
1st p. plur.	dormiríamos	habríamos dormido	
2nd p. plur.	dormiríais	habríais dormido	
3rd p. plur.	dormirían	habrían dormido	

Imperative	
Present	**Forms using the subjunctive stem**
duerme (tú)	**duerm**a (él, ella, usted)
dormid (vosotros)	**durm**amos (nosotros)
	duerman (ellos, ellas, ustedes)

OÍR

Irregular verb

The *stem** either adds ig in the 1st person singular of the present indicative and all forms of the present subjunctive, as well as some forms of the imperative or it changes to the *yod** in the present indicative and the imperative.

The yod which replaces the i of the *endings**

in the gerund, the preterit, the imperfect, and future subjunctive, marks the syllable break: oyó.

- Stem + ig
- Stem + y
- Spelling i › y before a, e

Impersonal mood

	Simple forms	Compound forms
Infinitive	oír	haber oído
Gerund	oyendo	habiendo oído
Past participle	oído	

Personal moods

	Indicative		Subjunctive	
	Simple forms	**Compound forms**	**Simple forms**	**Compound forms**
	Present	**Perfect**	**Present**	**Past**
1st p. sing.	oigo	he oído	oiga	haya oído
2nd p. sing.	oyes	has oído	oigas	hayas oído
3rd p. sing.	oye	ha oído	oiga	haya oído
1st p. plur.	oímos	hemos oído	oigamos	hayamos oído
2nd p. plur.	oís	habéis oído	oigáis	hayáis oído
3rd p. plur.	oyen	han oído	oigan	hayan oído
	Imperfect	**Past perfect**	**Imperfect**	**Past perfect**
1st p. sing.	oía	había oído	oyera	hubiera oído
2nd p. sing.	oías	habías oído	oyeras	hubieras oído
3rd p. sing.	oía	había oído	oyera	hubiera oído
1st p. plur.	oíamos	habíamos oído	oyéramos	hubiéramos oído
2nd p. plur.	oíais	habíais oído	oyerais	hubierais oído
3rd p. plur.	oían	habían oído	oyeran	hubieran oído
	Preterit	**Past anterior**		
1st p. sing.	oí	hube oído	oyese	hubiese oído
2nd p. sing.	oíste	hubiste oído	oyeses	hubieses oído
3rd p. sing.	oyó	hubo oído	oyese	hubiese oído
1st p. plur.	oímos	hubimos oído	oyésemos	hubiésemos oído
2nd p. plur.	oísteis	hubisteis oído	oyeseis	hubieseis oído
3rd p. plur.	oyeron	hubieron oído	oyesen	hubiesen oído
	Future	**Future perfect**	**Future**	**Future perfect**
1st p. sing.	oiré	habré oído	oyere	hubiere oído
2nd p. sing.	oirás	habrás oído	oyeres	hubieres oído
3rd p. sing.	oirá	habrá oído	oyere	hubiere oído
1st p. plur.	oiremos	habremos oído	oyéremos	hubiéremos oído
2nd p. plur.	oiréis	habréis oído	oyereis	hubiereis oído
3rd p. plur.	oirán	habrán oído	oyeren	hubieren oído
	Present conditional	**Conditional perfect**		
1st p. sing.	oiría	habría oído		
2nd p. sing.	oirías	habrías oído		
3rd p. sing.	oiría	habría oído		
1st p. plur.	oiríamos	habríamos oído		
2nd p. plur.	oiríais	habríais oído		
3rd p. plur.	oirían	habrían oído		

Imperative

Present	**Forms using the subjunctive stem**
oye (tú)	oiga (él, ella, usted)
oíd (vosotros)	oigamos (nosotros)
	oigan (ellos, ellas, ustedes)

CONDUCIR

Irregular verb

The c of the *stem** becomes zc in the present indicative, the present subjunctive, and in the forms of the imperative which use the subjunctive stem.

The strong form of the preterit, conduj applies both to the imperfect subjunctive and the future subjunctive.

■ Consonant change in the stem c › zc before a, o
■ Strong preterit: stem uc › uj

Impersonal mood		
	Simple forms	Compound forms
finitive	conducir	haber conducido
erund	conduciendo	habiendo conducido
st participle	conducido	

Personal moods				
	Indicative		Subjunctive	
	Simple forms	Compound forms	Simple forms	Compound forms
	Present	**Perfect**	**Present**	**Past**
st p. sing.	conduzco	he conducido	conduzca	haya conducido
nd p. sing.	conduces	has conducido	conduzcas	hayas conducido
rd p. sing.	conduce	ha conducido	conduzca	haya conducido
st p. plur.	conducimos	hemos conducido	conduzcamos	hayamos conducido
nd p. plur.	conducís	habéis conducido	conduzcáis	hayáis conducido
rd p. plur.	conducen	han conducido	conduzcan	hayan conducido
	Imperfect	**Past perfect**	**Imperfect**	**Past perfect**
t p. sing.	conducía	había conducido	condujera	hubiera conducido
nd p. sing.	conducías	habías conducido	condujeras	hubieras conducido
d p. sing.	conducía	había conducido	condujera	hubiera conducido
t p. plur.	conducíamos	habíamos conducido	condujéramos	hubiéramos conducido
nd p. plur.	conducíais	habíais conducido	condujerais	hubierais conducido
rd p. plur.	conducían	habían conducido	condujeran	hubieran conducido
	Preterit	**Past anterior**		
st p. sing.	conduje	hube conducido	condujese	hubiese conducido
nd p. sing.	condujiste	hubiste conducido	condujeses	hubieses conducido
d p. sing.	condujo	hubo conducido	condujese	hubiese conducido
st p. plur.	condujimos	hubimos conducido	condujésemos	hubiésemos conducido
nd p. plur.	condujisteis	hubisteis conducido	condujeseis	hubieseis conducido
d p. plur.	condujeron	hubieron conducido	condujesen	hubiesen conducido
	Future	**Future perfect**	**Future**	**Future perfect**
st p. sing.	conduciré	habré conducido	condujere	hubiere conducido
nd p. sing.	conducirás	habrás conducido	condujeres	hubieres conducido
d p. sing.	conducirá	habrá conducido	condujere	hubiere conducido
st p. plur.	conduciremos	habremos conducido	condujéremos	hubiéremos conducido
nd p. plur.	conduciréis	habréis conducido	condujereis	hubiereis conducido
rd p. plur.	conducirán	habrán conducido	condujeren	hubieren conducido
	Present conditional	**Conditional perfect**		
t p. sing.	conduciría	habría conducido		
nd p. sing.	conducirías	habrías conducido		
d p. sing.	conduciría	habría conducido		
t p. plur.	conduciríamos	habríamos conducido		
nd p. plur.	conduciríais	habríais conducido		
d p. plur.	conducirían	habrían conducido		

Imperative	
Present	**Forms using the subjunctive stem**
conduce (tú)	**conduzca** (él, ella, usted)
conducid (vosotros)	**conduzcamos** (nosotros)
	conduzcan (ellos, ellas, ustedes)

T R A E R

Irregular verb

The *stem** adds ig in the present indicative, the present subjunctive, and in the imperative.
The strong preterit applies to all forms of the imperfect subjunctive (traje**ra**/traje**se**).
The occurrence of the *yod** in the gerund marks the syllable break: tra**yendo** (see leer, p. 28).

■ Stem + ig
■ Strong preterit: tra › traj
■ Spelling i › y

Impersonal mood		
	Simple forms	Compound forms
Infinitive	traer	haber traído
Gerund	tra**yendo**	habiendo traído
Past participle	traído	

Personal moods			
Indicative		**Subjunctive**	
Simple forms	Compound forms	Simple forms	Compound forms
Present	**Perfect**	**Present**	**Past**
1st p. sing. **traigo**	he traído	**traiga**	haya traído
2nd p. sing. traes	has traído	**traigas**	hayas traído
3rd p. sing. trae	ha traído	**traiga**	haya traído
1st p. plur. traemos	hemos traído	**traigamos**	hayamos traído
2nd p. plur. traéis	habéis traído	**traigáis**	hayáis traído
3rd p. plur. traen	han traído	**traigan**	hayan traído
Imperfect	**Past perfect**	**Imperfect**	**Past perfect**
1st p. sing. traía	había traído	**trajera**	hubiera traído
2nd p. sing. traías	habías traído	**trajeras**	hubieras traído
3rd p. sing. traía	había traído	**trajera**	hubiera traído
1st p. plur. traíamos	habíamos traído	**trajéramos**	hubiéramos traído
2nd p. plur. traíais	habíais traído	**trajerais**	hubierais traído
3rd p. plur. traían	habían traído	**trajeran**	hubieran traído
Preterit	**Past anterior**		
1st p. sing. **traje**	hube traído	**trajese**	hubiese traído
2nd p. sing. **trajiste**	hubiste traído	**trajeses**	hubieses traído
3rd p. sing. **trajo**	hubo traído	**trajese**	hubiese traído
1st p. plur. **trajimos**	hubimos traído	**trajésemos**	hubiésemos traído
2nd p. plur. **trajisteis**	hubisteis traído	**trajeseis**	hubieseis traído
3rd p. plur. **trajeron**	hubieron traído	**trajesen**	hubiesen traído
Future	**Future perfect**	**Future**	**Future perfect**
1st p. sing. traeré	habré traído	**trajere**	hubiere traído
2nd p. sing. traerás	habrás traído	**trajeres**	hubieres traído
3rd p. sing. traerá	habrá traído	**trajere**	hubiere traído
1st p. plur. traeremos	habremos traído	**trajéremos**	hubiéremos traído
2nd p. plur. traeréis	habréis traído	**trajereis**	hubiereis traído
3rd p. plur. traerán	habrán traído	**trajeren**	hubieren traído
Present conditional	**Conditional perfect**		

Present conditional	Conditional perfect	Imperative	
1st p. sing. traería	habría traído	**Present**	**Forms using the subjunctive ste**
2nd p. sing. traerías	habrías traído	trae (tú)	**traiga** (él, ella, usted)
3rd p. sing. traería	habría traído	traed (vosotros)	**traigamos** (nosotros)
1st p. plur. traeríamos	habríamos traído		**traigan** (ellos, ellas, ustedes)
2nd p. plur. traeríais	habríais traído		
3rd p. plur. traerían	habrían traído		

PLACER

Irregular verb

The irregular forms of the preterit (plug**o**, plugu**ieron**) and the subjunctive (pl**e**ga, plugu**iera**...) are remnants of old Spanish.
- Vowel change in the *stem** a › u
- Consonant changes in the stem c › zc before **a**, **o** and c › g before **a**, **o**
- Spelling g › gu before **e**, **i**

Impersonal mood

	Simple forms	Compound forms
Infinitive	placer	haber placido
Gerund	placiendo	habiendo placido
Past participle	placido	

Personal moods

	Indicative		**Subjunctive**	
	Simple forms	Compound forms	Simple forms	Compound forms
	Present	**Perfect**	**Present**	**Past**
1st p. sing.	plazc**o**	he placido	plazc**a**	haya placido
2nd p. sing.	places	has placido	plazc**as**	hayas placido
3rd p. sing.	place	ha placido	plazc**a** o pl**egue**	haya placido
1st p. plur.	placemos	hemos placido	plazc**a**mos	hayamos placido
2nd p. plur.	placéis	habéis placido	plazc**á**is	hayáis placido
3rd p. plur.	placen	han placido	plazc**a**n	hayan placido
	Imperfect	**Past perfect**	**Imperfect**	**Past perfect**
1st p. sing.	placía	había placido	placiera	hubiera placido
2nd p. sing.	placías	habías placido	placieras	hubieras placido
3rd p. sing.	placía	había placido	placieraplaciese	hubiera placido
1st p. plur.	placíamos	habíamos placido	placiéramos	hubiéramos placido
2nd p. plur.	placíais	habíais placido	placierais	hubierais placido
3rd p. plur.	placían	habían placido	placieran	hubieran placido
	Preterit	**Past anterior**		
1st p. sing.	plací	hube placido	placiese	hubiese placido
2nd p. sing.	placiste	hubiste placido	placieses	hubieses placido
3rd p. sing.	plació o **plugo**	hubo placido	plugu**iera** o plugu**iese**	hubiese placido
1st p. plur.	placimos	hubimos placido	placiésemos	hubiésemos placido
2nd p. plur.	placisteis	hubisteis placido	placieseis	hubieseis placido
3rd p. plur.	placieron o plugu**ieron**	hubieron placido	placiesen	hubiesen placido
	Future	**Future perfect**	**Future**	**Future perfect**
1st p. sing.	placeré	habré placido	placiere	hubiere placido
2nd p. sing.	placerás	habrás placido	placieres	hubieres placido
3rd p. sing.	placerá	habrá placido	placiere o plugu**iere**	hubiere placido
1st p. plur.	placeremos	habremos placido	placiéremos	hubiéremos placido
2nd p. plur.	placeréis	habréis placido	placiereis	hubiereis placido
3rd p. plur.	placerán	habrán placido	placieren	hubieren placido
	Present conditional	**Conditional perfect**		
1st p. sing.	placería	habría placido		
2nd p. sing.	placerías	habrías placido		
3rd p. sing.	placería	habría placido		
1st p. plur.	placeríamos	habríamos placido		
2nd p. plur.	placeríais	habríais placido		
3rd p. plur.	placerían	habrían placido		

Imperative

Present	Forms using the subjunctive stem
place (tú)	plazc**a** (él, ella, usted)
placed (vosotros)	plazc**a**mos (nosotros)
	plazc**a**n (ellos, ellas, ustedes)

VALER

Irregular verb

A g is added to the *stem** in the 1st person singular in the present indicative, the present subjunctive, and the imperative. All forms of the future and present conditional are irregular and introduce a d. The 2nd person singular of the imperative is irregular. (See p. 127).

- Stem + g
- Irregular future and conditional: val › valdr (See p. 127)
- Irregular imperative: val

Impersonal mood		
	Simple forms	Compound forms
Infinitive	valer	haber valido
Gerund	valiendo	habiendo valido
Past participle	valido	

Personal moods				
	Indicative		Subjunctive	
	Simple forms	Compound forms	Simple forms	Compound forms
	Present	**Perfect**	**Present**	**Past**
1st p. sing.	**valg**o	he valido	**valg**a	haya valido
2nd p. sing.	vales	has valido	**valg**as	hayas valido
3rd p. sing.	vale	ha valido	**valg**a	haya valido
1st p. plur.	valemos	hemos valido	**valg**amos	hayamos valido
2nd p. plur.	valéis	habéis valido	**valg**áis	hayáis valido
3rd p. plur.	valen	han valido	**valg**an	hayan valido
	Imperfect	**Past perfect**	**Imperfect**	**Past perfect**
1st p. sing.	valía	había valido	valiera	hubiera valido
2nd p. sing.	valías	habías valido	valieras	hubieras valido
3rd p. sing.	valía	había valido	valiera	hubiera valido
1st p. plur.	valíamos	habíamos valido	valiéramos	hubiéramos valido
2nd p. plur.	valíais	habíais valido	valierais	hubierais valido
3rd p. plur.	valían	habían valido	valieran	hubieran valido
	Preterit	**Past anterior**		
1st p. sing.	valí	hube valido	valiese	hubiese valido
2nd p. sing.	valiste	hubiste valido	valieses	hubieses valido
3rd p. sing.	valió	hubo valido	valiese	hubiese valido
1st p. plur.	valimos	hubimos valido	valiésemos	hubiésemos valido
2nd p. plur.	valisteis	hubisteis valido	valieseis	hubieseis valido
3rd p. plur.	valieron	hubieron valido	valiesen	hubiesen valido
	Future	**Future perfect**	**Future**	**Future perfect**
1st p. sing.	**valdr**é	habré valido	valiere	hubiere valido
2nd p. sing.	**valdr**ás	habrás valido	valieres	hubieres valido
3rd p. sing.	**valdr**á	habrá valido	valiere	hubiere valido
1st p. plur.	**valdr**emos	habremos valido	valiéremos	hubiéremos valido
2nd p. plur.	**valdr**éis	habréis valido	valiereis	hubiereis valido
3rd p. plur.	**valdr**án	habrán valido	valieren	hubieren valido
	Present conditional	**Conditional perfect**		
1st p. sing.	**valdr**ía	habría valido		

Imperative	
Present	**Forms using the subjunctive stem**
val (tú)	**valg**a (él, ella, usted)
valed (vosotros)	**valg**amos (nosotros)
	valgan (ellos, ellas, ustedes)

Remaining present conditional forms:

	Present conditional	**Conditional perfect**
2nd p. sing.	**valdr**ías	habrías valido
3rd p. sing.	**valdr**ía	habría valido
1st p. plur.	**valdr**íamos	habríamos valido
2nd p. plur.	**valdr**íais	habríais valido
3rd p. plur.	**valdr**ían	habrían valido

Irregular verb

The o of the *ending** becomes a *yod** in the 1st person singular of the present indicative.
The strong preterit dar › di... dieron, applies to the imperfect subjunctive and future subjunctive
conjugations (diera, diese, diere...). (See p. 124.)
- Addition of the yod: doy
- Strong preterit: di

	Impersonal mood	
	Simple forms	Compound forms
Infinitive	dar	haber dado
Gerund	dando	habiendo dado
Past participle	dado	

Personal moods				
	Indicative		**Subjunctive**	
	Simple forms	Compound forms	Simple forms	Compound forms
	Present	**Perfect**	**Present**	**Past**
1st p. sing.	doy	he dado	dé	haya dado
2nd p. sing.	das	has dado	des	hayas dado
3rd p. sing.	da	ha dado	dé	haya dado
1st p. plur.	damos	hemos dado	demos	hayamos dado
2nd p. plur.	dais	habéis dado	deis	hayáis dado
3rd p. plur.	dan	han dado	den	hayan dado
	Imperfect	**Past perfect**	**Imperfect**	**Past perfect**
1st p. sing.	daba	había dado	diera	hubiera dado
2nd p. sing.	dabas	habías dado	dieras	hubieras dado
3rd p. sing.	daba	había dado	diera	hubiera dado
1st p. plur.	dábamos	habíamos dado	diéramos	hubiéramos dado
2nd p. plur.	dabais	habíais dado	dierais	hubierais dado
3rd p. plur.	daban	habían dado	dieran	hubieran dado
	Preterit	**Past anterior**		
1st p. sing.	di	hube dado	diese	hubiese dado
2nd p. sing.	diste	hubiste dado	dieses	hubieses dado
3rd p. sing.	dio	hubo dado	diese	hubiese dado
1st p. plur.	dimos	hubimos dado	diésemos	hubiésemos dado
2nd p. plur.	disteis	hubisteis dado	dieseis	hubieseis dado
3rd p. plur.	dieron	hubieron dado	diesen	hubiesen dado
	Future	**Future perfect**	**Future**	**Future perfect**
1st p. sing.	daré	habré dado	diere	hubiere dado
2nd p. sing.	darás	habrás dado	dieres	hubieres dado
3rd p. sing.	dará	habrá dado	diere	hubiere dado
1st p. plur.	daremos	habremos dado	diéremos	hubiéremos dado
2nd p. plur.	daréis	habréis dado	diereis	hubiereis dado
3rd p. plur.	darán	habrán dado	dieren	hubieren dado
	Present conditional	**Conditional perfect**		
1st p. sing.	daría	habría dado		
2nd p. sing.	darías	habrías dado		
3rd p. sing.	daría	habría dado		
1st p. plur.	daríamos	habríamos dado		
2nd p. plur.	daríais	habríais dado		
3rd p. plur.	darían	habrían dado		

Imperative

Present	Forms using the subjunctive stem
da (tú)	dé (él, ella, usted)
dad (vosotros)	demos (nosotros)
	den (ellos, ellas, ustedes)

ESTAR

Irregular verb

The **o** of the *ending** becomes a *yod** in the 1st person singular of the present indicative.
The strong preterit estar › estuv, applies to the imperfect and future subjunctive conjugations (estuviera, estuviere, estuviese...).
- Addition of the yod: est**oy**
- Strong preterit: est › estuv

	Impersonal mood			
	Simple forms		**Compound forms**	
Infinitive	estar		haber estado	
Gerund	estando		habiendo estado	
Past participle	estado			

Personal moods				
	Indicative		**Subjunctive**	
	Simple forms	**Compound forms**	**Simple forms**	**Compound forms**
	Present	**Perfect**	**Present**	**Past**
1st p. sing.	est**oy**	he estado	esté	haya estado
2nd p. sing.	estás	has estado	estés	hayas estado
3rd p. sing.	está	ha estado	esté	haya estado
1st p. plur.	estamos	hemos estado	estemos	hayamos estado
2nd p. plur.	estáis	habéis estado	estéis	hayáis estado
3rd p. plur.	están	han estado	estén	hayan estado
	Imperfect	**Past perfect**	**Imperfect**	**Past perfect**
1st p. sing.	estaba	había estado	estuviera	hubiera estado
2nd p. sing.	estabas	habías estado	estuvieras	hubieras estado
3rd p. sing.	estaba	había estado	estuviera	hubiera estado
1st p. plur.	estábamos	habíamos estado	estuviéramos	hubiéramos estado
2nd p. plur.	estabais	habíais estado	estuvierais	hubierais estado
3rd p. plur.	estaban	habían estado	estuvieran	hubieran estado
	Preterit	**Past anterior**		
1st p. sing.	estuve	hube estado	estuviese	hubiese estado
2nd p. sing.	estuviste	hubiste estado	estuvieses	hubieses estado
3rd p. sing.	estuvo	hubo estado	estuviese	hubiese estado
1st p. plur.	estuvimos	hubimos estado	estuviésemos	hubiésemos estado
2nd p. plur.	estuvisteis	hubisteis estado	estuvieseis	hubieseis estado
3rd p. plur.	estuvieron	hubieron estado	estuviesen	hubiesen estado
	Future	**Future perfect**	**Future**	**Future perfect**
1st p. sing.	estaré	habré estado	estuviere	hubiere estado
2nd p. sing.	estarás	habrás estado	estuvieres	hubieres estado
3rd p. sing.	estará	habrá estado	estuviere	hubiere estado
1st p. plur.	estaremos	habremos estado	estuviéremos	hubiéremos estado
2nd p. plur.	estaréis	habréis estado	estuviereis	hubiereis estado
3rd p. plur.	estarán	habrán estado	estuvieren	hubieren estado
	Present conditional	**Conditional perfect**		
1st p. sing.	estaría	habría estado		
2nd p. sing.	estarías	habrías estado		
3rd p. sing.	estaría	habría estado		
1st p. plur.	estaríamos	habríamos estado		
2nd p. plur.	estaríais	habríais estado		
3rd p. plur.	estarían	habrían estado		

Imperative

Present	**Forms using the subjunctive stem**
está (tú)	esté (él, ella, usted)
estad (vosotros)	estemos (nosotros)
	estén (ellos, ellas, ustedes)

S A L I R

Irregular verb

A g is added to the *stem** in the 1st person singular of the present indicative, the present subjunctive, and in the imperative. All forms of the future and present conditional are irregular and add a d. The 2nd person singular of the imperative is irregular. (See p. 127).

- Stem + g
- Irregular future and conditional: sal › saldr (See p. 127)
- Irregular imperative: sal

Impersonal mood		
	Simple forms	Compound forms
Infinitive	salir	haber salido
Gerund	saliendo	habiendo salido
Past participle	salido	

Personal moods				
	Indicative		**Subjunctive**	
	Simple forms	Compound forms	Simple forms	Compound forms
	Present	**Perfect**	**Present**	**Past**
1st p. sing.	**salgo**	he salido	**salga**	haya salido
2nd p. sing.	sales	has salido	**salga**s	hayas salido
3rd p. sing.	sale	ha salido	**salga**	haya salido
1st p. plur.	salimos	hemos salido	**salga**mos	hayamos salido
2nd p. plur.	salís	habéis salido	**salgá**is	hayáis salido
3rd p. plur.	salen	han salido	**salga**n	hayan salido
	Imperfect	**Past perfect**	**Imperfect**	**Past perfect**
1st p. sing.	salía	había salido	saliera	hubiera salido
2nd p. sing.	salías	habías salido	salieras	hubieras salido
3rd p. sing.	salía	había salido	saliera	hubiera salido
1st p. plur.	salíamos	habíamos salido	saliéramos	hubiéramos salido
2nd p. plur.	salíais	habíais salido	salierais	hubierais salido
3rd p. plur.	salían	habían salido	salieran	hubieran salido
	Preterit	**Past anterior**		
1st p. sing.	salí	hube salido	saliese	hubiese salido
2nd p. sing.	saliste	hubiste salido	salieses	hubieses salido
3rd p. sing.	salió	hubo salido	saliese	hubiese salido
1st p. plur.	salimos	hubimos salido	saliésemos	hubiésemos salido
2nd p. plur.	salisteis	hubisteis salido	salieseis	hubieseis salido
3rd p. plur.	salieron	hubieron salido	saliesen	hubiesen salido
	Future	**Future perfect**	**Future**	**Future perfect**
1st p. sing.	**saldré**	habré salido	saliere	hubiere salido
2nd p. sing.	**saldr**ás	habrás salido	salieres	hubieres salido
3rd p. sing.	**saldr**á	habrá salido	saliere	hubiere salido
1st p. plur.	**saldr**emos	habremos salido	saliéremos	hubiéremos salido
2nd p. plur.	**saldr**éis	habréis salido	saliereis	hubiereis salido
3rd p. plur.	**saldr**án	habrán salido	salieren	hubieren salido
	Present conditional	**Conditional perfect**		
1st p. sing.	**saldr**ía	habría salido		

Imperative	
Present	**Forms using the subjunctive stem**
sal (tú)	**salga** (él, ella, usted)
salid (vosotros)	**salga**mos (nosotros)
	salgan (ellos, ellas, ustedes)

2nd p. sing.	**saldr**ías	habrías salido
3rd p. sing.	**saldr**ía	habría salido
1st p. plur.	**saldr**íamos	habríamos salido
2nd p. plur.	**saldr**íais	habríais salido
3rd p. plur.	**saldr**ían	habrían salido

CABER

Irregular verb

- *Stem** cab › quep (in the present indicative, the present subjunctive, and the imperative)
- Strong preterit: cab › cup (See p. 118)
- Irregular future and conditional: cab › cabr (See p. 121)
- Spelling c › qu before e

Impersonal mood

	Simple forms	Compound forms
Infinitive	caber	haber cabido
Gerund	cabiendo	habiendo cabido
Past participle	cabido	

Personal moods

	Indicative		Subjunctive	
	Simple forms	Compound forms	Simple forms	Compound forms
	Present	**Perfect**	**Present**	**Past**
1st p. sing.	quepo	he cabido	quepa	haya cabido
2nd p. sing.	cabes	has cabido	quepas	hayas cabido
3rd p. sing.	cabe	ha cabido	quepa	haya cabido
1st p. plur.	cabemos	hemos cabido	quepamos	hayamos cabido
2nd p. plur.	cabéis	habéis cabido	quepáis	hayáis cabido
3rd p. plur.	caben	han cabido	quepan	hayan cabido
	Imperfect	**Past perfect**	**Imperfect**	**Past perfect**
1st p. sing.	cabía	había cabido	cupiera	hubiera cabido
2nd p. sing.	cabías	habías cabido	cupieras	hubieras cabido
3rd p. sing.	cabía	había cabido	cupiera	hubiera cabido
1st p. plur.	cabíamos	habíamos cabido	cupiéramos	hubiéramos cabido
2nd p. plur.	cabíais	habíais cabido	cupierais	hubierais cabido
3rd p. plur.	cabían	habían cabido	cupieran	hubieran cabido
	Preterit	**Past anterior**		
1st p. sing.	cupe	hube cabido	cupiese	hubiese cabido
2nd p. sing.	cupiste	hubiste cabido	cupieses	hubieses cabido
3rd p. sing.	cupo	hubo cabido	cupiese	hubiese cabido
1st p. plur.	cupimos	hubimos cabido	cupiésemos	hubiésemos cabido
2nd p. plur.	cupisteis	hubisteis cabido	cupieseis	hubieseis cabido
3rd p. plur.	cupieron	hubieron cabido	cupiesen	hubiesen cabido
	Future	**Future perfect**	**Future**	**Future perfect**
1st p. sing.	cabré	habré cabido	cupiere	hubiere cabido
2nd p. sing.	cabrás	habrás cabido	cupieres	hubieres cabido
3rd p. sing.	cabrá	habrá cabido	cupiere	hubiere cabido
1st p. plur.	cabremos	habremos cabido	cupiéremos	hubiéremos cabido
2nd p. plur.	cabréis	habréis cabido	cupiereis	hubiereis cabido
3rd p. plur.	cabrán	habrán cabido	cupieren	hubieren cabido
	Present conditional	**Conditional perfect**		
1st p. sing.	cabría	habría cabido		
2nd p. sing.	cabrías	habrías cabido		
3rd p. sing.	cabría	habría cabido		
1st p. plur.	cabríamos	habríamos cabido		
2nd p. plur.	cabríais	habríais cabido		
3rd p. plur.	cabrían	habrían cabido		

Imperative

Present	Forms using the subjunctive stem
cabe (tú)	quepa (él, ella, usted)
cabed (vosotros)	quepamos (nosotros)
	quepan (ellos, ellas, ustedes)

SABER

Irregular verb

- Irregular 1st person singular of the present indicative: sé
- Strong preterit sab › sup (See p. 118)
- Irregular present subjunctive and imperative: sab › sep
- Irregular future and conditional: sab › sabr

Impersonal mood

	Simple forms	Compound forms
Infinitive	saber	haber sabido
Gerund	sabiendo	habiendo sabido
Past participle	sabido	

Personal moods

	Indicative		Subjunctive	
	Simple forms	Compound forms	Simple forms	Compound forms
	Present	**Perfect**	**Present**	**Past**
1st p. sing.	sé	he sabido	sepa	haya sabido
2nd p. sing.	sabes	has sabido	sepas	hayas sabido
3rd p. sing.	sabe	ha sabido	sepa	haya sabido
1st p. plur.	sabemos	hemos sabido	sepamos	hayamos sabido
2nd p. plur.	sabéis	habéis sabido	sepáis	hayáis sabido
3rd p. plur.	saben	han sabido	sepan	hayan sabido
	Imperfect	**Past perfect**	**Imperfect**	**Past perfect**
1st p. sing.	sabía	había sabido	supiera	hubiera sabido
2nd p. sing.	sabías	habías sabido	supieras	hubieras sabido
3rd p. sing.	sabía	había sabido	supiera	hubiera sabido
1st p. plur.	sabíamos	habíamos sabido	supiéramos	hubiéramos sabido
2nd p. plur.	sabíais	habíais sabido	supierais	hubierais sabido
3rd p. plur.	sabían	habían sabido	supieran	hubieran sabido
	Preterit	**Past anterior**		
1st p. sing.	supe	hube sabido	supiese	hubiese sabido
2nd p. sing.	supiste	hubiste sabido	supieses	hubieses sabido
3rd p. sing.	supo	hubo sabido	supiese	hubiese sabido
1st p. plur.	supimos	hubimos sabido	supiésemos	hubiésemos sabido
2nd p. plur.	supisteis	hubisteis sabido	supieseis	hubieseis sabido
3rd p. plur.	supieron	hubieron sabido	supiesen	hubiesen sabido
	Future	**Future perfect**	**Future**	**Future perfect**
1st p. sing.	sabré	habré sabido	supiere	hubiere sabido
2nd p. sing.	sabrás	habrás sabido	supieres	hubieres sabido
3rd p. sing.	sabrá	habrá sabido	supiere	hubiere sabido
1st p. plur.	sabremos	habremos sabido	supiéremos	hubiéremos sabido
2nd p. plur.	sabréis	habréis sabido	supiereis	hubiereis sabido
3rd p. plur.	sabrán	habrán sabido	supieren	hubieren sabido
	Present conditional	**Conditional perfect**		
1st p. sing.	sabría	habría sabido		
2nd p. sing.	sabrías	habrías sabido		
3rd p. sing.	sabría	habría sabido		
1st p. plur.	sabríamos	habríamos sabido		
2nd p. plur.	sabríais	habríais sabido		
3rd p. plur.	sabrían	habrían sabido		

Imperative

Present	Forms using the subjunctive stem
sabe (tú)	sepa (él, ella, usted)
sabed (vosotros)	sepamos (nosotros)
	sepan (ellos, ellas, ustedes)

HACER

Irregular verb

- *Stem* + g (in the present indicative, the present subjunctive, and the imperative)
- Strong preterit: hac › hic (See p. 118)
- Irregular future and conditional: har
- Irregular 2nd person singular of the imperative: haz
- Spelling change: c › z before o
- Irregular past participle: hecho

Impersonal mood		
	Simple forms	Compound forms
Infinitive	hacer	haber **hecho**
Gerund	haciendo	habiendo **hecho**
Past participle	**hecho**	

Personal moods

	Indicative		Subjunctive	
	Simple forms	Compound forms	Simple forms	Compound forms
	Present	**Perfect**	**Present**	**Past**
1st p. sing.	hago	he **hecho**	haga	haya **hecho**
2nd p. sing.	haces	has **hecho**	hagas	hayas **hecho**
3rd p. sing.	hace	ha **hecho**	haga	haya **hecho**
1st p. plur.	hacemos	hemos **hecho**	hagamos	hayamos **hecho**
2nd p. plur.	hacéis	habéis **hecho**	hagáis	hayáis **hecho**
3rd p. plur.	hacen	han **hecho**	hagan	hayan **hecho**
	Imperfect	**Past perfect**	**Imperfect**	**Past perfect**
1st p. sing.	hacía	había **hecho**	hiciera	hubiera **hecho**
2nd p. sing.	hacías	habías **hecho**	hicieras	hubieras **hecho**
3rd p. sing.	hacía	había **hecho**	hiciera	hubiera **hecho**
1st p. plur.	hacíamos	habíamos **hecho**	hiciéramos	hubiéramos **hecho**
2nd p. plur.	hacíais	habíais **hecho**	hicierais	hubierais **hecho**
3rd p. plur.	hacían	habían **hecho**	hicieran	hubieran **hecho**
	Preterit	**Past anterior**		
1st p. sing.	hice	hube **hecho**	hiciese	hubiese **hecho**
2nd p. sing.	hiciste	hubiste **hecho**	hicieses	hubieses **hecho**
3rd p. sing.	hizo	hubo **hecho**	hiciese	hubiese **hecho**
1st p. plur.	hicimos	hubimos **hecho**	hiciésemos	hubiésemos **hecho**
2nd p. plur.	hicisteis	hubisteis **hecho**	hicieseis	hubieseis **hecho**
3rd p. plur.	hicieron	hubieron **hecho**	hiciesen	hubiesen **hecho**
	Future	**Future perfect**	**Future**	**Future perfect**
1st p. sing.	haré	habré **hecho**	hiciere	hubiere **hecho**
2nd p. sing.	harás	habrás **hecho**	hicieres	hubieres **hecho**
3rd p. sing.	hará	habrá **hecho**	hiciere	hubiere **hecho**
1st p. plur.	haremos	habremos **hecho**	hiciéremos	hubiéremos **hecho**
2nd p. plur.	haréis	habréis **hecho**	hiciereis	hubiereis **hecho**
3rd p. plur.	harán	habrán **hecho**	hicieren	hubieren **hecho**
	Present conditional	**Conditional perfect**		
1st p. sing.	haría	habría **hecho**		
2nd p. sing.	harías	habrías **hecho**		
3rd p. sing.	haría	habría **hecho**		
1st p. plur.	haríamos	habríamos **hecho**		
2nd p. plur.	haríais	habríais **hecho**		
3rd p. plur.	harían	habrían **hecho**		

Imperative

Present	Forms using the subjunctive stem
haz (tú)	**haga** (él, ella, usted)
haced (vosotros)	**hagamos** (nosotros)
	hagan (ellos, ellas, ustedes)

PONER

Irregular verb

- *Stem** + g (in the present indicative, the present subjunctive, and the imperative)
- Strong preterit: pon > pus (See p. 118)
- Irregular future and conditional: pondr (See p. 121)
- Irregular 2nd person singular of the imperative: pon
- Irregular past participle: puesto

Impersonal mood		
	Simple forms	Compound forms
Infinitive	poner	haber **puesto**
Gerund	poniendo	habiendo **puesto**
Past participle	**puesto**	

Personal moods			
	Indicative		**Subjunctive**

	Simple forms	Compound forms	Simple forms	Compound forms
	Present	**Perfect**	**Present**	**Past**
1st p. sing.	pongo	he puesto	ponga	haya puesto
2nd p. sing.	pones	has puesto	pongas	hayas puesto
3rd p. sing.	pone	ha puesto	ponga	haya puesto
1st p. plur.	ponemos	hemos puesto	pongamos	hayamos puesto
2nd p. plur.	ponéis	habéis puesto	pongáis	hayáis puesto
3rd p. plur.	ponen	han puesto	pongan	hayan puesto
	Imperfect	**Past perfect**	**Imperfect**	**Past perfect**
1st p. sing.	ponía	había puesto	pusiera	hubiera puesto
2nd p. sing.	ponías	habías puesto	pusieras	hubieras puesto
3rd p. sing.	ponía	había puesto	pusiera	hubiera puesto
1st p. plur.	poníamos	habíamos puesto	pusiéramos	hubiéramos puesto
2nd p. plur.	poníais	habíais puesto	pusierais	hubierais puesto
3rd p. plur.	ponían	habían puesto	pusieran	hubieran puesto
	Preterit	**Past anterior**		
1st p. sing.	puse	hube puesto	pusiese	hubiese puesto
2nd p. sing.	pusiste	hubiste puesto	pusieses	hubieses puesto
3rd p. sing.	puso	hubo puesto	pusiese	hubiese puesto
1st p. plur.	pusimos	hubimos puesto	pusiésemos	hubiésemos puesto
2nd p. plur.	pusisteis	hubisteis puesto	pusieseis	hubieseis puesto
3rd p. plur.	pusieron	hubieron puesto	pusiesen	hubiesen puesto
	Future	**Future perfect**	**Future**	**Future perfect**
1st p. sing.	pondré	habré puesto	pusiere	hubiere puesto
2nd p. sing.	pondrás	habrás puesto	pusieres	hubieres puesto
3rd p. sing.	pondrá	habrá puesto	pusiere	hubiere puesto
1st p. plur.	pondremos	habremos puesto	pusiéremos	hubiéremos puesto
2nd p. plur.	pondréis	habréis puesto	pusiereis	hubiereis puesto
3rd p. plur.	pondrán	habrán puesto	pusieren	hubieren puesto
	Present conditional	**Conditional perfect**		

			Imperative	
1st p. sing.	pondría	habría puesto	**Present**	**Forms using the subjunctive stem**
2nd p. sing.	pondrías	habrías puesto	pon (tú)	ponga (él, ella, usted)
3rd p. sing.	pondría	habría puesto	poned (vosotros)	pongamos (nosotros)
1st p. plur.	pondríamos	habríamos puesto		pongan (ellos, ellas, ustedes)
2nd p. plur.	pondríais	habríais puesto		
3rd p. plur.	pondrían	habrían puesto		

QUERER

Irregular verb

- *Diphthong**: e › ie (in the present indicative, the present subjunctive, and the imperative)
- Strong preterit: quer › quis (See p. 118)
- Irregular future and conditional: querr

Impersonal mood		
	Simple forms	Compound forms
Infinitive	querer	haber querido
Gerund	queriendo	habiendo querido
Past participle	querido	

Personal moods				
	Indicative		**Subjunctive**	
	Simple forms	Compound forms	Simple forms	Compound forms
	Present	**Perfect**	**Present**	**Past**
1st p. sing.	quiero	he querido	quiera	haya querido
2nd p. sing.	quieres	has querido	quieras	hayas querido
3rd p. sing.	quiere	ha querido	quiera	haya querido
1st p. plur.	queremos	hemos querido	queramos	hayamos querido
2nd p. plur.	queréis	habéis querido	queráis	hayáis querido
3rd p. plur.	quieren	han querido	quieran	hayan querido
	Imperfect	**Past perfect**	**Imperfect**	**Past perfect**
1st p. sing.	quería	había querido	quisiera	hubiera querido
2nd p. sing.	querías	habías querido	quisieras	hubieras querido
3rd p. sing.	quería	había querido	quisiera	hubiera querido
1st p. plur.	queríamos	habíamos querido	quisiéramos	hubiéramos querido
2nd p. plur.	queríais	habíais querido	quisierais	hubierais querido
3rd p. plur.	querían	habían querido	quisieran	hubieran querido
	Preterit	**Past anterior**		
1st p. sing.	quise	hube querido	quisiese	hubiese querido
2nd p. sing.	quisiste	hubiste querido	quisieses	hubieses querido
3rd p. sing.	quiso	hubo querido	quisiese	hubiese querido
1st p. plur.	quisimos	hubimos querido	quisiésemos	hubiésemos querido
2nd p. plur.	quisisteis	hubisteis querido	quisieseis	hubieseis querido
3rd p. plur.	quisieron	hubieron querido	quisiesen	hubiesen querido
	Future	**Future perfect**	**Future**	**Future perfect**
1st p. sing.	querré	habré querido	quisiere	hubiere querido
2nd p. sing.	querrás	habrás querido	quisieres	hubieres querido
3rd p. sing.	querrá	habrá querido	quisiere	hubiere querido
1st p. plur.	querremos	habremos querido	quisiéremos	hubiéremos querido
2nd p. plur.	querréis	habréis querido	quisiereis	hubiereis querido
3rd p. plur.	querrán	habrán querido	quisieren	hubieren querido
	Present conditional	**Conditional perfect**		
1st p. sing.	querría	habría querido		
2nd p. sing.	querrías	habrías querido		
3rd p. sing.	querría	habría querido		
1st p. plur.	querríamos	habríamos querido		
2nd p. plur.	querríais	habríais querido		
3rd p. plur.	querrían	habrían querido		

Imperative	
Present	**Forms using the subjunctive stem**
quiere (tú)	quiera (él, ella, usted)
quered (vosotros)	queramos (nosotros)
	quieran (ellos, ellas, ustedes)

Irregular verb

- *Diphthong**: o › ue (in the present indicative, the present subjunctive, and the imperative)
- Strong preterit: pod › pud (See p. 118)
- Irregular future and conditional: podr
- Irregular gerund: pudiendo

Impersonal mood		
	Simple forms	Compound forms
Infinitive	poder	haber podido
Gerund	**pudiendo**	habiendo podido
Past participle	podido	

Personal moods				
	Indicative		Subjunctive	
	Simple forms	Compound forms	Simple forms	Compound forms
	Present	**Perfect**	**Present**	**Past**
1st p. sing.	puedo	he podido	pueda	haya podido
2nd p. sing.	puedes	has podido	puedas	hayas podido
3rd p. sing.	puede	ha podido	pueda	haya podido
1st p. plur.	podemos	hemos podido	podamos	hayamos podido
2nd p. plur.	podéis	habéis podido	podáis	hayáis podido
3rd p. plur.	pueden	han podido	puedan	hayan podido
	Imperfect	**Past perfect**	**Imperfect**	**Past perfect**
1st p. sing.	podía	había podido	pudiera	hubiera podido
2nd p. sing.	podías	habías podido	pudieras	hubieras podido
3rd p. sing.	podía	había podido	pudiera	hubiera podido
1st p. plur.	podíamos	habíamos podido	pudiéramos	hubiéramos podido
2nd p. plur.	podíais	habíais podido	pudierais	hubierais podido
3rd p. plur.	podían	habían podido	pudieran	hubieran podido
	Preterit	**Past anterior**		
1st p. sing.	pude	hube podido	pudiese	hubiese podido
2nd p. sing.	pudiste	hubiste podido	pudieses	hubieses podido
3rd p. sing.	pudo	hubo podido	pudiese	hubiese podido
1st p. plur.	pudimos	hubimos podido	pudiésemos	hubiésemos podido
2nd p. plur.	pudisteis	hubisteis podido	pudieseis	hubieseis podido
3rd p. plur.	pudieron	hubieron podido	pudiesen	hubiesen podido
	Future	**Future perfect**	**Future**	**Future perfect**
1st p. sing.	podré	habré podido	pudiere	hubiere podido
2nd p. sing.	podrás	habrás podido	pudieres	hubieres podido
3rd p. sing.	podrá	habrá podido	pudiere	hubiere podido
1st p. plur.	podremos	habremos podido	pudiéremos	hubiéremos podido
2nd p. plur.	podréis	habréis podido	pudiereis	hubiereis podido
3rd p. plur.	podrán	habrán podido	pudieren	hubieren podido
	Present conditional	**Conditional perfect**		
1st p. sing.	podría	habría podido		
2nd p. sing.	podrías	habrías podido		
3rd p. sing.	podría	habría podido		
1st p. plur.	podríamos	habríamos podido		
2nd p. plur.	podríais	habríais podido		
3rd p. plur.	podrían	habrían podido		

Imperative	
Present	**Forms using the subjunctive stem**
puede (tú)	pueda (él, ella, usted)
poded (vosotros)	podamos (nosotros)
	puedan (ellos, ellas, ustedes)

TENER

Irregular verb

- *Diphthong**: e › ie (in the present indicative)
- *Stem** + g (in the present indicative, the present subjunctive, and the imperative)
- Strong preterit: ten › tuv (See p. 118)
- Irregular future and conditional: tendr
- Irregular 2nd person singular in the imperative: ten

Impersonal mood

	Simple forms	Compound forms
Infinitive	tener	haber tenido
Gerund	teniendo	habiendo tenido
Past participle	tenido	

Personal moods

	Indicative		Subjunctive	
	Simple forms	Compound forms	Simple forms	Compound forms
	Present	**Perfect**	**Present**	**Past**
1st p. sing.	tengo	he tenido	tenga	haya tenido
2nd p. sing.	tienes	has tenido	tengas	hayas tenido
3rd p. sing.	tiene	ha tenido	tenga	haya tenido
1st p. plur.	tenemos	hemos tenido	tengamos	hayamos tenido
2nd p. plur.	tenéis	habéis tenido	tengáis	hayáis tenido
3rd p. plur.	tienen	han tenido	tengan	hayan tenido
	Imperfect	**Past perfect**	**Imperfect**	**Past perfect**
1st p. sing.	tenía	había tenido	tuviera	hubiera tenido
2nd p. sing.	tenías	habías tenido	tuvieras	hubieras tenido
3rd p. sing.	tenía	había tenido	tuviera	hubiera tenido
1st p. plur.	teníamos	habíamos tenido	tuviéramos	hubiéramos tenido
2nd p. plur.	teníais	habíais tenido	tuvierais	hubierais tenido
3rd p. plur.	tenían	habían tenido	tuvieran	hubieran tenido
	Preterit	**Past anterior**		
1st p. sing.	tuve	hube tenido	tuviese	hubiese tenido
2nd p. sing.	tuviste	hubiste tenido	tuvieses	hubieses tenido
3rd p. sing.	tuvo	hubo tenido	tuviese	hubiese tenido
1st p. plur.	tuvimos	hubimos tenido	tuviésemos	hubiésemos tenido
2nd p. plur.	tuvisteis	hubisteis tenido	tuvieseis	hubieseis tenido
3rd p. plur.	tuvieron	hubieron tenido	tuviesen	hubiesen tenido
	Future	**Future perfect**	**Future**	**Future perfect**
1st p. sing.	tendré	habré tenido	tuviere	hubiere tenido
2nd p. sing.	tendrás	habrás tenido	tuvieres	hubieres tenido
3rd p. sing.	tendrá	habrá tenido	tuviere	hubiere tenido
1st p. plur.	tendremos	habremos tenido	tuviéremos	hubiéremos tenido
2nd p. plur.	tendréis	habréis tenido	tuviereis	hubiereis tenido
3rd p. plur.	tendrán	habrán tenido	tuvieren	hubieren tenido
	Present conditional	**Conditional perfect**		
1st p. sing.	tendría	habría tenido		
2nd p. sing.	tendrías	habrías tenido		
3rd p. sing.	tendría	habría tenido		
1st p. plur.	tendríamos	habríamos tenido		
2nd p. plur.	tendríais	habríais tenido		
3rd p. plur.	tendrían	habrían tenido		

Imperative

Present	**Forms using the subjunctive stem**
ten (tú)	tenga (él, ella, usted)
tened (vosotros)	tengamos (nosotros)
	tengan (ellos, ellas, ustedes)

VENIR

Irregular verb

- *Diphthong**: e › ie (in the present indicative)
- *Stem** + g (in the present indicative, the present subjunctive, and the imperative)
- Strong preterit: ven › vin (See p. 118)
- Irregular future and conditional: vendr
- Irregular 2nd person singular of the imperative: ven
- Irregular gerund: vin**iendo**

Impersonal mood

	Simple forms	Compound forms
Infinitive	venir	haber venido
Gerund	**viniendo**	habiendo venido
Past participle	venido	

Personal moods

	Indicative		Subjunctive	
	Simple forms	Compound forms	Simple forms	Compound forms
	Present	**Perfect**	**Present**	**Past**
1st p. sing.	ven**g**o	he venido	ven**g**a	haya venido
2nd p. sing.	v**ie**nes	has venido	ven**g**as	hayas venido
3rd p. sing.	v**ie**ne	ha venido	ven**g**a	haya venido
1st p. plur.	venimos	hemos venido	ven**g**amos	hayamos venido
2nd p. plur.	venís	habéis venido	ven**g**áis	hayáis venido
3rd p. plur.	v**ie**nen	han venido	ven**g**an	hayan venido
	Imperfect	**Past perfect**	**Imperfect**	**Past perfect**
1st p. sing.	venía	había venido	vin**ie**ra	hubiera venido
2nd p. sing.	venías	habías venido	vin**ie**ras	hubieras venido
3rd p. sing.	venía	había venido	vin**ie**ra	hubiera venido
1st p. plur.	veníamos	habíamos venido	vin**ié**ramos	hubiéramos venido
2nd p. plur.	veníais	habíais venido	vin**ie**rais	hubierais venido
3rd p. plur.	venían	habían venido	vin**ie**ran	hubieran venido
	Preterit	**Past anterior**		
1st p. sing.	vine	hube venido	vin**ie**se	hubiese venido
2nd p. sing.	viniste	hubiste venido	vin**ie**ses	hubieses venido
3rd p. sing.	vino	hubo venido	vin**ie**se	hubiese venido
1st p. plur.	vinimos	hubimos venido	vin**ié**semos	hubiésemos venido
2nd p. plur.	vinisteis	hubisteis venido	vin**ie**seis	hubieseis venido
3rd p. plur.	vinieron	hubieron venido	vin**ie**sen	hubiesen venido
	Future	**Future perfect**	**Future**	**Future perfect**
1st p. sing.	vend**r**é	habré venido	vin**ie**re	hubiere venido
2nd p. sing.	vend**r**ás	habrás venido	vin**ie**res	hubieres venido
3rd p. sing.	vend**r**á	habrá venido	vin**ie**re	hubiere venido
1st p. plur.	vend**r**emos	habremos venido	vin**ié**remos	hubiéremos venido
2nd p. plur.	vend**r**éis	habréis venido	vin**ie**reis	hubiereis venido
3rd p. plur.	vend**r**án	habrán venido	vin**ie**ren	hubieren venido
	Present conditional	**Conditional perfect**		
1st p. sing.	vend**r**ía	habría venido		
2nd p. sing.	vend**r**ías	habrías venido		
3rd p. sing.	vend**r**ía	habría venido		
1st p. plur.	vend**r**íamos	habríamos venido		
2nd p. plur.	vend**r**íais	habríais venido		
3rd p. plur.	vend**r**ían	habrían venido		

Imperative

Present	Forms using the subjunctive stem
ven (tú)	ven**g**a (él, ella, usted)
venid (vosotros)	ven**g**amos (nosotros)
	ven**g**an (ellos, ellas, ustedes)

DECIR

Irregular verb

- *Stem** + g (in the present indicative, the present subjunctive, and the imperative)
- Strong preterit: dec › dij (See p. 118)
- Irregular future and conditional: stem dir
- Monosyllabic imperative for the 2nd person singular: di
- Irregular gerund: dic**iendo**
- Irregular past participle: dicho

Impersonal mood		
	Simple forms	Compound forms
Infinitive	decir	haber **dicho**
Gerund	diciendo	habiendo **dicho**
Past participle	dicho	

Personal moods

	Indicative		Subjunctive	
	Simple forms	Compound forms	Simple forms	Compound forms
	Present	**Perfect**	**Present**	**Past**
1st p. sing.	digo	he **dicho**	diga	haya **dicho**
2nd p. sing.	dices	has **dicho**	digas	hayas **dicho**
3rd p. sing.	dice	ha **dicho**	diga	haya **dicho**
1st p. plur.	decimos	hemos **dicho**	digamos	hayamos **dicho**
2nd p. plur.	decís	habéis **dicho**	digáis	hayáis **dicho**
3rd p. plur.	dicen	han **dicho**	digan	hayan **dicho**
	Imperfect	**Past perfect**	**Imperfect**	**Past perfect**
1st p. sing.	decía	había **dicho**	dijera	hubiera **dicho**
2nd p. sing.	decías	habías **dicho**	dijeras	hubieras **dicho**
3rd p. sing.	decía	había **dicho**	dijera	hubiera **dicho**
1st p. plur.	decíamos	habíamos **dicho**	dijéramos	hubiéramos **dicho**
2nd p. plur.	decíais	habíais **dicho**	dijerais	hubierais **dicho**
3rd p. plur.	decían	habían **dicho**	dijeran	hubieran **dicho**
	Preterit	**Past anterior**		
1st p. sing.	dije	hube **dicho**	dijese	hubiese **dicho**
2nd p. sing.	dijiste	hubiste **dicho**	dijeses	hubieses **dicho**
3rd p. sing.	dijo	hubo **dicho**	dijese	hubiese **dicho**
1st p. plur.	dijimos	hubimos **dicho**	dijésemos	hubiésemos **dicho**
2nd p. plur.	dijisteis	hubisteis **dicho**	dijeseis	hubieseis **dicho**
3rd p. plur.	dijeron	hubieron **dicho**	dijesen	hubiesen **dicho**
	Future	**Future perfect**	**Future**	**Future perfect**
1st p. sing.	diré	habré **dicho**	dijere	hubiere **dicho**
2nd p. sing.	dirás	habrás **dicho**	dijeres	hubieres **dicho**
3rd p. sing.	dirá	habrá **dicho**	dijere	hubiere **dicho**
1st p. plur.	diremos	habremos **dicho**	dijéremos	hubiéremos **dicho**
2nd p. plur.	diréis	habréis **dicho**	dijereis	hubiereis **dicho**
3rd p. plur.	dirán	habrán **dicho**	dijeren	hubieren **dicho**
	Present conditional	**Conditional perfect**		
1st p. sing.	diría	habría **dicho**		
2nd p. sing.	dirías	habrías **dicho**		
3rd p. sing.	diría	habría **dicho**		
1st p. plur.	diríamos	habríamos **dicho**		
2nd p. plur.	diríais	habríais **dicho**		
3rd p. plur.	dirían	habrían **dicho**		

Imperative	
Present	**Forms using the subjunctive stem**
di (tú)	**diga** (él, ella, usted)
decid (vosotros)	**digamos** (nosotros)
	digan (ellos, ellas, ustedes)

VER

Irregular verb

- Contraction veer › ver (in the infinitive, the gerund, the present indicative, apart from the 1st person singular, and in the imperative)
- Monosyllabic preterit for the 1st and 3rd persons singular: vi, vio
- Irregular past participle: visto

Impersonal mood		
	Simple forms	Compound forms
Infinitive	ver	haber visto
Gerund	viendo	habiendo visto
Past participle	visto	

Personal moods				
	Indicative		Subjunctive	
	Simple forms	Compound forms	Simple forms	Compound forms
	Present	**Perfect**	**Present**	**Past**
1st p. sing.	veo	he visto	vea	haya visto
2nd p. sing.	ves	has visto	veas	hayas visto
3rd p. sing.	ve	ha visto	vea	haya visto
1st p. plur.	vemos	hemos visto	veamos	hayamos visto
2nd p. plur.	veis	habéis visto	veáis	hayáis visto
3rd p. plur.	ven	han visto	vean	hayan visto
	Imperfect	**Past perfect**	**Imperfect**	**Past perfect**
1st p. sing.	veía	había visto	viera	hubiera visto
2nd p. sing.	veías	habías visto	vieras	hubieras visto
3rd p. sing.	veía	había visto	viera	hubiera visto
1st p. plur.	veíamos	habíamos visto	viéramos	hubiéramos visto
2nd p. plur.	veíais	habíais visto	vierais	hubierais visto
3rd p. plur.	veían	habían visto	vieran	hubieran visto
	Preterit	**Past anterior**		
1st p. sing.	vi	hube visto	viese	hubiese visto
2nd p. sing.	viste	hubiste visto	vieses	hubieses visto
3rd p. sing.	vio	hubo visto	viese	hubiese visto
1st p. plur.	vimos	hubimos visto	viésemos	hubiésemos visto
2nd p. plur.	visteis	hubisteis visto	vieseis	hubieseis visto
3rd p. plur.	vieron	hubieron visto	viesen	hubiesen visto
	Future	**Future perfect**	**Future**	**Future perfect**
1st p. sing.	veré	habré visto	viere	hubiere visto
2nd p. sing.	verás	habrás visto	vieres	hubieres visto
3rd p. sing.	verá	habrá visto	viere	hubiere visto
1st p. plur.	veremos	habremos visto	viéremos	hubiéremos visto
2nd p. plur.	veréis	habréis visto	viereis	hubiereis visto
3rd p. plur.	verán	habrán visto	vieren	hubieren visto
	Present conditional	**Conditional perfect**		
1st p. sing.	vería	habría visto		
2nd p. sing.	verías	habrías visto		
3rd p. sing.	vería	habría visto		
1st p. plur.	veríamos	habríamos visto		
2nd p. plur.	veríais	habríais visto		
3rd p. plur.	verían	habrían visto		

Imperative	
Present	**Forms using the subjunctive stem**
ve (tú)	vea (él, ella, usted)
ved (vosotros)	veamos (nosotros)
	vean (ellos, ellas, ustedes)

HABER

Irregular verb

- *Impersonal* forms with the *yod* (in the present indicative and present subjunctive): hay, haya
- *Stem* + yod (in the present subjunctive and the imperative)
- Strong preterit: hab › hub (See p. 118)
- Irregular future and conditional: habr

Impersonal mood		
	Simple forms	Compound forms
Infinitive	haber	haber habido
Gerund	habiendo	habiendo habido
Past participle	habido	

Personal moods			
Indicative		**Subjunctive**	
Simple forms	Compound forms	Simple forms	Compound forms

	Indicative		Subjunctive	
	Present	**Perfect**	**Present**	**Past**
1st p. sing.	he	he habido	**haya**	haya habido
2nd p. sing.	has	has habido	**hay**as	hayas habido
3rd p. sing.	ha (**hay**)	ha habido	**haya**	haya habido
1st p. plur.	hemos	hemos habido	**hay**amos	hayamos habido
2nd p. plur.	habéis	habéis habido	**hay**áis	hayáis habido
3rd p. plur.	han	han habido	**hay**an	hayan habido
	Imperfect	**Past perfect**	**Imperfect**	**Past perfect**
1st p. sing.	había	había habido	**hubie**ra	hubiera habido
2nd p. sing.	habías	habías habido	**hubie**ras	hubieras habido
3rd p. sing.	había	había habido	**hubie**ra	hubiera habido
1st p. plur.	habíamos	habíamos habido	**hubié**ramos	hubiéramos habido
2nd p. plur.	habíais	habíais habido	**hubie**rais	hubierais habido
3rd p. plur.	habían	habían habido	**hubie**ran	hubieran habido
	Preterit	**Past anterior**		
1st p. sing.	**hube**	hube habido	**hubie**se	hubiese habido
2nd p. sing.	**hub**iste	hubiste habido	**hubie**ses	hubieses habido
3rd p. sing.	**hub**o	hubo habido	**hubie**se	hubiese habido
1st p. plur.	**hub**imos	hubimos habido	**hubié**semos	hubiésemos habido
2nd p. plur.	**hub**isteis	hubisteis habido	**hubie**seis	hubieseis habido
3rd p. plur.	**hub**ieron	hubieron habido	**hubie**sen	hubiesen habid
	Future	**Future perfect**	**Future**	**Future perfect**
1st p. sing.	**habr**é	habré habido	**hubie**re	hubiere habido
2nd p. sing.	**habr**ás	habrás habido	**hubie**res	hubieres habido
3rd p. sing.	**habr**á	habrá habido	**hubie**re	hubiere habido
1st p. plur.	**habr**emos	habremos habido	**hubié**remos	hubiéremos habido
2nd p. plur.	**habr**éis	habréis habido	**hubie**reis	hubiereis habido
3rd p. plur.	**habr**án	habrán habido	**hubie**ren	hubieren habido
	Present conditional	**Conditional perfect**		
1st p. sing.	**habr**ía	habría habido		
2nd p. sing.	**habr**ías	habrías habido		
3rd p. sing.	**habr**ía	habría habido		
1st p. plur.	**habr**íamos	habríamos habido		
2nd p. plur.	**habr**íais	habríais habido		
3rd p. plur.	**habr**ían	habrían habido		

Imperative	
Present	**Forms using the subjunctive stem**
he (tú)	**hay**a (él, ella, usted)
habed (vosotros)	**hay**amos (nosotros)
	hayan (ellos, ellas, ustedes)

I R

Irregular verb

- *Stem* + yod**: v**oy**
- Stem + yod (in the present subjunctive and the imperative): vay**a**
- Strong preterit: fu**i** (see ser)
- Irregular stem in the imperfect: ib**a**
- Gerund: **yendo**

Impersonal mood		
	Simple forms	Compound forms
Infinitive	ir	haber ido
Gerund	yendo	habiendo ido
Past participle	ido	

Personal moods			
Indicative		Subjunctive	
Simple forms	Compound forms	Simple forms	Compound forms
Present	**Perfect**	**Present**	**Past**
1st p. sing. voy	he ido	vaya	haya ido
2nd p. sing. vas	has ido	vayas	hayas ido
3rd p. sing. va	ha ido	vaya	haya ido
1st p. plur. vamos	hemos ido	vayamos	hayamos ido
2nd p. plur. vais	habéis ido	vayáis	hayáis ido
3rd p. plur. van	han ido	vayan	hayan ido
Imperfect	**Past perfect**	**Imperfect**	**Past perfect**
1st p. sing. iba	había ido	fuera	hubiera ido
2nd p. sing. ibas	habías ido	fueras	hubieras ido
3rd p. sing. iba	había ido	fuera	hubiera ido
1st p. plur. íbamos	habíamos ido	fuéramos	hubiéramos ido
2nd p. plur. ibais	habíais ido	fuerais	hubierais ido
3rd p. plur. iban	habían ido	fueran	hubieran ido
Preterit	**Past anterior**		
1st p. sing. fui	hube ido	fuese	hubiese ido
2nd p. sing. fuiste	hubiste ido	fueses	hubieses ido
3rd p. sing. fue	hubo ido	fuese	hubiese ido
1st p. plur. fuimos	hubimos ido	fuésemos	hubiésemos ido
2nd p. plur. fuisteis	hubisteis ido	fueseis	hubieseis ido
3rd p. plur. fueron	hubieron ido	fuesen	hubiesen ido
Future	**Future perfect**	**Future**	**Future perfect**
1st p. sing. iré	habré ido	fuere	hubiere ido
2nd p. sing. irás	habrás ido	fueres	hubieres ido
3rd p. sing. irá	habrá ido	fuere	hubiere ido
1st p. plur. iremos	habremos ido	fuéremos	hubiéremos ido
2nd p. plur. iréis	habréis ido	fuereis	hubiereis ido
3rd p. plur. irán	habrán ido	fueren	hubieren ido
Present conditional	**Conditional perfect**		
1st p. sing. iría	habría ido		
2nd p. sing. irías	habrías ido		
3rd p. sing. iría	habría ido		
1st p. plur. iríamos	habríamos ido		
2nd p. plur. iríais	habríais ido		
3rd p. plur. irían	habrían ido		

Imperative	
Present	**Forms using the subjunctive stem**
ve (tú)	vaya (él, ella, usted)
id (vosotros)	vayamos (nosotros)
	vayan (ellos, ellas, ustedes)

SER

Irregular verb

- *Stem* + yod**: s**oy**
- Strong preterit: f**ui** (see ir)
- Irregular stem in the imperfect: **era**
- Irregular past participle: sid**o**

Impersonal mood		
	Simple forms	Compound forms
Infinitive	ser	haber **sido**
Gerund	siendo	habiendo **sido**
Past participle	sido	

Personal moods				
	Indicative		Subjunctive	
	Simple forms	Compound forms	Simple forms	Compound forms
	Present	**Perfect**	**Present**	**Past**
1st p. sing.	soy	he **sido**	sea	haya **sido**
2nd p. sing.	eres	has **sido**	seas	hayas **sido**
3rd p. sing.	es	ha **sido**	sea	haya **sido**
1st p. plur.	somos	hemos **sido**	seamos	hayamos **sido**
2nd p. plur.	sois	habéis **sido**	seáis	hayáis **sido**
3rd p. plur.	son	han **sido**	sean	hayan **sido**
	Imperfect	**Past perfect**	**Imperfect**	**Past perfect**
1st p. sing.	era	había **sido**	fuera	hubiera **sido**
2nd p. sing.	eras	habías **sido**	fueras	hubieras **sido**
3rd p. sing.	era	había **sido**	fuera	hubiera **sido**
1st p. plur.	éramos	habíamos **sido**	fuéramos	hubiéramos **sido**
2nd p. plur.	erais	habíais **sido**	fuerais	hubierais **sido**
3rd p. plur.	eran	habían **sido**	fueran	hubieran **sido**
	Preterit	**Past anterior**		
1st p. sing.	fui	hube **sido**	fuese	hubiese **sido**
2nd p. sing.	fuiste	hubiste **sido**	fueses	hubieses **sido**
3rd p. sing.	fue	hubo **sido**	fuese	hubiese **sido**
1st p. plur.	fuimos	hubimos **sido**	fuésemos	hubiésemos **sido**
2nd p. plur.	fuisteis	hubisteis **sido**	fueseis	hubieseis **sido**
3rd p. plur.	fueron	hubieron **sido**	fuesen	hubiesen **sido**
	Future	**Future perfect**	**Future**	**Future perfect**
1st p. sing.	seré	habré **sido**	fuere	hubiere **sido**
2nd p. sing.	serás	habrás **sido**	fueres	hubieres **sido**
3rd p. sing.	será	habrá **sido**	fuere	hubiere **sido**
1st p. plur.	seremos	habremos **sido**	fuéremos	hubiéremos **sido**
2nd p. plur.	seréis	habréis **sido**	fuereis	hubiereis **sido**
3rd p. plur.	serán	habrán **sido**	fueren	hubieren **sido**
	Present conditional	**Conditional perfect**		
1st p. sing.	sería	habría **sido**		
2nd p. sing.	serías	habrías **sido**		
3rd p. sing.	sería	habría **sido**		
1st p. plur.	seríamos	habríamos **sido**		
2nd p. plur.	seríais	habríais **sido**		
3rd p. plur.	serían	habrían **sido**		

Imperative	
Present	**Forms using the subjunctive stem**
sé (tú)	sea (él, ella, usted)
sed (vosotros)	seamos (nosotros)
	sean (ellos, ellas, ustedes)

ABOLIR

Regular defective verb

The only forms of the verb in current use have an i in the *ending**. Only the 1st and 2nd person plural exist in the present indicative and there is no present subjunctive.

Impersonal mood

	Simple forms	Compound forms
Infinitive	abolir	haber abolido
Gerund	aboliendo	habiendo abolido
Past participle	abolido	

Personal moods

	Indicative		Subjunctive	
	Simple forms	Compound forms	Simple forms	Compound forms
	Present	**Perfect**	**Present**	**Past**
1st p. sing.	-	he abolido	-	haya abolido
2nd p. sing.	-	has abolido	-	hayas abolido
3rd p. sing.	-	ha abolido	-	haya abolido
1st p. plur.	abolimos	hemos abolido	-	hayamos abolido
2nd p. plur.	abolís	habéis abolido	-	hayáis abolido
3rd p. plur.	-	han abolido	-	hayan abolido
	Imperfect	**Past perfect**	**Imperfect**	**Past perfect**
1st p. sing.	abolía	había abolido	aboliera	hubiera abolido
2nd p. sing.	abolías	habías abolido	abolieras	hubieras abolido
3rd p. sing.	abolía	había abolido	aboliera	hubiera abolido
1st p. plur.	abolíamos	habíamos abolido	aboliéramos	hubiéramos abolido
2nd p. plur.	abolíais	habíais abolido	abolierais	hubierais abolido
3rd p. plur.	abolían	habían abolido	abolieran	hubieran abolido
	Preterit	**Past anterior**		
1st p. sing.	abolí	hube abolido	aboliese	hubiese abolido
2nd p. sing.	aboliste	hubiste abolido	abolieses	hubieses abolido
3rd p. sing.	abolió	hubo abolido	aboliese	hubiese abolido
1st p. plur.	abolimos	hubimos abolido	aboliésemos	hubiésemos abolido
2nd p. plur.	abolisteis	hubisteis abolido	abolieseis	hubieseis abolido
3rd p. plur.	abolieron	hubieron abolido	aboliesen	hubiesen abolido
	Future	**Future perfect**	**Future**	**Future perfect**
1st p. sing.	aboliré	habré abolido	aboliere	hubiere abolido*
2nd p. sing.	abolirás	habrás abolido	abolieres	hubieres abolido
3rd p. sing.	abolirá	habrá abolido	aboliere	hubiere abolido
1st p. plur.	aboliremos	habremos abolido	aboliéremos	hubiéremos abolido
2nd p. plur.	aboliréis	habréis abolido	aboliereis	hubiereis abolido
3rd p. plur.	abolirán	habrán abolido	abolieren	hubieren abolido
	Present conditional	**Conditional perfect**		
1st p. sing.	aboliría	habría abolido		
2nd p. sing.	abolirías	habrías abolido		
3rd p. sing.	aboliría	habría abolido		
1st p. plur.	aboliríamos	habríamos abolido		
2nd p. plur.	aboliríais	habríais abolido		
3rd p. plur.	abolirían	habrían abolido		

Imperative

Present	Forms using the subjunctive stem
- (tú)	- (él, ella, usted)
abolid (vosotros)	- (nosotros)
	- (ellos, ellas, ustedes)

BALBUCIR

Regular defective verb

This verb is replaced by balbucear in the following forms: 1st person singular in the present indicative, the whole of the present subjunctive and the forms of the imperative which use the subjunctive stem.

Impersonal mood		
	Simple forms	Compound forms
Infinitive	balbucir	haber balbucido
Gerund	balbuciendo	habiendo balbucido
Past participle	balbucido	

Personal moods				
	Indicative		**Subjunctive**	
	Simple forms	Compound forms	Simple forms	Compound forms
	Present	**Perfect**	**Present**	**Past**
1st p. sing.	-	he balbucido	-	haya balbucido
2nd p. sing.	balbuces	has balbucido	-	hayas balbucido
3rd p. sing.	balbuce	ha balbucido	-	haya balbucido
1st p. plur.	balbucimos	hemos balbucido	-	hayamos balbucido
2nd p. plur.	balbucís	habéis balbucido	-	hayáis balbucido
3rd p. plur.	balbucen	han balbucido	-	hayan balbucido
	Imperfect	**Past perfect**	**Imperfect**	**Past perfect**
1st p. sing.	balbucía	había balbucido	balbuciera	hubiera balbucido
2nd p. sing.	balbucías	habías balbucido	balbucieras	hubieras balbucido
3rd p. sing.	balbucía	había balbucido	balbuciera	hubiera balbucido
1st p. plur.	balbucíamos	habíamos balbucido	balbuciéramos	hubiéramos balbucido
2nd p. plur.	balbucíais	habíais balbucido	balbucierais	hubierais balbucido
3rd p. plur.	balbucían	habían balbucido	balbucieran	hubieran balbucido
	Preterit	**Past anterior**		
1st p. sing.	balbucí	hube balbucido	balbuciese	hubiese balbucido
2nd p. sing.	balbuciste	hubiste balbucido	balbucieses	hubieses balbucido
3rd p. sing.	balbució	hubo balbucido	balbuciese	hubiese balbucido
1st p. plur.	balbucimos	hubimos balbucido	balbuciésemos	hubiésemos balbucido
2nd p. plur.	balbucisteis	hubisteis balbucido	balbucieseis	hubieseis balbucido
3rd p. plur.	balbucieron	hubieron balbucido	balbuciesen	hubiesen balbucido
	Future	**Future perfect**	**Future**	**Future perfect**
1st p. sing.	balbuciré	habré balbucido	balbuciere	hubiere balbucido
2nd p. sing.	balbucirás	habrás balbucido	balbucieres	hubieres balbucido
3rd p. sing.	balbucirá	habrá balbucido	balbuciere	hubiere balbucido
1st p. plur.	balbuciremos	habremos balbucido	balbuciéremos	hubiéremos balbucido
2nd p. plur.	balbuciréis	habréis balbucido	balbuciereis	hubiereis balbucido
3rd p. plur.	balbucirán	habrán balbucido	balbucieren	hubieren balbucido
	Present conditional	**Conditional perfect**		
1st p. sing.	balbuciría	habría balbucido		
2nd p. sing.	balbucirías	habrías balbucido		
3rd p. sing.	balbuciría	habría balbucido		
1st p. plur.	balbuciríamos	habríamos balbucido		
2nd p. plur.	balbuciríais	habríais balbucido		
3rd p. plur.	balbucirían	habrían balbucido		

Imperative	
Present	**Forms using the subjunctive stem**
balbuce (tú)	- (él, ella, usted)
balbucid (vosotros)	- (nosotros)
	- (ellos, ellas, ustedes)

DESOLAR

Regular defective verb

The **o** in the stem changes to **ue** in the present indicative, the present subjunctive, and the imperative.

	Impersonal mood	
	Simple forms	Compound forms
finitive	desolar	haber desolado
•rund	desolando	habiendo desolado
st participle	desolado	

	Personal moods			
	Indicative		**Subjunctive**	
	Simple forms	Compound forms	Simple forms	Compound forms
	Present	**Perfect**	**Present**	**Past**
st p. sing.	desuelo	he desolado	desuele	haya desolado
nd p. sing.	desuelas	has desolado	desueles	hayas desolado
rd p. sing.	desuela	ha desolado	desuele	haya desolado
st p. plur.	desolamos	hemos desolado	desolemos	hayamos desolado
nd p. plur.	desoláis	habéis desolado	desoléis	hayáis desolado
rd p. plur.	desuelan	han desolado	desuelen	hayan desolado
	Imperfect	**Past perfect**	**Imperfect**	**Past perfect**
st p. sing.	desolaba	había desolado	desolara	hubiera desolado
nd p. sing.	desolabas	habías desolado	desolaras	hubieras desolado
rd p. sing.	desolaba	había desolado	desolara	hubiera desolado
st p. plur.	desolábamos	habíamos desolado	desoláramos	hubiéramos desolado
nd p. plur.	desolabais	habíais desolado	desolarais	hubierais desolado
rd p. plur.	desolaban	habían desolado	desolaran	hubieran desolado
	Preterit	**Past anterior**		
st p. sing.	desolé	hube desolado	desolase	hubiese desolado
nd p. sing.	desolaste	hubiste desolado	desolases	hubieses desolado
rd p. sing.	desoló	hubo desolado	desolase	hubiese desolado
st p. plur.	desolamos	hubimos desolado	desolásemos	hubiésemos desolado
nd p. plur.	desolasteis	hubisteis desolado	desolaseis	hubieseis desolado
rd p. plur.	desolaron	hubieron desolado	desolasen	hubiesen desolado
	Future	**Future perfect**	**Future**	**Future perfect**
st p. sing.	desolaré	habré desolado	desolare	hubiere desolado
nd p. sing.	desolarás	habrás desolado	desolares	hubieres desolado
rd p. sing.	desolará	habrá desolado	desolare	hubiere desolado
st p. plur.	desolaremos	habremos desolado	desoláremos	hubiéremos desolado
nd p. plur.	desolaréis	habréis desolado	desolareis	hubiereis desolado
rd p. plur.	desolarán	habrán desolado	desolaren	hubieren desolado
	Present conditional	**Conditional perfect**		
st p. sing.	desolaría	habría desolado		
nd p. sing.	desolarías	habrías desolado		
rd p. sing.	desolaría	habría desolado		
st p. plur.	desolaríamos	habríamos desolado		
nd p. plur.	desolaríais	habríais desolado		
rd p. plur.	desolarían	habrían desolado		

Imperative

Present	Forms using the subjunctive stem
desuela (tú)	desuele (él, ella, usted)
desolad (vosotros)	desolemos (nosotros)
	desuelen (ellos, ellas, ustedes)

SOLER

Defective verb

This verb is only used in the present and imperfect indicative and the present subjunctive.
■ Irregular: *diphthong** o › ue

Impersonal mood		
	Simple forms	Compound forms
Infinitive	soler	-
Gerund	-	-
Past participle	-	-

Personal moods

	Indicative		Subjunctive	
	Simple forms	Compound forms	Simple forms	Compound forms
	Present	**Perfect**	**Present**	**Past**
1st p. sing.	suelo	-	suela	-
2nd p. sing.	sueles	-	suelas	-
3rd p. sing.	suele	-	suela	-
1st p. plur.	solemos	-	solamos	-
2nd p. plur.	soléis	-	soláis	-
3rd p. plur.	suelen	-	suelan	-
	Imperfect	**Past perfect**	**Imperfect**	**Past perfect**
1st p. sing.	solía	-	-	-
2nd p. sing.	solías	-	-	-
3rd p. sing.	solía	-	-	-
1st p. plur.	solíamos	-	-	-
2nd p. plur.	solíais	-	-	-
3rd p. plur.	solían	-	-	-
	Preterit	**Past anterior**		
1st p. sing.	-	-	-	-
2nd p. sing.	-	-	-	-
3rd p. sing.	-	-	-	-
1st p. plur.	-	-	-	-
2nd p. plur.	-	-	-	-
3rd p. plur.	-	-	-	-
	Future	**Future perfect**	**Future**	**Future perfect**
1st p. sing.	-	-	-	-
2nd p. sing.	-	-	-	-
3rd p. sing.	-	-	-	-
1st p. plur.	-	-	-	-
2nd p. plur.	-	-	-	-
3rd p. plur.	-	-	-	-
	Present conditional	**Conditional perfect**		
1st p. sing.	-	-		
2nd p. sing.	-	-		
3rd p. sing.	-	-		
1st p. plur.	-	-		
2nd p. plur.	-	-		
3rd p. plur.	-	-		

Imperative	
Present	**Forms using the subjunctive stem**
- (tú)	- (él, ella, usted)
- (vosotros)	- (nosotros)
	- (ellos, ellas, ustedes)

Grammar
summary

THE SPANISH VERB

As with every word in a language, a verb is made up of:

- lexical information which provides the sense or the meaning of the verb;
- grammatical information which shows we are dealing with a verb.

In Spanish, the subject personal pronoun is optional.

1 Formation

Let's take the form cant<u>as</u>.

It is made of

- a *stem** cant, which holds the meaning of **singing**. This gives us the meaning of the verb, the action that the *speaker** wants to talk about;

- an *ending** <u>-as</u>, which supplies information about the *mood** (indicative), the *aspect** (simple form), the tense (present), and the person (2nd person singular).

In the ending -as, the vowel <u>-a-</u> tells us that the verb belongs to the first group of verbs ending in <u>-ar</u>.

This is the main difference in the way that Spanish and English verbs behave. Spanish verbs inflect and contain the grammatical information in the ending, unlike English verbs which need a subject personal pronoun to specify the subject of the verb.

If we take cantas, all the grammatical information is contained within the inflected verb, including the fact that it is in the 2nd person singular. Spanish verbs have six possible inflections which make the use of the subject personal pronoun redundant.

These inflected forms of the Spanish verb are inherited from Latin.

Latin: *canto, cantas, cantat, cantamus, cantatis, cantant.*

Spanish: canto, cantas, canta, cantamos, cantáis, cantan.

Compare the English which just uses the infinit form of the verb plus the subject personal p noun to denote the speaker (apart from in the person singular which adds an 's').

English: *I sing, you sing, he/she sings, we sing, y sing, they sing*

2 Usage

We need different types of words to make se tences: articles, nouns, adjectives, verbs, adver etc. These different types are called Parts Speech.

Each verb expresses an action or a state wh applies to a person or a thing.

Cantas.
You sing.

I am saying that a person 'tú' sings (the action)

La casa estaba en llamas.
The house was on fire.

I am describing the state that a thing 'la casa' v in.

La casa está en llamas.
The house is on fire.

If the tense in the sentence is changed, or the verb changes. The verb holds the inform tion about the tense. It can tell you whether t action is in the past, the present or the future. addition to this, a verb describes the tempo flow (or lack of it) of an action as it unfolds. Th is referred to as the 'grammatical aspect.' See 116.

VOSEO

Voseo (use of the vos form of address) is one of the forms widely used in Latin American Spanish, especially in Argentina and Uruguay, for addressing someone directly. Vos is used as the familiar form of address and usted is the polite form. The plural of both vos and usted is ustedes.

Voseo does not exist in peninsular Spanish and certain Latin American countries – Chile, Bolivia, Colombia and Peru – use the tú form instead.

1 Formation

Voseo affects the present indicative form and the imperative. The subject personal pronoun is vos.

In the present subjunctive and the negative imperative (no + subjunctive), both the vos form and the tú form more commonly used in Peninsular Spanish can be used.

Peninsular Spanish	Latin American Spanish	Translation
tú forms	vos forms	
Present indicative		
(tú) amas	(vos) amás	you love
(tú) temes	(vos) temés	you fear
(tú) partes	(vos) partís	you leave
Imperative		
(tú) ama	(vos) amá	love!
(tú) teme	(vos) temé	fear!
(tú) parte	(vos) partí	leave!
Subjunctive		
(tú) ames	(vos) amés	that you love
(tú) temas	(vos) temás	that you fear
(tú) partas	(vos) partás	that you leave

2 Usage

Below is a conversation between two friends who haven't seen each other in a number of years and meet in an area of Buenos Aires (Argentina).

– ¿En qué andás? ¡Tanto tiempo!
– Soy arquitecto. ¿Y vos? Contame de vos, ¿qué hiciste todo este tiempo? ¿Te casaste, tenés pibes? ¿Seguís en el barrio?

- *What are you up to these days? It's been a long time!*
- *I'm an architect. How about you? Tell me about you. What have you been up to all this time? Are you married? Do you have any kids? Are you still living in the same area?*

Spanish has six personal pronouns which can be the subject of a verb. They are the 1st, 2nd, 3rd person singular and the 1st, 2nd, 3rd person plural.

1 Formation

yo tú él/ella/usted nosotros/nosotras vosotros/ vosotras ellos/ellas/ustedes
me te le/lo/la lo/le/la usted nos os los/las los/las ustedes
me te le le usted nos os les les ustedes
mí ti él/ella/ello/sí usted nosotros/nosotras vosotros/ vosotras ellos/ellas/sí ustedes
fl me te se se usted nos os se se ustedes

Throughout a large part of Spanish-speaking Latin America, vos is the preferred familiar form. (See p. 101)

The Spanish verb holds the subject information in the *ending**, whereas in English, the verb must be accompanied by a subject personal pronoun 'I,' 'you,' 'he'...

Viene.
He is coming.

2 Usage

In context, subject personal pronouns in Spanish are not directly equivalent to personal pronouns in English. For example, yo is not always equivalent to 'I;' él is not always equivalent to 'he'...

They would normally translate by object personal pronouns: **me**, **you**, **him/her**, **us**, **you**, **them**. If using a subject personal pronoun, the relevant auxiliary must also be used.

– ¿Quién lo dijo? – Yo.
– *Who said that? – Me./I did.*

– ¿Quién llama? – Él.
– *Who's calling? – Him./He is.*

In English, you can't just reply 'I' or 'he' in the examples above: 'Who said that?' 'I.' You either have to use the object personal pronoun 'me' or use the subject personal pronoun together with the relevant auxiliary 'do' or 'have': 'Who said that?' 'I did.'

In English, the subject personal pronouns are dependent on the verb, whereas in Spanish they are not.

In Spanish, subject personal pronouns are only used when you want to emphasize the person:

Tú sales mientras que yo me quedo a dormir.
You go out while I stay and have a sleep.

Yo pienso que es inútil.
I think there's no point.

They are used to avoid ambiguity as more than one subject can have the same inflected verb form:

Ella no se atrevió a contestar.
She didn't dare reply.

Here, as there are several possible subjects (el hombre, la mujer, usted...) of the inflected form 'atrevió', a subject personal pronoun such as 'él, ella, usted...' is needed to clarify the actual subject of the verb.

OBJECT PERSONAL PRONOUNS

Direct object pronouns can go before or after the verb. They can also be preceded by a preposition as in English.
The order of direct object pronouns in Spanish is invariable: indirect object pronoun followed by direct object pronoun.

1 Function

■ They refer to the person or thing directly affected by the action of the verb.

Subo la maleta.
I'll take the suitcase up.

La subo.
direct object of verb
I'll take it up.

■ They refer to the recipient of the action.

Doy un consejo a mi hija.
I give my daughter some advice.

Le doy un consejo.
indirect object of verb
I give her some advice.

2 Position

■ When the verb is conjugated in the indicative or the subjunctive, the pronoun precedes the verb unlike in English where the pronoun comes after the verb.

Quiero que me lo digas.
I want you to tell me it.

■ When the verb is in the infinitive or gerund, the direct object pronoun is tagged on to the end of the infinitve. This feature is called *enclisis**.

Habrá que decírselo.
We'll need to tell him.

■ This attachment is also used with imperatives.

No tires lo útil, recíclalo.
Don't throw away something that can be used. Recycle it.

■ Note that the order of object pronouns is always the same in Spanish. The indirect pronoun is followed by the direct pronoun. In English, both orders are acceptable.

Mi madre se lo presta.
(indirect pronoun + direct pronoun)

My mother lends it to him.

(direct object pronoun + indirect object pronoun)

My mother lends him it.

(indirect object pronoun + direct object pronoun)

■ In constructions which have an **auxiliary + infinitive verb**/**present participle**, adding the pronoun to the end of the verb is not compulsory.

Ella me lo estaba explicando.
Ella estaba explicándomelo.
She was explaining it to me.

Direct object pronouns which are preceded by a preposition (a mí, a ti, a él...) are known as '**tonic pronouns**,' as opposed to the others (me, te, se, le, la, lo...) which are called '**atonic pronouns**.' Where the pronoun has been tagged on to the end of the verb, this will affect the stress and may require a written accent to be added or a different syllable to be stressed.

No te preocupes por mí.
Don't worry about me.

Ven conmigo.
Come with me.

For a table of pronouns, see p. 102.

MOOD

When constructing a verb, the mood is the first stage of a complex process. This is then followed by the choice of *voice**, *aspect**, tense and subject.

1 Formation

The impersonal mood

This covers the infinitive, the gerund and the past participle. At this point, no tense is yet involved. In order to form a tense, impersonal verbs need an *auxiliary**. (See p. 105)

fi	temer	to fear
	temiendo	fearing
	temido	feared

Personal moods

These are: the imperative, the subjunctive and the indicative.

- The imperative just has one simple tense: the present.

¡Cantemos!
Let's sing!

The subjunctive can use three tenses: the present, the past and the future. Each simple verb form has a corresponding compound form. (See *Aspect**, p. 116) The subjunctive mood, however, cannot behave independently. It is always dependent on the main action expressed in the indicative in the *main clause**.

Quiero que vengas.
I want you to come.

The subjunctive form vengas is dependent on the main verb quiero. (See p. 125)

- In the indicative, the action expressed by the verb is complete and doesn't depend on any thing else.

Most forms of the verb are autonomous in this way. They fall into three time periods: the present, the past and the future with five simple tenses and five compound tenses. (See p. 116)

– ¿Quieres más azúcar?
– Sí, quiero.

– *Would you like more sugar?*
– *Yes, please.*

2 Usage

The mood describes the speaker's attitude to an actual event. No act or fact is ever real or not real as such. The speaker's feelings and state of mind always have some bearing on the way something is presented.

I hope he'll remember to come.

This can have two possible renditions in Spanish.

Espero que se acordará de venir.

Whatever the outcome, the speaker's choice of the indicative gives a positive note to the statement. He wants to believe that it is quite likely that the person referred to will remember to come.

Espero que se acuerde de venir.

By choosing to use the subjunctive in the sentence above, the speaker introduces an element of doubt into the same event, making it sound more hypothetical. He knows that there is some chance that this event will not occur.

THE IMPERSONAL MOOD

The impersonal mood includes the following verb forms: infinitive, gerund and past participle.
These verb forms never have an inflected *ending** of their own.
Neither can they place an action in the past, present or future by themselves.

1 Formation

	Spanish	English
Infinitive	jugar/comer/pedir/	to play/eat/ask for
Gerund	jugando/comiendo/pidiendo	playing/eating/asking for
Past participle	jugado/comido/pedido	played/eaten/asked for

The infinitive and the gerund are used to form compound forms, just as in English.

haber pedido *to have asked for*

habiendo jugado *having played*

2 Usage

■ These three forms (cantar, cantando, cantado) are not purely verb forms.

As with English, Spanish has nominalized verbs which can function as nouns or adjectives.

Hemos comido asado de cordero.
[Noun]

We had a lamb roast.

¿Te gustan las castañas asadas?
[Adjective]

Do you like roast chestnuts?

■ In Spanish, infinitives can be used as nouns whereas English tends to use the present participle in this way.

Nos vamos descubriendo a través de su atento escuchar.
We are getting to know each other through his careful listening.

■ The subject and tense are provided by the accompanying verbs (the *auxiliary** verbs).

Si quieres puedo explicártelo.
I can explain it to you, if you like.

■ These forms provide the information on the action taking place.

Voy a comer.
Future action. (See p. 107)

I am going to eat.

Estoy leyendo.
Action currently taking place. (See p. 109)

I am reading.

¿Qué tal has dormido?
Past/completed action. (See p. 111)

Did you sleep well?

THE INFINITIVE

The infinitive in Spanish falls into three groups of verbs with the following endings: -ar, -er and -ir.
The infinitive is used mainly to form the simple future and the conditional. (See p. 121)

1 Formation

stem*	ar	amar	to love
stem*	er	temer	to fear
stem*	ir	subir	to go up

Present and past infinitives

Spanish uses both a present infinitive and a past infinitive.

Quiere irse ahora mismo.
She wants to leave immediately.

Pienso haber terminado los deberes.
I'm planning on having finished my homework.

Formation of future tenses

The simple future and the conditional are formed using the infinitive form of the verb. (See p. 121)

amaré, **I will love**, amaría, **I would love**, etc.

2 Usage

■ The infinitive can be used as an imperative to give instructions.

¡Callaros!
Be quiet!

■ The infinitive can also have the role of a noun.

In this case, it needs to be preceded by a determiner (e.g. an article, a possessive adjective or demonstrative pronoun). Here, English normally uses the present participle in this role.

El ladrar (*barking*), el vivir (*living*), tu andar (*your way of walking*)...

There are some nominal infinitives which even admit a plural form.

Los deberes (*homework*), los seres humanos (*human beings*), los placeres (*pleasures*)...

■ The infinitive can fulfill several functions within a sentence. It can be the subject of the verb, the direct object or the indirect object.

Afirmar eso es ridículo.
(Subject of the verb es.)
Saying that is ridiculous.

Ella sabe mentir.
(Direct object of the verb sabe.)
She knows how to lie.

Dudaron en llamarnos.
(Indirect object of the verb dudaron.)
They hesitated to call us.

VERB PATTERNS USING THE INFINITIVE

The infinitive does not give any information on time or person.
It supplies information on the sequence of events. The use of the infinitive indicates that the action has not yet taken place.

Usage

The use of the infinitive in verb patterns suggests that an action will take place. The time of the action, however, will be shown by the *auxiliary** (the past, present or future). English sometimes mirrors this use of the infinitive but also often uses a structure with the present participle, examples of which are shown in the right-hand column.

■ ir a + infinitive

to be going to fi
Vamos a escribirles.
We are going to write to them.

■ ponerse a + infinitive

to start to fi
Se puso a llover.
It started to rain.

■ meterse a + infinitive

to begin to fi
Se metió a invertir en Bolsa.
He began to invest in the Stock Market.

■ haber de + infinitive

to have to fi
Es tu padre quien ha de hacerlo.
It's your father who has to do it.

■ haber que + infinitive

should fi
Habrá que decírselo.
We should tell them.

■ estar para + infinitive

to be about to fi
Está para llorar.
He's about to cry.

■ tener que + infinitive

to have to fi
Tienes que cumplir.
You have to do your duty.

■ echarse a + infinitive

to start
Se echó a reír.
He started laughing.

■ llegar a + infinitive

to end up
Llegó a ser un gran médico.
He ended up becoming a great doctor.

■ dejar de + infinitive

to stop
Andando el tiempo, dejamos de escribirles.
As time went by, we stopped writing to them.

■ romper a + infinitive

to burst out
Rompió a llorar.
He burst out crying.

■ acostumbrarse a + infinitive

to get used to
Se acostumbró a madrugar.
She got used to getting up early.

■ lanzarse a + infinitive

to rush into
Se lanzó a comprarlo.
He rushed into buying it.

THE GERUND

The gerund is formed from the infinitive *stem** plus the ending **-ando** or **-iendo**. English uses the present participle (-ing) in a similar way.
In Spanish, the use of the gerund always describes an action which is still in progress.

1 Formation

Regular gerunds

*Stem** + ending

am**ar**	**ando**	*loving*
	→ am**ando**	
tem**er**	**iendo**	*fearing*
	→ tem**iendo**	
sub**ir**	**iendo**	*going up*
	→ sub**iendo**	

As in English, the gerund can have both a simple form and a compound form.

Diciendo	Habiendo dicho
Saying	*Having said*

Regular gerunds which change their spelling: i, e › y

These gerund forms are still regular. The presence of the *yod** just leads to a change in spelling. The yod marks the syllable break between the vowel of the *stem** and the i of the *ending**. Thus, the following case of having three vowels together is avoided: ca/ i/ endo.

caer (49) *to fall* → ca**yendo**

oír (58) *to hear* → o**yendo**

ir (77) *to go* → **yendo**

Irregular gerunds

decir	*to say*	dic**iendo**

dormir	*to sleep*	durm**iendo**
morir	*to die*	mur**iendo**
pedir	*to ask for*	pid**iendo**
poder	*to be able to*	pud**iendo**
reír	*to laugh*	r**iendo**
seguir	*to follow*	sigu**iendo**
sentir	*to feel*	sint**iendo**
venir	*to come*	vin**iendo**

Added to these are any derivatives of these verbs and irregular verbs which modify their spelling changing the e to i as per the pedir (39) model.

Also added to these are any derivatives of these verbs and regular verbs or irregular verbs which involve a spelling change according to the huir (52) model.

2 Usage

When it is used after a conjugated verb, it serves to complete the action described by the verb. The action depicted by the gerund is secondary to that of the main verb.

Le hablaba procurando no asustarla.
He spoke to her trying not to frighten her.

In sentences which use a gerund clause, the subject always goes in the second part of the sentence.

Estando él ausente, no me apetece ir a esa fiesta.
With him not going, I don't feel like going to that party.

English would more naturally use an **if** clause in such cases.

VERB PATTERNS USING THE GERUND

In a verb pattern, the role of the gerund is to express an action that is in the process of taking place, regardless of the tense of the *auxiliary**, be it past, present or future.

Usage

■ estar + gerund

This structure is used whenever an action is still taking place. In English, the usual way of rendering this is with the structure **'to be + -ing'**.

¿Me estabas esperando?
Were you waiting for me?

■ ir + gerund

This structure is used to express the duration of an action and places the emphasis on the unfolding of the events. English would normally resort to an adverb or adverbial phrase such as **gradually**, **little by little**.

Los primos fueron conociéndose.
Gradually, the cousins got to know each other.

■ venir + gerund

This structure is used when the action begins in the past and continues right up to the present moment. Its use emphasizes that the action is prolonged over a period of time.

Vengo diciéndole desde hace un mes que se equivoca, pero ella no me hace caso.
I've been telling her for a month that she's wrong, but she won't listen to me.

■ seguir + gerund

The action began in the past but continues into the present. In English, this is often rendered by verbs such as **to continue to be**, **to remain**, **to be still**.

Su pasión sigue siendo el chocolate.
Chocolate remains/is still her passion.

■ llevar + temporal clause + gerund

A temporal clause, or an indication of time, is inserted between the auxiliary verb and the gerund. This structure serves to emphasize the amount of time that has elapsed since the start of the action. Length of time is usually expressed in English by the preposition **for**.

Los pacientes llevan una hora esperando al médico.
The patients have been waiting to see the doctor for an hour.

■ andar + gerund

The structure describes an action which is ongoing and often suggests negative connotations. English usually uses the preposition **for** to express the duration of an action.

Anda buscando trabajo desde hace un año.
She has been looking for work for a year.

THE PAST PARTICIPLE

The past participle is used to form compound tenses in the *active voice**.
The *auxiliary verbs** used are haber and sometimes tener.
The auxiliaries ser and estar are used to form the *passive voice**. (See p. 113)

1 Formation

Regular past participles

*Stem** + ending

am<u>ar</u>	<u>ado</u>	
	→ am<u>ado</u>	*loved*
tem<u>er</u>	<u>ido</u>	
	→ tem<u>ido</u>	*feared*
sub<u>ir</u>	<u>ido</u>	
	→ sub<u>ido</u>	*gone up*

Irregular past participles

abrir	*to open*	abierto
cubrir	*to cover*	cubierto
decir	*to say*	dicho
escribir	*to write*	escrito
hacer	*to do*	hecho
morir	*to die*	muerto
poner	*to put*	puesto
pudrir	*to rot*	podrido
romper	*to break*	roto
satisfacer	*to satisfy*	satisfecho
ver	*to see*	visto
volver	*to return*	vuelto

2 Usage

■ When it is used with the auxiliary haber, the past participle never inflects.

Cuando llegues, habremos cenado.
→ invariable past participle
When you arrive, we will have eaten.
→ **to have** + invariable past participle

■ In Spanish, when the past participle is preceded by the auxiliary haber, it never changes its ending regardless of any direct object in the sentence. The same is true for English.

¿Cuántos libros has leído?
How many books have you read?

Te devuelvo los que he leído.
I'm bringing you back the ones I have read.

Me los he leído antes de comprarlos.
I read them before buying them.

■ With certain verbs, the past participle does agree in gender and number.

A Carmen le gusta andar descalza por casa.
Carmen likes to walk around the house barefoot.

VERB PATTERNS USING THE PAST PARTICIPLE

The past participle serves to complete the verbal action. Spanish uses it in this way in a variety of verb patterns.
In these cases, English would naturally use 'to be' or 'to have' + past participle.

Usage

In verb patterns, the past participle shows that an action is completed, regardless of the tense of the *auxiliary verb** (whether this is in the past, present or future).

As it takes on an adjectival role, it agrees in gender and number.

andar + past participle

Ahora mi hermana anda muy ocupada.
My sister is really busy right now.

dejar + past participle

He dejado dicho que no me despierten.
I've left a message not to be woken.

ir + past participle

Ya van vendidos diez cuadros.
We've sold ten paintings already.

llevar + past participle

Llevo tres páginas leídas.
I've already read three pages.

quedarse + past participle

Con tu respuesta me quedo satisfecha.
I'm satisfied with your reply.

resultar + past participle

En la colisión resultaron heridas diez personas.
Ten people were hurt in the accident.

seguir + past participle

A pesar de mis consejos, sigue despistada.
Despite my advice, she's still distracted.

traer + past participle

Trae puesta su chaqueta nueva.
He's wearing his new jacket.

VERBS WITH TWO PAST PARTICIPLE FORMS

Some Spanish verbs have two possible past participle forms, one regular, one irregular.
- The regular one is used to form compound tenses and is invariable.
- The irregular form, is used like an adjective and so agrees with the noun in gender and number.

1 Formation

Verb	Translation	Regular past participle	Irregular past participle
absorber	to absorb	absorbido	absorto
afligir	to afflict	afligido	aflicto
atender	to see to	atendido	atento
comprimir	to compress	comprimido	compreso
confesar	to confess	confesado	confeso
confundir	to confuse	confundido	confuso
convencer	to convince	convencido	convicto
convertir	to convert	convertido	converso
corregir	to correct	corregido	correcto
despertar	to wake up	despertado	despierto
difundir	to spread	difundido	difuso
dividir	to divide	dividido	diviso
elegir	to choose	elegido	electo
enjugar	to dry	enjugado	enjuto
excluir	to exclude	excluido	excluso
expresar	to express	expresado	expreso
extender	to extend	extendido	extenso
fijar	to fix	fijado	fijo
incluir	to include	incluido	incluso
salvar	to save	salvado	salvo
soltar	to let go	soltado	suelto
suprimir	to suppress	suprimido	supreso
suspender	to suspend	suspendido	suspenso
sustituir	to substitute	sustituido	sustituto
torcer	to twist	torcido	tuerto

2 Usage

- A past participle is invariable.

El profesor todavía no ha fijado la fecha del examen.
The teacher hasn't fixed the date of the examination yet.

- An adjective agrees with the noun in gender and number.

A veces se despierta con una idea fija en la cabeza.
Sometimes, he wakes up with a fixed idea in his head.

- Either form of the past participle can be used in the following cases:

freír *to fry* → freído/ frito

imprimir *to print* → imprimido/ impreso

- The *passive voice** is not used as frequently in Spanish as it is in English.
- In English, the passive is always formed with the *auxiliary verb** 'to be' + past participle.
- Spanish can use either ser or estar to form the passive.

1 Ser + past participle

In Spanish, the passive is formed using the auxiliary verb ser followed by a past participle. The past participle, in this case, agrees in number and gender with the subject.

La ministra fue acusada de traición por los periodistas.
The minister was accused of treachery by the journalists.

In the above sentence, we can see the following:

- a patient: la ministra (the subject of the verb);

- an agent: los periodistas (the object of the verb preceded by the preposition por).

In Spanish, the construction ser + past participle depicts the action as it is happening (in the present, past or future). It describes the actual action performed by the agent on the patient. In this example, the focus of the action is the point when the minister is accused (in a newspaper article, a statement, etc.).

Sometimes, the agent isn't specified and remains implicit.

La ministra fue acusada de traición.
The minister was accused of treachery.

2 Estar + past participle

In Spanish, the auxiliary verb estar can be followed by a past participle. In this case, the past participle agrees with the subject in gender and number. Estar + past participle is used to express the result of an action.

La ministra está acusada de traición.
The minister is accused of treachery.

Here, está acusada depicts the situation; the state in which the minister finds herself. The actual act of accusing someone, involving an agent and a patient, is expressed by ser + past participle. When estar is used, the focus is just on the action.

Compare the following:

La puerta fue cerrada.	La puerta está cerrada.
The door _____.	*The door _____.*

3 The passive with estar

Note: certain verbs (acompañar, dominar, ocupar...) prefer to use estar to form the passive.

When these verbs are in the passive, they don't only express the action performed by an agent on the patient but also give us the completed action.

El rey está acompañado por la reina.
The king is accompanied by the queen.

What is peculiar about this structure, is that the action of the agent (la reina) is a continuing one. That is, the action continues beyond the result, el rey está acompañado.

El hotel estaba ocupado por gente ruidosa.
The hotel was occupied by noisy people.

In this example also, with the result of the action already established (el hotel estaba ocupado), the agent (gente ruidosa) continues its action on the patient (el hotel). The action is ongoing.

In English, adjectives describing the subject are introduced by the verb 'to be.'
In Spanish, they can be introduced by either ser or estar.

1 Using ser

El café es amargo.
Coffee is bitter.

By preceding the adjective with ser, we are saying that the characteristic is intrinsic to the subject and is a permanent condition. This is not something that can be changed. Coffee is bitter; that is part of its nature.

2 Using estar

Este café está amargo.
This coffee is/tastes bitter.

By using estar, we are saying that the quality is not a permanent one but is a temporary state dependent on the circumstances. The reason is known and it is possible to change the state. For example, the coffee is bitter because it doesn't have enough sugar but this is something that can be changed.

- If the characteristic expressed by the adjective is temporary and dependent on circumstances ➜ estar
- If the characteristic expressed by the adjective is permanent and not affected by circumstances ➜ ser

3 Using ser or estar

In principle, all adjectives can take ser or estar, but the meaning of the phrase changes according to which verb is used.

■ ser ciego	*to be blind (permanent state)*
estar ciego	*to be blinded by something (temporary state)*

■ ser claro	*to be light (not dark)*
estar claro	*to be clear (meaning)*
■ ser feliz	*to be happy (characteristic)*
estar feliz	*to be feeling happy (due to specific circumstances)*
■ ser guapo	*to be good-looking (by nature)*
estar guapo	*to look smart (for an occasion)*
■ ser joven	*to be young (not old)*
estar joven	*to look or feel young (for your age)*
■ ser limpio	*to be clean and tidy (by nature)*
estar limpio	*to be clean (after washing or cleaning)*
■ ser listo	*to be clever (by nature)*
estar listo	*to be ready (to do something)*
■ ser malo	*to be naughty (by nature)*
estar malo	*to be ill (due to circumstances)*
■ ser sucio	*to be dirty and untidy (by nature)*
estar sucio	*to be dirty (because it's been dirtied)*

Note

- **Some adjectives can only take ser.**

cierto *(true)*, concreto *(specific)*, culto *(educated)*, desdichado *(unfortunate)*, infeliz *(unhappy)*, dichoso *(happy)*, evidente *(clear)*, posible *(possible)*, imposible *(impossible)*...

- **Some adjectives can only take estar.**

contento *(happy)*, desierto *(deserted)*, enfermo *(ill)*, lleno *(full)*, vacío *(empty)*, satisfecho *(satisfied)*, solo *(alone)*...

ER AND ESTAR + PREPOSITIONS

Both these verbs are often used followed by a preposition and this lexical unit is known as a *verbal phrase**.

Usage

er + preposition

ser de + noun: **to belong to, to be from, to be (made of)**

ta casa es de mi abuela.
is house is my grandmother's.

de la provincia de Valencia.
e is from the province of Valencia.

de oro.
s (made of) gold.

ser para + infinitive: **to be for**

te botón es para apagar la luz.
is button is for switching the light off.

star + preposition

estar a: used with dates

tamos a 12 de febrero.
s February 12.

estar de

• with an activity: estar de vacaciones (*to be on*

vacation), estar de viaje (*to be on a trip*)...

• indicating a position: estar de rodillas (*to be kneeling*), estar de pie (*to be standing up*)...

■ estar para: **to be about to, to be in the mood for, to be in a position to**

Hoy no estoy para bromas.
I'm not in the mood for jokes today.

Mi abuelo ya no está para caminar tanto.
My grandfather can't walk that much anymore.

■ estar por

• **to be in love with someone**

Se ve clarísimo que Pedro está por ti.
It's obvious that Pedro is in love with you.

• **to need** + -ing, **to still need to be** + past participle

La habitación está por limpiar.
The room still needs cleaning.

• **to be about to**

Casi estaba por darte la razón.
I was nearly about to say you were right.

115

A S P E C T

Aspect* refers to the nature of the action described by the verb. There are three aspects: indefinite (or simple), complete (or present perfect), continuing (or progressive).
With Spanish verbs, the choice of aspect is made by selecting either the simple verb or the compound form with haber.

1 Formation

In Spanish, all forms of the verb can have a simple and a compound form apart from the imperative.

In the *active voice**, compound tenses are formed in the following way.

The auxiliary haber + past participle of the relevant verb
➜ the auxiliary is conjugated (mood, tense, person)
➜ the past participle is invariable

In this case, the past participle is always invariable in Spanish.

Hemos bajado.
We went down.

The *auxiliary** supplies the grammatical information, while the past participle gives the lexical information, that is, the information about what is happening.

Each simple form has a corresponding compound form.

	Simple forms	Compound forms
Impersonal mood *	dormir	haber dormido
	durmiendo	habiendo dormido
Personal mood*		
	duermo	he dormido
	dormía	había dormido
	dormí	hube dormido
	dormiré	habré dormido
	dormiría	habría dormido

Simple forms	Compound forms
duerma	haya dormido
durmiera	hubiera dormido
durmiese	hubiese dormido
durmiere	hubiere dormido

2 Usage

The speaker can present an action and the agent of the action in two ways.

He can either describe an action as it takes or took place, and describe the speaker in action using the past, the present or the future.

➜ Simple form

Adela se cayó de la silla.
Adela fell off her chair.

Or he can describe a completed action, when the speaker is no longer performing the action, again using the past, present or future.

➜ Compound form

Cuando llegues, habremos cenado.
When you arrive, we will have had supper.

As a rule, nothing should come between the auxiliary and the past participle. The adverb goes before or after the verb structure.

He dormido muy bien.
I slept really well.

Nunca lo habría dicho.
I would never have guessed it.

THE PRESENT INDICATIVE

> Formation: the same irregular forms of the present indicative are found in the subjunctive and the imperative.

1 Formation

Regular verbs

→ *Stem** + ending. With regular verbs, the stem remains the same and the ending is conjugated.

Verbs ending in	ar	er	ir
(Yo)	o	o	o
(Tú)	as	es	es
(Él, ella, usted)	a	e	e
(Nosotros)	amos	emos	imos
(Vosotros)	áis	éis	ís
(Ellos, ellas, ustedes)	an	en	en

Irregular verbs

1st person ending in go: caigo, digo, hago, oigo, pongo, salgo, tengo, traigo, valgo, vengo.

1st person with a *yod**: soy, estoy, voy, doy and hay (*impersonal** form).

1st person with zc: conozco, luzco, nazco.

1st person irregular: quepo (caber), he (haber), sé (saber), veo (ver).

With verbs that contain a *diphthong**, modifying either the vowel or the consonant, the irregular form always applies to four forms: the 1st, 2nd and 3rd person singular and the 3rd person plural.

Verbs containing a diphthong: e › ie (pienso), o › ue (duermo).

Verbs which modify the vowel: e › i (pido), o › u (pudro).

Verbs which modify the consonant: insert the yod, concluyo (concluir).

acertar (22)	colgar (30)	pedir (39)
acierto	cuelgo	pido
aciertas	cuelgas	pides
acierta	cuelga	pide
acertamos	colgamos	pedimos
acertáis	colgáis	pedís
aciertan	cuelgan	piden

2 Usage

- As in English, the present is used to describe an action taking place at the time of speaking.

El claxon de este coche hace mucho ruido.
The horn on this car is very loud.

- In cases like proverbs, the present is used to express a general truth that transcends time. This is known as the atemporal present.

Ojos que no ven, corazón que no siente.
Out of sight, out of mind.

- The present is also used to describe a regular action.

Los miércoles vamos al cine.
We go to the movies on Wednesdays.

THE PRETERIT

There are three types of preterit:
- Regular 'weak' preterits: the *stem** of the verb remains unchanged and the accent falls on the *ending**.
- Preterits where the vowel in the stem modifies (e › i): the accent falls on the ending.
- Sixteen 'strong' verbs: the accent falls on the last syllable of the stem in the 1st and 3rd person singular.

The preterit is regularly used, both in written and spoken Spanish, to express a completed action.

1 Formation

Regular verbs

These are the most common forms in Spanish.

➜ *Stem** + ending.

Verbs ending in	ar	er ir
(Yo)	é	í
(Tú)	aste	iste
(Él, ella, usted)	ó	ió
(Nosotros)	amos	imos
(Vosotros)	asteis	isteis
(Ellos, ellas, ustedes)	aron	ieron

Verbs which modify the vowel

The stem modifies but the accent falls on the ending as in regular verbs.

This irregularity only applies to two forms: 3rd person singular and 3rd person plural.

pedir (39) ➜ pidió, pidieron

sentir (55) ➜ sintió, sintieron

dormir (57) ➜ durmió, durmieron

Strong preterits

➜ *Stem** + ending.

(Yo)	e
(Tú)	iste
(Él, ella, usted)	o
(Nosotros)	imos
(Vosotros)	isteis
(Ellos, ellas, ustedes)	(i)eron

Note:

The modified stem applies to all six forms.

The ending is the same for all three groups.

The accent falls on the stem in the 1st and 3rd person singular.

■ Verbs which change the vowel to a

traer	traje trajo

■ Verbs which change the vowel u

andar	anduve anduvo
caber	cupe cupo
conducir	conduje condujo
estar	estuve estuvo
haber	hube hubo
poder	pude pudo
poner	puse puso
saber	supe supo
tener	tuve tuvo

■ Verbs which change the vowel o i

dar	di dio
decir	dije dijo
ir ser	fui fue
hacer	hice hizo
querer	quise quiso
venir	vine vino

* and ser are the same in the preterit.

2 Usage

Some common uses of the preterit

The preterit is the tense used for describing actions in the past. Unlike with the present perfect tense, the event described by the preterit is completely divorced from the present. With the preterit, the *speaker** establishes that the present from which he is speaking is completely cut off from the action in the past he is describing.

The description usually just conveys the facts.

Este cuento se publicó en El País.
This story was published in El País.

Ayer me anunció que se iba a casar.
Yesterday, she told me she was getting married.

The preterit is also the tense commonly used in fairy tales.

La princesa se pinchó el dedo y cayó en un profundo sueño.
The princess pricked her finger and fell into a deep sleep.

The preterit is often used in the press to report events.

Aquí mismo se produjo una colisión de ocho vehículos.
There was an eight-vehicle collision right here.

Note: Spanish can also use the present perfect to express a past event.

Compare the following:

Mi padre murió en junio de 2005.	Mi padre ha muerto.
My father died in June 2005.	*My father has died.*

By using the preterit, mi padre murió, the speaker is expressing a past event, which is over and is cut off from the present from which he is speaking. With the present perfect tense (the auxiliary haber conjugated in the present + the past participle muerto), the speaker describes an event that is over – a completed action – but which conveys that the event is still connected to the present time as he speaks and still has some impact on the way he feels about it.

THE IMPERFECT

The use of the imperfect tense is basically the same in Spanish as in English.

1 Formation

Regular verbs

→ Regular *stem** + ending

Verbs ending in	ar	er / ir
(Yo)	aba	ía
(Tú)	abas	ías
(Él, ella, usted)	aba	ía
(Nosotros)	ábamos	íamos
(Vosotros)	abais	íais
(Ellos, ellas, ustedes)	aban	ían

jugar (34)	cocer (36)	distinguir (20)
jugaba	cocía	distinguía
jugabas	cocías	distinguías
jugaba	cocía	distinguía
jugábamos	cocíamos	distinguíamos
jugabais	cocíais	distinguíais
jugaban	cocían	distinguían

Irregular verbs

→ Irregular *stem** + ending

ir (77)	ser (78)	ver (75)
iba	era	veía
ibas	eras	veías
iba	era	veía
íbamos	éramos	veíamos
ibais	erais	veíais
iban	eran	veían

2 Usage

The narrative tense

The imperfect is the narrative tense which the narrator uses to retell an event that was taking place in the past.

Oíamos el ruido de una fiesta lejana.
We could hear the noise coming from a party in the distance.

Descriptions in the past

The imperfect is the tense used for describing things with reference to the past.

Era un hombre de unos treinta años.
He was a man of about thirty.

Describing regular actions in the past

The imperfect is used to describe an action which was a regular occurrence in the past.

Su tía pasaba los días y las veladas ante la televisión.
Her aunt spent her days and evenings in front of the television.

THE FUTURE AND THE CONDITIONAL

In the indicative, the future and the conditional are formed with the infinitive. This way of forming future tenses is a common feature across *romance languages**. Note, however, that Spanish prefers the subjunctive in subordinate relative clauses where English would use a when + infinitive clause.

1 Formation

Regular verbs

In the indicative, the future and the conditional are formed from the infinitive of the verb. The *endings** for the future tense come from the old conjugation of the verb haber. The endings for the conditional, ía, ías, etc., are borrowed from the indicative form of the imperfect. (See p. 120)

Infinitive +	Future	Conditional
	é	ía
	ás	ías
	á	ía
	emos	íamos
	éis	íais
	án	ían

Irregular verbs

Verbs which have an irregular future and conditional are also irregular in the preterit (apart from salir). Their *stem** often ends in a series of consonants: br, dr, rr.

Infinitive	Future	Conditional
caber	cabré	cabría
decir	diré	diría
haber	habré	habría
hacer	haré	haría

poder	podré	podría
poner	pondré	pondría
querer	querré	querría
saber	sabré	sabría
salir	saldré	saldría
tener	tendré	tendría
valer	valdré	valdría
venir	vendré	vendría

haber (76)	
Future	Conditional
habré	habría
habrás	habrías
habrá	habría
habremos	habríamos
habréis	habríais
habrán	habrían

2 Usage

The future

■ As in English, the future tense is used in Spanish to express an event that is yet to take place.

Speaking in the present, the speaker uses the future tense to express an action that is very likely to happen.

Mañana estaré ahí.
I'll be there tomorrow.

- The future serves to express conjecture or probability speaking from the present time.

In English, this is something that is usually expressed by the structure '**must** + infinitive.'

Ella tendrá catorce años.
She must be fourteen.

- In the subordinate temporal clause, cuando + subjunctive in Spanish is rendered by **when** + infinitive in English.

Avísame cuando llegues.
cuando + subjunctive

Let me know when you arrive.
when + infinitive

- In a subordinate relative clause introduced by **who**, **which** + infinitive in English, Spanish prefers the subjunctive.

Los que saquen el billete esta semana, se beneficiarán de un 15% de descuento.
People who buy their ticket this week will benefit from a 15 % discount.

The present conditional

Just as in English, the event described in th conditional is subject to a prior event which usually expressed in a subordinate clause intro duced by si + imperfect subjunctive.

Si cambiaras de opinión sobre mi hermano, podría mos salir con él.
If you changed your mind about my brother, we could go out with him.

The action podríamos salir con él cannot ta place unless a prior action, si cambiaras de op nión, takes place.

- The present conditional of some verbs can k replaced by the imperfect subjunctive. Th substitution feature is particular to Spanish.

deber	debería	debiera
poder	podría	pudiera
querer	querría	quisiera
saber	sabría	supiera
valer	valdría	valiera

Quisiera saber cómo llegó usted hasta aquí.
I would like to know how you got this far.

THE FUTURE PERFECT

The future perfect can be used in two ways in Spanish. It can describe an action that will take place and be completed in the future or it can be used to express possibility.

Formation

with all tenses in the *active voice**, the future perfect is formed with the *auxiliary** haber followed by the past participle which is invariable.

The auxiliary haber is conjugated in the future: habré, habrás, habrá, habremos, habréis, habrán.

Compound verb forms express an action in its completed state whereas simple verb forms describe an action as it took place. The difference between them is a question of *aspect**. **(See p. 5)**

cantarás.
you will sing.

habrás cantado.
you will have sung.

2 Usage

■ The future perfect allows us to express an action that will be completed in the future.

No te preocupes: para cuando ellas lleguen yo ya me habré ido.
Don't worry. By the time they arrive, I will have already left.

The key point expressed by ya me habré ido isn't the actual fact of leaving as much as that at the moment in question, the action will already be completed. The person will have already left.

■ This verbal structure allows us to speculate about future events and express probability as an alternative to using the verb deber de.

- ¿Marta?... ¿Estás ahí?... Bueno, habrás salido...
- *Marta?... Are you there?... Oh well, you must have gone out...*

In English, this sort of speculation is rendered by the verbal structure **must have + past participle**.

THE SUBJUNCTIVE

Just as the indicative, the subjunctive also has both simple and compound forms. For the difference between simple and compound forms, see *aspect**, p. ***.
A *subordinate clause** is always dependent on a *main clause** which contains a verb in the indicative. The subjunctive mood, although more rare and mainly reserved for formal contexts in English, is widely used in Spanish to discuss potential or hypothetical events.

1 Formation

The present subjunctive

■ **Regular verbs:** *stem** **+ ending**

Infinitives ending in	ar	er/ir
(Yo)	e	a
(Tú)	es	as
(Él ella usted)	e	a
(Nosotros)	emos	amos
(Vosotros)	éis	áis
(Ellos ellas ustedes)	en	an

■ The subjunctive brings in many orthographical changes.

sacar › saque (13)

vencer › venza (14)

proteger › proteja (17), etc.

■ Irregular verbs are also affected by these orthographical changes.

comenzar › comience (23)

■ **Irregular verbs: irregular stem + ending**

If the first person of the present indicative is irregular, the subjunctive form is also irregular.

■ The *tonic accent** or stress produces a *diphthong** in the same forms as the present indicative, that is in the 1st, 2nd and 3rd person

singular and the 3rd person plural.

acertar › acierte (22)

sonar › suene (28)

■ For verbs where the vowel changes, the who conjugation is irregular.

pedir › pida (39)

sentir › sienta (55)

■ For verbs where the consonant changes in th 1st person, the change applies to the who conjugation.

nacer › nazca (44)

lucir › luzca (47)

The imperfect subjunctive

The imperfect subjunctive is formed in the sam way for both regular and irregular verbs. It formed by taking the 3rd person plural of th preterit and taking off the ending ron. This giv us a new *stem** from which to conjugate all th forms. Spanish has two alternative subjuncti forms, the ra ending and the se ending, which ca be used interchangeably.

	amar	hacer	pedir
	amaron	hicieron	pidieron
stem*	ama	hicie	pidie

The following endings are added to the ne stems:

ra, ras, ra, ramos, rais, ran ➜ imperfect subjuncti (ra form) se, ses, se, semos, seis, sen → imperfect subjunctive (se form)

The future subjunctive is formed in the same way.

re, res, re, remos, reis, ren → future subjunctive (re form)

Note

In the 1st person plural, there is a written accent on the last vowel of the *stem**.

2 Usage

The subordinate clause

Spanish uses the subjunctive in subordinate clauses to refer to an event which may or may not happen. Here, English would more naturally use an infinitive as use of the subjunctive would seem very formal.

We want   _you to tell the truth._

fi

Verbs and verbal phrases

■ The subjunctive is used after verbs that express feelings or wishes.

• Expressing wishes: querer que (*to want* + infinitive), desear que (*to wish that*)...

• Expressing orders: mandar que/ordenar que (*to order* + infinitive), decir que (*to tell* + infinitive), rogar que (*to ask/beg* + infinitive)...

• Forbidding something: prohibir que (*to forbid* + infinitive), impedir que (*to not allow* + infinitive)...

• Expressing need: es necesario que, es preciso que, hace falta que... (*to need* + infinitive)...

• Expressing agreement: permitir que (*to allow* + infinitive)...

Quiero que digas la verdad.
I want you to tell the truth.

The use of the subjunctive conveys that the action, which in the sentence above is digas, may or may not happen. There is no guarantee that the person referred to will tell the truth.

■ The subjunctive is used after verbs or verbal phrases that cast hesitation or doubt on whether the action will take place.

• Expressing preferences: preferir que, me parece mejor que...

Prefiero que no digas nada.
I would rather you didn't say anything.

The speaker expresses a preference for one of the two possible actions that may be taken. The person he is addressing may opt either to say something or not and the speaker has no guarantee that his preference will be adhered to. All this is conveyed through the use of the subjuntive mood.

• Expressing possibility: quizás + subjunctive → *maybe* + future indicative (in English).

Quizás esté con nosotros en Navidad.
Maybe he will spend Christmas with us.

• Expressing wishes: ojalá + subjunctive → *to hope that...* (in English).

¡Ojalá esté con nosotros en Navidad!
I really hope he spends Christmas with us!

Spanish has prescribed rules for the sequence of tenses.

Usage

Rules of agreement

When the verb in the *subordinate clause** is in the subjunctive, the tense (present subjunctive or imperfect subjunctive) is determined by the tense of the verb in the *main clause**. This is known as 'tense agreement.'

- Main clause in the indicative (simple present and present perfect, simple future and future perfect) or in the imperative.

→ Subordinate clause in the present subjunctive.

- Main clause in the indicative (imperfect, past perfect, preterit, past anterior, present conditional and conditional perfect).

→ Subordinate clause in the imperfect subjunctive.

Example

Su madre está dando las órdenes para que se sirva la cena.
Her mother is asking for dinner to be served.

If the tense of the main clause is changed (present → past), the following happens in both languages.

Spanish

Su madre estaba dando las órdenes para que se <u>sirviera</u> la cena.

English

Her mother asked that dinner should be served.

- Note: When the verb in the main clause is in the present perfect, the imperfect subjunctive is normally used in the subordinate clause.

Me ha seguido sin que me diera cuenta.
He followed me without my realizing.

- Verbs introduced by phrases like como si, igual que si, lo mismo que si are always followed by the imperfect subjunctive or the past perfect subjunctive.

In these cases, the tense of the indicative verb in the main clause (whether it is present, imperfect, preterit, future...) doesn't have any bearing on the tense of the subordinate verb.

Hacen/Hacían/Hicieron/Harán como si no nos conociéramos.
They behave/were behaving/behaved/will behave as if we didn't know each other.

THE IMPERATIVE

This *mood** only exists in the present in Spanish.
There is the imperative used to issue orders and give instructions and the negative imperative.
The verb forms used for the negative imperative are based on the subjunctive.
For polite and familiar forms of the imperative, see p. 101.

Formation

The imperative

- The two forms which are specific to the imperative are the familiar form of the 2nd person singular (tú) and the 2nd person plural (vosotros).

- The imperative of the familiar form of the 2nd person singular is formed by taking the present indicative of the same person, cant<u>as</u> and dropping the <u>s</u> → cant<u>a</u> = *sing* (**you**).

- The imperative of the familiar form of the 2nd person plural is formed by taking the infinitive form, canta<u>r</u> and replacing the <u>r</u> of the *ending** with <u>d</u> → canta<u>d</u> = *sing* (**you + you**).

- The other forms are based on the present subjunctive.

Usted → cant<u>e</u> *Sing, Miss!*

Nosotros → cant<u>emos</u> *Let us sing!*

Ustedes → cant<u>en</u> *Sing, Ladies!*

Summary

	amar (1)	temer (2)	partir (3)
<u>s</u>	am<u>a</u>	tem<u>e</u>	part<u>e</u>
	am<u>e</u>	tem<u>a</u>	part<u>a</u>
	am<u>emos</u>	tem<u>amos</u>	part<u>amos</u>
<u>r</u> <u>d</u>	am<u>ad</u>	tem<u>ed</u>	part<u>id</u>
	am<u>en</u>	tem<u>an</u>	part<u>an</u>

Object pronouns are attached to the end of the verb. (See *enclisis**, p. 103)

For pronominal verb conjugations, see p. 129.

Irregular forms only apply to the 2nd person singular.

decir → di	haber → he	hacer → haz
say	*have*	*do*
ir → ve	poner → pon	salir → sal
go	*put*	*get out*
ser → sé	tener → ten	venir → ven
be	*hold*	*come*

The negative imperative

In Spanish, the negative imperative is always formed from the subjunctive. All the verb forms are preceded by no.

Negative imperative

(Tú)	digas	*don't say*
(Usted)	diga	*don't say (sir)*
(Nosotros)	digamos	*let's not say*
(Vosotros)	digáis	*don't say (children)*
(Ustedes)	digan	*don't say (gentlemen)*

IMPERSONAL AND DEFECTIVE VERBS

Some verbs are only ever used in the *impersonal mood** and in the 3rd person singular. These are called impersonal verbs.

Others are only ever used in certain indicative and subjunctive tenses and do not have a *passive voice** or a compound form. These are called defective verbs.

They undergo the same spelling changes and irregularities as verbs of the same conjugation.

Usage

Natural phenomena

acaecer	to happen
acontecer	to take place
amanecer	to get light
anochecer	to get dark
atardecer	to get dark
clarear	
diluviar	to pour with rain
gotear	to spit
granizar	to hail
helar	to freeze
llover	to rain
lloviznar	to drizzle
nevar	to snow
relampaguear	to flash (lightning)
tronar	to thunder
ventear	to be windy

Impersonal usage

Some verbs can be used impersonally in some contexts. Where time is involved, English uses structures with **ago**, **for** or **since**.

haber

Hay, hubo, había, habrá: *there is*, *there was*, *there was*, *there will be*.

Tiempo ha.
A long time ago.

hacer + temporal clause.

Hace dos años que no nos vemos.
We haven't seen each other for two years.

Where possibility is expressed, English uses **might**.

poder

Puede que nos olvide.
He might forget us.

It seems (that) is another way of expressing other impersonal Spanish verbs.

resultar

Resulta que con el calor que hacía, se desmayó.
It seems it was so hot that she fainted.

parecer

Parece que no habrá guerra.
It seems (that) there won't be a war.

Defective verbs

These are verbs which have limited forms. There are both regular and irregular defective verbs.

atañer: *to concern* (only used in the 3rd person singular and plural)

Son problemas que sólo atañen a la familia.
They are problems that only concern the family.

soler (82): *to usually do sthg/ used to do sthg* (basically used in the infinitive, present indicative, present subjunctive, and imperfect indicative)

Solíamos salir por la noche.
We used to go out at night.

Soler and acostumbrar (*to usually do sthg*) are peculiar in that they don't have a compound form or a *passive voice** (ser + past participle). This is what makes them defective verbs.

Mi hermana acostumbraba a pasear todas las mañanas.
My sister used to go for a walk every morning.

PRONOMINAL VERBS

Pronominal verbs are verbs in which the subject also appears as the object of the verb, often in the form of a personal pronoun, which in the indicative and subjunctive goes before the verb.

In the imperative, the pronoun is added on enclitically to the end of the verb. (See *enclisis** p. 103).

Formation

Example: despertarse

	Present indicative	Imperative	Translation
(yo)	despierto		I wake up
(tú)	despiertas	despiérta	you wake up/ wake up
(él, ella, usted)	despierta	despiérte	s/ he wakes up/ you wake up/ wake up
(nosotros)	despertamos	despertémo	we wake up/ let's wake up
(vosotros)	despertáis	desperta	you wake up/ wake up
(ellos, ellas, ustedes)	despiertan	despiérten	they/ you wake up/ wake up

In the imperative, the 1st person plural (nosotros) drops the s from the ending and the 2nd person plural (vosotros) drops the d.

The enclitic pronoun can also be added to the infinitive in Spanish.

despertarse ➜ to wake up

Puedo despertarte.
I can wake you up.

In the gerund, both structures (with or without the enclitic pronoun) are possible in *verbal** *phrases** of the type 'auxiliary** + gerund.' (See p. 103).

¿Estabas esperándome?
Were you waiting for me?

2 Usage

■ Spanish pronominal verbs are often translated by intransitive verbs in English. With reflexive verbs, the reflexive pronouns me, te, se, etc. would be translated by **myself, yourself, himself,** etc. in English.

concluirse	to end
despedirse	to say goodbye
divorciarse	to get divorced
enamorarse	to fall in love
fijarse	to note
mudarse	to move (house)
parecerse	to look like
quedarse	to stay
volverse	to come back

PREPOSITIONS

A verb can have several types of complement.
In Spanish, as in English, *prepositions** can introduce a wide range of complements.

The role of prepositions

Adverbial phrases

Prepositions can introduce an *adverbial phrase**.

Nos recibieron en el salón.
They received us in the living room.

Verb system

Prepositions fall within 'the verb system.' They introduce the objects of the verb.

Pienso en mi abuela.
I'm thinking about my grandmother.

Spanish prepositions can be grouped in opposing pairs: a/de (**to/from**); con/sin (**with/without**); por/para (**for**, **by/for**, **towards**); desde/hasta (**since/until**); sobre/bajo (**on/under**); delante de/detrás de (**in front of/behind**); dentro de/fuera de (**inside**, **within/outside**), etc.

■ a/de

A always indicates movement towards somebody, something or some target whether it is physical or to do with time. On the other hand, de indicates movement away from somebody, something or some action.

Voy a casa.
I'm going home.

Vengo de casa.
I've come from home.

Se puso a llorar.
He started crying.

Acabo de volver.
I have just come back.

■ con/sin

Con and sin allow a whole range of objects to be added to the verb.

Ven con tus amigos.
Come with your friends.

Pedro irá con Lola.
Pedro will go with Lola.

Salió sin paraguas.
He went out without an umbrella.

■ para/por

Para implies a place, a target to be reached or something that you are aiming for.

Por, on the other hand, is used to show where the activity is taking place. Por also often introduces a reason or the agent of a passive structure. (See p. 113).

Salgo para Londres.
I'm leaving for London.

He venido para ayudarte.
I've come to help you.

Nos paseamos por el campo.
We went for walks in the country.

La puerta fue cerrada por el profesor.
The door was closed by the teacher.

■ desde/hasta

Desde always indicates a specific point in the past when the action started whereas hasta specifies the point where the action ends.

Desde ayer resulta imposible aparcar en este barrio.
Since yesterday, it's impossible to park in this area.

Fuimos desde el parque hasta la iglesia.
We went from the park to the church.

■ en

En is a multi-purpose preposition. It always introduces some sort of area where you are or where your thoughts are.

Estoy en casa.
I'm at home.

Estaba enfrascado en su lectura.
He was lost in his reading.

Dictionary

of verb structures

Countries and regions

Am	Latin America
Esp	Spain

Subject fields

COMM	commerce
FIN	finance
LAW	law
RELIG	religion
SCH	school

Other abbreviations

fig	figurative
inf	informal
v ind	indirect verb
v + prep	verb + preposition
vp + prep	pronominal verb + preposition
vulg	vulgar

DICTIONARY

A

abandonarse [01]
■ **abandonarse a** vp + prep 1. (despair, pain) to succumb to (drink, drugs) to give oneself over to • acabó abandonándose aquel ritmo irresistible he ended up surrendering to the irresistible rhythm

abastecerse [45]
■ **abastecerse de** vp + prep to stock up on • abastecerse de combustible to stock up on gas

abonarse [01]
■ **abonarse a** vp + prep 1. to subscribe to • ¿cómo me abono a la lista de difusión? how can I get on the mailing list? 2. to buy a season ticket for • me he abonado a la ópera I've bought a season ticket for the opera

abrigarse [19]
■ **abrigarse de** vp + prep 1. to shelter from • entró en un portal para abrigarse de la lluvia he went into a doorway to shelter from the rain 2. to wrap up against • los hombres prehistóricos se abrigaban del frio con pieles de animales prehistoric man wore animal skins to wrap up against the cold

abrirse [03]
■ **abrirse a** vp + prep to open up to • le cuesta abrirse a la gente que no conoce bien he finds it hard to open up to people he doesn't know
■ **abrirse con** vp + prep to confide in • conmigo se abre porque nuestra relación se basa en la mutua confianza he confides in me because our relationship is based on mutual trust

abstenerse [72]
■ **abstenerse de** vp + prep to refrain from • se abstuvo de hacer cualquier comentario she refrained from commenting

abundar [01]
■ **abundar en** v + prep to abound with • la región abunda en riquezas the area abounds with riches

abusar [01]
■ **abusar de** v + prep to take advantage of • estás abusando de mi you're taking advantage of me • no hay que abusar del alcohol you shouldn't drink too much • no abuses de mi paciencia don't try my patience

acabar [01]
■ **acabar con** v + prep 1. (violence, crime) to put an end to • hay que acabar con el problema de la droga we have to put an end to the drugs problem 2. (patience) to exhaust • acabó con mi paciencia he exhausted my patience 3. (kill) to do away with • acabaron con el enemigo they did away with the enemy
■ **acabar de** v + prep 1. • acabar de hacer algo to have just done something : acabo de llegar I've just arrived 2. • no acabar de hacer algo : no acabo de entender su reacción I can't quite understand his reaction
■ **acabar en** v + prep to end in • las palabras que acaban en "n" words ending in "n" • acabó en la cárcel he ended up in prison
■ **acabar por** v + prep to end up • acabaron por ceder they ended up giving in

acceder [02]
■ **acceder a** v + prep 1. to get into, to gain admittance to • no tiene la nota exigida para acceder a la universidad he doesn't have the required grades to get into college 2. to agree to • el gobierno accedió a todas las demandas de los sindicatos the government agreed to all the labor unions' demands

acercarse [13]
■ **acercarse a** vp + prep 1. to go up to • se acercó a la ventana she went up to the window • no te acerques al perro don't get too close to the dog 2. to get nearer to • se van acercando a un compromiso they are getting nearer to reaching an agreement

acertar [22]
■ **acertar a** v + prep 1. to be right to • acertaste al decírselo you were right to tell her 2. to manage to • los cientificos no acertaron a dar una explicación racional del fenómeno scientists couldn't manage to find a rational explanation for the phenomenon
■ **acertar con** v + prep to get right • acertó con la respuesta he got the answer right
■ **acertar con** OR **en** v + prep to get right • el director ha acertado en el reparto the director got the casting right

acobardarse [01]
■ **acobardarse ante** vp + prep to shrink back from • no se acobarda ante nada ni ante nadie he doesn't shrink back from anything or anyone

acogerse [17]

■ **acogerse a** *vp + prep* to take refuge in • se acogió a la inmunidad diplomática para eludir sus responsabilidades he took refuge in diplomatic immunity to evade his responsibilities

acometer [02]

■ **acometer contra** *v + prep* to hurtle into • el toro acometió contra la barrera the bull hurtled into the barrier

acomodarse [01]

■ **acomodarse en** *vp + prep* to settle down in • se acomodó en el sillón he settled down in the armchair

acordarse [28]

■ **acordarse de** *vp + prep* **1.** *(recall)* to remember • me acuerdo de sus sabios consejos I remember his words of wisdom • ¿no te acuerdas de mí? don't you remember me? **2.** *(not forget)* to remember • acuérdate de llevar el traje a la tintorería remember to take your suit back to the dry cleaner's

acostumbrarse [01]

■ **acostumbrarse a** *vp + prep* **1.** to get used to • se acostumbró poco a poco a su presencia she gradually got used to him being there **2.** to get in the habit of • me he acostumbrado a acostarme temprano I've got in the habit of going to bed early

actuar [9]

■ **actuar de** *v + prep* to act as • las puertas actúan de tabiques móviles the doors act as movable partitions

acudir [03]

■ **acudir a** *v + prep* **1.** to attend • no se disculpó por no haber acudido a la reunión he didn't apologize for not attending the meeting **2.** to turn up • más de un 20 millones de electores acudieron a las urnas over 20 million voters turned up to vote **3.** to go to • los demandantes han acudido al tribunal the plaintiffs went to court

adherirse [55]

■ **adherirse a** *vp + prep* to support • no me adhiero a tu propuesta I don't support your proposal

admirarse [01]

■ **admirarse de** *vp + prep* **1.** to be amazed by • todos se admiraban de la ingenuidad de sus preguntas everyone was amazed by how naive his questions were **2.** to admire • me admiro de su capacidad de trabajar en varios proyectos a la vez I'd admire her ability to work on several projects at once

adueñarse [01]

■ **adueñarse de** *vp + prep* to take over • las multinacionales se están adueñando del mercado multinationals are taking over the market

afanarse [01]

■ **afanarse por** *vp + prep* to do everything one can to • las empresas se afanan por aumentar la rentabilidad companies are doing everything they can to increase profits

afianzarse [16]

■ **afianzarse en** *vp + prep* to consolidate • el equipo australiano se afianza en el liderato del campeonato the Australian team consolidate their lead in the championship

aficionar [01]

■ **aficionarse a** *vp + prep* to become keen on • poco a poco se fue aficionando a la ópera he gradually became keen on opera

afiliarse [08]

■ **afiliarse a** *vp + prep* to join, to become a member of • quisiera afiliarme a un club de golf I'd like to join a golf club • de muy joven se afilió a un partido ecologista she joined a green party when she was very young

agarrarse [01]

■ **agarrarse a** *vp + prep* **1.** to grab, to hold on to • agárrate a la primera oportunidad que se te presente grab the first opportunity that comes your way **2.** to use • se agarra a cualquier pretexto para no ir a la escuela he'll use any excuse not to go to school

ahondar [01]

■ **ahondar en** *v + prep* **1.** to penetrate deep into • hay que ahondar más en la roca we have to penetrate deeper into the rock **2.** *fig* to go deeper into • desea ahondar en el conocimiento del tema he wants to go deeper into the subject

ajustarse [01]

■ **ajustarse a** *vp + prep* **1.** to comply with • los cursos se ajustan al programa pedagógico establecido por el ministerio the courses comply with the educational program established by the ministry **2.** to be in line with • la traducción no se ajusta al texto original the translation isn't in line with the original text

alardear [01]

alardear de *v + prep* to brag about • alardea de que sus padres son inmensamente ricos he brags about his parents being filthy rich

alcanzar [16]

alcanzar a *v + prep* to manage to • no alcanzo a comprender porque te quejas tanto I can't quite understand why you complain so much

alcanzar para *v + prep* to be enough for • las provisiones alcanzarán para toda la semana the supplies will be enough for the whole week

alegrarse [01]

alegrarse de OR **por** *vp + prep* **1.** to be pleased about • me alegro de tu nominación al puesto I'm pleased you've been nominated for the post **2.** to be very happy for • me alegro muchísimo por ti I'm very happy for you

aliarse [07]

aliarse con *vp + prep* to form an alliance with • los atenienses se aliaron con los espartanos the Athenians formed an alliance with the Spartans

alimentarse [01]

alimentarse con *vp + prep* to run on • el aparato se alimenta con la corriente de la línea telefónica the device runs on power from the telephone line

alimentarse de *vp + prep* to live on • el oso panda se alimenta de brotes de bambú pandas live on bamboo shoots

alternar [01]

alternar con *v + prep* **1.** to socialize with • prefiere no alternar con los compañeros fuera del trabajo he prefers not to socialize with colleagues outside work **2.** to alternate with • su locura alterna con períodos de lucidez her madness alternates with lucid periods

aludir [03]

aludir a *v + prep* **1.** to refer to • no aludo a nadie en particular I'm not referring to anyone in particular **2.** to allude to *fml,* to mention • el presidente evitó aludir a la crisis ministerial the president avoided alluding to the ministerial crisis

ampararse [01]

ampararse de OR **contra** *vp + prep* **1.** *(rain)* to shelter from **2.** *(sun)* to protect oneself from • llevaba un sombrero para ampararse de los rayos del sol she was wearing a hat to protect herself from the sun's rays

ampararse en *vp + prep* **1.** to have recourse to • el abogado se amparó en el artículo 12 del código penal the lawyer had recourse to article 12 of the penal code **2.** to take refuge in • en la red muchos sueltan comentarios irresponsables amparándose en el anonimato many people post irresponsible comments on the net taking refuge in anonimity

andar [54]

andar a *v + prep* • andaban a puñetazos they were always fighting • andaban a gritos they were always shouting

andar en *v + prep* **1.** to be mixed up in • andan en un turbio asunto de drogas they are mixed up in some shady drugs deal **2.** to rummage around in • no quiero que andes en mis cosas I don't want you rummaging around in my things

andar por *v + prep* • andará por los sesenta años he must be about seventy • andamos por los mil números vendidos we must have sold about a thousand issues

andar tras OR **detrás de** *v + prep* **1.** to be after • anda tras las huellas de sus padres biológicos he's trying to trace his biological parents **2.** *(ideal, dream)* to be pursuing • andaba detrás de un ideal she was pursuing an ideal

andarse con *vp + prep* • ¡ándate con cuidado! take care! • siempre os andáis con misterios you're always hiding something

andarse sin *vp + prep* to be without • anda sin trabajo he doesn't have any work, he's without work

anidar [01]

anidar en *v + prep fig* to stay at • mientras no encuentre piso anidaré en casa de unos amigos while I don't find a flat, I'll stay at my friends'

anteponerse [69]

anteponerse a *vp + prep* to come before • nada se antepone a su vida profesional, ni siquiera su familia nothing comes before his work, not even his family

anticiparse [01]

anticiparse a *vp + prep* **1.** to be ahead of • es un científico que se anticipó a su tiempo he's a scientist who was ahead of his time **2.** • anticiparse a hacer algo to rush into doing something : no hay que anticiparse a tomar decisiones we mustn't rush into any decisions

apartarse [01]

■ **apartarse de** *vp* + *prep* **1.** to be apart from • no se aparta ni un momento de su hermano gemelo he's never apart from his twin brother **2.** *(subject)* to get off **3.** *(thread, plot)* to lose • no te apartes del hilo del razonamiento don't lose the thread of the argument **4.** *(world, society)* to cut oneself off from • decidió apartarse del mundo y vivir en un monasterio he decided to cut himself off from the world and go and live in a monastery

apasionarse [01]

■ **apasionarse por** OR **con** *vp* + *prep* to be mad about • se apasiona por la informática he's mad about computers

apechugar [19]

■ **apechugar con** *v* + *prep* **1.** *inf* to end up with • siempre me toca apechugar con las tareas más desagradables I always end up with the worst tasks **2.** *inf* to live with • tendrá que apechugar con sus errores she'll have to live with her mistakes

apegarse [19]

■ **apegarse a** *vp* + *prep* to become attached to • poco a poco los europeos se han ido apegando al euro Europeans have gradually become attached to the euro

apelar [01]

■ **apelar a** *v* + *prep* **1.** to resort to • apelar a la violencia no es una solución resorting to violence isn't a solution **2.** to appeal to • el presidente se dirigió a los huelguistas y apeló a su sentido común the president addressed the strikers and appealed to their common sense

■ **apelar ante** *v* + *prep* to appeal to • las victimas apelaron ante el Tribunal de Apelaciones the victims appealed to the Court of Appeals

■ **apelar contra** *v* + *prep* to appeal against • los inculpados han apelado contra la sentencia the accused have appealed against the sentence

apercibirse [03]

■ **apercibirse de** *vp* + *prep* to notice • se apercibió de que alguien la estaba siguiendo she noticed that someone was following her

apestar [01]

■ **apestar a** *v* + *prep* to stink of • este cuarto apesta a tabaco this room stinks of cigarettes

apiadarse [01]

■ **apiadarse de** *vp* + *prep* to take pity on • los secuestradores se apiadaron de los rehenes y los liberaron the kidnappers took pity on the hostages and freed them

aplicarse [13]

■ **aplicarse a** *vp* + *prep* to apply to • la regla general no se aplica a este caso preciso the general rule doesn't apply to this particular case

■ **aplicarse en** *vp* + *prep* to apply oneself to • se aplica en estudiar para aprobar she applies herself to her studies to pass her exams

apoderarse [01]

■ **apoderarse de** *vp* + *prep* to seize • los ladrones se apoderaron de todos los objetos de valor the burglars seized all the valuables

apostar [28]

■ **apostar por** *v* + *prep* to bet on • aposté por el caballo ganador I bet on the winning horse

apoyarse [01]

■ **apoyarse en** *vp* + *prep* to be based on • sus conclusiones se apoyan en los resultados de años de investigación his conclusions are based on the results of years of research

apropiarse [08]

■ **apropiarse de** *vp* + *prep* to take, to appropriate *fml* • los colonos se apropiaron de las tierras más fértiles the settlers appropriated the most fertile lands

aprovecharse [01]

■ **aprovecharse de** *vp* + *prep* to take advantage of • los timadores se aprovecharon de su ingenuidad the swindlers took advantage of her naivety

apuntarse [01]

■ **apuntarse a** *vp* + *prep* to put one's name down for, to be up for • ¿quién se apunta a la excursión? who's interested in going on the trip? • Gregorio se apunta siempre a todas las fiestas Gregorio's always up for going to a party

armarse [01]

■ **armarse de** *vp* + *prep* to summon up • ¡hay que armarse de paciencia! you have to summon up all your patience!

armonizar [16]

■ **armonizar con** *v* + *prep* to go with • este vino armoniza perfectamente con todo tipo de pescados y ariscos this wine goes perfectly with all types of fish and afood

rremeter [02]

■ **arremeter contra** *v + prep* **1.** to charge against • el ro arremetió contra el caballo the bull charged against e horse **2.** *fig* to attack • los manifestantes arremetieron ontra los símbolos estadounidenses the demonstrators tacked the American symbols

rrepentirse [55]

■ **arrepentirse de** *vp + prep* to regret • no me repiento de nada de lo que he hecho I don't regret nything I've done

rriesgarse [19]

■ **arriesgarse a** *vp + prep* to risk • los expertos no se riesgaron a realizar un pronóstico de la situación experts ouldn't risk forecasting the situation

rrimarse [01]

■ **arrimarse a** *vp + prep* to move closer to • si tienes frío, rimate al fuego if you're cold, move closer to the fire

scender [26]

■ **ascender a** *v + prep* to come to • los daños causados or el terremoto ascienden a cientos de millones de euros e damage done by the earthquake comes to hundreds of illions of euros

segurarse [01]

■ **asegurarse de** *vp + prep* to make sure that • se eguró de que nadie la hubiera seguido hasta allí she ade sure no one had followed her there • asegúrate de errar la puerta make sure you close the door

■ **asegurarse contra** *vp + prep* to insure oneself against este asegurador ofrece varias coberturas para asegurarse ontra robo this insurer offers various policies that insure ou against theft

sentir [55]

■ **asentir a** *v + prep* to agree to • el acusado asintió a odo the accused agreed to everything

sesorarse [01]

■ **asesorarse en** *vp + prep* to take advice on • han ecidido contratar los servicios de una empresa privada ara asesorarse en materia de seguridad they have decided enlist the services of a private company to take advice on ecurity matters

■ **asesorarse de** OR **con** *vp + prep* to consult • es importante asesorarse con profesionales del sector it is important to consult professionals in the field

asombrarse [01]

■ **asombrarse de** *vp + prep* to be surprised to • se asombró de encontrarme allí she was surprised to find me there

aspirar [01]

■ **aspirar a** *v + prep* to aspire to • la película aspira al máximo galardón en el certamen the film aspires to the highest award in the competition

asustarse [01]

■ **asustarse de** OR **por** *vp + prep* to be frightened of • no se asusta de nada ni de nadie she's not frightened of anything or anyone

atender [26]

■ **atender a** *v + prep* to pay attention to • atiende a lo que te digo pay attention to what I'm saying

■ **atender por** *v + prep* to answer to the name of • el perro atiende por "Campeón" the dog answers to the name of "Campeón"

atenerse [72]

■ **atenerse a** *vp + prep* **1.** to stick to • aténgase a las indicaciones que aparecen en el formulario stick to the instructions on the form • son mentiras que no se atienen a la realidad they are lies beyond the confines of reality **2.** to abide by • el moderador del foro prohibió la participación de varios participantes por no haberse atenido a las normas the chair of the forum prevented several people from participating for not having abided by the rules

atentar [01]

■ **atentar contra** *v + prep (life, person)* • han atentado varias veces contra su vida several attempts have been made on his life

atiborrarse [01]

■ **atiborrarse de** *vp + prep inf & fig* to stuff oneself with • los niños se atiborraron de caramelos the children stuffed themselves with sweets

atinar [01]

■ **atinar a** *v + prep* to manage to • no atino a encontrar una explicación verosímil al fenómeno I can't manage to find a credible explanation for the phenomenon

■ **atinar con** *v + prep* to find • no atinaba con las palabras exactas she couldn't find the right words

atracar [13]
■ **atracar en** *v + prep* to dock • el buque atracó en el puerto the ship docked in the port
■ **atracarse de** *vp + prep inf* to stuff oneself with • nos atracamos de chocolate we stuffed ourselves with chocolate

atreverse [02]
■ **atreverse a** *vp + prep* to dare • no se atrevió a confesarle la verdad she didn't dare tell him the truth

avenirse [73]
■ **avenirse a** *vp + prep* to agree to • finalmente se avinieron a firmar el acuerdo they finally agreed to sign to contract

aventurarse [01]
■ **aventurarse a** *vp + prep* to risk • se aventuraron a realizar aquella expedición sin un guía they risked going on the expedition without a guide

avergonzarse [32]
■ **avergonzarse de** *vp + prep* to be ashamed of • deberías avergonzarte de haber actuado así you should be ashamed of having behaved like that

ayudarse [01]
■ **ayudarse de** or **con** *vp + prep* to use • este invertebrado se ayuda de sus tentáculos para desplazarse this invertebrate uses its tentacles to move around

B, C

bajar [01]
■ **bajar(se) de** *v + prep* to get off • los pasajeros bajaron del avión the passengers got off the plane

basarse [01]
■ **basarse en** *vp + prep* **1.** *(theory, work)* to be based on **2.** *(person)* to base one's argument on • ¿en qué te basas para afirmar esto? what grounds do you have for confirming that?

bastar [01]
■ **bastar con** *v + prep* to be enough • bastará con que se lo digas telling her will be enough • bastaba con decirlo you should have just said

beber [02]
■ **beber a** or **por** *v + prep* to drink to • bebimos a salud de los novios we drank to the bride and groom health

beneficiarse [08]
■ **beneficiarse de** *vp + prep* to benefit from • lo parados se benefician de un descuento del 25 % th unemployed benefit from a 25 % discount

brindar [01]
■ **brindar por** *v + prep* to drink to • los invitado brindaron por los novios the guests drank to the brid and groom
■ **brindarse a** *vp + prep* to offer to • se brindó acompañarla a casa he offered to walk her home

burlarse [01]
■ **burlarse de** *vp + prep* to make fun of • la gente tomaba por loco y se burlaba de sus ideas people thoug he was mad and made fun of his ideas

cachondearse [01]
■ **cachondearse de** *vp + prep vulg* to make fun o • tengo la impresión de que se están cachondeando d nosotros I have a feeling they're making fun of us

caer [49]
■ **caer en** *v + prep* • cae en domingo it falls on a Sunda • caer en la cuenta to catch on, to get it

calar [01]
■ **calar en** *v + prep* to have an effect on • su mensaje n acaba de calar en la opinión pública his message hasn really had an effect on public opinion

cambiar [08]
■ **cambiar de** *v + prep* to change • cambi constantemente de parecer she's constantly changing h opinion • tendrías que cambiar de velocidades en la cuest you should really change gear when you're going uphill
■ **cambiarse de** *vp + prep* to change • se cambió d zapatos para estar más cómoda she changed her shoes be more comfortable

cansarse [01]
■ **cansarse de** *vp + prep* **1.** to get bored of • empieza cansarse de su oficio she's beginning to get bored of h job **2.** *fig* to get tired of • me cansé de esperar y me fui I g tired of waiting and left

carecer [45]

■ **carecer de** *v + prep* to lack • la región carece de interés turístico the area lacks any tourist attractions

cargar [19]

■ **cargar con** *v + prep* **1.** to carry • cargó con los dos sacos he carried both the sacks • tiene que cargar solo con el fardo he has to carry the bundle by himself **2.** *(responsibility)* to take • no pienso cargar con toda la responsabilidad del fracaso del proyecto there's no way I'm taking all the blame for the project failing **3.** to pay for, to cover the cost of • ya cargaré yo con la bebida I'll pay for the drinks **4.** to bear • cada uno debe cargar con las consecuencias de sus actos everyone must bear the consequences of their actions **5.** *(accompany)* to take with • como no puede dejar sola a su madre, tiene que cargar con ella as he can't leave his mother on her own, he has to take her everywhere with him

■ **cargar contra** *v + prep* to attack • los soldados cargaron contra el enemigo the soldiers attacked the enemy

■ **cargarse de** *vp + prep (responsibilities, debts)* to get weighed down with • el cielo se cargó de nubes the sky clouded over

cebarse [02]

■ **cebarse en** *vp + prep* to savage • la oposición se ha cebado en las declaraciones del primer ministro the opposition savaged the prime minister's statement

ceder [02]

■ **ceder a** OR **ante** *v + prep* to give in to • el gobierno acabó cediendo ante la presión de los sindicatos the government ended up giving in to pressure from the labor unions

■ **ceder en** *v + prep* to give way on • no cedió en ningún punto en las negociaciones he didn't give way on any point in the negotiations

cejar [01]

■ **cejar en** *v + prep* to give up on • no cejaba en sus intentos por convencernos he wouldn't give up trying to convince us • no cejaré en mi empeño I'll never give up

centrarse [01]

■ **centrarse en** *vp + prep* to concentrate on • céntrate en lo que realmente es importante concentrate on what is really important

ceñirse [39]

■ **ceñirse a** *vp + prep* to stick to • cíñete a lo realmente importante stick to what is really important

cerciorarse [01]

■ **cerciorarse de** *vp + prep* to make sure that • me cercioré de que no hubiera nadie I made sure there was no one there

cerrarse [22]

■ **cerrarse a** *vp + prep* to close one's mind to • no hay que cerrarse a ninguna posibilidad we must keep an open mind about things

cesar [01]

■ **cesar de** *v + prep* to stop • el bebé no cesaba de llorar the baby wouldn't stop crying

chiflarse [01]

■ **chiflarse por** *vp + prep inf* **1.** to go crazy over • se chifla por cualquier cosa que tenga relación con el esoterismo he goes crazy over anything esoteric • mi hermano se chifla por las motos my brother is crazy about motorbikes **2.** to fall for • se ha chiflado por un hombre mayor que ella she's fallen for an older man

chochear [01]

■ **chochear por** *vp + prep inf* **1.** to dote on • nuestro vecino chochea por su nieta our neighbor dotes on his grandaughter **2.** to be crazy about • reconozco que chocheo por los videojuegos I know I'm crazy about videogames

chulear [01]

■ **chulear de** *v + prep* to brag about • chulea de conocer a un ministro he brags about knowing a government minister

cifrar [01]

■ **cifrarse en** *vp + prep* to amount to • las pérdidas de la empresa se cifran en millones de euros the company's losses amount to millions of euros

circunscribirse [03]

■ **circunscribirse a** *vp + prep* to be limited to, to be restricted to • es un problema que no se circunscribe solamente al ámbito familiar it is a problem that is not limited to families

clamar [01]

■ **clamar a** *v + prep* to appeal to • clamó a la clemencia de los jueces she appealed for mercy from the judges

■ **clamar contra** *v* + *prep* to protest against • numerosos eran los que clamaban contra la injusticia there were many people who protested against injustice

clasificarse [13]

■ **clasificarse para** *vp* + *prep* to get through to, to qualify for • nuestro equipo se ha clasificado para la final our team has got through to the final

claudicar [13]

■ **claudicar de** *v* + *prep* **1.** to abandon, to renounce *fml* • acabó claudicando de sus ideas y convicciones de juventud he ended up abandoning the ideas and convictions of his youth **2.** to go back on • el gobierno ha claudicado de sus promesas electorales the government has gone back on its electoral promises

codearse [01]

■ **codearse con** *vp* + *prep* to rub shoulders with • dicen que ahora se codea con la nobleza apparently he rubs shoulders with nobility these days

cogerse [17]

■ **cogerse a** OR **de** *vp* + *prep* to hold on to • me tuve que coger a su brazo para no caerme I had to hold on to his arm so as not to fall

coincidir [03]

■ **coincidir con** *v* + *prep* **1.** to agree with • en eso coincido contigo I agree with you on that **2.** to bump into • coincidí con unos amigos que no había visto desde hacía tiempo en una inauguración I bumped into some friends I hadn't seen in a long time at a launch

■ **coincidir en** *v* + *prep* to agree that • todos coinciden en que no es posible continuar así everyone agrees that we can't carry on like this

colaborar [01]

■ **colaborar a** *v* + *prep* to contribute to, to help • este tipo de actos vandálicos colabora a generar un clima de inseguridad entre la población this type of destructive behavior helps to create a climate of insecurity in the population

■ **colaborar con** *v* + *prep* to collaborate with • se negó a colaborar con la policía he refused to collaborate with the police

■ **colaborar en** *v* + *prep* to work on, to collaborate on • varios laboratorios colaboran en la investigación sobre la enfermedad de Alzheimer several laboratories are collaborating on the research into Alzheimer's

colarse [01]

■ **colarse en** *vp* + *prep* **1.** *(room, building)* to sneak into **2.** *(party)* to crash • lograron colarse en la fiesta they managed to crash the party

colgar [30]

■ **colgar de** *v* + *prep* to hang from • una preciosa araña colgaba del techo a beautiful chandelier was hanging from the ceiling

■ **colgarse de** *vp* + *prep* to hang off • ¡no te cuelgues de esa rama, que se puede romper! don't hang off that branch, it might break!

comenzar [23]

■ **comenzar a** *v* + *prep* to start • de repente comenzó a llover it suddenly started raining

comerciar [08]

■ **comerciar con** *v* + *prep* to trade in • comercia con piedras preciosas he trades in precious stones

compadecerse [45]

■ **compadecerse de** *vp* + *prep* to feel sorry for • me compadezco de estas pobres gentes I feel sorry for these poor people

compaginarse [01]

■ **compaginarse con** *vp* + *prep* to go with • sus actos no se compaginan con sus palabras his actions don't go with his words

compararse [01]

■ **compararse con** *vp* + *prep* to be compared to • la situación actual no se puede comparar con la que precedió a la revolución the current situation cannot be compared to the one before the revolution

competer [02]

■ **competer a** *v* + *prep* to be up to • es una decisión que sólo te compete a ti it's a decision that is entirely up to you

competir [39]

■ **competir con** *v* + *prep* to compete with OR against • los españoles compiten con otros equipos europeos por el título the Spanish are competing with other European teams for the title • una empresa española que compite con las multinacionales a Spanish company which competes with the multinationals

■ **competir por** *v* + *prep* to compete for, to be in competition for • tres empresas compiten por liderar el mercado mundial de las telecomunicaciones three companies are in competition to be the world market leader in telecommunications

complacerse [44]

■ **complacerse en** *vp* + *prep* to be pleased to, to have pleasure in *fml* • me complazco en anunciarle que su obra ha sido seleccionada para el certamen it gives me great pleasure to tell you that your work has been selected for the competition

componerse [69]

■ **componerse de** *vp* + *prep* to consist of • el examen se compone de tres partes the exam consists of three parts

comprometerse [02]

■ **comprometerse a** *vp* + *prep* to promise to, to commit oneself to • se comprometió a ayudarnos he promised to help us

■ **comprometerse con** *vp* + *prep* to be committed to • está comprometido con la defensa del medio ambiente he's committed to the protection of the environment

■ **comprometerse en** *vp* + *prep* to commit oneself to • el presidente llama a los paises ricos a comprometerse en la lucha contra pobreza the president is calling on wealthy nations to commit themselves to the fight against poverty

comulgar [19]

■ **comulgar con** *v* + *prep* to share • no comulgo con su manera de ver las cosas I don't share her view of things

comunicar [13]

■ **comunicar con** *v* + *prep* **1.** to communicate with • comunica con sus amigos por mensajes de texto he communicates with his friends via text messages **2.** *(two rooms)* to be off • el lavadero comunica con la cocina the utility room is off the kitchen **3.** *(two places, roads)* to be connected to • el rio comunica con el mar the river flows into the sea

concentrarse [01]

■ **concentrarse en** *vp* + *prep* **1.** to concentrate on • concéntrate en lo que haces concentrate on what you are doing **2.** to gather • miles de personas se concentran en la capital para protestar thousands of people are gathered in the capital to protest

concernir [27]

■ **concernir a** *v* + *prep* to concern • la droga es un problema que nos concierne a todos drugs are a problem that concern us all

conciliarse [08]

■ **conciliarse con** *vp* + *prep* to be reconciled with • la nueva ley contiene disposiciones que no pueden conciliarse con las de la ley anterior there are regulations in the new law that cannot be reconciled with the ones in the previous law

concluir [52]

■ **concluir por** *v* + *prep* to end up • ambas partes concluyeron por aceptar un compromiso both sides ended up accepting a compromise

concurrir [03]

■ **concurrir a** *v* + *prep* to contribute to • numerosos factores han concurrido a este resultado numerous factors have contributed to this result

condescender [26]

■ **condescender a** *v* + *prep* to consent to • no puedo menos que condescender a una petición tan justa consenting to such a reasonable request is the least I can do

confesarse [22]

■ **confesarse de** *vp* + *prep* (RELIG) to confess • se confesó de sus pecados she confessed her sins

confiar [07]

■ **confiar en** *v* + *prep* to trust • confio totalmente en ella I trust her completely • confio en verle mañana I trust I'll see you tomorrow • confio en que ganemos I'm confident we'll win

confluir [52]

■ **confluir en** *v* + *prep* **1.** *(people)* to converge on • miles de manifestantes confluyeron en la plaza mayor thousands of demonstrators converged on the main square **2.** *(parties, sides)* to agree on • todos los interesados confluyen en un mismo punto all interested parties agree on the same point

conformarse [01]

■ **conformarse con** *vp* + *prep* to be satisfied with • me conformo con que todo siga tal como ahora I'm satisfied with things carrying on as they are • nuestro equipo tuvo que conformarse con un empate our team had to settle for a draw

confundir [03]

■ **confundirse con** *vp* + *prep* to be mistaken for • el perdón no debe confundirse con el olvido forgiveness shouldn't be mistaken for forgetfulness

■ **confundirse en** OR **entre** *vp* + *prep* **1.** *(escape)* to disappear into • el ladrón huyó y se confundió entre la multitud the thief escaped and disappeared into the crowd **2.** *(so as not to be recognized)* to mingle with • al rey le gustaba confundirse de vez en cuando con el pueblo now and again, the king liked to mingle with the people

congraciarse [08]

■ **congraciarse con** *vp* + *prep* to win over • la sociedad anunció el reparto de 1.500 millones de euros entre sus accionistas para congraciarse con los inversores the company announced that it would be sharing out 1,500 million euros among its shareholders to win over investors

congratularse [01]

■ **congratularse de** *vp* + *prep* to be pleased about • nos congratulamos de tu recuperación we're pleased you've made a good recovery • nos congratulamos de que el problema haya sido por fin solventado we are pleased that the problem has finally been solved

■ **congratularse por** *vp* + *prep* • me congratulo por el éxito de tu libro congratulations on the success of your book

consentir [55]

■ **consentir en** *v* + *prep* to agree to • el gobierno acabó consitiendo en que el tema fuera sometido a referéndum the government ended up agreeing to a referendum on the subject

consistir [03]

■ **consistir en** *v* + *prep* to consist of • el premio consiste en un crucero para dos personas por el Caribe the prize consists of a cruise for two in the Caribbean • su tarea consistirá en ampliar la cartera de clientes de la empresa your duties will involve increasing the company's client portfolio

constar [01]

■ **constar de** *v* + *prep* to consist of • el curso consta de dos módulos the course consists of two modules • el proceso de selección consta de varias partes the selection process consists of several parts

■ **constar en** *v* + *prep* • según consta en las actas as stated in the minutes

constituirse [52]

■ **constituirse de** *vp* + *prep* to be made up of • todo objeto de estudio se constituye de dos elementos: el

empìrico y el teórico all research objects are made up of two elements: the empirical and the theoretical

contactar [01]

■ **contactar con** *v* + *prep* to contact, to get in touch with • si tiene cualquier problema, contacte con nosotros if you have any problems, please contact us

contagiarse [08]

■ **contagiarse con** *vp* + *prep* to become infected with, to catch • evitar contagiarse con el virus avoid becoming infected with the virus

contar [28]

■ **contar con** *v* + *prep* **1.** to count on • puedes contar conmigo you can count on me • no contaba con esto I wasn't expecting this **2.** to have • cuentas con dos horas para hacerlo you have two hours to do it in

contentarse [01]

■ **contentarse con** *vp* + *prep* to be happy with • me contento con que me des la mitad I'm happy with you just giving me half • se contenta con poco she's easy to please

contribuir [52]

■ **contribuir a** *v* + *prep* to help • es un alimento que contribuye a reducir el colesterol it's a food that helps reduce cholesterol

■ **contribuir con** *v* + *prep* to contribute • cada uno contribuyó al regalo con diez euros everyone contributed ten euros to the present

convencer [14]

■ **convencerse de** *v* + *prep* to convince oneself that • intenta convencerse de que puede ganar she's trying to convince herself that she can win

convenir [73]

■ **convenir en** *v* + *prep* **1.** *(decide)* to agree • convenimos en reunirnos we agreed to have a meeting **2.** *(accept)* • convenir en que to admit : convengo en que, por una vez tienes razón I admit that, for once, you're right

converger [17]

■ **converger en** *v* + *prep* to lead to • diferentes teorias convergen a una misma conclusión different theories all lead to the same conclusion

convertirse [55]

■ **convertirse a** *vp* + *prep* to convert to • se ha convertido al budismo he's converted to Buddhism

convertirse en *vp + prep* to become • el festival se a convertido en cita obligada para cinéfilos the festival as become a must for movie buffs

onvidar [01]

convidar a *v + prep* to be conducive to • este buen empo convida a pasear this lovely weather is conducive » going for walks

orresponder [02]

corresponder a *v + prep (compensate for)* to repay • me vitó para corresponder a mi favor she paid to repay the vor I'd done for her

corresponderse con *vp + prep (write to)* to correspond ith • mi hijo se corresponde con un chico australiano my on corresponds with an Australian boy

otizarse [16]

cotizarse a *vp + prep (bonds, shares)* to be quoted at • las cciones de esta empresa se cotizan a más de 67 euros this ompany's shares are quoted at over 67 euros

reer [12]

creer en *v + prep* to believe in • a pesar de todo, sigo reyendo en el ser humano despite everything, I still believe human beings

ristalizarse [16]

cristalizarse en *vp + prep* to develop into • todas las ensiones se cristalizaron en un movimiento revolucionario l the tensions developed into a revolutionary movement

ruzarse [16]

cruzarse con *vp + prep* to pass • me crucé con la ecina I passed my neighbor

uadrar [01]

cuadrar con *v + prep* to tally with • su declaración o cuadra con los hechos his statement doesn't tally with le facts

ubrirse [03]

cubrirse de *vp + prep* to cover oneself in • en aquella casión el ejército español se cubrió de gloria on that ccasion, the Spanish army covered itself in glory

uidar [01]

cuidar de *v + prep* to look after • ¿quién va a cuidar el perro cuando estemos de vacaciones? who is going to ok after the dog while we're on vacation?

cuidarse de *vp + prep* to be careful to, to make sure that • para mantener el suspense, se cuidó de decir si aceptaría o no la invitación to keep the suspense, she was careful not to say whether she would go or not

culminar [01]

■ **culminar con** *v + prep* to finish with, to culminate in • el acto conmemorativo culminó con un baile popular the commemorative ceremony finished with a popular dance

cumplir [03]

■ **cumplir con** *v + prep* **1.** *(duty)* to do one's duty by • considero haber cumplido contigo I think I've done my duty by you • por mi parte yo he cumplido con mi deber I've done my duty **2.** *(promise)* to keep • cumplió con su promesa he kept his promise • cumplir con la palabra to keep one's word **3.** *(aims, objectives)* to meet, to achieve • la empresa ha cumplido con todos sus objetivos the company has achieved all its aims

curarse [01]

■ **curarse de** *vp + prep* to recover from • se curó de su enfermedad sin recurrir a ningún tratamiento she recovered from her illness without having any treatment

D

dar [63]

■ **dar a** *v + prep* **1.** *(building, front)* to face **2.** *(window, balcony)* to look out onto **3.** *(door)* to open onto • la fachada principal da al este the main façade faces east • la ventana da al patio the window looks out onto the courtyard • la puerta da a la calle the door opens onto the street **4.** *(operate)* • dale a la manilla turn the handle • hay que dar al botón you have to press the switch

■ **dar con** *v + prep* **1.** *(solution, answer)* to find, to hit upon something • he dado con la solución I've hit upon the solution **2.** *(meet)* to bump into • di con él al salir de aquí I bumped into him when I left here

■ **dar para** *v + prep* to be enough for • esa tela no da para una falda that material isn't enough for a skirt

■ **darse a** *vp + prep (drink, drugs)* to turn to • se dio a la bebida he turned to drink

■ **darse de** *vp + prep (consider oneself)* • dárselas de : se las da de listo he reckons he's clever; se las da de valiente he reckons he's brave

■ **darse por** *vp + prep* to consider oneself • puedes darte por suspendido you can consider yourself suspended

datar [01]

■ **datar de** *v + prep* to date from • la torre data de la época mudéjar the tower dates from the Mudejar era

deber [02]

■ **deber de** *v + prep (expressing probability)* • deben de ser las siete it must be seven o'clock • no debe de haber nadie en casa there can't be anyone at home

■ **deberse a** *vp + prep* 1. to be due to • el retraso se debe a la huelga the delay must be due to the strike 2. to devote oneself to • dice que se debe a sus hijos she says she's devoted to her children

dedicarse [13]

■ **dedicarse a** *vp + prep* 1. *(work as)* to do • ¿a qué te dedicas? what do you do for a living? 2. *(activities)* to spend time on • se dedica a promover la práctica del deporte en las escuelas he spends his time on promoting sports in schools 3. *(people)* to devote oneself to • toda su vida se dedicó a los pobres all his life he's devoted himself to the poor

defender [26]

■ **defenderse de** *vp + prep* 1. *(danger)* to defend oneself from • un pequeño roedor que se sube a los árboles para defenderse de los predadores a small rodent that climbs trees to defend itself from predators 2. *(cold, elements)* to protect oneself from • se defendieron como pudieron del frío they did their best to protect themselves from the cold

degenerar [01]

■ **degenerar en** *v + prep* to degenerate into • la manifestación degeneró en enfrentamientos con la policía the demonstration degenerated into clashes with police

dejar [01]

■ **dejar de** *v + prep* 1. to stop • ¡deja de gritar! stop shouting! 2. *(not forget, stop)* • ¡no dejes de escribirme! don't forget to write • no dejaremos de venir a verte we'll still come and visit

■ **dejarse de** *vp + prep* to stop • ¡déjate de tonterías! stop messing around!

depender [02]

■ **depender de** *v + prep* to depend on • todo depende de ti it all depends on you

derivar [02]

■ **derivar de** *v + prep* to come from, to derive from *fml* el español que hoy hablamos deriva directamente del lati the Spanish we speak today is directly derived from Latin

■ **derivar en** *v + prep (end in)* to result in • la manifestació derivó en una batalla con los agentes del orden th demonstration resulted in a battle with the police officers

desasirse [03]

■ **desasirse de** *vp + prep* to let go of • no es fáci desasirse de costumbres tan arraigadas it isn't easy to le go of such deep-rooted customs

descargarse [19]

■ **descargarse con** *vp + prep* to let rip • el cineast se descargó con la crítica the moviemaker let rip at th critics

desconectarse [01]

■ **desconectarse de** *vp + prep* to switch off from esta isla es un paraíso para quienes deseen desconectarse durante unos días del mundo this island is paradise fo anyone who wants to switch off from the world for a fev days

desconfiar [07]

■ **desconfiar de** *v + prep* to distrust, to not trust desconfía hasta de su propia sombra he doesn't even trus his own shadow • desconfiaba de los que querían ayudarl he distrusted those who wanted to help him

descubrirse [03]

■ **descubrirse ante** *vp + prep fig* to take one's ha off to • me descubro ante su talento I take my hat off t his talent

desdecir [74]

■ **desdecir de** *v + prep* to clash with, not to go with • l sobrecargada cúpula desdice de la sencillez arquitectura del resto del edificio the ornate dome clashes with th architectural simplicity of the rest of the building

■ **desdecirse de** *vp + prep* to go back on • se h desdicho de sus declaraciones anteriores she's gone bac on her previous statement

desembarazarse [16]

■ **desembarazarse de** *vp + prep* to get rid of • ¿acas quieres desembarazarte de mí? so you want to get rid o me, do you?

esembocar [13]

desembocar en *v + prep* **1.** *(river)* to flow into • el jo desemboca en el Atlántico the Tajo flows into the antic **2.** *(road)* to lead to **3.** *(talks)* to lead to, to result in • las gociaciones no desembocaron en ningún acuerdo the gotiations didn't result in an agreement

esengañarse [01]

desengañarse de *vp + prep* to become disillusioned nuestra época se ha desengañado de las utopías our neration has become disillusioned with the idea of a rfect world • desengáñate stop kidding yourself

esentenderse [26]

desentenderse de *vp + prep* to have nothing to with, to wash one's hands of *inf* • las autoridades se esentendieron del problema the authorities have washed eir hands of the problem • los jóvenes se desentienden e la participación ciudadana young people don't want to ow about civic duties

esfallecer [45]

desfallecer de *v + prep* to faint • desfallecíamos e cansancio we felt faint with exhaustion • estuvieron a unto de desfallecer de inanición they nearly passed out th hunger

eshacerse [68]

deshacerse de *vp + prep* to get rid of • el asesino se eshizo del cadáver the murderer got rid of the body

deshacerse en *vp + prep* **1.** *(praise, insults)* to heap • la itica se ha deshecho en elogios ante su última película e critics heaped praise on his latest film **2.** *(apology)* • se eshizo en excusas por no haberme felicitado por mi umpleaños she was extremely apologetic for forgetting to sh me a happy birthday

esinteresarse [01]

desinteresarse de OR **por** *vp + prep* to show no terest • se desinteresa de sus amigos/del trabajo he ows no interest in his friends/his work

esistir [03]

desistir de *v + prep* to give up • desistió de la idea e entrar al seminario he gave up the idea of entering the iesthood

esligar [19]

desligarse de *vp + prep fig* to distance oneself from se ha ido desligando del grupo he's gradually distanced mself from the group

despacharse [01]

■ **despacharse con** *vp + prep* • se despachó a gusto con su mejor amiga she let off steam with her best friend

despedirse [39]

■ **despedirse de** *vp + prep* **1.** to say goodbye to • antes de irse se despidió de todos los invitados before she left, she said goodbye to all the guests **2.** *(forget)* to kiss goodbye to • si no apruebas, despídete de la moto if you fail your exams, you can kiss goodbye to the motorbike

despegarse [19]

■ **despegarse de** *vp + prep* **1.** *(omelette, pancake)* to come unstuck from • te darás cuenta que ya está cuando veas que se despega de la sartén you'll know it's done when you see it comes unstuck from the frying pan **2.** *(person)* • en toda la tarde no se despegó del sofá he didn't get off the sofa the whole afternoon • no se despega de su madre she won't leave her mother's side

despojarse [01]

■ **despojarse de** *vp + prep* to give up, to renounce *fml* • se despojó de todas sus riquezas she renounced all her wealth

desprenderse [02]

■ **desprenderse de** *vp + prep* **1.** *(paper)* to peel off, to come off • el papel pintado se desprende fácilmente de la pared wallpaper peels off the wall easily **2.** *(conclude)* to be clear • de sus palabras se desprende que no está dispuesto a ceder ni un ápice from what he says, it is clear that he is not prepared to give an inch **3.** *(obligations, duties)* to get out of • no es nada fácil desprenderse de algunas obligaciones it's not easy to get out of some of your commitments

despreocuparse [01]

■ **despreocuparse de** *vp + prep* not to worry about, not to have anything to do with • yo prefiero despreocuparme de todo lo que tiene que ver con el aspecto financiero del proyecto I prefer not to have anything to do with the financial side of the project

despuntar [01]

■ **despuntar entre** *v + prep* to stand out among • esta joven atleta despunta entre los grandes atletas de su categoría this young athlete stands out among the great athletes in her event • la espectacular cúpula de cristal despunta entre los tejados de la ciudad the spectacular glass dome stands out amidst the city's rooftops

■ **despuntar por** *v + prep* to stand out for • no despunta precisamente por su inteligencia he doesn't exactly stand out for his intelligence

desquitarse [01]
■ **desquitarse de** *vp + prep* to get one's own back • pienso desquitarme de ese agravio I plan to get my own back for that insult

destacarse [13]
■ **destacarse de** *vp + prep* to stand out from • un artista que se destaca de sus coetáneos por su originalidad an artist who stands out from his contemporaries because of this originality

■ **destacarse por** *vp + prep* to be remarkable for, to stand out because of • la región destaca por su patrimonio histórico y artístico the area is remarkable for its history and artistic heritage

desvelarse [01]
■ **desvelarse por** *vp + prep* to live for • se desvela por sus hijos she lives for her children

desviarse [07]
■ **desviarse de** *vp + prep* 1. *(path)* to detour from • se desviaron del camino para tomar un atajo they detoured from the path to take a shortcut 2. *(subject, idea)* to get sidetracked from, to stray from • no te desvies del tema don't get sidetracked • se desvió de su propósito he lost sight of his aim

desvincularse [01]
■ **desvincularse de** *vp + prep* 1. *(friends, acquaintances)* to dissociate oneself from • poco a poco se fue desvinculando de sus antiguas amistades he gradually dissociated himself from his old acquaintances 2. *(duties, obligations)* to drop • no puede desvincularse unilateralmente de sus obligaciones you can't just drop your obligations when you want to

desvivirse [03]
■ **desvivirse por** *vp + prep* 1. to live for • se desvivia por sus hijos she lived for her children 2. • desvivirse por hacer algo to go out of one's way to : no comprendo a las personas que se desviven por acumular riquezas y poder I can't understand people who go out of their way to become rich and powerful

determinarse [01]
■ **determinarse a** *vp + prep* to make up one's mind to • se determinó a hacer todo lo posible she made up her mind to do everything possible

diferenciarse [08]
■ **diferenciarse de** *vp + prep* to differ from • lo humanos nos diferenciamos de los animales en el us de la razón we humans differ from animals in our abili to reason

diferir [55]
■ **diferir de** *v + prep* to disagree with • en este tem difiero de mis compañeros I disagree with my friends o this subject • mi punto de vista difiere diametralmente de suyo my point of view is diametrically opposed to yours

dimitir [03]
■ **dimitir de** *v + prep* to resign • el escándalo lo h obligado a dimitir de su cargo de ministro the scanda forced him to resign his ministerial post

diplomarse [01]
■ **diplomarse en** *vp + prep* to graduate in • se acab de diplomar en ingenieria he has just graduated i engineering

dirigirse [18]
■ **dirigirse a** *vp + prep* 1. *(train, coach)* to head for • venia d Burgos y se dirigia a Toledo it was on its way from Burgo and heading for Toledo 2. *(be intended for)* to be aimed at • e una serie que se dirige al público adolescente it's a serie aimed at young people 3. *(communicate with)* to contact, to wri to • sirvanse dirigirse al servicio de reclamaciones pleas contact the complaints department

■ **dirigirse hacia** *vp + prep* to head for • se dirigi lentamente hacia la puerta she slowly headed for the doc

discrepar [01]
■ **discrepar de** *v + prep* to differ from, to disagree wi • discrepamos radicalmente de sus opiniones our opinior are radically different to theirs

disculparse [01]
■ **disculparse por** *vp + prep* to apologize • se disculp por la reacción que habia tenido she apologized for h reaction

discutir [03]
■ **discutir de** OR **sobre** *v + prep* to argue about • l participantes al coloquio discutieron sobre la viabilida del proyecto the people attending the symposium argue about the viability of the project

disfrazarse [16]

disfrazarse de *vp + prep* to dress up as • los niños se disfrazaron de indios y vaqueros the children dressed up as cowboys and indians

disfrutar [01]

disfrutar de *v + prep* 1. *(privileges, health)* to enjoy, to have • disfrutan de un trato de favor they enjoy preferential treatment • disfruta de una envidiable salud para su edad he is in enviable good health for his age 2. *(benefit from)* to enjoy • disfruta de las pequeñas cosas que te ofrece la vida enjoy the little things that life brings • disfrutamos de unas merecidas vacaciones we enjoyed a well-deserved holiday

disponer [69]

disponer de *v + prep* to have • el hotel dispone de todas las comodidades the hotel has all the amenities

disponerse a *vp + prep* to get ready to • me disponía a salir cuando sonó el teléfono I was getting ready to go out when the telephone rang

divagar [19]

divagar sobre *v + prep* to muse over • no tengo tiempo para divagar sobre lo humano y lo divino I don't have time to muse over the human and the divine

doblarse [01]

doblarse a OR **ante** *vp + prep (pressure, demands)* to give in to • nunca se dobló ante las presiones del poder he never gave in to the pressures of power • terminó doblándose ante aquella justa demanda he ended up giving in to that reasonable request

doblegarse [19]

doblegarse a OR **ante** *vp + prep* to give in to, to yield to • a menudo es necesario doblegarse a las exigencias del cliente it's often necessary to give in to clients' demands • el gobierno no tuvo más remedio que doblegarse ante la presión de la calle the government had no choice but to give in to public pressure

dolerse [35]

dolerse de OR **por** *vp + prep* to complain about • el delantero centro se dolía de la pierna derecha the center forward was complaining about his right leg

dudar [01]

dudar de *v + prep (mistrust)* to doubt • duda de todo y de todos he doubts everything and everyone

dudar sobre *v + prep (not be sure)* to doubt, to question • dudo sobre sus verdaderos motivos I question his true motives

E

echar [01]

echar a *v + prep* to start • echó a correr he started running

echar por *v + prep inf (follow)* to head along • echa por el camino de la izquierda head along the path on the left

echarse a *vp + prep* 1. to start • se echó a reír she burst out laughing 2. *(embark on)* to hit • nos echamos a la carretera de buena mañana we hit the road early in the morning

ejercer [14]

ejercer de *v + prep* to practice • ejerce de abogado he practices law

ejercitarse [01]

ejercitarse en *vp + prep* to practice • deberías ejercitarte más en hablar en público you should practice speaking in public more

elevarse [01]

elevarse a *vp + prep* to amount to • los daños causados por el terremoto se elevan a mil millones de euros the damage caused by the earthquake amounts to a billion euros

elucubrar [01]

elucubrar sobre *v + prep* to reflect on • no tiene mucho sentido elucubrar sobre este tema there's little point reflecting on this subject

emanar [01]

emanar de *v + prep* to emanate from • valiosas propuestas han emanado de ese primer encuentro internacional valuable suggestions have emanated from that first international meeting

embadurnar [01]

embadurnarse de *vp + prep* to smear oneself with • los soldados se embadurnaron de barro para camuflarse the soldiers smeared themselves in mud to camouflage themselves

embarcarse [13]

embarcarse en *vp + prep fig* to embark on • hay que evitar como sea embarcarse en una aventura militar de resultados inciertos we have to avoid at all costs embarking on a military venture with an uncertain outcome

empaparse [01]

■ **empaparse de** *vp + prep* to soak up • fui allì a vivir una temporada para empaparme del ambiente I went to live there a while to soak up the atmosphere

emparentar [01]

■ **emparentar con** *v + prep* to become related to • gracias a aquella boda emparentó con la aristocracia thanks to that wedding, she became related to the aristocracy

empecinarse [01]

■ **empecinarse en** *vp + prep* to persist in • se empecina a hacer las cosas sin escuchar los consejos de los demás he persists in doing things without listening to other people's advice

empeñarse [01]

■ **empeñarse en** *vp + prep* **1.** to persist in • no te empeñes en convencerme, no vale la pena don't keep trying to convince me, you're wasting your time **2.** • empeñarse en hacer algo to be set on doing something : por mucho que se empeñaba en olvidarla, seguìa amándola however set he was on forgetting her, he still loved her

emperrarse [01]

■ **emperrarse en** *vp + prep* to get it into one's head to • cuando se emperra en hacer algo, no hay manera de disuadirlo when he gets it into his head to do something, there's no stopping him

empezar [23]

■ **empezar a** *v + prep* to start • empieza a hacer frìo it's starting to get cold

■ **empezar por** *v + prep* to begin by • empecemos por hacer un inventario detallado let's begin by making a detailed inventory

enamorarse [01]

■ **enamorarse de** *vp + prep* to fall in love with • se enamoró de ella la primera vez que la vio he fell in love with her the first time he saw her

encaminarse [01]

■ **encaminarse a** OR **hacia** *vp + prep* to set off for OR towards • los peregrinos se encaminaron hacia la ermita the pilgrims set off towards the chapel

encamotarse [01]

■ **encamotarse de** *vp + prep (Am) inf* to fall in love with • el chico se encamotó de su profesora de matemáticas the boy fell in love with his math teacher

encapricharse [01]

■ **encapricharse con** *vp + prep (be determined)* to set one's mind on • se encaprichó con ser cantante she set her mind on becoming a singer

■ **encapricharse con** OR **de** *vp + prep* **1.** *(person)* to become infatuated with **2.** *(thing)* to take a liking to • se encaprichó de un hombre casado she became infatuated with a married man • tu hijo se ha encaprichado con el juguete de ese niño your son's taken a liking to that boy's toy

encararse [01]

■ **encararse con** *vp + prep (oppose)* to stand up to • se encaró a su jefe he stood up to his boss

encargar [19]

■ **encargarse de** *vp + prep (be responsible for)* to take care of • yo me encargo de traer las bebidas I'll take care of the drinks

encariñarse [01]

■ **encariñarse con** *vp + prep* to become fond of • he acabado encariñándome con el perro I've ended up becoming fond of the dog

encarnizarse [16]

■ **encarnizarse con** *vp + prep* to befall • parece como si la desgracia se hubiera encarnizado con ellos it seemed bad luck had befallen them

encomendarse [22]

■ **encomendarse a** *vp + prep* **1.** *(person)* to entrust oneself to • me encomiendo a vosotros para que me aconsejéis I'm entrusting myself to you for your advice **2.** *(God, Saint)* to commend oneself to • se encomendó a Santa Rita she commended herself to Saint Rita

encontrarse [28]

■ **encontrarse con** *vp + prep* to bump into • me encontré con el vecino en el ascensor I bumped into my neighbor in the elevator

enfrascarse [13]

■ **enfrascarse en** *vp + prep* **1.** *(activity, work)* to become engrossed in • nada mejor que enfrascarse en la lectura

los clásicos there's nothing like becoming engrossed
reading the classics **2.** *(argument, discussion)* to become
embroiled in • se enfrascaron en una larga discusión they
came embroiled in a long argument

afrentarse [01]

■ **enfrentarse a** *vp + prep* to face • nuestra empresa
enfrenta a una grave crisis our company is facing a
serious crisis

■ **enfrentarse con** *vp + prep* to clash with • grupos de
jóvenes se enfrentaron con las fuerzas del orden groups of
youths clashed with police

engancharse [01]

■ **engancharse a** *vp + prep inf* to be hooked on • me
he enganchado a la telenovela esa y no me pierdo ni un
episodio I'm hooked on that soap and don't miss a single
episode

enorgullecerse [45]

■ **enorgullecerse de** *vp + prep* to be proud of • nos
enorgullecemos de la confianza que nos otorgan los
clientes we're proud of the trust our clients put in us • me
enorgullezco de considerarlo como a un amigo I'm proud
to call him a friend

enredarse [01]

■ **enredarse a** *vp + prep* to get into • nos enredamos a
clasificar las fotos y pasamos la tarde haciéndolo we got
into sorting out our photos and spent the whole afternoon
doing it

■ **enredarse con** *vp + prep inf* to get involved with • se
ha enredado con un compañero de trabajo she's gotten
involved with a work colleague

enrollarse [01]

■ **enrollarse con** *vp + prep inf* **1.** *(in a relationship)* to get
involved with • se enrolló con una amiga de su hermana he
got involved with one of his sister's friends **2.** *(speak)* to have
a chat • cada vez que me ve se enrolla conmigo every time
she sees me she stops for a chat

ensañarse [01]

■ **ensañarse con** *vp + prep* to treat appallingly • la
policía se ensañó contra los manifestantes the police
treated the demonstrators appallingly • el temporal se
ensaña con el litoral vasco the storm is unleashing itself on
the Basque coastline

ensimismarse [01]

■ **ensimismarse en** *vp + prep* to become absorbed in
• tiene tendencia a ensimismarse en sus pensamientos he
has a tendency to become self-absorbed • se ensimismó en
la contemplación del horizonte she became absorbed in
looking at the horizon

entender [26]

■ **entender de** OR **en** *v + prep* to know about • ¿tu
entiendes de informática? do you know anything about
computers?

enterar [01]

■ **enterarse de** *vp + prep* **1.** *(news, event)* to hear • me
enteré de que te habías mudado I heard you'd moved • ¿te
has enterado de lo que ha pasado en Madagascar? have
you heard what's happened in Madagascar? **2.** *(ask)* to find
out • intenta enterarte del precio try and find out the price
3. *(discover)* to find out about • como se entere de esto, te va
a matar if he finds out about this, he'll kill you

entrar [01]

■ **entrar a** *v + prep* to start • entró a trabajar en la
empresa el mes pasado he started working at the company
last month

■ **entrar de** *v + prep* to start as • entró de telefonista
y ahora es director he started as a telephone operator and
now he's the director

■ **entrar en** *v + prep* • no entramos todos en tu coche
we can't all fit in your car • ¿cuántas peras entran en un kilo?
how many pears do you get in a kilo? • esto no entraba en
mis cálculos I hadn't allowed for this in my calculations

entregarse [19]

■ **entregarse a** *vp + prep* **1.** to surrender to, to give
oneself up • el asesino decidió entregarse a la justicia the
murderer decided to give himself up **2.** to devote oneself to
• se entrega por completo a su trabajo she devotes herself
completely to her work **3.** *(emotionally, sexually)* to give oneself
to, to surrender to • se entregó a aquel hombre en cuerpo
y alma she gave herself to that man body and soul **4.** to give
oneself over to, to take to *inf* • se entregó a la bebida he
took to drink

entremeterse [02]

■ **entremeterse en** *vp + prep* to meddle in • no
soporto a la gente que se entremete en los asuntos que

no son de su incumbencia I can't stand people who meddle in affairs that don't concern them

entretenerse [72]

■ **entretenerse con** *vp + prep* to amuse oneself with • a esta edad los niños se entretienen con cualquier cosa at this age, children amuse themselves with anything

entristecerse [45]

■ **entristecerse por** OR **con** *vp + prep* to be saddened by • se entristeció con la noticia she was saddened by the news

entrometerse [02]

■ **entrometerse en** *vp + prep* 1. to meddle in • siempre anda entrometiéndose en mis asuntos she's always meddling in my affairs 2. to butt in • un desconocido se entrometió en nuestra charla someone we didn't know butted in our conversation

entroncar [13]

■ **entroncar con** *v + prep* 1. (person) to become related to 2. (work) to be related to • con aquella boda entroncó con la familia real española with that marriage, she became related to the Spanish royal family • su obra entronca con la tradición romántica his work is related to the romantic tradition 3. (road) to connect with, to meet • la N-12 entronca con la A-6 the N-12 meets the A-6

entusiasmarse [01]

■ **entusiasmarse con** *vp + prep* to become excited by • todos se entusiasmaron con la propuesta they all became excited by the proposal

enzarzarse [16]

■ **enzarzarse en** *vp + prep* to become embroiled in • se enzarzaron en una interminable disputa dialéctica they became embroiled in an endless dialectical argument

equivaler [02]

■ **equivaler a** *v + prep* to amount to • eso equivaldría a reconocer vuestro error that would amount to admitting your mistake

equivocarse [13]

■ **equivocarse con** *vp + prep* to be wrong about • me equivoqué con él, en realidad es simpatiquísimo I was wrong about him, he's actually really funny

■ **equivocarse de** *vp + prep* to get wrong • nos equivocamos de día we got the day wrong

escandalizarse [16]

■ **escandalizarse de** OR **por** *vp + prep* to be shock with OR by • parece mentira que todavía haya gente que escandalice por estas cosas it's incredible that some peo are still shocked by these things

escapar [01]

■ **escapar a** *v + prep* to escape • le era imposible escap a la vigilancia de sus padres it was impossible to escape parents' watchful eye

■ **escapar de** *v + prep* 1. to escape from • varios pres han escapado de una cárcel de alta seguridad seve prisoners have escaped from a high-security prison 2. (dec danger) to escape • escapó de la muerte por los pelos narrowly escaped death

escaquearse [01]

■ **escaquearse de** *vp + prep inf* to get out of • siemp se escaquea de las tareas duras he always manages to out of the difficult tasks • ¡esta vez no te vas a escaque de lavar los platos! you're not getting out of doing t dishes this time

esconderse [02]

■ **esconderse de** *vp + prep* to hide from • busca esconderse de la vista de los curiosos she was trying to hi from curious onlookers • se escondía de sus perseguidor he was hiding from the people who were after him

esforzarse [16]

■ **esforzarse en** OR **por** *vp + prep* to try hard to, to one's best to • se esfuerzan por ofrecer una imagen positi they are trying hard to present a positive image

esmerarse [01]

■ **esmerarse en** *vp + prep* 1. (be dedicated) to take gr pains over • se esmera en el trabajo she takes great pa over her work 2. (put effort into) • esmerarse en hacer algo try hard with, to make a real effort with : esmérate en hac buena letra make a real effort with your handwriting

especializarse [16]

■ **especializarse en** *vp + prep* to specialize in • licenció en medicina y luego se especializó en pediatría graduated in medicine and then specialized in pediatrics

especular [01]

■ **especular con** OR **en** *v + prep* (FIN & COMM) to specula in • especula en divisas he speculates in foreign exchang

especular sobre *v + prep (consider)* to speculate about los científicos especulan sobre la posible existencia de vida extraterrestre scientists speculate about the possible existence of extraterrestrial life

estar [64]

estar a *v + prep* **1.** *(currency)* to be worth • ¿a cuánto está el dólar? how much is the dollar worth? **2.** *(with dates)* to be • hoy estamos a 13 de julio it's July 13 today

estar de *v + prep* **1.** *(in a post)* to be • está de director de la agencia he is the director of the agency **2.** *(indicating mood)* to be • hoy estoy de buen/mal humor I'm in a good/bad mood today

estar en *v + prep* **1.** *(problem, difficulty)* to be, to lie in • el problema está en la fecha it's the date that's the problem **2.** *(think)* • estar en que to reckon : estoy en que no vendrá I reckon he won't come

estar para *v + prep (indicating mood, state)* to be in the mood for • no estoy para bromas I'm not in the mood for jokes

estar por *v + prep* **1.** *(indicating a future action)* • el trabajo más difícil todavía está por hacer the most difficult work is still ahead of us • eso está por ver that remains to be seen **2.** *(indicating an imminent action)* to be about to • estaba por irme cuando llegaste I was about to leave when you arrived • estuve por pegarle I was on the verge of hitting him

estirar [01]

estirar de *v + prep* to pull on • no estires de la cuerda don't pull on the rope

estremecerse [45]

estremecerse de *vp + prep (fear, cold)* to shudder with • al oír la noticia nos estremecimos todos de espanto we all shuddered with horror when we heard the news • notó una corriente de aire y se estremeció de frío she felt a draft that made her shudder

estribar [01]

estribar en *v + prep* to lie in • la diferencia no estriba tanto en la calidad como en el precio the difference lies more in the price than the quality

excusarse [01]

excusarse por *vp + prep* • excusarse (con alguien) por algo to apologize (to somebody) for something : se excusaron con nosotros por haber llegado tan tarde they apologized to us for arriving so late

expansionarse [01]

■ **expansionarse con** *vp + prep* to open up to • se expansiona fácilmente con los desconocidos she finds it easy to open up to strangers

explayarse [01]

■ **explayarse con** *vp + prep* to open up to • no es conveniente explayarse con cualquiera it isn't advisable to open up to just anyone

exponerse [69]

■ **exponerse a** *vp + prep* to expose oneself to • el presidente no teme exponerse a las críticas the president isn't afraid of being exposed to criticism

extralimitarse [01]

■ **extralimitarse en** *vp + prep* to exceed one's authority • acusan a la comisión de haberse extralimitado en sus funciones the commission is accused of exceeding its authority

extrañarse [01]

■ **extrañarse de** *vp + prep* to be surprised at • a mi edad ya no me extraño de nada at my age, nothing surprises me anymore

F

faltar [01]

■ **faltar a** *v + prep* **1.** *(promise, agreement)* to break • faltó a su palabra he broke his word **2.** *(offend)* to be rude to • no consentiré que faltes a tus padres I won't allow you to be rude to your parents

familiarizarse [16]

■ **familiarizarse con** *vp + prep* to familiarize oneself with • me prestó un móvil para que fuera familiarizándome con su utilización he lent me a cellphone so that I could familiarize myself with how to use it

fiarse [07]

■ **fiarse de** *vp + prep* to trust • no me fío ni un pelo del jardinero I don't trust the gardener in the slightest

fijarse [01]

■ **fijarse en** *vp + prep* **1.** to pay attention to • en el supermercado tienes que fijarte en la fecha de caducidad de los productos at the supermarket, you have to pay attention to the use-by dates on products **2.** to notice • nadie se fijó en ella durante la fiesta nobody took any notice of her at the party • fíjate en lo que pasa cuando pulsas el botón derecho del ratón watch what happens when you right-click on the mouse

fisgar [19]

■ **fisgar en** *v* + *prep* to pry • ¡deja de fisgar en mis cosas! stop prying into my affairs!

flojear [01]

■ **flojear en** *v* + *prep* to be weak in • mi hijo flojea en física y química my son is weak in physics and chemistry

fundarse [01]

■ **fundarse en** *vp* + *prep* to base oneself on • ¿en qué te fundas para hacer tales afirmaciones? what are you basing your assertions on?

fungir [18]

■ **fungir de** *v* + *prep (Am)* to act as • en el improvisado escenario hay una tela roja que funge de telón on the improvised stage, a piece of red material acts as the curtain

G, H

gozar [16]

■ **gozar con** *v* + *prep* to relish • gozaba con la idea de encontrarse cerca de su amada he was relishing the idea of being near his loved one

■ **gozar de** *v* + *prep* to enjoy • un cantante que goza de gran popularidad entre los jóvenes a singer who enjoys enormous popularity among the young

graduarse [09]

■ **graduarse en** *vp* + *prep* to graduate in • se graduó en ciencias políticas she graduated in political science

guardarse [01]

■ **guardarse de** *vp* + *prep* to be careful with • guárdate de los aduladores be careful with flatterers

guarecer [45]

■ **guarecerse de** *v* + *prep* to shelter from • buscaron una cueva para guarecerse del frío they looked for a cave to shelter from the cold

guasearse [01]

■ **guasearse de** *vp* + *prep inf* to make fun of • tengo la impresión de que os estáis guaseando de mí I have a feeling you're making fun of me

guiarse [07]

■ **guiarse por** *vp* + *prep* to follow • yo me guío siempre por el instinto I always follow my instinct

haber [76]

■ **haber de** *v* + *prep* **1.** *(expressing obligation)* to have to • has de trabajar más you have to work harder **2.** *(expressing probability)* • ha de ser su hermano he must be her brother • han de ser las tres it must be about three

habituarse [09]

■ **habituarse a** *vp* + *prep* **1.** *(become accustomed to)* to get used to • mi abuela no acaba de habituarse al euro my grandmother can't quite get used to the euro • no me habitúo a vivir solo I can't get used to living on my own **2.** *(habit, addiction)* to get in the habit of • de jovencita se habituó a fumar un paquete diario when she was young she got in the habit of smoking a packet a day

hablar [01]

■ **hablar de** *v* + *prep* to talk about • hablamos de todo y de nada we talked about everything and nothing

■ **hablarse con** *vp* + *prep* to speak to • hace un año que no me hablo con mi hermano I haven't spoken to my brother for a year

hacer [68]

■ **hacer de** *v* + *prep* **1.** *(act as)* to serve as • un sofá que también hace de cama a sofa which serves as a bed **2.** *(be employed as)* to work as • hace de cajera she works as a cashier **3.** *(in a film or play)* to play • en su última película hace de vampiro he plays a vampire in his latest film

■ **hacerse a** *vp* + *prep (become accustomed to)* to get used to • no acabo de hacerme al nuevo piso I can't quite get used to the new flat

■ **hacerse con** *vp* + *prep* **1.** *(gain)* to take • se hicieron con todo el dinero they took all the money • los rebeldes se han hecho con el poder the rebels have taken power **2.** *(obtain)* to get • habrá que hacerse con víveres para la expedición we'll have to get provisions for the expedition

hartarse [01]

■ **hartarse de** *vp* + *prep* **1.** *(food)* to stuff oneself with • las pasadas Navidades nos hartamos de dulces last Christmas we stuffed ourselves with sweet things **2.** *(tire of)* to get fed up of • me harté de esperar y me fui I got fed up of waiting and left **3.** *(do in excess)* to have one's fill of • durante las vacaciones nos hartamos de visitar museos during the holidays we had our fill of going round museums

stiarse [07]

■**astiarse de** *vp + prep* to get fed up with • el niño
hastió pronto de los juguetes the boy soon got fed up
h his toys

ncharse [01]

■**incharse a** or **de** *vp + prep* **1.** *(food)* to stuff oneself
h • nos hinchamos de marisco we stuffed ourselves with
afood **2.** *(work)* to do something non-stop • me hincho a
rar y todo por un sueldo miserable I work non-stop and
for a paltry wage

ir [52]

■**uir de** *v + prep* to flee from • la famosa actriz huía
los periodistas the famous actress was fleeing from
e press

I

entificarse [13]

■**dentificarse con** *vp + prep* to identify with • el
blico se identifica con el personaje principal the public
ntifies with the main character

ualarse [01]

■**gualarse a** or **con** *vp + prep* to match, to equal
ingún competidor puede igualarse con nosotros no
mpetitor can match us

sionarse [01]

■**lusionarse con** *vp + prep* to get one's hopes up
h • no te ilusiones con ese chico porque ya tiene
via don't get your hopes up with that guy because he
eady has a girlfriend • se ilusionaba con la posibilidad
ganar el campeonato he had his heart set on winning
e championship

plicarse [13]

■**mplicarse en** *vp + prep* to get involved in • lo mejor
que no te impliques en este asunto the best thing for you
not to get involved in this matter

pregnarse [01]

■**mpregnarse de** *vp + prep* to immerse oneself in •
abó impregnándose de la cultura del país he ended up
mersing himself in the culture of the country

cautarse [01]

■**ncautarse de** *vp + prep* (LAW) to seize • los aduaneros
incautaron de casi una tonelada de cocaína customs
icers seized nearly a ton of cocaine

incidir [03]

■ **incidir en** *v + prep* **1.** to fall into, to make • no incidas
en los mismos errores don't fall into the same mistake
2. to insist on • incidió en la importancia de extremar las
precauciones she insisted on the importance of taking the
maximum precautions **3.** *(influence)* to have a bearing on •
es un factor que no incide en los resultados it is a factor
that has no bearing on the results **4.** *(in an operation)* to cut, to
make an incision in *fml* • el cirujano incidió en el brazo the
surgeon made an incision in the arm

inclinar [01]

■ **inclinarse a** *vp + prep (tend to)* to be inclined to •
me inclino a pensar que nos ha mentido acerca de sus
verdaderos motivos I'm inclined to think that he has lied to
us about his real motives

■ **inclinarse ante** *vp + prep (as a mark of respect)* to bow •
el embajador se inclinó ante la reina the ambassador bowed
before the queen

■**inclinarse por** *vp + prep (prefer)* to favor •
personalmente me inclino por esta última teoría
personally, I favor this last theory

incomodarse [01]

■ **incomodarse por** *vp + prep* to take offense at • creo
que se incomodó por lo que le dijiste I think he took offense
at what you said to him

incorporarse [01]

■ **incorporarse a** *vp + prep* **1.** to join • rechazó la oferta
de incorporarse al comité he refused the offer to join the
committee **2.** *(work)* to start **3.** *(post)* to take up • ¿cuándo te
incorporas a tu nuevo trabajo? when are you starting your
new job?

incumbir [03]

■ **incumbir a** *v + prep* to rest with • la responsabilidad
incumbe al fabricante the responsibility rests with the
manufacturer

incurrir [03]

■ **incurrir en** *v + prep* **1.** to fall into, to make • no vuelvas
a incurrir en la misma equivocación don't make the same
mistake again **2.** to incur • al casarse en secreto con la
princesa incurrió en la ira del rey by secretly marrying the
princess, he incurred the king's wrath

indignarse [01]

■ **indignarse con** or **por** *vp + prep* to be outraged by
• la población se ha indignado con la nueva subida del
precio de la gasolina people are outraged by the new rise

in gas prices • numerosos son los que se indignan por el maltrato dado a los emigrantes many people are outraged by the ill-treatment of emigrants

inflarse [01]

■ **inflarse de** *vp + prep inf* to stuff oneself with • nos inflamos de langostinos we stuffed ourselves with king prawns

influir [52]

■ **influir en** *v + prep* to have an influence on, to have a bearing on • la alimentación influye en el rendimiento físico e intelectual food has a bearing on physical and mental performance

informarse [01]

■ **informarse de** *vp + prep* to find out about, to look into • la próxima vez infórmate un poco más del tema antes de abrir la boca next time find out a bit more about the subject before opening your mouth

■ **informarse sobre** *vp + prep* to inquire about • nos informamos sobre los riesgos reales we inquired about the actual risks

inhibirse [03]

■ **inhibirse de** *vp + prep* to get out of • esta vez no te vas a inhibir de tus responsabilidades you're not getting out of your responsibilities this time

iniciarse [08]

■ **iniciarse en** *vp + prep* to start learning • he comprado unos videos para iniciarme en la guitarra I've bought some videos to start learning the guitar

injerirse [55]

■ **injerirse en** *vp + prep* to interfere in • la Unión Europea ha decidido no injerirse en el proceso democrático del país independizado the European Union has decided not to interfere in the democratic process of the newly-independent country

inmiscuirse [52]

■ **inmiscuirse en** *vp + prep* to interfere in, to meddle in • ¡no vuelvas a inmiscuirte en mis asuntos! don't meddle in my affairs again!

inscribir [03]

■ **inscribirse en** *vp + prep* **1.** *(list)* to put one's name down on • se ha inscrito en la lista de espera he's put his name down on the waiting list **2.** *(course)* to enroll in • me he inscrito

a un curso de cocina I've enrolled in a cookery course **3.** *(cl* to join, to become a member of • se inscribió en un club golf he joined a golf club

insistir [03]

■ **insistir en** *v + prep* to insist on • no insistas en es punto don't insist on this point

inspirarse [01]

■ **inspirarse en** *vp + prep* to be inspired by • el aut se ha inspirado en una historia real the author was inspir by a true story

integrarse [01]

■ **integrarse en** *vp + prep* to fit in with • le cos bastante integrarse en el equipo he found it quite diffic to fit in with the team

interceder [02]

■ **interceder por** *v + prep* to intercede • nunca poc agradecerle lo bastante haber intercedido por mí en t delicado asunto I'll never be able to thank her enough f having interceded on my behalf in such a delicate matter

interesarse [01]

■ **interesarse en** *vp + prep* to be interested ir me intereso por todo lo que concierne a Egipto y l faraones I'm interested in everything to do with Egypt a the pharaoes

■ **interesarse por** *vp + prep* **1.** to be interested in • interesa por la política he's interested in politics **2.** *(pers health)* to care about • me intereso por tu salud I care abc your health

interferir [27]

■ **interferir en** *v + prep* **1.** *(get in the way of)* to interfe with • no quiero que nada interfiera en mis planes I do want anything interfering with my plans **2.** *(affairs, business)* interfere in, to meddle in • no interfieras en mis asunt don't meddle in my affairs **3.** *(interrupt)* to intervene • dejaba de interferir en el debate he kept intervening the debate

interponerse [69]

■ **interponerse en** *vp + prep* to intervene • Europa quiere interponerse en el conflicto Europe doesn't want intervene in the conflict

■ **interponerse entre** *vp + prep* to come between • n dejaré a nadie interponerse entre nosotros I won't alle anyone to come between us

intervenir [73]

intervenir en *v* + *prep* to take part in • preferì no ntervenir en el debate I preferred not to take part in the debate

intimar [01]

intimar con *v* + *prep* to be close to • nunca intimé con él, pero siempre le tuve un real afecto I was never really close to him but I was always very fond of him

involucrarse [01]

involucrarse en *vp* + *prep* to become involved in • te consejo que no te involucres en ese tipo de asuntos my advice is not to become involved in that sort of thing

ir [77]

ir a *v* + *prep (followed by an infinitive, expressing the immediate future)* • voy a decirselo a mi padre I'm going to tell my father • va a llover it's going to rain

ir con *v* + *prep* **1.** *(dressed in)* to wear • hay que ir con corbata you have to wear a tie **2.** *(match)* to go with • el color del sofá no va con las cortinas the color of the sofa doesn't go with the curtains **3.** *(be intended for)* to be aimed at • eso no va contigo that wasn't aimed at you

ir de *v* + *prep* **1.** *(deal with)* to be about • ¿de qué va la pelicula? what's the film about? **2.** *(be dressed in)* to wear • siempre va de azul he always wears blue **3.** *fig (pretend to be)* • va de listo/intelectual he thinks he's clever/intellectual • pero ¿tú de qué vas? who do you think you are?

ir en *v* + *prep (be dressed in)* to be wearing • iba en camiseta he was wearing a shirt

ir por *v* + *prep* **1.** *(collect)* to pick up • si quieres yo iré por el niño I'll go and pick the boy up if you like **2.** *(reach)* • voy por la mitad del libro I'm halfway through the book **3.** *(be intended for)* to be aimed at • lo que he dicho no va por nadie en particular what I said isn't aimed at anyone in particular • no mires al techo que esto va por ti don't look up at the ceiling, this applies to you **4.** *(serve as recompense for)* • eso va por lo que tú me hiciste that's for what you did for me

J, L

jactarse [01]

jactarse de *vp* + *prep* to boast about, to boast that • se jactaba de ser el único que se había atrevido a saltar he boasted about being the only one who had dared jump

juntarse [01]

juntarse con *vp* + *prep* **1.** to get together with • se juntaron con unos amigos para ir a tomar unas copas they got together with some friends to go for a drink **2.** to be seeing • se ha juntado con una chica que conoció durante las vacaciones he's seeing a girl who he met on vacation

lamentarse [01]

lamentarse de OR **por** *vp* + *prep* to complain about • se lamenta continuamente de su suerte he's constantly complaining about his luck

lanzarse [16]

lanzarse a *vp* + *prep* to set out to, to embark upon • la empresa piensa lanzarse a la conquista del mercado americano the company plans to set out to conquer the American market

lanzarse sobre *vp* + *prep* to pounce on • dos individuos se lanzaron sobre mi two individuals pounced on me

liarse [07]

liarse a *vp* + *prep* to get tied up • se liaron a clasificar las fotos they got tied up sorting out the photos • se liaron a puñetazos they started punching each other

liarse con *vp* + *prep inf* to become involved with • se ha liado con un compañero de trabajo she's become involved with a work colleague

liarse en *vp* + *prep* to get involved in • nos liamos en discusiones absurdas we get involved in these ridiculous arguments

liberar [01]

liberarse de *vp* + *prep* to free oneself from • le fue difícil liberarse de la influencia de su familia she found it hard to free herself from her family's influence

librarse [01]

librarse de *vp* + *prep* **1.** to escape • gracias a su abogado se libró de la cárcel thanks to his attorney, he escaped a jail sentence • ¡de buena te libraste! you had a lucky escape! **2.** to get out of • nos libramos de ir a la reunión we got out of going to the meeting **3.** to get rid of • no conseguí librarme de aquel pesado en toda la noche I didn't manage to get rid of that pain all night

licenciarse [08]

licenciarse en *vp* + *prep* (SCH) to get a degree • se licenció en psicología en 1997 she got a degree in psychology in 1997

lidiar [08]

lidiar con *v* + *prep* to do battle with • el torero saltó a la arena dispuesto a lidiar con el imponente toro the bullfighter jumped into the ring ready to do battle with the imposing bull

ligar [19]

■ **ligar con** *v + prep inf* to pick up • en la discoteca ligamos con unas chicas muy majas at the disco, we picked up these really nice girls

limitarse [01]

■ **limitarse a** *vp + prep* • el portavoz del gobierno se limitó a leer una declaración the government spokesperson just read out a statement

llegar [19]

■ **llegar a** *v + prep* 1. to reach • no llegó a la cima he didn't reach the summit • no llego al estante de arriba I can't reach the top shelf 2. • llegar a (ser) algo to become : llegarás a presidente you'll be president one day : llegó a ser muy popular he became very popular 3. • llegar a hacer algo to go as far as : no llegué a confesárselo I never got as far as confessing it : no llegamos a conocernos we never got to meet each other

■ **llegar hasta** *v + prep* to come down/up to • el abrigo le llega hasta la rodilla her coat comes down to her knees

■ **llegarse a** *vp + prep* to go over to • paseando nos llegamos al castillo we walked over to the castle

llenarse [01]

■ **llenarse de** *vp + prep* 1. to get covered in • se le llenó la cara de granos his face got covered in pimples 2. to fill with • las calles se llenaron de gente the streets filled with people

lucirse [47]

■ **lucirse en** *vp + prep* • la célebre actriz se lució en la fiesta the famous actress paraded herself at the party • el equipo local se lució en el último encuentro the local team excelled

M

mantenerse [72]

■ **mantenerse con** OR **de** *vp + prep* to live off • los miembros de la tribu se mantienen de la caza y la pesca the tribe members live off hunting and fishing

mentalizar [16]

■ **mentalizar de** *vp + prep* to prepare oneself mentally • empieza a mentalizarte de que nada volverá a ser igual

start mentally preparing yourself for the fact that nothing will be the same again

meterse [02]

■ **meterse a** *vp + prep* 1. to become • se metió a periodista he became a journalist • su hijo se ha metido a cura her son has become a priest 2. to start • se metió a invertir en bolsa she started investing on the Stock Exchange

■ **meterse con** *vp + prep inf* 1. to pick on • los otros niños se meten con él the other boys pick on him 2. (annoy) to pick a fight • no te metas conmigo, que no estoy de humor leave me alone, I'm not in the mood

■ **meterse en** *vp + prep inf* to get involved in • no te metas en los asuntos de los demás don't poke your nose in other people's business • siempre te estás metiendo en problemas you're always getting into trouble

mezclar [01]

■ **mezclarse con** *vp + prep* 1. (join) to mingle with • se mezcló con un grupo de invitados y se coló en la fiesta he mingled with a group of guests and slipped into the party 2. (combine) to mix, to blend • un ritmo novedoso en el que el tango se mezcla perfectamente con el jazz a novel rhythm in which the tango blends perfectly with jazz

■ **mezclarse en** *vp + prep* to get involved in • no te mezcles en lo que no te importa don't get involved in things that don't concern you

mirar [01]

■ **mirar a** *v + prep* 1. to overlook • tiene un precioso apartamento con una gran terraza que mira al mar she has a beautiful apartment with a large roof terrace overlooking the sea 2. to lead out to • la puerta de la cocina da al jardín the kitchen door leads out into the garden

■ **mirar por** *v + prep* to think of • mira sólo por sus intereses he only thinks of his own interests

molestarse [01]

■ **molestarse en** *vp + prep* to bother • ni se molestó en mirar quién entraba she didn't even bother to see who was coming in

■ **molestarse por** *vp + prep* to worry about • no te molestes por mì don't worry about me

montar [01]

■ **montar a** *v + prep* (horse) to ride • montaba a caballo como una auténtica amazona she rode a horse like a true horsewoman

montar en *v + prep (bike)* to ride • a los tres años ya bía montar en bicicleta he could already ride a bike at ree (years old)

orirse [57]

morirse de *vp + prep* to die of • se murió de un infarto died of a heart attack

morirse por *vp + prep fig* to be dying to • me muero or ir a esa fiesta I'm dying to go to that party

udar [01]

mudar de *v + prep (state)* to change • los camaleones ueden mudar de color chameleons can change color

mudarse de *vp + prep (clothes)* to change • se mudó de pa he changed his clothes

urmurar [01]

murmurar de OR **sobre** *v + prep* to gossip about • importa un comino que murmuren de ella she couldn't re less if people gossip about her

N, O

egarse [24]

negarse a *vp + prep* to refuse • algunos soldados se garon a obedecer las órdenes some soldiers refused to bey orders

utrirse [03]

nutrirse de OR **con** *vp + prep* to feed on • las hembras e los mosquitos se nutren con sangre female mosquitos ed on blood • se nutre sólo de alimentos biológicos he ly eats organic food

bcecarse [13]

obcecarse con OR **por** *vp + prep* to be blinded by no te dejes obcecar por la cólera don't let yourself be inded by rage

obcecarse en *vp + prep* to persist in • se obcecaron seguir un camino equivocado they persisted in going wn the wrong path

bedecer [45]

obedecer a *v + prep* to be due to • un comportamiento ue obedece a un instinto natural de defensa behavior hich is due to a natural instinct to defend yourself

bligar [19]

obligarse a *vp + prep* **1.**to force oneself to • se obligó

a levantarse antes de que amaneciera he forced himself to get up before dawn **2.** to undertake to • me he obligado a escribirle y pienso hacerlo I've undertaken to write to him and I plan on doing so

obsesionarse [08]

■ **obsesionarse con** *vp + prep* to become obsessed with • no hay que obsesionarse con los resultados you shouldn't get obsessed with results

obstinarse [01]

■ **obstinarse en** *vp + prep* to insist on • se obstinaba en su mutismo he was determined to remain silent • obstinarse en hacer algo to insist on doing something : el acusado se obstina en proclamar su inocencia the accused insists on proclaiming his innocence

ocuparse [01]

■ **ocuparse de** *vp + prep* to deal with • ocúpate de tus cosas you deal with your own things • ¡ocúpate de lo tuyo! mind your own business!

oficiar [08]

■ **oficiar de** *v + prep* to officiate as • me pidieron que oficiara de moderador en el debate I was asked to officiate as mediator in the debate

ofrecerse [45]

■ **ofrecerse a** OR **para** *vp + prep* to offer to • se ofreció a ayudarme she offered to help me

ofuscarse [13]

■ **ofuscarse con** *vp + prep* to become obssessed with • el tirano se ofuscó con el poder the tyrant became obssessed with power

oler [37]

■ **oler a** *v + prep* to smell of • las sábanas huelen a lavanda the sheets smell of lavender • la habitación huele a tabaco the room smells of smoke

olvidarse [01]

■ **olvidarse de** *vp + prep* to forget • se olvidó de cerrar la puerta she forgot to close the door • me olvidé de que el lunes no tenías clase I forgot you didn't have school on Mondays

oponerse [69]

■ **oponerse a** *vp + prep* to oppose • nadie se opuso a la propuesta noboby opposed the proposal

optar [01]

■ **optar a** *v* + *prep* to apply for • es la primera vez que opto a una beca it's the first time I've applied for a scholarship

■ **optar por** *v* + *prep* to choose to • optaron por no decir nada they chose to say nothing

P

padecer [45]

■ **padecer de** *v* + *prep* to suffer from • en primavera padezco de fiebre del heno I suffer from hayfever in spring

parapetarse [01]

■ **parapetarse tras** *vp* + *prep* to take refuge in • justificaba su silencio parapetándose tras el secreto profesional she took refuge in professional secrecy as a justification of her silence

parar [01]

■ **parar de** *v* + *prep* to stop • no para de llover it won't stop raining

participar [01]

■ **participar de** *v* + *prep* to share • participo de tus ideas I share your ideas

■ **participar en** *v* + *prep* 1. to take part in, to participate in *fml* • numerosos científicos han participado en el proyecto many scientists have participated in the project • miles de personas participaron en la maratón thousands of people took part in the marathon 2. *(benefit from)* to have a share in • los empleados participan en los beneficios de la empresa the employees have a share in the company's profits

partir [03]

■ **partir de** *v* + *prep* to start from, to take as a starting point • si partimos de los resultados arrojados por las encuestas... if we take the results of the surveys as a starting point...

pasar [01]

■ **pasar a** *v* + *prep* *(change subject, activity)* to move on • pasemos a otra cosa let's move on to something else

■ **pasar de** *v* + *prep* 1. to be over, to be more than • pasan de veinte there's over twenty • no pasa de los cuarenta he can't be more than forty 2. *inf (not be interested in)* • paso de ir al cine I can't be bothered with the cinema

■ **pasar por** *v* + *prep* 1. *(be considered)* • pasa por tonto pe[ro] es muy listo he might pretend to be stupid but he's actual[ly] very clever 2. *(experience)* to go through • está pasando por u[n] momento difícil she's going through a difficult patch

■ **pasar sin** *v* + *prep* to go without, to manage witho[ut] • habrá que pasar sin carne we'll have to go without meat [•] no puedo pasar sin hablar I can't manage without talking

■ **pasarse a** *vp* + *prep* to go over to • algunos se pasar[on] al enemigo some went over to the enemy

■ **pasarse de** *vp* + *prep* *(go too far)* • a veces te pasas [de] bueno sometimes you're too kind for your own good • ¡n[o] te pases de listo! don't try and be too clever!

pavonearse [01]

■ **pavonearse de** *vp* + *prep* to brag about • francament[e] no sé de que te pavoneas quite frankly, I don't know wha[t] you're bragging about

pecar [13]

■ **pecar de** *v* + *prep* to be • pecó de prudente she wa[s] a little over-cautious

pensar [22]

■ **pensar en** *v* + *prep* *(person)* to think about • pensab[a] en su amada día y noche he thought about his loved on[e] day and night

■ **pensar sobre** *v* + *prep* *(consider)* to think about • piens[a] un poco sobre lo que te acabo de decir have a little thin[k] about what I've just said

percatarse [01]

■ **percatarse de** *vp* + *prep* to notice • no me percaté d[e] ningún cambio I didn't even notice any change

perdurar [01]

■ **perdurar en** *v* + *prep* to still exist • esta superstició[n] perdura en las mentalidades this superstition still exists [in] people's minds

perseverar [01]

■ **perseverar en** *v* + *prep* to persist with • perseveró e[n] su error he persisted with his mistake

persistir [03]

■ **persistir en** *v* + *prep* to persist in • persistía en s[u] actitud he persists in his attitude • persiste en no quere[r] decir nada she persists in refusing to say anything

persuadirse [03]

■ **persuadirse de** *vp + prep* to be persuaded of • acabó persuadiéndose de la gravedad del tema in the end, he was persuaded of the seriousness of the matter

pertenecer [45]

■ **pertenecer a** *v + prep* **1.** *(be property of)* to belong to • a quién pertenece este paraguas? who does this umbrella belong to? **2.** *(club, group)* to belong to, to be a member of • el candidato no pertenece a ningún grupo político the candidate doesn't belong to any political group • pertenece a una coral she's a member of a choir

pirrarse [01]

■ **pirrarse por** *vp + prep inf* **1.** *(thing)* to be crazy about • me pirro por los sudoku I'm crazy about sudoku **2.** *(person)* to have a crush on • se pirró por un compañero de trabajo he had a real crush on someone at work

pitorrearse [01]

■ **pitorrearse de** *vp + prep* to make fun of • no soporto que se pitorreen de mí I can't stand people making fun of me

poder [71]

■ **poder con** *v + prep* **1.** to handle, to beat • nadie podrá conmigo no one will be able to beat me **2.** to manage, to cope with • ella sola no podrá con la mudanza she won't be able to manage the move on her own **3.** *inf (subject, task)* to get to grips with **4.** *(person)* to stand • de pequeño no podía con las matemáticas I couldn't get to grips with math when I was young • no puedo con su novio I can't stand her boyfriend

polarizarse [16]

■ **polarizarse en** *vp + prep* to become polarized into • las opiniones se han polarizado en dos posiciones extremas opinions have become polarized into two extremes

polemizar [16]

■ **polemizar sobre** *v + prep* to argue about • no pienso polemizar más en este asunto I have no intention of arguing about this matter anymore

ponerse [69]

■ **ponerse a** *vp + prep* to start • se puso a llorar she started crying

porfiar [07]

■ **porfiar en** *v + prep* to persist in • porfió en no querer disculparse he obstinately refused to apologize • porfiaron en el error they persisted with their mistake

preguntar [01]

■ **preguntar por** *v + prep* **1.** *(look for)* to ask for • ¿alguien ha preguntando por mí? did anyone ask for me? **2.** *(be interested in)* to ask about • Isabel me ha preguntado por ti Isabel asked me how you were

prendarse [01]

■ **prendarse de** *vp + prep* to fall for • la primera vez que la vio se prendó de ella he fell for her the first time he set eyes on her

preocuparse [01]

■ **preocuparse de** *vp + prep* **1.** to worry about • no te preocupes de la presentación, de eso ya me encargo yo don't worry about the presentation, I'll take care of that • no me preocupo del qué dirán I don't worry about what people might say **2.** to make sure • preocúpate de que nadie entre make sure no one comes in

■ **preocuparse por** *vp + prep* to worry about, to be concerned about • me preocupo por su salud I'm concerned about his health • no te preocupes por nada don't worry about anything

prepararse [01]

■ **prepararse a** or **para** *vp + prep* **1.** *(with noun)* to get ready for, to prepare for **2.** *(with verb)* to get ready to, to prepare to • la ciudad se prepara para acoger a miles de visitantes the city is preparing to receive thousands of visitors

prescindir [03]

■ **prescindir de** *v + prep* **1.** to do without • vivo en el campo y no puedo prescindir del coche I live in the country and I can't do without a car **2.** to leave aside • prescindiendo de un par de detalles, el resto me parece perfecto aside from a couple of details, the rest looks great

prestarse [01]

■ **prestarse a** *vp + prep* **1.** *(volunteer)* to offer to • se prestó a ayudarme she offered to help me **2.** *(to be likely to)* to be open to • esto se presta a confusión this is open to misinterpretation

presumir [03]

■ **presumir de** *v + prep (show off)* • presume de tener un descapotable he loves letting people know he has a convertible • presume de listo he thinks he's clever

prevalecer [45]

■ **prevalecer sobre** *v + prep* to prevail over • soñaba con una sociedad en que la justicia prevaleciera sobre los intereses económicos he dreamt of a society in which justice prevailed over financial concerns

primar [01]
■ **primar sobre** *v* + *prep* to take precedence over • para mi la calidad prima sobre la cantidad for me, quality takes precedence over quantity

privar [01]
■ **privarse de** *vp* + *prep* to deprive oneself of • durante las últimas vacaciones no nos privamos de nada on our last vacation we didn't deprive ourselves of anything

probar [28]
■ **probar a** *v* + *prep* to try • prueba a hablar con él try talking to him

proceder [45]
■ **proceder a** *v* + *prep* to begin, to proceed to *fml* • procedieron a contar los votos they began counting the votes

■ **proceder de** *v* + *prep* **1.** *(have as its origin)* to come from • la energia de las estrellas procede de la fusión termonuclear the energy of the stars comes from thermonuclear fusion **2.** *(be natives of)* to be from • sus abuelos procedían de Galicia her grandparents were from Galicia **3.** *(be made in)* to come from • una gran parte de productos manufacturados procede del Sureste Asiático many manufactured products come from South-East Asia

prodigarse [19]
■ **prodigarse en** *vp* + *prep* to be lavish with • la critica se prodigó en elogios the critics were lavish with their praise • no suele prodigarse en las explicaciones he's not usually very forthcoming with explanations

profundizar [16]
■ **profundizar en** *v* + *prep* to go into in depth • habria que profundizar en algunos aspectos de la cuestión we should go into some aspects of the issue in depth

pronunciarse [08]
■ **pronunciarse sobre** *vp* + *prep* to comment on • prefiero no pronunciarme sobre tan delicado tema I'd rather not comment on such a delicate matter

propasarse [01]
■ **propasarse con** *vp* + *prep* **1.** to overdo it with • no hay que propasarse con el alcohol you shouldn't overdo it with drink **2.** to make a pass at • intentó propasarse con ella he tried to make a pass at her

prorrumpir [03]
■ **prorrumpir en** *v* + *prep* to burst into • prorrump en sollozos she broke into sobs • la sala prorrumpió aplausos the theater burst into applause

protestar [01]
■ **protestar contra** or **por** *v* + *prep* to protest abo • los consumidores protestan por la subida de los preci consumers are protesting about the price rises

proveerse [12]
■ **proveerse de** *vp* + *prep* **1.** to equip oneself w • se han provisto de linternas para explorar la cue they've equipped themselves with lanterns to explore t caves **2.** to obtain • varios municipios tienen dificultad para proveerse de agua potable several municipiti experience difficulty in obtaining drinking water

provenir [73]
■ **provenir de** *v* + *prep* **1.** *(in space)* to come from • es tradición proviene de Estados Unidos this tradition com from the United States **2.** *(in time)* to date from • much nombres de calle provienen de la Edad Media many stre names date from the Middle Ages

Q, R

quedar [01]
■ **quedar con** *v* + *prep* to arrange to meet • he quedac con Luisa a las 10 delante del teatro I've arranged to me Luisa at 10 outside the theater

■ **quedar en** *v* + *prep* **1.** • hemos quedado en el cii we've arranged to meet at the cinema **2.** *(decide)* • habiamo quedado en vernos a las 7 we'd agreed to meet at 7 • ¿ qué quedamos? so, what shall we do then?

■ **quedar por** *v* + *prep* *(remain)* • nos quedan todav muchos lugares por visitar we still have a lot of places visit

■ **quedarse con** *vp* + *prep* **1.** *(retain)* to keep • quédes con el cambio keep the change **2.** *(choose)* to keep • ¿cc cuál te quedaste? which one did you decide to keep? **3.** *(mock)* to make fun of • ¡te estás quedando conmigo! are yo making fun of me?

quejarse [01]
■ **quejarse por** or **de** *vp* + *prep* to complain about varios clientes se quejaron del servicio several custome complained about the service

dicar [13]

■ **adicar en** *v* + *prep (problem, difficulty)* to lie in • el rdadero problema radica en la falta de comunicación the l problem lies in the lack of communication

mificarse [13]

■ **amificarse en** *vp* + *prep* to branch out into • movimiento artístico se ramificó en dos escuelas e artistic movement branched out into two schools of ught

tificarse [13]

■ **atificarse en** *vp* + *prep* to reaffirm • el testigo se tificó en la primera versión de los hechos the witness affirmed his initial version of the facts

yar [01]

■ **rayar en** *v* + *prep* to border on • raya en lo ridículo it's rdering on the ridiculous

afirmarse [01]

■ **reafirmarse en** *vp* + *prep* to reaffirm • los peritos se tificaron en su convencimiento the experts reaffirmed eir conviction

bajarse [01]

■ **rebajarse a** *vp* + *prep* to lower oneself to • no pienso bajarme a pedirle perdón I've no intention of lowering yself to apologize to him

bosar [01]

■ **rebosar de** *v* + *prep* to brim with, to burst with • los ños rebosan de energía the children are bursting with ergy

caer [49]

■ **recaer en** *v* + *prep* to relapse into • lo más difícil es itar recaer en la droga the most difficult thing is to avoid apsing into taking drugs

■ **recaer sobre** *v* + *prep* to fall on • las sospechas cayeron inmediatamente sobre un vecino de la víctima spicion immediately fell on one of the victim's neighbors

celar [01]

■ **recelar de** *v* + *prep* to be suspicious of • recelo de los pertos I'm suspicious of experts

cobrarse [01]

■ **recobrarse de** *vp* + *prep* to recover from, to get over todavía no me he recobrado del susto I haven't got over

the shock yet • no acaba de recobrarse de la muerte de su esposa he can't quite get over his wife's death

reconcomerse [02]

■ **reconcomerse de** *vp* + *prep* to be consumed by • se reconcomía de celos he was consumed by jealousy

recuperarse [01]

■ **recuperarse de** *vp* + *prep* to recover from • se está recuperando de la intervención quirúrgica she's recovering from her operation

recurrir [03]

■ **recurrir a** *v* + *prep* to resort to • la actriz afirmó no haber recurrido a la cirugía estética the actress confirmed that she hadn't resorted to cosmetic surgery

reducirse [47]

■ **reducirse a** *vp* + *prep* to come down to • la película se reduce a una serie de escenas yuxtapuestas the film comes down to a series of juxtaposed scenes

redundar [01]

■ **redundar en** *v* + *prep* • esto redunda en beneficio de todos this will benefit everyone

referirse [55]

■ **referirse a** *vp* + *prep* to refer to • ¿a qué te refieres? what do you mean? • en lo que se refiere a los datos personales. no se comunicarán a terceros as far as personal details are concerned, they will not be divulged to third parties

refugiarse [08]

■ **refugiarse de** *vp* + *prep* 1. *(from problems, work)* to take refuge from 2. *(from rain, storm)* to shelter from • se refugiaron de la lluvia en una cueva they sheltered from the rain in a cave

regirse [40]

■ **regirse por** *vp* + *prep* to be governed by • me rijo por mi instinto I follow my instinct

regocijarse [01]

■ **regocijarse con** OR **de** *vp* + *prep* to delight in • me regocijo de saber que eres feliz I'm delighted to know you're happy

reincorporarse [01]

■ **reincorporarse a** *vp* + *prep* 1. to return • miles de alumnos se reincorporaron a sus actividades escolares thousands of students have returned to school **2.** to rejoin • se negaban a reincorporarse al ejército they refused to rejoin the army

reintegrarse [01]

■ **reintegrarse a** *vp + prep* **1.** to return • le propusieron reintegrarse al cargo they suggested he returned to his post **2.** to reintegrate • tiene dificultades para reintegrarse a la sociedad it's difficult for him to reintegrate into society

reír [42]

■ **reír** or **reírse de** *v + prep* **1.** *(have fun)* to laugh at • se puede reír de todo pero no con cualquiera you can laugh at anything but not with just anyone **2.** *(mock)* to laugh at • todos se reían de él everyone laughed at him

relacionarse [08]

■ **relacionarse con** *vp + prep* to mix with • no me relaciono con ese tipo de gente I don't mix with those sort of people

remitirse [03]

■ **remitirse a** *vp + prep* to refer to • me remito a los hechos I refer to the facts

remontarse [01]

■ **remontarse a** *vp + prep fig* to go back to, to date from • una tradición que se remonta al siglo II a tradition that goes back to the second Century

rendirse [39]

■ **rendirse a** or **ante** *vp + prep* to surrender to, to accept • acabó rindiéndose ante la evidencia in the end she had to accept the evidence

renegar [24]

■ **renegar de** *v + prep* **1.** *(principles)* to renounce **2.** *(family, roots)* to disown, to turn one's back on • no reniego de mis humildes orígenes campesinos I would never turn my back on my humble peasant background

renunciar [08]

■ **renunciar a** *v + prep* **1.** *(abandon)* to renounce • las bandas armadas aceptaron renunciar a la violencia the armed gangs agreed to renounce violence **2.** *(refuse)* to decline • el presidente saliente renunció a presentarse de nuevo a las elecciones the outgoing president declined to stand for re-election

reparar [01]

■ **reparar en** *v + prep* to notice • reparé en este deta mucho más tarde I only noticed that detail later on • repararon en gastos they spared no expense

repercutir [03]

■ **repercutir en** *v + prep* to have an impact on, to ha repercussions on • la subida del petróleo repercute en precio de venta the increase in oil prices has repercussio on the sale price

reponerse [69]

■ **reponerse de** *vp + prep* to recover from • tardó reponerse de aquella enorme decepción it took her a wh to recover from that huge disappointment

resarcirse [15]

■ **resarcirse de** *vp + prep* to make up for • imposib resarcirse de tal pérdida you couldn't begin to make for such a loss

resentirse [55]

■ **resentirse de** *vp + prep* to suffer from • el jugad se resiente todavía del tobillo the player is still sufferir from his ankle injury

resguardarse [01]

■ **resguardarse de** *vp + prep* to protect oneself fro • llevaba un grueso abrigo y guantes para resguardar del frío she was wearing a thick coat and gloves to prote herself from the cold

residir [03]

■ **residir en** *v + prep* **1.** to live in • reside en Chile he liv in Chile • reside en la calle Arenal, número 1 she lives number 1, Arenal Street **2.** *(problem, difficulty)* to lie in • la clav de su éxito reside en su facilidad de manejo the key to success lies in that it's easy to use

resignarse [01]

■ **resignarse a** *vp + prep* to resign oneself to • no m resigno a la soledad I can't resign myself to being alone

resistir [03]

■ **resistir a** *v + prep* to resist • no resistí a la tentación couldn't resist the temptation

■ **resistirse a** *vp + prep* to be reluctant to • me resisto creerlo I find it hard to believe

resolverse [35]

■ **resolverse a** *vp + prep* to decide to, to resolve to *fml* • después de pensarlo mucho finalmente se resolvió a llamarla after a lot of thought, he finally decided to call her

respaldarse [01]

■ **respaldarse en** *vp + prep* 1. to sit back in • se respaldó en la butaca he sat back in the armchair 2. *fig* to lean on • a tu edad no puedes continuar respaldándote en tu familia you can't expect your family to keep supporting you at your age

responder [02]

■ **responder a** *v + prep* 1. *(question, need)* to answer • el candidato respondió a todas las preguntas the candidate answered all the questions • esta ley responde a una necesidad this law meets a need 2. *(treatment)* to respond to • el paciente no responde a los antibióticos the patient isn't responding to antibiotics

■ **responder de** *v + prep* to take responsibility for, to be responsible for • ¿quién va a responder de las consecuencias? who is going to be responsible for the consequences?

■ **responder por** *v + prep* to vouch for • yo no respondo por él I'm not going to vouch for him

responsabilizarse [16]

■ **responsabilizarse de** *vp + prep* to take responsibility for • debes responsabilizarte de tus actos you should take responsibility for your actions

resumirse [03]

■ **resumirse en** *vp + prep* to amount to • mi patrimonio se resume en mi casa y mi coche my worldly possessions amount to my house and my car

retorcerse [45]

■ **retorcerse de** *vp + prep* to writhe • se retorcía de dolor she was writhing in pain

retractarse [01]

■ **retractarse de** *vp + prep* to withdraw • el acusado se retractó de sus declaraciones anteriores the accused withdrew his earlier statement

retroceder [45]

■ **retroceder ante** *v + prep* to back down • no retrocede ante nada he never backs down on anything

reventar [22]

■ **reventar por** *v + prep inf* to be bursting to, to be dying to • reventaba por anunciarle la noticia she was dying to tell him the news

■ **reventarse a** *vp + prep (make effort)* • me reviento a trabajar I work my butt off

revolver [35]

■ **revolver en** *v + prep* to rummage around in • ¿quién ha estado revolviendo en mis cosas? who's been rummaging around in my things?

rivalizar [16]

■ **rivalizar con** *v + prep* to compete with • nuestros productos no pueden rivalizar con los asiáticos our products cannot compete with Asian ones

■ **rivalizar en** *v + prep* to rival each other in • ambas hermanas rivalizan en simpatia e inteligencia both sisters rival each other in sympathy and intelligence

rodearse [01]

■ **rodearse de** *vp + prep* to surround oneself with • ha sabido rodearse de un fenomenal equipo de colaboradores he's been able to surround himself with an incredible team of collaborators

romper [02]

■ **romper a** *v + prep (start)* to burst into • rompió a llorar he burst into tears

■ **romper con** *v + prep (end a relationship)* to split up with • ha roto con su novio she's split up with her boyfriend

rozarse [16]

■ **rozarse con** *vp + prep fig* to mix with • yo no me rozo con ese tipo de individuos I don't mix with those sort of people

S

saber [67]

■ **saber a** *v + prep* to taste of • el vino sabe a fresas the wine tastes of strawberries • el asado sabe a quemado the roast tastes burnt • eso me supo a disculpa that sounded like an excuse to me

■ **saber de** *v + prep* 1. to know about • sabe mucho de informática he knows a lot about computers 2. to hear from

• ¿qué sabes de Carmen? hace mucho que no la veo have you heard from Carmen? I haven't seen her in ages

sacrificarse [13]

■ **sacrificarse por** *vp* + *prep* to sacrifice oneself for • muchos fueron los que se sacrificaron por la patria there were many who sacrificed themselves for their country

saldarse [01]

■ **saldarse con** *vp* + *prep* to end in • la experiencia se saldó con un rotundo fracaso the experience ended in total failure

salir [65]

■ **salir a** *v* + *prep* to take after • este niño ha salido a su padre this boy takes after his father

■ **salir a** OR **por** *v* + *prep (cost)* • la cena nos salió por 25 euros cada uno the meal worked out at 25 euros each • nos va salir muy caro it's going to work out too expensive

■ **salir con** *v* + *prep (have a relationship with)* to date • sale con su vecina he's dating a neighbor

■ **salir de** *v* + *prep* to get out of • el gobierno no sabe qué hacer para salir de la situación the government doesn't know what to do to get out of the situation

■ **salirse de** *vp* + *prep* **1.** *(leave)* to come off • se salió de la autopista he came off the freeway **2.** *(depart)* to leave • no estaba de acuerdo con el nuevo presidente y se salió del partido he didn't agree with the new president and he left the party **3.** *(derail)* to come off • el tren se salió de la vía the train came off the rails **4.** *(by accident)* to come off • dio un volantazo para no salirse de la carretera he swerved so as not to come off the road **5.** *(ramble)* to go off • no te salgas del tema keep to the point **6.** *(spill)* • el agua se salió de la bañera the bath water overflowed

salvarse [01]

■ **salvarse de** *vp* + *prep* to escape • pocos libros se salvaron de la quema few books escaped the fire

seguir [41]

■ **seguir a** *v* + *prep* to follow • la primavera sigue al invierno spring follows winter

separarse [01]

■ **separarse de** *vp* + *prep* **1.** *(couple)* to separate from, to split up with • se acaba de separar de su marido she's just split up with her husband • nunca se separa de su móvil he's never without his mobile **2.** *(move away from)* to split up

from, to leave • por favor, no se separen del grupo please stay with the group

ser [78]

■ **ser de** *v* + *prep* **1.** *(indicating origin)* to be from • yo soy d Buenos Aires I'm from Buenos Aires **2.** *(indicating material)* t be made of • el reloj es de oro the watch is made of gol **3.** *(indicating property)* to belong to • ese libro es de mi herman that book is my brother's, that book belongs to my brothe **4.** *(indicating role)* to be from • él es de la junta municipal he from the local government

■ **ser para** *v* + *prep* **1.** *(indicating use, purpose)* to be for • est trapo es para limpiar los cristales this cloth is for cleanin the windows **2.** *(indicating suitability)* to be for • este libro no e para los niños this book isn't for children

servir [03]

■ **servir de** *v* + *prep* to serve as • es muy útil y ademá sirve de adorno it's very useful and it serves as a ornament

■ **servir para** *v* + *prep* to be useful for • esto no sirv para nada this is no use for anything

■ **servirse de** *vp* + *prep* to take advantage of • tengo l impresión de que se ha servido de ti I've got a feeling he' taken advantage of you

simpatizar [16]

■ **simpatizar con** *v* + *prep* **1.** to take to • enseguida simpaticé con ellos I soon took to them **2.** to be sympatheti to • no simpatizo con sus ideas revolucionarias I'm no sympathetic to their revolutionary ideas

sincerarse [01]

■ **sincerarse con** *vp* + *prep* to be honest with, to talk to si sientes la necesidad de sincerarte con alguien, aquí estoy if you need to talk to anyone, I'm here for you

sintonizar [16]

■ **sintonizar en** *v* + *prep* • sintonizar en algo to tune int something : un autor teatral que ha sabido sintonizar co el público en casi todo a playwright who has been able t tune into the audience on many levels

sobreponerse [69]

■ **sobreponerse a** *vp* + *prep* to get over • no se ha sobrepuesto el fracaso de su último espectáculo he hasn' gotten over the fact that his last show failed

obresalir [65]

obresalir de OR **entre** v + prep to stand out from • un artista que sobresale entre sus contemporáneos he's artist who stands out from his contemporaries

brevivir [03]

obrevivir a v + prep to survive • ha sobrevivido a ios atentados he has survived various attempts on his

ltarse [28]

oltarse a vp + prep to start • a los diez meses el niño se soltó a andar at ten months the boy already started lking

oltarse en [28] vp + prep to gain confidence in • se soltando en inglés she's gaining confidence in speaking glish

meterse [02]

ometerse a vp + prep 1. to submit to • le cuesta meterse a la autoridad she has a problem with authority el conductor no aceptó someterse a la prueba de oholemia the driver refused to take the breathalyzer test o undergo • deberá someterse a una operación a corazón ierto he will have to undergo open heart surgery

nar [28]

sonar a v + prep to sound like • lo que dijo sonaba a rdad what he said sounded like the truth

ñar [28]

soñar con v + prep 1. (while asleep) to dream about desire) to dream of • anoche soñé contigo I dreamt about u last night • sueño con viajar a Australia I dream of ing to Australia

spechar [01]

sospechar de v + prep to suspect • la policia sospecha él the police suspect him

bir [03]

subir a v + prep 1. to go up to • subió al décimo so a pie he walked up to the tenth floor 2. to give up os escaladores españoles han desistido de subir al imanjaro the Spanish climbers gave up trying to climb imanjaro 3. to get on • le da miedo subir a los aviones e's frightened of getting on a plane

subirse a v + prep 1. to climb on • al ver al ratón se subió una silla when she saw the mouse, she climbed on a chair o climb up • el gato se subió al manzano the cat climbed up the apple tree 3. to get in • vamos, súbete al coche come on, get in the car

subscribirse see suscribirse

suceder [45]

■ **suceder a** v + prep to follow • a la guerra sucedieron años terribles the war was followed by some terrible years

sucumbir [03]

■ **sucumbir a** v + prep to succumb to • era dificil no sucumbir a su encanto it was difficult not to succumb to her charms

sufrir [03]

■ **sufrir de** v + prep to suffer from • sufre de asma she suffers from asthma • sufro del corazón I have a heart problem

sujetarse [01]

■ **sujetarse a** OR **de** vp + prep to hold on tight to • sujétate fuerte a la barra hold on tight to the bar

sumarse [01]

■ **sumarse a** vp + prep 1. to add to • una plaga de langostas se ha sumado al problema de la sequia a plague of locusts has added to the drought problem 2. to join • los estudiantes se sumaron a la manifestación the students joined the demonstration

sumergirse [03]

■ **sumergirse en** vp + prep to immerse oneself in • se sumergió en sus cristalinas aguas del lago she immersed herself in the crystal-clear waters of the lake • volvio a sumergirse en sus recuerdos she immersed herself in her memories again

sumirse [03]

■ **sumirse en** vp + prep to become absorbed in • durante unos segundos se sumió en sus pensamientos/ ensoñaciones for a few seconds, she became absorbed in her thoughts/dreams

supeditarse [01]

■ **supeditarse a** vp + prep to abide by • habrá que supeditarse a las normas vigentes we'll have to abide by the regulations currently in force

surtirse [03]

■ **surtirse de** vp + prep to provide oneself with, to get • excavaron un pozo para surtirse de agua they dug a well to get water for themselves

suscribirse, subscribirse [03]
■ **suscribirse a, subscribirse a** *vp* + *prep* **1.** to subscribe to • por favor, introduzca su email para suscribirse a nuestra lista please enter your email address to subscribe to our list **2.** (COMM) to take out • me he suscrito a un seguro de vida I've taken out life insurance

suspirar [01]
■ **suspirar por** *v* + *prep* **1.** to long for, to yearn for *fml* • suspiraba por su vecina he longed for his neighbor **2.** to be dying for • suspiro por un vaso de agua I'm dying for a glass of water

sustraerse [60]
■ **sustraerse a** OR **de** *vp* + *prep* to avoid • esta vez no podrá sustraerse de la justicia he won't be able to avoid justice this time

T

temer [02]
■ **temer por** *v* + *prep* to fear for • teme por sus hijos she fears for her children

tender [26]
■ **tender a** *v* + *prep* **1.** (*fact*) to tend to • la historia tiende a repetirse history tends to repeat itself • tiendo a engordar I have a tendency to put on weight **2.** (*color*) to verge on • el vestido es de un amarillo que tiende a verde the dress is a yellow verging on green, the dress is a yellowy-green

teñirse [39]
■ **teñirse de** *vp* + *prep* to dye one's hair • se tiñe de rubio/moreno she dyes her hair blond/brown

terciar [08]
■ **terciar en** *v* + *prep* to intervene in • decidi terciar en la conversación para dejar clara mi postura I decided to intervene in the conversation to make my position clear

terminar [01]
■ **terminar con** *v* + *prep* to put an end to, to finish off • hemos terminado con este tema we've put an end to this matter
■ **terminar de** *v* + *prep* to end up as • terminó de conserje en un hotel de mala muerte he ended up as a receptionist in a dive of a hotel

■ **terminar en** *v* + *prep* to end up in • la discusi terminó en pelea the argument ended up in a fight
■ **terminar por** *v* + *prep* to end up • terminó p convencerme he ended up convincing me

titularse [01]
■ **titularse en** *vp* + *prep* to get a degree in, to gradua in • en 1999 se tituló en psicologia en la Universidad Zaragoza in 1999, he got a degree in psychology fro Zaragoza University

tirar [01]
■ **tirar a** *v* + *prep* **1.** (*person*) to take after, to look like • tira su abuela he takes after his grandmother **2.** (*color*) • el vestic es azul tirando a verde the dress is greenish blue

tocar [13]
■ **tocar a** *v* + *prep* • tocamos a seis gambas por cabe we get six prawns each

tontear [01]
■ **tontear con** *v* + *prep* to flirt with • tontea con tod los chicos she flirts with all the guys

toparse [01]
■ **toparse con** *vp* + *prep* to bump into, to meet • se top con su ex en una fiesta she bumped into her ex at a part

trabajar [01]
■ **trabajar de** *v* + *prep* to work as • trabaja de camare he works as a waiter

traficar [13]
■ **traficar con** OR **en** *v* + *prep* to traffic in • aqu hombre traficaba con drogas that man used to traffic drugs

transformarse [01]
■ **transformarse en** *vp* + *prep* to convert into • el sof se transforma en cama the sofa converts into a bed

transigir [18]
■ **transigir con** *v* + *prep* to tolerate • lo siento pero n transijo con algunas cosas I'm sorry but there are certai things I will not tolerate
■ **transigir en** *v* + *prep* to give way on, to give in on • n estoy dispuesto a transigir en ese punto I'm not prepare to give in on that point

trascender, transcender [26]

■ **trascender a, transcender a** *v + prep* **1.** *(pass to)* to extend to • el lenguaje de los jóvenes ha trascendido a otros ámbitos the way young people speak has extended to other areas **2.** *(reach)* to spread to • el descontento de los jubilados ha trascendido al resto de los ciudadanos retirees' dissatisfaction has spread to the rest of the population

tratar [01]

■ **tratar de** *v + prep* **1.** *(subject)* to deal with • la película trata de problemas muy actuales the movie deals with very current problems **2.** • tratar de hacer algo to try to do something : trata de explicárselo de nuevo try to explain it to him again

■ **tratarse con** *vp + prep (person)* to have anything to do with • no me trato con individuos de su calaña I don't have anything to do with people of that type

■ **tratarse de** *vp + prep* to be about • ¿de qué se trata? what is it about?

triunfar [01]

■ **triunfar sobre** *v + prep* to triumph over • gracias a la educación se puede triunfar sobre la ignorancia thanks to education, we can overcome ignorance

tropezar [23]

■ **tropezar con** *v + prep* **1.** *(table, door)* to bump into **2.** *(problems, difficulties)* to encounter • tropecé con la mesita bumped into the bedside table • el proyecto tropezó con numerosas dificultades the project encountered many difficulties

■ **tropezarse con** *vp + prep inf (person)* to bump into • me tropecé con él en el pasillo I bumped into him in the corridor

U, V

ufanarse [01]

■ **ufanarse de** *vp + prep* to boast about • no sé de qué te ufanas I don't know what you're boasting about

unirse [03]

■ **unirse a** *vp + prep* to join • ¿queréis uniros a nosotros? would you like to join us?

valer [62]

■ **valer para** *v + prep* to be good for • esto no vale para nada this is no good for anything

■ **valerse de** *vp + prep* to use • se ha valido de sus conocidos para obtener un empleo she used her contacts to get a job

vanagloriarse [08]

■ **vanagloriarse de** *vp + prep* to show off about, to boast about • se vanagloriaba de su boyante situación financiera she showed off about her buoyant financial situation

variar [08]

■ **variar de** *v + prep* **1.** *(shape, appearance)* to change **2.** *(price, temperature)* to vary from • ha variado de color y de forma it's changed color and shape • los síntomas varían de una persona a otra the symptoms vary from one person to another

velar [01]

■ **velar por** *v + prep* to safeguard • vela por los intereses de su empresa he safeguards his company's interests

vengarse [19]

■ **vengarse de** *vp + prep* to take revenge on • prometió vengarse de quienes le habían humillado he promised to take revenge on those who had humilliated him

venir [73]

■ **venir a** *v + prep* to work out at • viene a ser lo mismo it's the same thing in the end • el viaje nos vino a costar unos 1.000 euros the trip worked out at 1,000 euros

■ **venir de** *v + prep* **1.** *(airplane)* to come from • ¿a qué hora llega el avión que viene de Buenos Aires? what time does the plane from Buenos Aires arrive? **2.** *(have as origin)* to come from • esta palabra viene del latín this word comes from Latin

■ **venir con** *v + prep* • no me vengas con historias I don't want to hear your excuses

versar [01]

■ **versar sobre** *v + prep* to deal with, to be on • su último ensayo versa sobre el arte africano his latest essay is on African art

verse [75]

■ **verse con** *vp + prep (meet up with)* to see • me veo a menudo con Tomás I often see Tomás

vestir [39]

■ **vestir de** *v + prep* to wear • siempre viste de azul she always wears blue

■ **vestirse de** *vp* + *prep* **1.** to wear • se vistió de negro para ir al entierro she wore black for the funeral **2.** to dress up as • se vistió de hada she dressed up as a fairy

viciarse [08]

■ **viciarse con** *vp* + *prep* to become addicted to • acabó viciándose con el juego he ended up becoming addicted to gambling

vivir [03]

■ **vivir de** *v* + *prep* to live off • vive de lo que le dan sus padres she lives off what her parents give her

volcarse [13]

■ **volcarse con** OR **en** *vp* + *prep* **1.** *(work, activity)* to throw oneself into **2.** *(children)* to devote oneself to • desde entonces se vuelca en sus hijos/en su trabajo she's devoted herself to her children since then • después de la muerte de su marido, se volcó en su trabajo after her husband's death, she threw herself into her work

volver [35]

■ **volver a** *v* + *prep* **1.** *(do again)* • vuelve a llover it's raining again • volver a leer algo to re-read something **2.** *(return to)* to go back to • volvamos a nuestro tema let's go back to what we were talking about

■ **volverse a** *vp* + *prep (return)* to go back • me vuelvo a casa I'm going back home

■ **volverse contra** OR **en contra de** *vp* + *prep* to turn against • la opinión pública se volvió contra él public opinion turned against him

■ **volverse de** *vp* + *prep* to go back to • hace ya un año que nos volvimos de Madrid al pueblo it's a year already since we left Madrid and went back to the country

votar [01]

■ **votar por** *v* + *prep* to vote for • ¿por quién votaste en las últimas elecciones? who did you vote for in the last elections?

Z

zambullirse [03]

■ **zambullirse en** *vp* + *prep* **1.** to dive in • se zambulló en la piscina she dived into the pool **2.** *fig* to immerse oneself in • una visita que le permitirá zambullirse en una cultura milenaria a visit which will allow you to immerse yourself in a thousand-year-old culture

VERBS WITH AN INDIRECT OBJECT

Verbs like gustar

a mí me gusta'

(A mí)	me gusta	I like
(A ti)	te gusta	you like
(A él, a ella, a usted)	le gusta	he/she likes, you like (formal)
(A nosotros)	nos gusta	we like
(A vosotros)	os gusta	you like
(A ellos, a ellas, a ustedes)	les gusta	they/you (formal) like

abrumar [01]
v ind to overwhelm • el trabajo me abruma I'm overwhelmed by work

aburrir [3]
v ind to bore • me aburren sus temas de conversación I'm bored by his conversation topics

acongojar [01]
v ind to distress • la acongoja la soledad she gets distressed by being alone

alegrar [01]
v ind to make somebody happy • me alegra que hayas aprobado el examen I'm pleased you passed your exam

apenar [01]
v ind to sadden, to make somebody sad • me apena que no seas feliz it saddens me to see you unhappy

apetecer [45]
v ind to feel like • ¿te apetece un café? do you feel like a coffee? • me apetece salir I feel like going out

asombrar [01]
v ind to astonish, to amaze • me asombra tu sangre fría I'm amazed at how calm you are

caer [49]
v ind • me cae bien I like him • me cae mal I don't like her

chiflar [01]
v ind inf to love • me chiflan las patatas fritas I love French fries

compensar [01]
v ind • por lo que me pagan, no me compensa pasar tanto tiempo en ello for what I'm paid, it's not worth spending so much time on it • ver a sus hijos felices le compensaba de tantos sacrificios seeing her children happy was enough reward for all the sacrifices she'd made

complacer [61]
v ind to please • me complace que te guste I'm pleased you like it • me complace conocerla pleased to meet you • me complace verlo I'm pleased to see him

constar [01]
v ind • me consta que ha llegado I'm sure he's arrived

costar [28]
v ind • me cuesta creerlo I find it hard to believe

dañar [01]
v ind to hurt • me dañaron sus palabras I was hurt by what he said

encantar [01]
v ind to love • me encanta tu nuevo peinado I love your new hairstyle • nos encantan las tapas we love tapas • a mi hermana le encanta bailar my sister loves dancing

extrañar [01]
v ind to surprise • me extrañó verte aquí I was surprised to see you here

faltar [01]
v ind to lack • le falta confianza he lacks confidence

fascinar [01]
v ind to love, to be crazy about • me fascinan los coches deportivos I love sports cars

gustar [01]
v ind • me gusta esa chica I like that girl • me gusta el deporte I like sports • a mi hermano le gustan mucho las motos my brother really likes motorbikes • ¿te gusta ir al cine? do you like going to the movies?

ilusionar [01]
v ind • me ilusiona verte I'm really excited about seeing you, I'm really looking forward to see you

importar [01]
v ind to matter • me importas mucho you mean a lot to me, you really matter to me

pesar [01]

v ind • me pesa habérselo dicho I regret having told him

placer [61]

v ind • me place presentarles al nuevo director I am pleased to introduce the new director

preocupar [01]

v ind • no le preocupa lo que piensen los demás she's not bothered about what other people think

sobrar [01]

v ind • ¿te sobra un sello? do you have a spare stamp?

tocar [29]

v ind • le ha tocado la lotería he's won the lottery • le ha tocado sufrir mucho he's been through a lot

Verbs like ocurrírsele algo a uno

(A mi)	se me ocurre	*I think, it occurs to me (formal)*
(A ti)	se te ocurre	*you think, it occurs to you (formal)*
(A él, a ella, a usted)	se le ocurre	*he/she thinks, you think it occurs to him/her/you (formal)*
(A nosotros, a nosotras)	se nos ocurre	*we think, it occurs to us (formal)*
(A vosotros, a vosotras)	se os ocurre	*you think, it occurs to you (formal)*
(A ellos, a ellas, a ustedes)	se les ocurre	*they think, it occurs to them (formal)*

antojarse [01]

vp • antojársele a alguien (hacer) algo to have a feeling th
• se le antojó que alguien quería asesinarlo he had a feelir that someone wanted to kill him

apañarse [01]

vp inf • apañárselas para hacer algo *fig* to manage howeve you can to do something • apáñatelas para que mañana trabajo esté terminado you'll have to manage however yo can to get the work done by tomorrow

dar [63]

vt • darle a alguien por hacer algo to decide to do something to get it into your head to do something • le ha dado pc dejarse la barba he's decided to grow a beard

figurarse [01]

vp • figurársele a alguien algo • se le figuraba que queri engañarla she had a feeling that he was trying to chea on her

hacerse [68]

vp • hacérsele + adj + a alguien • se me hace difícil creerl I find it hard to believe • me voy que se me hace tarde I'r going because it's getting late

ingeniarse [08]

vp • ingeniárselas para hacer algo to manage to d something • siempre se las ingenia para no pagar he alway manages to get away without paying

ocurrirse [03]

vp • ocurrírsele algo a alguien to think of something • n se me ocurre ninguna solución I can't think of a solution se me ocurre una idea I have an idea

olvidarse [01]

vp • olvidársele algo a alguien to forget something • se no olvidó llamarte we forgot to call you • se le olvidó lo qu quería decir she forgot what she wanted to say • se le olvid el paraguas en el taxi she left her umbrella in the taxi

Index

acabar 01
acabarse 01
acabildar 01
acachetar 01
acachetear 01
academizar 16
acaecer 45
acalabrotar 01
acalambrarse 01
acalenturarse 01
acallar 01
acalorarse 01
acamalar 01
acamar 01
acamarse 01
acamellonar 01
acampanar 01
acampanarse 01
acampar 01
acanalar 01
acanallar 01
acanallarse 01
acantonar 01
acantonarse 01
acaparar 01
acapujar 01
acapullarse 01
acaramelar 01
acaramelarse 01
acardenalar 01
acardenalarse 01
acardenillarse 01
acariciar 08
acariciarse 08
acarralar 01
acarrear 01
acarroñarse 01
acartonar 01
acartonarse 01
acatar 01
acatarrar 01

acatarrarse 01
acaudalar 01
acaudillar 01
acceder 02
accidentar 01
accidentarse 01
accionar 01
acechar 01
acecinar 01
acecinarse 01
acedar 01
acedarse 01
aceitar 01
acelerar 01
acelerarse 01
acendrar 01
acenefar 01
acentuar 09
acentuarse 09
acepar 01
acepillar 01
aceptar 01
acercar 13
acercarse 13
acerrojar 01
acertar 22
acetificar 13
acetilar 01
acetrinar 01
achabacanar 01
achabacanarse 01
achacar 13
achaflanar 01
achamparse 01
achancharse 01
achantar 01
achantarse 01
achaparrarse 01
acharar 01
acharolar 01
achatar 01

achatarse 01
achatarrar 01
achicar 13
achicarse 13
achicharrar 01
achicharrarse 01
achicharronarse 01
achicopalarse 01
achiguarse 11
achinar 01
achiquitar 01
achiquitarse 01
achispar 01
achisparse 01
achocar 13
achocharse 01
achoclonarse 01
acholar 01
acholarse 01
achubascarse 13
achuchar 01
achucharse 01
achucharrar 01
achucharrarse 01
achucutar 01
achucuyar 01
achulaparse 01
achularse 01
achunchar 01
achuncharse 01
achurar 01
acibarar 01
acicalar 01
acicalarse 01
acicatear 01
acidificar 13
acidular 01
aciguatarse 01
acitronar 01
aclamar 01
aclarar 01

aclararse **01**
aclimatar **01**
aclimatarse **01**
acobardar **01**
acobardarse **01**
acobijar **01**
acocear **01**
acochambrar **01**
acochinar **01**
acochinarse **01**
acodalar **01**
acodar **01**
acodarse **01**
acoderar **01**
acodillar **01**
acoger **17**
acogollar **01**
acogotar **01**
acojinar **01**
acojonar **01**
acojonarse **01**
acolar **01**
acolchar **01**
acolitar **01**
acollar **01**
acollarar **01**
acollararse **01**
acomedirse **39**
acometer **02**
acomodar **01**
acomodarse **01**
acompañar **01**
acompañarse **01**
acompasar **01**
acomplejar **01**
acomplejarse **01**
acomunarse **01**
aconchabarse **01**
aconchar **01**
aconcharse **01**
acondicionar **01**

acondicionarse **01**
acongojar **01**
acongojarse **01**
aconsejar **01**
aconsejarse **01**
aconsonantar **01**
acontecer **45**
acopar **01**
acoparse **01**
acopiar **08**
acoplar **01**
acoplarse **01**
acoquinar **01**
acoquinarse **01**
acorazar **16**
acorazarse **16**
acorchar **01**
acorcharse **01**
acordar **28**
acordarse **28**
acordelar **01**
acordonar **01**
acornar **28**
acornear **01**
acorralar **01**
acorrer **02**
acortar **01**
acortarse **01**
acosar **01**
acosijar **01**
acostar **28**
acostarse **28**
acostumbrar **01**
acostumbrarse **01**
acotar **01**
acotejar **01**
acoyundar **01**
acoyuntar **01**
acrecentar **22**
acrecentarse **22**
acrecer **45**

acreditar **01**
acreditarse **01**
acribar **01**
acribillar **01**
acriminar **01**
acriollarse **01**
acrisolar **01**
acristalar **01**
acromatizar **16**
activar **01**
activarse **01**
actualizar **16**
actuar **09**
acuadrillar **01**
acuartelar **01**
acuartelarse **01**
acuartillar **01**
acuatizar **16**
acuchillar **01**
acuciar **08**
acuclillarse **01**
acudir **03**
acuilmarse **01**
acuitar **01**
acuitarse **01**
acular **01**
acularse **01**
acumular **01**
acumularse **01**
acunar **01**
acuñar **01**
acurrucarse **13**
acurrullar **01**
acusar **01**
acusarse **01**
adamascar **13**
adaptar **01**
adaptarse **01**
adargar **19**
adecenar **01**
adecentar **01**

adecentarse 01	adormilar 01	afianzar 16
adecuar 10	adormilarse 01	afianzarse 16
adecuarse 10	adornar 01	aficionar 01
adehesar 01	adornarse 01	aficionarse 01
adelantar 01	adosar 01	afiebrarse 01
adelantarse 01	adquirir 38	afilar 01
adelgazar 16	adrizar 16	afilarse 01
adelgazarse 16	adscribir 03	afiliar 08
ademar 01	adsorber 02	afiliarse 08
adentellar 01	aduanar 01	afiligranar 01
aderezar 16	aducir 59	afinar 01
adestrar 22	adujar 01	afinarse 01
adeudar 01	adujarse 01	afincar 13
adeudarse 01	adular 01	afincarse 13
adherir 55	adulterar 01	afirmar 01
adiar 07	adulzar 16	afistularse 01
adicionar 01	adulzorar 01	aflamencarse 13
adiestrar 01	adumbrar 01	aflatarse 01
adiestrarse 01	adunar 01	aflautar 01
adinerarse 01	adundarse 01	afligir 18
adir 03	advenir 73	afligirse 18
adivinar 01	adverar 01	aflojar 01
adivinarse 01	adverbializar 16	aflojarse 01
adjetivar 01	adversar 01	aflorar 01
adjudicar 13	advertir 55	afluir 52
adjudicarse 13	aerificar 13	afofarse 01
adjuntar 01	aerotransportar 01	afollar 28
adminicular 01	afamar 01	afollarse 28
administrar 01	afamarse 01	afondar 01
administrarse 01	afanar 01	afondarse 01
admirar 01	afanarse 01	aforar 28
admitir 03	afarolarse 01	aforrar 01
adobar 01	afear 01	aforrarse 01
adocenar 01	afearse 01	afoscarse 13
adocenarse 01	afeccionarse 01	afrailar 01
adoctrinar 01	afectar 01	afrancesar 01
adoptar 01	afeitar 01	afrancesarse 01
adoquinar 01	afeitarse 01	afrenillar 01
adorar 01	afelpar 01	afrentar 01
adormecer 45	afeminar 01	afrentarse 01
adormecerse 45	aferrar 01	afretar 01

icanizar 16
ontar 01
silar 01
bachar 01
bacharse 01
chaparse 01
char 01
charse 01
lerar 01
muzar 16
ngrenarse 01
rbillar 01
rrar 01
rrarse 01
rrochar 01
rrotar 01
rrotarse 01
sajar 01
ucharse 01
villar 01
zapar 01
zaparse 01
nciar 08
nciarse 08
gantar 01
gantarse 01
ipollar 01
ipollarse 01
izar 16
otar 01
tanar 01
tanarse 01
tar 01
tarse 01
omerar 01
omerarse 01
utinar 01
biar 08
biarse 08
lparse 01
nizar 16

agorar 31
agorgojarse 01
agostar 01
agostarse 01
agotar 01
agotarse 01
agraciar 08
agradar 01
agradecer 45
agramar 01
agramilar 01
agrandar 01
agrandarse 01
agranujarse 01
agravar 01
agravarse 01
agraviar 08
agraviarse 08
agrazar 16
agredir 79
agregar 19
agregarse 19
agremiar 08
agremiarse 08
agriar 07
agriarse 07
agrietar 01
agrietarse 01
agringarse 19
agrisar 01
agrisarse 01
agrumar 01
agrumarse 01
agrupar 01
agruparse 01
aguachar 01
aguacharse 01
aguacharnar 01
aguachinar 01
aguaitar 01
aguantar 01

aguantarse 01
aguar 11
aguarse 11
aguardar 01
aguazar 16
agudizar 16
agudizarse 16
aguerrir 79
aguijar 01
aguijonear 01
aguizgar 19
agujerar 01
agujerarse 01
agujerear 01
agujerearse 01
agusanarse 01
aguzar 16
ahechar 01
ahelear 01
aherrojar 01
aherrumbrar 01
aherrumbrarse 01
ahervorarse 01
ahijar 06
ahilar 06
ahilarse 06
ahincar 06
ahincarse 06
ahitarse 06
ahocinarse 01
ahogar 19
ahogarse 19
ahondar 01
ahorcajarse 01
ahorcar 13
ahorcarse 13
ahormar 01
ahornar 01
ahornarse 01
ahorquillar 01
ahorrar 01

ahorrarse 01
ahuecar 13
ahuecarse 13
ahuesarse 01
ahuevar 01
ahuevarse 01
ahumar 05
ahumarse 05
ahuyentar 01
ahuyentarse 01
airar 04
airarse 04
airear 01
airearse 01
aislar 04
aislarse 04
ajamonarse 01
ajar 01
ajarse 01
ajardinar 01
ajear 01
ajetrearse 01
ajobar 01
ajornalar 01
ajuiciar 08
ajumarse 01
ajuntar 01
ajuntarse 01
ajustar 01
ajustarse 01
ajusticiar 08
alabar 01
alabarse 01
alabear 01
alabearse 01
alacranear 01
alambicar 13
alambrar 01
alamparse 01
alancear 01
alardear 01

alargar 19
alargarse 19
alarmar 01
alarmarse 01
albardar 01
albardear 01
albear 01
albergar 19
albergarse 19
alborear 01
alborotar 01
alborotarse 01
alborozar 16
alborozarse 16
alburear 01
alcahuetear 01
alcalinizar 16
alcalizar 16
alcanforar 01
alcantarillar 01
alcanzar 16
alcanzarse 16
alcoholar 01
alcoholizar 16
alcoholizarse 16
alcorzar 16
aldabear 01
alear 01
alebrarse 01
alebrestarse 01
aleccionar 01
alegar 19
alegorizar 16
alegrar 01
alegrarse 01
alejar 01
alejarse 01
alelar 01
alelarse 01
alentar 22
alentarse 22

alertar 01
aletargar 19
aletargarse 19
aletear 01
alfabetizar 16
alfeñicarse 13
alfilerar 01
alfombrar 01
alforzar 16
algaliar 08
algodonar 01
alhajar 01
alheñar 01
alheñarse 01
aliar 07
aliarse 07
alicatar 01
alicortar 01
alienar 01
alienarse 01
aligerar 01
alijar 01
alijarar 01
alimentar 01
alimentarse 01
alimonarse 01
alindar 01
alinderar 01
alinear 01
alinearse 01
aliñar 01
alisar 01
alisarse 01
alistar 01
alistarse 01
alivianar 01
alivianarse 01
aliviar 08
aliviarse 08
aljofarar 01
aljofifar 01

llanar 01
llanarse 01
llegar 19
lmacenar 01
lmacenarse 01
lmadiarse 08
lmagrar 01
lmarbatar 01
lmenar 01
lmibarar 01
lmidonar 01
lmizclar 01
lmogavarear 01
lmohadillar 01
lmohazar 16
lmonedear 01
lmorzar 33
locar 13
lojar 01
lojarse 01
lomar 01
loquecerse 45
lotar 01
lpargatar 01
lquilar 01
lquitarar 01
lquitranar 01
lterar 01
lterarse 01
lternar 01
lternarse 01
ltivarse 01
lucinar 01
lujar 01
lumbrar 01
lumbrarse 01
luminar 01
lunarse 01
lunizar 16
lustrar 01
lzaprimar 01

alzar 16
alzarse 16
amachetear 01
amacizar 16
amacollar 01
amacollarse 01
amadrigar 19
amadrigarse 19
amadrinar 01
amaestrar 01
amagar 19
amainar 01
amajadar 01
amalayar 01
amalgamar 01
amamantar 01
amancebarse 01
amancillar 01
amanecer 45
amanecerse 45
amanerarse 01
amanojar 01
amansar 01
amansarse 01
amanzanar 01
amañar 01
amar 01
amarse 01
amarar 01
amarchantarse 01
amargar 19
amargarse 19
amarguear 01
amariconar 01
amariconarse 01
amarillear 03
amarillecer 45
amarinar 01
amaromar 01
amarrar 01
amarrarse 01

amarrocar 13
amartelar 01
amartelarse 01
amartillar 01
amasar 01
amasijar 01
amayorazgar 19
ambarar 01
ambicionar 01
ambientar 01
ambientarse 01
amblar 01
amedrentar 01
amedrentarse 01
amelar 01
amelgar 19
amenazar 16
amenguar 11
amenizar 16
americanizar 16
ameritar 01
amerizar 16
ametrallar 01
amigarse 19
amilanar 01
amilanarse 01
amillarar 01
aminorar 01
amistar 01
amistarse 01
amnistiar 07
amoblar 01
amodorrar 01
amodorrarse 01
amogollonarse 01
amohinar 04
amohinarse 04
amojamar 01
amojamarse 01
amojonar 01
amolar 28

amolarse 28
amoldar 01
amoldarse 01
amollar 01
amononar 01
amononarse 01
amonedar 01
amonestar 01
amontonar 01
amontonarse 01
amoratar 01
amoratarse 01
amordazar 16
amorecer 45
amorrar 01
amorrarse 01
amorronar 01
amortajar 01
amortecer 45
amortecerse 45
amortiguar 11
amortiguarse 11
amortizar 16
amoscarse 13
amostazar 16
amostazarse 16
amotinar 01
amotinarse 01
amparar 01
ampararse 01
ampliar 07
amplificar 13
ampollar 01
ampollarse 01
amputar 01
amueblar 01
amuelar 01
amuermar 01
amuermarse 01
amugronar 01
amugronarse 01

amularse 01
amunicionar 01
amurallar 01
amurar 01
amurrarse 01
amusgar 19
amustiar 08
anadear 01
analizar 16
anarquizar 16
anarquizarse 16
anastomosarse 01
anatematizar 16
anatomizar 16
anclar 01
anclarse 01
ancorar 01
andaluzarse 16
andamiar 08
andar 54
andarse 54
anegar 19
anegarse 19
anejar 01
anestesiar 08
anexar 01
anexionar 01
anexionarse 01
anglicanizar 16
angostarse 01
angustiar 08
angustiarse 08
anhelar 01
anidar 01
anillar 01
animalizar 16
animalizarse 16
animar 01
animarse 01
aniñarse 01
aniquilar 01

anochecer 45
anonadar 01
anotar 01
anotarse 01
anquear 01
anquilosar 01
anquilosarse 01
ansiar 07
antagallar 01
antagonizar 16
anteceder 02
antedatar 01
antelar 01
anteponer 69
anteponerse 69
antever 75
anticipar 01
anticiparse 01
anticuar 10
anticuarse 10
antipatizar 16
antojarse 01
antologar 19
anualizar 16
anublar 01
anublarse 01
anudar 01
anudarse 01
anular 01
anularse 01
anunciar 08
anunciarse 08
añadir 03
añejar 01
añejarse 01
añilar 01
añorar 01
aojar 01
aovar 01
apabullar 01
apabullarse 01

aportillar **01**
aposentar **01**
aposentarse **01**
apostar **28**
apostarse **28**
apostatar **01**
apostemar **01**
apostemarse **01**
apostillar **01**
apostillarse **01**
apostolizar **16**
apostrofar **01**
apotrerar **01**
apoyar **01**
apoyarse **01**
apozarse **16**
apreciar **08**
apreciarse **08**
aprehender **02**
apremiar **08**
aprender **02**
aprenderse **02**
apresar **01**
aprestar **01**
aprestarse **01**
apresurar **01**
apresurarse **01**
apretar **22**
apretarse **22**
apretujar **01**
apretujarse **01**
apriscar **13**
apriscarse **13**
aprisionar **01**
aproar **01**
aprobar **28**
aprontar **01**
aprontarse **01**
apropiar **08**
aprovechar **01**
aprovecharse **01**

aprovisionar **01**
aprovisionarse **01**
aproximar **01**
aproximarse **01**
apulgarar **01**
apunarse **01**
apuntalar **01**
apuntar **01**
apuntarse **01**
apuntillar **01**
apuñalar **01**
apuñear **01**
apurar **01**
apurarse **01**
apurruñar **01**
aquejar **01**
aquerenciarse **08**
aquietar **01**
aquietarse **01**
aquilatar **01**
arabizar **16**
arabizarse **16**
arañar **01**
arañarse **01**
arar **01**
arbitrar **01**
arbolar **01**
arbolarse **01**
arborecer **45**
arborizar **16**
arcaizar **16**
archivar **01**
arcillar **01**
arder **02**
arderse **02**
arenar **01**
arencar **13**
arengar **19**
arfar **01**
argamasar **01**
argayar **01**

argentar **01**
argentinizar **16**
argüir **53**
argumentar **01**
aricar **13**
aridecer **45**
aridecerse **45**
aristocratizar **16**
armar **01**
armarse **01**
armonizar **16**
aromar **01**
aromatizar **16**
arpegiar **08**
arponar **01**
arponear **01**
arquear **01**
arquearse **01**
arrabiatar **01**
arracimarse **01**
arraigar **19**
arraigarse **19**
arramblar **01**
arramblarse **01**
arrancar **13**
arrancarse **13**
arranchar **01**
arrasar **01**
arrasarse **01**
arrascar **13**
arrastrar **01**
arrastrarse **01**
arrear **01**
arrebañar **01**
arrebatar **01**
arrebatarse **01**
arrebiatar **01**
arrebiatarse **01**
arrebolar **01**
arrebolarse **01**
arrebozar **16**

rebozarse 16
rebujar 01
rebujarse 01
rechar 01
recharse 01
reciar 08
recirse 79
redrar 01
redrarse 01
reglar 01
reglarse 01
rejacar 13
rejerar 01
rejuntar 01
rejuntarse 01
rellanarse 01
remangar 19
remangarse 19
remeter 02
remolinar 01
remolinarse 01
rempujar 01
rendar 22
repanchigarse 19
repentirse 55
restar 01
restarse 01
riar 07
riarse 07
ribar 01
riesgar 19
riesgarse 19
rimar 01
rimarse 01
rinconar 01
rinconarse 01
riostrar 01
riscar 13
riscarse 13
rizar 16
robar 01

arrobarse 01
arrocinar 01
arrocinarse 01
arrodillar 01
arrodillarse 01
arrodrigar 19
arrodrigonar 01
arrogarse 19
arrojar 01
arrojarse 01
arrollar 01
arromanzar 16
arronzar 16
arropar 01
arroparse 01
arrostrar 01
arroyar 01
arroyarse 01
arruar 09
arrufar 01
arrufarse 01
arrugar 19
arrugarse 19
arruinar 01
arruinarse 01
arrullar 01
arrumar 01
arrumbar 01
arrumbarse 01
artesonar 01
articular 01
artigar 19
artillar 01
asaetear 01
asalariar 08
asaltar 01
asar 01
ascender 26
asear 01
asearse 01
asechar 01

asedar 01
asediar 08
asegurar 01
asegurarse 01
asemejar 01
asemejarse 01
asenderear 01
asentar 22
asentarse 22
asentir 55
aseptizar 16
aserenar 01
aserenarse 01
aseriarse 08
aserrar 22
aserruchar 01
asesinar 01
asesorar 01
asesorarse 01
asestar 01
aseverar 01
asfaltar 01
asfixiar 08
asfixiarse 08
asignar 01
asilar 01
asilarse 01
asimilar 01
asimilarse 01
asir 51
asirse 51
asistir 03
asnear 01
asociar 08
asociarse 08
asolanar 01
asolar 28
asolarse 28
asolear 01
asolearse 01
asomar 01

asomarse 01
asombrar 01
asombrarse 01
asonantar 01
asonar 28
asorochar 01
asorocharse 01
aspar 01
asparse 01
asperjar 01
aspirar 01
asquear 01
asquearse 01
astillar 01
astillarse 01
astreñir 39
astringir 18
astrologar 19
asumir 03
asurar 01
asurcar 13
asustar 01
asustarse 01
atabalear 01
atablar 01
atacar 13
atafagar 19
atafagarse 19
atagallar 01
atajar 01
atajarse 01
atalajar 01
atalayar 01
atañer 02
atar 01
atarse 01
atarantar 01
atarazar 16
atardecer 45
atarear 01
atarearse 01

atarquinar 01
atarquinarse 01
atarragar 19
atarrayar 01
atarugar 19
atarugarse 19
atasajar 01
atascar 13
atascarse 13
ataviar 07
ataviarse 07
atediar 08
atemorizar 16
atemorizarse 16
atemperar 01
atemperarse 01
atenazar 16
atender 26
atenderse 26
atenebrarse 01
atentar 01
atenuar 09
atenuarse 09
aterirse 79
aterrajar 01
aterrar 22
aterrarse 22
aterrizar 16
aterronar 01
aterronarse 01
aterrorizar 16
aterrorizarse 16
atesorar 01
atestar 22
atestarse 22
atestiguar 11
atezar 16
atezarse 16
atiborrar 01
atiborrarse 01
atiesar 01

atildar 01
atildarse 01
atinar 01
atinconar 01
atiplar 01
atiplarse 01
atipujarse 01
atirantar 01
atisbar 01
atizar 16
atizarse 16
atizonar 01
atizonarse 01
atoar 01
atochar 01
atocharse 01
atocinar 01
atocinarse 01
atollarse 01
atolondrar 01
atolondrarse 01
atomizar 16
atontar 01
atontarse 01
atontolinar 01
atorar 01
atorarse 01
atormentar 01
atormentarse 01
atornillar 01
atorrar 01
atortolar 01
atortolarse 01
atortujar 01
atosigar 19
atosigarse 19
atracar 13
atracarse 13
atraer 60
atrafagar 19
atragantar 01

gantarse **01**
illar **04**
amparse **01**
ncar **13**
ncarse **13**
apar **01**
asar **01**
asarse **01**
avesar **22**
avesarse **22**
echar **01**
everse **02**
buir **52**
buirse **52**
bular **01**
bularse **01**
incar **13**
ncherar **01**
ncherarse **01**
ochar **01**
ofiar **08**
ofiarse **08**
onar **28**
opar **01**
opellar **01**
opellarse **01**
fiar **01**
farse **01**
rdir **03**
rdirse **03**
rrullar **01**
rrullarse **01**
rullar **01**
rullarse **01**
sar **01**
sarse **01**
itar **01**
urar **01**
lar **05**
nentar **01**
ar **05**

aunarse **05**
aupar **05**
aureolar **01**
aurificar **13**
auscultar **01**
ausentarse **01**
auspiciar **08**
autenticar **13**
autentificar **13**
autoafirmarse **01**
autocensurarse **01**
autodefenderse **26**
autodefinirse **03**
autodestruirse **52**
autodeterminarse **01**
autodisolverse **35**
autoeditar **01**
autoemplearse **01**
autoengañarse **01**
autoevaluarse **09**
autoexcluirse **52**
autofinanciarse **08**
autogestionar **01**
autogestionarse **01**
autografiar **07**
autoinculparse **01**
autolimitarse **01**
automarginarse **01**
automatizar **16**
automedicarse **13**
autoparodiarse **08**
autopsiar **08**
autorizar **16**
autorregularse **01**
autosugestionarse **01**
auxiliar **08**
avalar **01**
avalorar **01**
avaluar **09**
avanzar **16**
avasallar **01**

avasallarse **01**
avecinarse **01**
avecindarse **01**
avejentar **01**
avejentarse **01**
avejigar **19**
avejigarse **19**
avellanar **01**
avellanarse **01**
avenar **01**
avenir **73**
avenirse **73**
aventajar **01**
aventar **22**
aventarse **22**
aventurar **01**
aventurarse **01**
avergonzar **32**
avergonzarse **32**
averiar **08**
averiarse **08**
averiguar **11**
avezar **16**
avezarse **16**
aviar **07**
aviarse **07**
aviejar **01**
aviejarse **01**
avillanar **01**
avillanarse **01**
avinagrar **01**
avinagrarse **01**
avisar **01**
avispar **01**
avisparse **01**
avistar **01**
avistarse **01**
avituallar **01**
avivar **01**
avivarse **01**
avizorar **01**

avocar 13
axiomatizar 16
ayudar 01
ayudarse 01
ayunar 01
ayuntarse 01
azacanear 01
azafranar 01
azarar 01
azararse 01
azarear 01
azarearse 01
azoar 01
azogar 19
azolvar 01
azolvarse 01
azorar 01
azorarse 01
azorrarse 01
azorrillar 01
azorrillarse 01
azotar 01
azotarse 01
azucarar 01
azucararse 01
azufrar 01
azular 01
azulear 01
azulejar 01
azumagarse 19
azuzar 16

B

babear 01
babosear 01
bacharse 01
bachatear 01
bachear 01
bachearse 01
bachillerear 01
bagar 19

bagayear 01
bailar 01
bailotear 01
bajar 01
bajarse 01
bajonear 01
bajonearse 01
balacear 01
baladrar 01
baladronear 01
balancear 01
balancearse 01
balar 01
balastar 01
balbucear 01
balbucir 80
balcanizar 16
balconear 01
baldar 01
baldarse 01
baldear 01
baldonar 01
baldosar 01
balear 01
balitar 01
balizar 16
bambalear 01
bambolear 01
bambolearse 01
banalizar 16
bancar 13
bancarse 13
bancarizar 16
bandear 01
bandearse 01
banderillear 01
banquear 01
bañar 01
bañarse 01
baquear 01
baquetear 01

barajar 01
baratear 01
barbear 01
barbechar 01
barbotar 01
barbullar 01
bardar 01
barloar 01
barloventear 01
barnizar 16
barquear 01
barrenar 01
barrer 02
barretear 01
barritar 01
barroquizar 16
barroquizarse 16
barruntar 01
barzonear 01
basar 01
bascular 01
basquear 01
bastar 01
bastarse 01
bastardear 01
bastear 01
bastimentar 01
bastonear 01
basurear 01
batallar 01
batanar 01
batanear 01
batear 01
batir 03
batirse 03
batojar 01
batuquear 01
bautizar 16
bazucar 13
bazuquear 01
beatificar 13

eber 02
eberse 02
eborrotear 01
ecar 13
ecerrear 01
efar 01
ejuquear 01
eldar 22
ellaquear 01
endecir 74
eneficiar 08
eneficiarse 08
ermejear 01
errear 01
esar 01
esarse 01
esotear 01
estializar 16
estializarse 16
esuquear 01
esuquearse 01
icicletear 01
ieldar 01
ienquerer 70
ienquistar 01
ienquistarse 01
ienvivir 03
ifurcarse 13
igardear 01
inar 01
iografiar 07
ipolarizar 16
irlar 01
isar 01
isbisar 01
isbisear 01
iselar 01
izarrear 01
izcar 13
izcochar 01
izquear 01

blandear 01
blandearse 01
blandir 79
blanquear 01
blanquecer 45
blasfemar 01
blasonar 01
blindar 01
blocar 13
blofear 01
bloquear 01
bloquearse 01
blufear 01
bobear 01
bobinar 01
bocadear 01
bocelar 01
bochar 01
bochinchear 01
bocinar 01
bogar 19
boicotear 01
boycotear 01
bojar 01
bolacear 01
bolchevizar 16
bolear 01
bolearse 01
boletear 01
bolichear 01
bollar 01
bolsear 01
bolsiquear 01
boludear 01
bombardear 01
bombear 01
bonificar 13
boquear 01
borbollar 01
borbollonear 01
borbotar 01

borbotear 01
bordar 01
bordear 01
bordonear 01
bornear 01
bornearse 01
borrajear 01
borrar 01
borrarse 01
borronear 01
bosquejar 01
bostezar 16
botanear 01
botar 01
botarse 01
boxear 01
boyar 01
bracear 01
bramar 01
brasear 01
bravear 01
bravuconear 01
brear 01
bregar 19
bricolar 01
brillar 01
brincar 13
brindar 01
briscar 13
brocearse 01
bromar 01
bromear 01
broncear 01
broncearse 01
bronquear 01
brotar 01
brotarse 01
brujear 01
brujulear 01
bruñir 03
brutalizar 16

pturar 01
racolear 01
racterizar 16
racterizarse 16
rambolear 01
ramelizar 16
ratular 01
rbonatar 01
rbonizar 16
rbonizarse 16
rburar 01
rcajearse 01
rcomer 02
rcomerse 02
rdar 01
rear 01
rearse 01
renar 01
rgar 19
rgarse 19
rgosear 01
riar 08
riarse 08
ricaturar 01
ricaturizar 16
rmenar 01
rnear 01
rnerear 01
rpir 03
rraspear 01
rretear 01
rrochar 01
rrozar 16
rtear 01
rtearse 01
rtografiar 07
sar 01
sarse 01
scabelear 01
scar 13
scarse 13

cascotear 01
castañetear 01
castellanizar 16
castigar 19
castigarse 19
castrar 01
catalanizar 16
catalanizarse 16
catalizar 16
catalogar 19
catapultar 01
catar 01
catatar 01
catear 01
categorizar 16
catequizar 16
cauchutar 01
caucionar 01
causar 01
cauterizar 16
cautivar 01
cavar 01
cavilar 01
cazar 16
cazoletear 01
cazumbrar 01
cebar 01
cebarse 01
cecear 01
cecinar 01
cedacear 01
ceder 02
cegar 24
cegarse 24
cejar 01
celar 01
celebrar 01
celebrarse 01
cellisquear 01
cementar 01
cenar 01

cencerrear 01
censar 01
censurar 01
centellear 01
centonar 01
centralizar 16
centrar 01
centrarse 01
centrifugar 19
centuplicar 13
ceñir 39
ceñirse 39
cepillar 01
cepillarse 01
cercar 13
cercenar 01
cerchar 01
cerciorarse 01
cerdear 01
cerner 26
cerner 26
cernerse 26
cernir 27
cerotear 01
cerrar 22
cerrarse 22
certificar 13
cesantear 01
cesar 01
chacharear 01
chacotear 01
chafallar 01
chafar 01
chafarrinar 01
chaflanar 01
chalanear 01
chalar 01
chalarse 01
chamarilear 01
chambear 01
chambonear 01

champurrar 01
chamullar 01
chamuscar 13
chamuscarse 13
chamuyar 01
chancar 13
chancear 01
chanchullar 01
chancletear 01
chanelar 01
changar 19
changuear 01
chantajear 01
chapalear 01
chapar 01
chaparrear 01
chapecar 13
chapodar 01
chapotear 01
chapucear 01
chapurrar 01
chapurrear 01
chapuzar 16
chapuzarse 16
chaquetear 01
charlar 01
charlatanear 01
charlotear 01
charolar 01
charquear 01
charranear 01
chascar 13
chasquear 01
chatear 01
checar 13
chequear 01
chicanear 01
chichear 01
chichonear 01
chiclear 01
chicolear 01

chicotear 01
chiflar 01
chiflarse 01
chilenizar 16
chillar 01
chimar 01
chimbar 01
chimiscolear 01
chinchar 01
chincharse 01
chinchinear 01
chinchorrear 01
chinear 01
chinganear 01
chingar 19
chingarse 19
chiquear 01
chiquitear 01
chiripear 01
chirlar 01
chirriar 07
chisguetear 01
chismear 01
chismorrear 01
chisparse 01
chispear 01
chisporrotear 01
chistar 01
chivar 01
chivarse 01
chivatear 01
chocar 13
chocarrear 01
chochar 01
chochear 01
chollar 01
chorar 01
chorear 01
choricear 01
chorizar 16
chorrear 01

chorrearse 01
chozpar 01
chucear 01
chuchear 01
chufletear 01
chulear 01
chulearse 01
chumarse 01
chumbar 01
chupar 01
chuparse 01
chupetear 01
churrasquear 01
churruscar 13
churruscarse 13
churruscarse 13
chutar 01
chutarse 01
ciar 07
cicatear 01
cicatrizar 16
cifrar 01
cilindrar 01
cimbrar 01
cimbrarse 01
cimbrear 01
cimbrearse 01
cimentar 22
cincelar 01
cinchar 01
cinematografiar 07
cinglar 01
cintilar 01
circular 01
circuncidar 01
circundar 01
circunferir 55
circunnavegar 19
circunscribir 03
circunvalar 01
circunvenir 73

cunvolar 01
ujear 01
car 13
carse 13
ar 01
arse 01
vilizar 16
vilizarse 16
allar 01
añar 01
amar 01
amorear 01
arear 01
arearse 01
arecer 45
arificar 13
arificarse 13
asificar 13
asificarse 13
audicar 13
austrar 01
ausular 01
ausurar 01
avar 01
avarse 01
avetear 01
matizar 16
sar 01
onar 01
oquear 01
orar 01
proformar 01
proformizar 16
orurar 01
accionar 01
acervar 01
adunar 01
adunarse 01
adyuvar 01
agular 01
agularse 01

coaligar 19
coaligarse 19
coartar 01
cobijar 01
cobijarse 01
cobrar 01
cobrarse 01
cocear 01
cocer 36
cocerse 36
cocinar 01
cocinarse 01
codear 01
codiciar 08
codificar 13
codillear 01
codirigir 18
coeditar 01
coercer 14
coescribir 03
coexistir 03
coextenderse 26
cofinanciar 08
coger 17
cogerse 17
cohabitar 01
cohechar 01
coheredar 01
cohesionar 01
cohibir 03
cohibirse 03
cohobar 01
cohonestar 01
coimear 01
coincidir 03
coinquinar 01
cojear 01
cojudear 01
colaborar 01
colacionar 01
colapsar 01

colapsarse 01
colar 28
colarse 28
colchar 01
colear 01
colearse 01
coleccionar 01
colectar 01
colectivizar 16
colegiarse 08
colegir 40
colgar 30
colgarse 30
colicuar 10
colicuarse 10
colicuecer 45
coligar 19
coligarse 19
colisionar 01
colmar 01
colocar 13
colocarse 13
colonizar 16
colorar 01
colorear 01
colorir 79
columbrar 01
columpiar 08
columpiarse 08
comadrear 01
comandar 01
comanditar 01
comarcar 13
combar 01
combarse 01
combatir 03
combinar 01
combinarse 01
comedirse 39
comentar 01
comenzar 23

nfirmar 01
nfirmarse 01
nfiscar 13
nfitar 01
nfluir 52
nformar 01
nformarse 01
nfortar 01
nfraternar 01
nfraternizar 16
nfrontar 01
nfundir 03
nfundirse 03
nfutar 01
ngelar 01
ngelarse 01
ngeniar 08
ngestionar 01
ngestionarse 01
nglomerar 01
nglomerarse 01
nglutinar 01
nglutinarse 01
ngojar 01
ngojarse 01
ngraciar 08
ngraciarse 08
ngratular 01
ngratularse 01
ngregar 19
ngregarse 19
njeturar 01
njugar 19
njuntar 01
njuntarse 01
njuramentar 01
njuramentarse 01
njurar 01
njurarse 01
nllevar 01
nmemorar 01

conmensurar 01
conminar 01
conmocionar 01
conmover 35
conmoverse 35
conmutar 01
connaturalizarse 16
connotar 01
conocer 46
conocerse 46
conquistar 01
consagrar 01
consagrarse 01
conseguir 41
consensuar 09
consentir 55
conservar 01
conservarse 01
considerar 01
considerarse 01
consignar 01
consolar 28
consolarse 28
consolidar 01
consolidarse 01
conspirar 01
constar 01
constatar 01
constelar 01
consternar 01
consternarse 01
constiparse 01
constitucionalizar 16
constituir 52
constituirse 52
constreñir 39
costreñir 39
construir 52
consultar 01
consumar 01
consumir 03

consumirse 03
contabilizar 16
contactar 01
contagiar 08
contagiarse 08
contaminar 01
contaminarse 01
contar 28
contarse 28
contemplar 01
contemporizar 16
contender 26
contener 72
contenerse 72
contentar 01
contentarse 01
contestar 01
contextualizar 16
continuar 09
contonearse 01
contornar 01
contornear 01
contorsionarse 01
contraatacar 13
contrabalancear 01
contrabandear 01
contrabracear 01
contracalcar 13
contrachapar 01
contrachapear 01
contradecir 74
contradecirse 74
contraer 60
contraerse 60
contrafallar 01
contragolpear 01
contrahacer 68
contraindicar 13
contramandar 01
contramanifestar 22
contramatar 01

contramatarse 01
contraminar 01
contrapasar 01
contrapesar 01
contraponer 69
contraponerse 69
contraprogramar 01
contrapuntear 01
contrapuntearse 01
contrariar 07
contrarrestar 01
contrastar 01
contratar 01
contravenir 73
contribuir 52
contristar 01
contristarse 01
controlar 01
controlarse 01
controvertir 55
contundir 03
conturbar 01
contusionar 01
convalecer 45
convalidar 01
convencer 14
convencerse 14
convenir 73
converger 17
convergir 18
conversar 01
convertir 27
convertirse 27
convidar 01
convivir 03
convocar 13
convoyar 01
convulsionar 01
cooperar 01
cooptar 01
coordinar 01

copar 01
coparse 01
copear 01
copiar 08
copinar 01
coplear 01
copresidir 03
coproducir 59
coprotagonizar 16
copular 01
copularse 1
coquear 01
coquetear 01
coquizar 16
corchar 01
corcovar 01
corcovear 01
corear 01
corlar 01
corlear 01
cornear 01
coronar 01
coronarse 01
corporeizar 16
corporeizarse 16
correar 01
corregir 40
correlacionar 01
correr 02
correrse 02
corresponder 02
corresponderse 02
corresponsabilizarse 16
corretear 01
corroborar 01
corroer 50
corroerse 50
corromper 02
corromperse 02
cortar 01
cortarse 01

cortejar 01
cortocircuitar 01
coruscar 13
corvar 01
corvetear 01
cosechar 01
coser 02
cosificar 13
cosquillar 01
cosquillear 01
costar 28
costear 01
costearse 01
cotejar 01
cotillear 01
cotizar 16
cotizarse 16
cotorrear 01
coyotear 01
craquear 01
crear 01
crearse 01
crecer 45
crecerse 45
creer 12
creerse 12
cremar 01
creosotar 01
crepitar 01
criar 07
criarse 07
cribar 01
criminalizar 16
criminar 01
crispar 01
crisparse 01
cristalizar 16
cristalizarse 16
cristianar 01
cristianizar 16
criticar 13

croar 01
crocitar 01
cromar 01
cromolitografiar 07
cronometrar 01
crotorar 01
crucificar 13
crujir 03
crujirse 03
cruzar 16
cruzarse 16
cuadrar 01
cuadrarse 01
cuadricular 01
cuadruplicar 13
cuadruplicarse 13
cuajar 01
cuajarse 01
cualificar 13
cuantificar 13
cuartar 01
cuartear 01
cuartearse 01
cuartelar 01
cuatrerear 01
cuatrodoblar 01
cubanizar 16
cubanizarse 16
cubicar 13
cubilar 01
cubiletear 01
cubrir 03
cubrirse 03
cucar 13
cuchichear 01
cuchichiar 08
cuchuchear 01
cuchufletear 01
cuentear 01
cuerear 01
cuerpear 01

cuestionar 01
cuestionarse 01
cuidar 01
cuidarse 01
culear 01
culebrear 01
culminar 01
culpabilizar 16
culpar 01
cultivar 01
culturizar 16
culturizarse 16
cumplimentar 01
cumplir 03
cumplirse 03
cundir 03
cunear 01
cunearse 01
curar 01
curarse 01
curiosear 01
currar 01
currarse 01
currelar 01
curruscar 13
cursar 01
curtir 03
curtirse 03
curvar 01
curvarse 01
custodiar 08
cuzquear 01

D

dactilografiar 07
dallear 01
damasquinar 01
damnificar 13
danzar 16
dañar 01
dañarse 01

dar 63
darse 63
datar 01
deambular 01
debatir 03
debatirse 03
debelar 01
deber 02
deberse 02
debilitar 01
debilitarse 01
debitar 01
debutar 01
decaer 49
decalcificar 13
decampar 01
decantar 01
decantarse 01
decapar 01
decapitar 01
decapsular 01
decepcionar 01
decidir 03
decidirse 03
decir 74
decirse 74
declamar 01
declarar 01
declararse 01
declinar 01
decolar 01
decomisar 01
deconstruir 52
decorar 01
decrecer 45
decrepitar 01
decretar 01
decuplar 01
decuplicar 13
dedicar 13
deducir 59

defecar 13	demorar 01	derechizar 16
defender 26	demorarse 01	derechizarse 16
defenderse 26	demostrar 28	derivar 01
defenestrar 01	demudar 01	derogar 19
definir 03	demultiplicar 13	derramar 01
definirse 03	denegar 24	derramarse 01
deflactar 01	denguear 01	derrapar 01
deflagrar 01	denigrar 01	derrengar 19
defoliar 08	denominar 01	derrengarse 19
deforestar 01	denominarse 01	derretir 39
deformar 01	denostar 28	derretirse 39
deformarse 01	denotar 01	derribar 01
defraudar 01	densificar 13	derrocar 13
degenerar 01	densificarse 13	derrochar 01
degenerarse 01	dentalizar 16	derrotar 01
deglutir 03	dentalizarse 16	derrotarse 01
degollar 31	dentar 22	derrubiar 08
degradar 01	dentellar 01	derruir 52
degradarse 01	dentellear 01	derrumbar 01
degustar 01	denudar 01	derrumbarse 01
deificar 13	denunciar 08	desabastecer 45
dejar 01	deparar 01	desabollar 01
dejarse 01	departir 03	desabonarse 01
delatar 01	depauperar 01	desabotonar 01
delegar 19	depauperarse 01	desabotonarse 01
deleitar 01	depender 02	desabrigar 19
deleitarse 01	depilar 01	desabrigarse 19
deletrear 01	deplorar 01	desabrir 03
deliberar 01	deponer 69	desabrirse 03
delimitar 01	deportar 01	desabrochar 01
delinear 01	depositar 01	desabrocharse 01
delinquir 21	depositarse 01	desacalorarse 01
delirar 01	depravar 01	desacatar 01
demacrar 01	depravarse 01	desacelerar 01
demacrarse 01	deprecar 13	desacelerarse 01
demandar 01	depreciar 08	desacertar 22
demarcar 13	depreciarse 08	desacidificar 13
demasiarse 07	depredar 01	desaclimatar 01
demeritar 01	deprimir 03	desaclimatarse 01
democratizar 16	deprimirse 03	desacomodar 01
demoler 35	depurar 01	desacomodarse 01

desacompañar 01
desacompasar 01
desaconsejar 01
desacoplar 01
desacordar 28
desacordarse 28
desacostumbrar 01
desacostumbrarse 01
desacralizar 16
desacreditar 01
desacreditarse 01
desactivar 01
desacuartelar 01
desadeudar 01
desadeudarse 01
desadoquinar 01
desadormecer 45
desadormecerse 45
desaduanar 01
desadvertir 55
desafanarse 01
desaferrar 22
desafiar 07
desafiarse 07
desafilar 01
desafilarse 01
desafinar 01
desafinarse 01
desaforar 01
desaforarse 01
desagarrar 01
desagotar 01
desagraciar 08
desagradar 01
desagradecer 45
desagraviar 08
desagregar 19
desagregarse 19
desaguar 11
desaguarse 11
desahijar 06

desahijarse 06
desahogar 19
desahogarse 19
desahuciar 08
desahumar 05
desainar 04
desairar 04
desajustar 01
desajustarse 01
desalabear 01
desalar 01
desalbardar 01
desalentar 22
desalentarse 22
desalinear 01
desalinearse 01
desalinizar 16
desaliñar 01
desalmidonar 01
desalojar 01
desalquilar 01
desalquilarse 01
desalquitranar 01
desalterar 01
desamar 01
desamarrar 01
desambiguar 11
desamelgar 19
desamorar 01
desamorarse 01
desamortizar 16
desamparar 01
desamueblar 01
desanclar 01
desandar 54
desangrar 01
desangrarse 01
desanidar 01
desanimar 01
desanimarse 01
desanudar 01

desanudarse 01
desaparear 01
desaparecer 45
desaparejar 01
desapasionar 01
desapasionarse 01
desaplomar 01
desaplomarse 01
desapoderar 01
desapolillar 01
desapolillarse 01
desaporcar 13
desaprender 02
desapretar 22
desapretarse 22
desaprobar 28
desaprovechar 01
desapuntalar 01
desapuntar 01
desapuntarse 01
desarbolar 01
desarbolarse 01
desarenar 01
desargentar 01
desarmar 01
desarmarse 01
desarmonizar 16
desaromatizarse 16
desarraigar 19
desarraigarse 19
desarreglar 01
desarreglarse 01
desarrendar 22
desarrimar 01
desarrollar 01
desarrollarse 01
desarropar 01
desarroparse 01
desarrugar 19
desarrugarse 19
desarrumar 01

desarticular 01
desarticularse 01
desartillar 01
desarzonar 01
desasear 01
desasimilar 01
desasir 51
desasirse 51
desasistir 03
desasnar 01
desasociar 08
desasosegar 24
desasosegarse 24
desatar 01
desatarse 01
desatascar 13
desatascarse 13
desatender 26
desaterrar 22
desatinar 01
desatollar 01
desatorar 01
desatornillar 01
desatracar 13
desatraillar 04
desatrancar 13
desaturdir 03
desaturdirse 03
desautorizar 16
desavenir 73
desaviar 07
desayunar 01
desayunarse 01
desazogar 19
desazolvar 01
desazonar 01
desazonarse 01
desbancar 13
desbandarse 01
desbarajustar 01
desabarajustarse 01

desbaratar 01
desbaratarse 01
desbarbar 01
desbarbarse 01
desbarbillar 01
desbardar 01
desbarrancarse 13
desbarrar 01
desbastar 01
desbastarse 01
desbautizar 16
desbecerrar 01
desbloquear 01
desbloquearse 01
desbocar 13
desbocarse 13
desbolar 01
desbordar 01
desbordarse 01
desborrar 01
desbotonar 01
desbotonarse 01
desbravar 01
desbravarse 01
desbravecer 45
desbravecerse 45
desbridar 01
desbriznar 01
desbrozar 16
desbullar 01
desburocratizar 16
descabalar 01
descabalarse 01
descabalgar 19
descabellar 01
descabellarse 01
descabezar 16
descabezarse 16
descabritar 01
descachar 01
descacharrar 01

descacharrarse 01
descachazar 16
descaderar 01
descaderarse 01
descadillar 01
descaecer 45
descafeinar 04
descafilar 01
descalabazarse 16
descalabrar 01
descalabrarse 01
descalaminar 01
descalcificar 13
descalcificarse 13
descalificar 13
descalzar 16
descalzarse 16
descamar 01
descamarse 01
descambiar 08
descaminar 01
descaminarse 01
descamisar 01
descamisarse 01
descampar 01
descansar 01
descantillar 01
descantillarse 01
descantonar 01
descañonar 01
descapirotar 01
descapitalizar 16
descapitalizarse 16
descapotar 01
descararse 01
descarbonatar 01
descarburar 01
descargar 19
descargarse 19
descarnar 01
descarnarse 01

escarozar 16
escarriar 07
escarriarse 07
escarrilar 01
escartar 01
escartarse 01
escasar 01
escasarse 01
escascar 13
escascarse 13
escascarar 01
escascararse 01
escascarillar 01
escascarillarse 01
escaspar 01
escastar 01
escatolizar 16
escebar 01
escender 26
escentralizar 16
escentralizarse 16
escentrar 01
escentrarse 01
escepar 01
escercar 13
escerebrar 01
escerebrarse 01
escerezar 16
escerrajar 01
eschavetarse 01
escifrar 01
escimbrar 01
escinchar 01
esclasificar 13
esclavar 01
escoagular 01
escobajar 01
escocar 13
escocarse 13
escodificar 13
escogotar 01

descojonarse 01
descolar 01
descolchar 01
descolgar 30
descolgarse 30
descollar 28
descolmillar 01
descolocar 13
descolocarse 13
descolonizar 16
descolorar 01
descolorarse 01
descolorir 79
descolorirse 79
descombrar 01
descomedirse 39
descompasarse 01
descompensar 01
descompensarse 01
descomponer 69
descomponerse 69
descomprimir 03
descomulgar 19
desconcentrar 01
desconcentrarse 01
desconceptuar 09
desconcertar 22
desconcertarse 22
desconchar 01
desconcharse 01
desconchinflar 01
desconchinflarse 01
desconectar 01
desconectarse 01
desconfiar 07
desconformar 01
descongelar 01
descongelarse 01
descongestionar 01
descongestionarse 01
desconocer 46

desconsiderar 01
desconsolar 28
descontaminar 01
descontar 28
descontentar 01
descontextualizar 16
descontrolar 01
descontrolarse 01
desconvenir 73
desconvocar 13
descorazonar 01
descorazonarse 01
descorchar 01
descordar 28
descornar 28
descornarse 28
descoronar 01
descorrer 02
descortezar 16
descoser 02
descoserse 02
descostillarse 01
descostrar 01
descotar 01
descoyuntar 01
descoyuntarse 01
descremar 01
descrestar 01
describir 03
descrismar 01
descrismarse 01
descristianizar 16
descruzar 16
descuadernar 01
descuadernarse 01
descuadrillarse 01
descuajar 01
descuajarse 01
descuajaringar 19
descuajaringarse 19
descuajeringar 19

descuajeringarse 19
descuartizar 16
descubrir 03
descubrirse 03
descuerar 01
descuidar 01
descuidarse 01
descular 01
desculatar 01
desdecir 74
desdecirse 74
desdentar 22
desdeñar 01
desdevanar 01
desdibujar 01
desdibujarse 01
desdoblar 01
desdoblarse 01
desdorar 01
desdramatizar 16
desear 01
desecar 13
desecarse 13
desechar 01
deselectrizar 16
desellar 01
desembalar 01
desembaldosar 01
desembanastar 01
desembarazar 16
desembarcar 13
desembargar 19
desembarrancar 13
desembarrar 01
desembaular 05
desembebecerse 45
desembelesarse 01
desembocar 13
desembojar 01
desembolsar 01
desemborrachar 01

desemboscarse 13
desembotar 01
desembragar 19
desembravecer 45
desembravecerse 45
desembrear 01
desembriagar 19
desembridar 01
desembrollar 01
desembrozar 16
desembrujar 01
desembuchar 01
desemejar 01
desempacar 13
desempacarse 13
desempachar 01
desempacharse 01
desempalmar 01
desempañar 01
desempapelar 01
desempaquetar 01
desemparejar 01
desemparejarse 01
desemparvar 01
desempastar 01
desempatar 01
desempedrar 22
desempeñar 01
desempeñarse 01
desemperezarse 16
desempernar 01
desemplumar 01
desempolvar 01
desemponzoñar 01
desempotrar 01
desempuñar 01
desenastar 01
desencabalgar 19
desencabestrar 01
desencadenar 01
desencadenarse 01

desencajar 01
desencajarse 01
desencajonar 01
desencallar 01
desencantar 01
desencapar 01
desencapillar 01
desencapotar 01
desencapotarse 01
desencarcelar 01
desencargar 19
desencarpetar 01
desencasquillar 01
desencenagar 19
desencerrar 22
desenchufar 01
desenclavar 01
desenclavijar 01
desencobrar 01
desencofrar 01
desencoger 17
desencogerse 17
desencolar 01
desencolarse 01
desencolerizar 16
desencolerizarse 16
desenconar 01
desenconarse 01
desencontrarse 28
desencordelar 01
desencorvar 01
desencrespar 01
desencuadernar 01
desencuadernarse 01
desendemoniar 08
desendiablar 01
desendiosar 01
desenfadar 01
desenfadarse 01
desenfilar 01
desenfocar 13

desgarrarse 01
desgastar 01
desgastarse 01
desgerminar 01
desglasar 01
desglosar 01
desgobernar 22
desgobernarse 22
desgomar 01
desgonzar 16
desgonzarse 16
desgoznar 01
desgraciar 08
desgraciarse 08
desgramar 01
desgranar 01
desgranarse 01
desgrasar 01
desgravar 01
desgravarse 01
desgreñar 01
desgreñarse 01
desguañangar 19
desguañingar 19
desguarnecer 45
desguazar 16
desguindar 01
desguindarse 01
desguinzar 16
deshabitar 01
deshabituar 09
deshabituarse 09
deshacer 68
deshacerse 68
deshebillar 01
deshebrar 01
deshechizar 16
deshelar 22
deshelarse 22
desherbar 22
desheredar 01

deshermanar 01
deshermanarse 01
desherrar 22
desherrumbrar 01
deshidratar 01
deshidratarse 01
deshidrogenar 01
deshijar 01
deshilachar 01
deshilacharse 01
deshilar 01
deshilvanar 01
deshincar 13
deshinchar 01
deshincharse 01
deshipnotizar 16
deshipotecar 13
deshojar 01
deshojarse 01
deshollejar 01
deshollinar 01
deshonorar 01
deshonorarse 01
deshonrar 01
deshornar 01
deshuesar 01
deshuevarse 01
deshumanizar 16
deshumanizarse 16
deshumedecer 45
deshumidificar 13
desideologizar 16
designar 01
desilusionar 01
desilusionarse 01
desimanar 01
desimantar 01
desimponer 69
desimpresionar 01
desimpresionarse 01
desincentivar 01

desincorporar 01
desincorporarse 01
desincrustar 01
desinfectar 01
desinflamar 01
desinflamarse 01
desinflar 01
desinflarse 01
desinformar 01
desinsectar 01
desintegrar 01
desintegrarse 01
desinteresarse 01
desintoxicar 13
desintoxicarse 13
desinvertir 55
desistir 03
desjarretar 01
desjugar 19
desjuntar 01
deslabonar 01
desladrillar 01
deslastrar 01
deslavar 01
deslavazar 16
deslazar 16
deslechugar 19
deslechuguillar 01
deslegitimar 01
desleír 42
desleírse 42
deslendrar 22
deslenguar 11
deslenguarse 11
desliar 07
desliarse 07
desligar 19
desligarse 19
deslindar 01
desliñar 01
deslizar 16

deslizarse 16
deslomar 01
deslomarse 01
deslucir 47
deslumbrar 01
deslustrar 01
desmadejar 01
desmadejarse 01
desmadrar 01
desmadrarse 01
desmagnetizar 16
desmajolar 28
desmalezar 16
desmallar 01
desmamar 01
desmamonar 01
desmanarse 01
desmanchar 01
desmancharse 01
desmandarse 01
desmanear 01
desmangar 19
desmantecar 13
desmantelar 01
desmaquillar 01
desmarcar 13
desmarcarse 13
desmarojar 01
desmatar 01
desmayar 01
desmayarse 01
desmedirse 39
desmejorar 01
desmejorarse 01
desmelenar 01
desmelenarse 01
desmembrar 22
desmembrarse 22
desmemoriarse 08
desmentir 55
desmenuzar 16

desmeollar 01
desmerecer 45
desmigajar 01
desmigajarse 01
desmigar 19
desmigarse 19
desmilitarizar 16
desmitificar 13
desmochar 01
desmogar 19
desmoldar 01
desmonetizar 16
desmontar 01
desmoñar 01
desmoralizar 16
desmoralizarse 16
desmoronar 01
desmoronarse 01
desmotar 01
desmotivar 01
desmovilizar 16
desmultiplicar 13
desnacionalizar 16
desnarigar 19
desnatar 01
desnaturalizar 16
desnazificar 13
desnitrificar 13
desnivelar 01
desnivelarse 01
desnucar 13
desnucarse 13
desnuclearizar 16
desnudar 01
desnudarse 01
desnutrirse 03
desobedecer 45
desobstruir 52
desocupar 01
desocuparse 01
desodorar 01

desodorizar 16
desoír 58
desojar 01
desojarse 01
desolar 81
desolarse 81
desoldar 28
desollar 28
desollarse 28
desopilar 01
desoprimir 03
desorbitar 01
desorbitarse 01
desordenar 01
desordenarse 01
desorejar 01
desorganizar 16
desorganizarse 16
desorientar 01
desorientarse 01
desorillar 01
desortijar 01
desosar 28
desovar 01
desovillar 01
desoxidar 01
desoxigenar 01
despabilar 01
despabilarse 01
despachar 01
despacharse 01
despachurrar 01
despajar 01
despaldar 01
despaldillar 01
despaletillar 01
despalillar 01
despalmar 01
despampanar 01
despampanarse 01
despampanillar 01

despanchurrar 01
despanzurrar 01
despanzurrarse 01
despapar 01
desparasitar 01
desparedar 01
desparejar 01
desparpajar 01
desparramar 01
desparramarse 01
desparvar 01
despatarrar 01
despatarrarse 01
despatillar 01
despavesar 01
despavonar 01
despavorir 79
despavorirse 79
despearse 01
despechar 01
despechugar 19
despechugarse 19
despedazar 16
despedir 39
despedirse 39
despedrar 22
despedregar 19
despegar 19
despegarse 19
despeinar 01
despeinarse 01
despejar 01
despejarse 01
despellejar 01
despellejarse 01
despelotar 01
despelotarse 01
despeluznar 16
despeluznarse 16
despenalizar 16
despenar 01

despeñar 01
despeñarse 01
despepitar 01
despepitarse 01
desperdiciar 08
desperdigar 19
desperdigarse 19
desperecer 45
desperezarse 16
desperfilar 01
despernancarse 13
despernar 22
despersonalizar 16
despersonalizarse 16
despertar 22
despertarse 22
despestañar 01
despezonar 01
despezonarse 01
despezuñarse 01
despicar 13
despicarse 13
despichar 01
despicharse 01
despiezar 16
despilarar 01
despilfarrar 01
despimpollar 01
despinochar 01
despintar 01
despintarse 01
despinzar 16
despiojar 01
despiolar 01
despistar 01
despistarse 01
despistolizar 16
desplacer 61
desplantar 01
desplantarse 01
desplatar 01

desplatear 01
desplazar 16
desplazarse 16
desplegar 24
desplegarse 24
despleguetear 01
desplomar 01
desplomarse 01
desplumar 01
desplumarse 01
despoblar 28
despoblarse 28
despoetizar 16
despojar 01
despolarizar 16
despolitizar 16
despolvar 01
despolvorear 01
despopularizar 16
desportillar 01
desportillarse 01
desposar 01
desposarse 01
desposeer 12
despostar 01
despotizar 16
despotricar 13
despreciar 08
desprecintar 01
desprender 02
desprenderse 02
despreocuparse 01
despresar 01
desprestigiar 08
desprestigiarse 08
despresurizar 16
despresurizarse 16
desprogramar 01
desproporcionar 01
desproveer 12
despulpar 01

despumar 01
despuntar 01
despuntarse 01
desquebrajar 01
desquebrajarse 01
desquejar 01
desquerer 70
desquiciar 08
desquiciarse 08
desquijarar 01
desquijerar 01
desrabar 01
desrabotar 01
desramar 01
desratizar 16
desregular 01
desrielar 01
desriñonar 01
desriñonarse 01
desriscarse 13
desrizar 16
desrizarse 16
desroblar 01
desrodrigar 19
destacar 13
destacarse 13
destajar 01
destallar 01
destalonar 01
destapar 01
destaparse 01
destapiar 08
destaponar 01
destarar 01
destazar 16
destechar 01
destejar 01
destejer 02
destellar 01
destemplar 01
destemplarse 01

destender 26
destensar 01
destensarse 01
desteñir 39
desteñirse 39
desternerar 01
desterrar 22
desterronar 01
destetar 01
destetarse 01
destilar 01
destilarse 01
destinar 01
destituir 52
destocar 13
destocarse 13
destorcer 36
destorcerse 36
destornillar 01
destornillarse 01
destrabar 01
destrabarse 01
destramar 01
destrenzar 16
destripar 01
destriunfar 01
destrizar 16
destrocar 29
destronar 01
destroncar 13
destrozar 16
destrozarse 16
destruir 52
destruirse 52
destusar 01
desubicar 13
desubicarse 13
desuerar 01
desulfurar 01
desuncir 15
desunir 03

desunirse 03
desuñar 01
desurdir 03
desusar 01
desustanciar 08
desvahar 01
desvainar 01
desvalijar 01
desvalorar 01
desvalorarse 01
desvalorizar 16
desvalorizarse 16
desvanecer 45
desvanecerse 45
desvarar 01
desvariar 07
desvastigar 19
desvedar 01
desvelar 01
desvelarse 01
desvenar 01
desvencijar 01
desvencijarse 01
desvendar 01
desventar 22
desvertebrarse 01
desvestir 39
desvestirse 39
desviar 07
desviarse 07
desvincular 01
desvirar 01
desvirgar 19
desvirtuar 09
desvitalizar 16
desvitrificar 13
desvolcanarse 01
desyemar 01
desyerbar 01
desyugar 19
deszulacar 13

deszumar 01
detallar 01
detectar 01
detener 72
detenerse 72
detentar 01
deterger 17
deteriorar 01
deteriorarse 01
determinar 01
determinarse 01
detestar 01
detonar 01
detractar 01
detraer 60
devalar 01
devaluar 09
devaluarse 09
devanar 01
devanarse 01
devanear 01
devastar 01
develar 01
devengar 19
devenir 73
devolver 35
devolverse 35
devorar 01
diablear 01
diagnosticar 13
dializar 16
dialogar 19
diamantar 01
dibujar 01
dibujarse 01
dictaminar 01
dictar 01
diezmar 01
difamar 01
diferenciar 08
diferenciarse 08

diferir 55
dificultar 01
difluir 52
difractar 01
difuminar 01
difuminarse 01
difundir 03
difundirse 03
digerir 55
digitalizar 16
digitar 01
dignarse 01
dignificar 13
dilapidar 01
dilatar 01
dilatarse 01
diligenciar 08
dilucidar 01
diluir 52
diluirse 52
diluviar 08
dimitir 03
dinamitar 01
dinamizar 16
diñar 01
diplomar 01
diplomarse 01
diptongar 19
diputar 01
direccionar 01
dirigir 18
dirimir 03
discar 13
discernir 27
disciplinar 01
disciplinarse 01
discontinuar 09
discordar 28
discrepar 01
discretear 01
discriminar 01

disculpar 01
disculparse 01
discurrir 03
discursear 01
discutir 03
disecar 13
diseccionar 01
diseminar 01
diseminarse 01
disentir 55
diseñar 01
disertar 01
disfrazar 16
disfrutar 01
disgregar 19
disgregarse 19
disgustar 01
disgustarse 01
disidir 03
disimilar 01
disimular 01
disipar 01
disiparse 01
dislocar 13
dislocarse 13
disminuir 52
disociar 08
disociarse 08
disolver 35
disolverse 35
disonar 28
disparar 01
dispararse 01
disparatar 01
dispensar 01
dispersar 01
dispersarse 01
displacer 61
disponer 69
disputar 01
disputarse 01

embadurnarse 01
embaír 79
embalar 01
embalarse 01
embaldosar 01
emballenar 01
embalsamar 01
embalsar 01
embalsarse 01
embanastar 01
embancarse 13
embanderar 01
embanquetar 01
embarazar 16
embarbascarse 13
embarbecer 45
embarbillar 01
embarcar 13
embarcarse 13
embardar 01
embargar 19
embarrancar 13
embarrancarse 13
embarrar 01
embarrarse 01
embarrilar 01
embarullar 01
embarullarse 01
embastar 01
embastecer 45
embastecerse 45
embaucar 13
embaular 05
embazar 16
embazarse 16
embebecer 45
embebecerse 45
embeber 02
embelecar 13
embelesar 01
embelesarse 01

embellaquecerse 45
embellecer 45
embellecerse 45
embermejar 03
embermejecer 45
emberrenchinarse 01
emberrincharse 01
embestir 39
embetunar 01
embicar 13
embicharse 01
embijar 01
embizcar 13
emblandecer 45
emblandecerse 45
emblanquecer 45
embobar 01
embobarse 01
embobecer 45
embocar 13
embocinarse 01
embochinarse 01
embodegar 19
embojar 01
embolar 01
embolarse 01
embolismar 01
embolsar 01
embolsarse 01
embonar 01
emboñigar 19
emboquillar 01
emborrachar 01
emborracharse 01
emborrar 01
emborrascarse 13
emborrazar 16
emborricarse 13
emborrizar 16
emborronar 01
emboscar 13

emboscarse 13
embosquecer 45
embostar 01
embotar 01
embotarse 01
embotellar 01
embotellarse 01
embotijar 01
embotijarse 01
embovedar 01
embozalar 01
embozar 16
embozarse 16
embragar 19
embravecer 45
embravecerse 45
embrazar 16
embrear 01
embreñarse 01
embriagar 19
embriagarse 19
embridar 01
embrocar 13
embrochalar 01
embrollar 01
embrollarse 01
embromar 01
embromarse 01
embroquetar 01
embrujar 01
embrutecer 45
embrutecerse 45
embuchar 01
embudar 01
embullar 01
emburujar 01
emburujarse 01
embutir 03
embutirse 03
emerger 17
emigrar 01

emitir 03

emocionar 01

emocionarse 01

empacar 13

empacarse 13

empachar 01

empacharse 01

empadronar 01

empadronarse 01

empajar 01

empajarse 01

empalagar 19

empalar 01

empalarse 01

empaliar 08

empalizar 16

empalmar 01

empanar 01

empanarse 01

empanizar 16

empantanar 01

empantanarse 01

empañar 01

empapar 01

empaparse 01

empapelar 01

empapirotarse 01

empaquetar 01

empaquetarse 01

emparamar 01

emparamarse 01

emparchar 01

empardar 01

emparedar 01

emparejar 01

emparejarse 01

emparentar 22

emparrar 01

emparrillar 01

emparvar 01

empastar 01

empastarse 01

empastelar 01

empastillar 01

empastillarse 01

empatar 01

empatarse 01

empatizar 16

empavar 01

empavarse 01

empavesar 01

empavonar 01

empavonarse 01

empecinar 01

empedar 01

empedarse 01

empedernir 79

empedernirse 79

empedrar 22

empegar 19

empelechar 01

empellar 01

empellejar 01

empeller 02

empelotarse 01

empenachar 01

empentar 01

empeñar 01

empeñarse 01

empeorar 01

empequeñecer 45

empequeñecerse 45

emperchar 01

emperdigar 19

emperejilarse 01

emperezarse 16

empergaminar 01

emperifollar 01

emperifollarse 01

empernar 01

empertigar 01

empezar 23

empicarse en *or* con 23

empicotar 01

empilar 01

empilcharse 01

empiltrarse 01

empinar 01

empinarse 01

empingorotar 01

empingorotarse 01

empiparse 01

empitonar 01

empizarrar 01

emplastar 01

emplastecer 45

emplazar 16

emplear 01

emplearse 01

emplebeyecer 45

emplomar 01

emplumar 01

emplumecer 45

empobrecer 45

empobrecerse 45

empodrecer 45

empodrecerse 45

empollar 01

empollarse 01

empolvar 01

empolvarse 01

empolvorar 03

empolvorizar 16

emponcharse 01

emponzoñar 01

empopar 01

emporcar 29

emporcarse 29

emporrarse 01

empotrar 01

empotrarse 01

empozar 16

empozarse 16

empradizar 16
emprender 02
empreñar 01
empreñarse 01
emprestar 01
emprimar 01
empujar 01
empulgar 19
empuntar 01
empuntarse 01
empuñar 01
emular 01
emulsionar 01
enaceitar 01
enaceitarse 01
enaguachar 01
enaguacharse 01
enaguar 11
enaguazar 16
enajenar 01
enajenarse 01
enalbar 01
enalbardar 01
enaltecer 45
enaltecerse 45
enamorar 01
enamorarse 01
enamoricarse 13
enamoriscarse 01
enancarse 13
enanchar 01
enarbolar 01
enarbolarse 01
enarcar 13
enardecer 45
enardecerse 45
enarenar 01
enarenarse 01
enastar 01
encabalgar 19
encaballar 01

encabestrar 01
encabestrarse 01
encabezar 16
encabritarse 01
encabronarse 01
encachar 01
encadenar 01
encadenarse 01
encajar 01
encajarse 01
encajonar 01
encajonarse 01
encalabozar 16
encalabrinar 01
encalabrinarse 01
encalar 01
encallar 01
encallarse 01
encallecer 45
encallecerse 45
encalmarse 01
encalomar 01
encalvecer 45
encamarse 01
encambijar 01
encaminar 01
encaminarse 01
encamisar 01
encamotarse 01
encampanar 01
encampanarse 01
encanalar 03
encanalizar 16
encanallar 01
encanallarse 01
encanar 01
encanastar 01
encancerarse 01
encandecer 45
encandelar 01
encandelillar 01

encandilar 01
encandilarse 01
encanecer 45
encanecerse 45
encanijarse 01
encanillar 01
encantar 01
encanutar 01
encañar 01
encañonar 01
encapachar 01
encaparazonar 01
encapillar 01
encapillarse 01
encapirotar 01
encapotar 01
encapotarse 01
encapricharse 01
encapuchar 03
encapucharse 03
encapuzar 16
encapuzarse 16
encaramar 01
encaramarse 01
encarar 01
encarcelar 01
encarecer 45
encarecerse 45
encargar 19
encargarse 19
encariñar 01
encarnar 01
encarnarse 01
encarnecer 45
encarnizar 16
encarpetar 01
encarrilar 01
encarrilarse 01
encarroñar 01
encarroñarse 01
encarrujarse 01

encartar 01
encartonar 01
encascabelar 01
encascotar 01
encasillar 01
encasillarse 01
encasquetar 01
encasquetarse 01
encasquillar 01
encasquillarse 01
encastillar 01
encastillarse 01
encastrar 01
encauchar 01
encausar 01
encausticar 13
encauzar 16
encebadar 01
encebadarse 01
encebollar 01
enceguecer 45
encelar 01
encelarse 01
encellar 01
encenagarse 19
encender 26
encenderse 26
encenizar 16
encentar 22
encepar 01
enceparse 01
encerar 01
encerotar 01
encerrar 22
encerrarse 22
encespedar 01
encestar 01
enchalecar 13
enchancletar 01
enchapar 01
encharcar 13

encharcarse 13
enchicharse 01
enchilar 01
enchilarse 01
enchinar 01
enchinchar 01
enchincharse 01
enchiquerar 01
enchironar 01
enchivarse 01
enchuecar 13
enchufar 01
enchufarse 01
encimar 01
encintar 01
encismar 01
encizañar 01
enclaustrar 01
enclaustrarse 01
enclavar 01
enclavarse 01
enclavijar 01
enclocar 29
encobrar 01
encocorar 01
encofrar 01
encoger 17
encogerse 17
encolar 01
encolerizar 16
encolerizarse 16
encomendar 22
encomiar 08
encompadrar 01
enconar 01
enconarse 01
encontrar 28
encontrarse 28
encoñarse 01
encopetar 01
encopetarse 01

encorajinar 01
encorajinarse 01
encorar 28
encorbatarse 01
encorchar 01
encorchetar 01
encordar 28
encordarse 28
encordelar 01
encordonar 01
encorozar 16
encorralar 01
encorsetar 01
encorvar 01
encorvarse 01
encostalar 01
encostrar 28
encostrarse 28
encovar 28
encrasar 01
encrespar 01
encresparse 01
encriptar 01
encristalar 01
encrudecerse 45
encuadernar 01
encuadrar 01
encuadrarse 01
encubar 01
encubrir 03
encuerar 01
encuestar 01
encularse 01
encumbrar 01
encumbrarse 01
encunar 01
encurtir 03
endemoniar 01
endentar 22
endentecer 45
enderezar 16

enderezarse 16	enfrascar 13	engordarse 01
endeudar 01	enfrenar 01	engoznar 01
endeudarse 01	enfrentar 01	engrampar 01
endiablar 01	enfrentarse 01	engranar 01
endilgar 01	enfriar 07	engrandecer 45
endiñar 01	enfriarse 07	engrandecerse 45
endiosar 01	enfrontar 01	engrapar 01
endiosarse 01	enfundar 01	engrasar 01
endomingar 19	enfundarse 01	engrasarse 01
endomingarse 19	enfurecer 45	engreír 42
endosar 01	enfurecerse 45	engreírse 42
endoselar 01	enfurruñarse 01	engrescar 13
endrogarse 19	enfurtir 03	engrescarse 13
endulzar 16	engafar 01	engrifarse 01
endurar 01	engaitar 01	engrillar 01
endurecer 45	engalanar 01	engrillarse 01
endurecerse 45	engalanarse 01	engringarse 19
enemistar 01	engalgar 19	engriparse 01
enemistarse 01	engallarse 01	engrosar 28
enervar 01	enganchar 01	engrosarse 28
enfadar 01	engancharse 01	engrudar 01
enfadarse 01	engañar 01	engrudarse 01
enfaldar 01	engañarse 01	engrupir 03
enfangar 19	engarabitarse 01	enguachinar 01
enfangarse 19	engargolar 01	engualdrapar 01
enfardar 01	engarrotar 01	engualichar 01
enfardelar 01	engarzar 16	enguantarse 01
enfatizar 16	engastar 01	enguatar 01
enfermar 01	engatillar 01	enguijarrar 01
enfermarse 01	engatusar 01	enguirnaldar 01
enfervorizar 16	engavillar 01	engullir 03
enfervorizarse 16	engazar 16	enharinar 01
enfeudar 01	engendrar 01	enhebrar 01
enfiestarse 01	englobar 01	enherbolar 01
enfilar 01	engolfar 01	enhilar 01
enfistolarse 01	engolfarse 01	enhornar 01
enflaquecer 45	engolosinar 01	enjabonar 01
enflautar 01	engomar 01	enjabonarse 01
enfocar 13	engominar 01	enjaezar 16
enfoscar 13	engominarse 01	enjalbegar 19
enfoscarse 13	engordar 01	enjalmar 01

enjambrar 01
enjaquimar 01
enjarciar 08
enjaretar 01
enjaular 01
enjaularse 01
enjebar 01
enjertar 01
enjimelgar 19
enjoyar 01
enjoyarse 01
enjuagar 19
enjuagarse 19
enjugar 19
enjugarse 19
enjuiciar 08
enlabiar 08
enladrillar 01
enlagunar 01
enlardar 01
enlatar 01
enlazar 16
enlazarse 16
enlegamar 01
enligar 19
enligarse 19
enllantar 01
enlobreguecer 45
enlodar 03
enlodazar 16
enlomar 01
enlomarse 01
enloquecer 45
enlosar 01
enlozar 16
enlucir 47
enlustrecer 45
enlutar 01
enlutarse 01
enmaderar 01
enmadrarse 01

enmallarse 01
enmangar 19
enmantar 01
enmantecar 13
enmarañar 01
enmarañarse 01
enmararse 01
enmarcar 13
enmarcarse 13
enmaridar 01
enmarillecerse 45
enmaromar 01
enmascarar 01
enmascararse 01
enmasillar 01
enmelar 22
enmendar 22
enmendarse 22
enmicar 13
enmohecer 45
enmohecerse 45
enmollecerse 45
enmontarse 01
enmoquetar 01
enmudecer 45
enmugrar 01
enmugrarse 01
enmugrecer 45
enmugrecerse 45
enmuinarse 01
ennegrecer 45
ennegrecerse 45
ennoblecer 45
enojar 01
enojarse 01
enorgullecer 45
enquiciar 08
enquistarse 01
enrabiar 08
enrabiarse 08
enraizar 16

enraizarse 16
enramar 01
enranciar 08
enranciarse 08
enrarecer 45
enrarecerse 45
enrasar 01
enrayar 01
enredar 01
enredarse 01
enrejar 01
enriar 07
enrielar 01
enripiar 08
enriquecer 45
enriquecerse 45
enriscarse 13
enristrar 01
enrocar 13
enrocarse 13
enrodrigar 19
enrodrigonar 19
enrojecer 45
enrojecerse 45
enrolar 01
enrollar 01
enrollarse 01
enromar 01
enronquecer 45
enronquecerse 45
enroscar 13
enroscarse 13
enrostrar 01
enrubiar 08
enrubiarse 08
enrular 01
enrularse 01
ensabanar 01
ensabanarse 01
ensacar 13
ensalivar 01

ensalmar 01
ensalzar 16
ensambenitar 01
ensamblar 01
ensanchar 01
ensancharse 01
ensandecer 45
ensangrentar 22
ensangrentarse 22
ensañarse 01
ensarmentar 22
ensartar 01
ensartarse 01
ensayar 01
ensebar 01
ensenar 01
enseñar 01
enseñarse 01
enserar 01
enseriarse 08
ensilar 01
ensillar 01
ensilvecerse 45
ensimismarse 01
ensoberbecer 45
ensoberbecerse 45
ensogar 19
ensombrecer 45
ensombrecerse 45
ensopar 01
ensoparse 01
ensordecer 45
ensortijar 01
ensortijarse 01
ensuciar 08
ensuciarse 08
entablar 01
entablarse 01
entablerarse 01
entablillar 01
entalamar 01

entalegar 19
entalegarse 19
entalingar 19
entallar 01
entallecer 45
entapar 01
entapizar 16
entapujar 01
entarimar 01
entarquinar 01
entarugar 19
entechar 01
entender 26
entenderse 26
entenebrecer 45
entenebrecerse 45
enterar 01
enterarse 01
entercarse 13
enternecer 45
enternecerse 45
enterrar 22
enterrarse 22
entesar 01
entibar 01
entibiar 08
entibiarse 08
entinar 01
entintar 01
entintarse 01
entiznar 01
entoldar 01
entoldarse 01
entomizar 16
entonar 01
entonarse 01
entonelar 01
entongar 19
entontar 01
entontarse 01
entontecer 45

entontecerse 45
entorchar 01
entorilar 01
entornar 01
entorpecer 45
entortar 28
entosigar 19
entramar 01
entrampar 01
entramparse 01
entrañar 01
entrañarse 01
entrar 01
entreabrir 03
entreabrirse 03
entreayudarse 01
entrecavar 01
entrecerrar 22
entrechocar 13
entrechocarse 13
entrecomar 01
entrecomillar 01
entrecortar 01
entrecortarse 01
entrecruzar 16
entrecruzarse 16
entredecir 74
entregar 19
entregarse 19
entrejuntar 01
entrelazar 16
entrelazarse 16
entrelinear 01
entrelucir 47
entremeter 02
entremezclar 01
entremezclarse 01
entrenar 01
entrenarse 01
entreoír 58
entrepelar 01

trerrenglonar 01
tresacar 13
tretallar 01
tretejer 02
tretener 72
tretenerse 72
trever 75
treverse 75
treverar 01
treverarse 01
trevistar 01
trevistarse 01
tristecer 45
trojar 01
trometerse 02
tromparse 01
tronar 01
troncar 13
tronizar 16
truchar 01
trujar 01
tubar 01
tullecer 45
tumecer 45
tumecerse 45
tumirse 03
tunicar 13
tupir 03
turbiar 08
turbiarse 08
tusiasmar 01
tusiasmarse 01
uclear 01
umerar 01
unciar 08
vainar 01
valentonar 01
valentonarse 01
vanecer 45
vanecerse 45
varar 01

envararse 01
envasar 01
envedijarse 01
envejecer 45
envejecerse 45
envenenar 01
envenenarse 01
enverar 01
enverdecer 45
envergar 19
enviar 07
enviciar 08
enviciarse 08
envidar 01
envidiar 08
envigar 19
envilecer 45
envilecerse 45
envinagrar 01
envinar 01
enviscar 13
enviscarse 13
enviudar 01
envolver 35
envolverse 35
enyerbar 01
enyesar 01
enyetar 01
enyodar 01
enyugar 19
enyuntar 01
enzainarse 01
enzarzar 16
enzunchar 01
enzurdecer 45
enzurizar 16
enzurronar 01
epatar 01
epilogar 19
epitomar 01
equidistar 01

equilibrar 01
equilibrarse 01
equipar 01
equiparse 01
equiparar 01
equipararse 01
equiponderar 01
equivocar 13
equivocarse 13
ergotizar 16
erguir 56
erguirse 56
erigir 18
erizar 16
erizarse 16
erogar 19
erosionar 01
erosionarse 01
erotizar 16
erradicar 13
errar 25
eructar 01
esbozar 16
escabechar 01
escabullirse 03
escachar 01
escacharrar 01
escacharrarse 01
escalar 01
escaldar 01
escaldarse 01
escalfar 01
escalonar 01
escalpar 01
escamar 01
escamondar 01
escamotear 01
escampar 01
escamujar 01
escanciar 08
escandalizar 16

escandalizarse 16	escodar 01	escurrirse 03
escandallar 01	escofinar 01	esdrujulizar 16
escandir 03	escoger 17	esfacelarse 01
escanear 01	escolarizar 16	esforzar 33
escantillar 01	escoliar 08	esforzarse 33
escapar 01	escollar 01	esfumar 01
escaparse 01	escoltar 01	esfumarse 01
escaquearse 01	escombrar 01	esfuminar 01
escarabajear 01	esconder 02	esgrafiar 07
escaramucear 01	esconderse 02	esgrimir 03
escaramuzar 16	escoñar 01	esguazar 16
escarapelar 01	escoñarse 01	eslabonar 01
escarapelarse 01	escopetear 01	eslavizar 16
escarbar 01	escopetearse 01	eslingar 19
escarbarse 01	escoplear 01	esmachar 01
escarchar 01	escorar 01	esmaltar 01
escardar 01	escorarse 01	esmerarse 01
escardillar 01	escoriar 08	esmerilar 01
escariar 08	escorificar 13	esnifar 01
escarificar 13	escorzar 16	espabilar 01
escarificarse 13	escoscarse 13	espabilarse 01
escarizar 16	escotar 01	espachurrar 01
escarmenar 01	escrachar 01	espaciar 08
escarmentar 22	escracharse 01	espaciarse 08
escarnecer 45	escribir 03	espaldear 01
escarolar 01	escribirse 03	espaldonarse 01
escarpar 01	escriturar 01	espantar 01
escarrancharse 01	escrutar 01	espantarse 01
escarzar 16	escuadrar 01	españolear 01
escasear 01	escuadronar 01	españolizar 16
escatimar 01	escuchar 01	españolizarse 16
escayolar 01	escucharse 01	esparcir 15
escenificar 13	escudar 01	esparcirse 15
escindir 03	escuderear 01	esparrancarse 13
escindirse 03	escudillar 01	espatarrarse 01
esclarecer 45	escudriñar 01	especializar 16
esclavizar 16	escueznar 01	especializarse 16
escobar 01	esculcar 13	especificar 13
escobillar 01	esculpir 03	especular 01
escocer 36	escupir 03	espejear 01
escocerse 36	escurrir 03	espeluzar 16

peluznar 01
peranzar 16
peranzarse 16
perar 01
perarse 01
pesar 01
pesarse 01
petar 01
piar 07
pichar 01
pigar 19
pigarse 19
pinar 01
pirar 01
piritualizar 16
pitar 01
plender 02
polear 01
poliar 08
polvorear 01
ponjar 01
ponjarse 01
ponsorizar 16
portear 01
posar 01
printar 01
pulgar 19
pumajear 01
pumar 01
purrear 03
purriar 08
putar 01
quematizar 16
quiar 07
quilar 01
quilmar 01
quinar 01
quinzar 16
quivar 01
quivarse 01
tabilizar 16

estabilizarse 16
establecer 45
establecerse 45
estabular 01
estacar 13
estacarse 13
estacionar 01
estacionarse 01
estafar 01
estallar 01
estambrar 01
estampar 01
estamparse 01
estampillar 01
estancar 13
estancarse 13
estandardizar 16
estandarizar 16
estañar 01
estaquear 01
estaquillar 01
estar 64
estarse 64
estarcir 03
estatalizar 16
estatificar 13
estatizar 16
estatuir 52
estelarizar 16
esterar 01
estercolar 01
estereotipar 01
esterificar 13
esterilizar 16
estezar 16
estibar 01
estigmatizar 16
estilar 01
estilarse 01
estilizar 16
estilizarse 16

estimar 01
estimarse 01
estimular 01
estipendiar 08
estipular 01
estirar 01
estirarse 01
estofar 01
estomagar 19
estoquear 01
estorbar 01
estornudar 01
estovar 01
estragar 19
estragarse 19
estrangular 01
estrangularse 01
estraperlear 01
estratificar 13
estratificarse 13
estrechar 01
estrecharse 01
estregar 24
estregarse 24
estrellar 01
estrellarse 01
estremecer 45
estremecerse 45
estrenar 01
estrenarse 01
estreñir 39
estresar 01
estresarse 01
estriar 07
estriarse 07
estridular 01
estropear 01
estropearse 01
estroquear 01
estructurar 01
estrujar 01

estrujarse 01
estucar 13
estudiar 08
estudiarse 08
estuprar 01
eterificar 13
eterizar 16
eternizar 16
eternizarse 16
etimologizar 16
etiquetar 01
europeizar 16
europeizarse 16
euscaldunizar 16
euskaldunizar 16
evacuar 10
evadir 03
evadirse 03
evaluar 09
evangelizar 16
evaporar 01
evaporarse 01
evaporizar 16
evidenciar 08
evidenciarse 08
evitar 01
evitarse 01
evocar 13
evolucionar 01
exacerbar 01
exacerbarse 01
exagerar 01
exaltar 01
exaltarse 01
examinar 01
examinarse 01
exasperar 01
exasperarse 01
excarcelar 01
excarcelarse 01
excavar 01

exceder 02
excederse 02
exceptuar 09
exceptuarse 09
excitar 01
excitarse 01
exclamar 01
exclamarse 01
exclaustrar 01
excluir 52
excluirse 52
excomulgar 19
excoriar 08
excoriarse 08
excrementar 01
excretar 01
exculpar 01
exculparse de
excusar 01
excusarse 01
execrar 01
exentar 01
exfoliar 08
exfoliarse 08
exhalar 01
exheredar 01
exhibir 03
exhibirse 03
exhortar 01
exhumar 01
exigir 18
exilar 01
exiliar 08
exiliarse 08
eximir 03
eximirse 03
existir 03
exonerar 01
exorbitar 01
exorcizar 16
exornar 01

expandir 03
expandirse 03
expansionar 01
expansionarse 01
expatriar 08
expatriarse 08
expectorar 01
expedientar 01
expedir 39
expedirse 39
expeler 02
expender 02
expensar 01
experimentar 01
expiar 07
expirar 01
explanar 01
explayar 01
explayarse 01
explicar 13
explicarse 13
explicitar 01
explicotear 01
explorar 01
explosionar 01
explotar 01
expoliar 08
exponer 69
exponerse 69
exportar 01
expresar 01
expresarse 01
exprimir 03
expropiar 08
expugnar 01
expulsar 01
expurgar 19
extasiar 07
extasiarse 07
extender 26
extenderse 26

xtenuar 09
xtenuarse 09
xteriorizar 16
xterminar 01
xternalizar 16
xternar 01
xtinguir 20
xtinguirse 20
xtirpar 01
xtornar 01
xtorsionar 01
xtractar 01
xtradir 03
xtraditar 01
xtraer 60
xtralimitarse 01
xtranjerizar 16
xtrañar 01
xtrañarse 01
xtrapolar 01
xtravasarse 01
xtravenarse 01
xtraviar 07
xtraviarse 07
xtremar 01
xtremarse 01
xtrudir 03
xudar 01
xulcerar 01
xultar 01
yacular 01
yectar 01

abricar 13
abular 01
achear 01
achendear 01
acilitar 01
acturar 01
acultar 01

faenar 01
fagocitar 01
fajar 01
fajarse 01
faldear 01
fallar 01
fallecer 45
falopear 01
falopearse 01
falsear 01
falsificar 13
faltar 01
familiarizar 16
fanatizar 16
fanfarrear 01
fanfarronear 01
fantasear 01
fardar 01
farfullar 01
farolear 01
farrear 01
farsear 01
fascinar 01
fastidiar 08
fastidiarse 08
fatigar 19
fatigarse 19
faulear 01
favorecer 45
faxear 01
fayuquear 01
falluquear 01
fechar 01
fecundar 01
fecundizar 16
federalizar 16
federar 01
federarse 01
felicitar 01
felicitarse 01
feminizar 16

feminizarse 16
fenecer 45
feriar 08
fermentar 01
fertilizar 16
festejar 01
festejarse 01
festinar 01
festonear 01
fiar 07
fiarse 07
fibrilar 01
fichar 01
fidelizar 16
figurar 01
figurarse 01
fijar 01
fijarse 01
fildear 01
filetear 01
filiar 08
filiarse 08
filmar 01
filosofar 01
filtrar 01
filtrarse 01
finalizar 16
financiar 08
finar 01
fincar 13
fingir 18
fingirse 18
finiquitar 01
fintar 01
firmar 01
fiscalizar 16
fisgar 19
fisgonear 01
fisionar 01
flagelar 01
flagelarse 01

flambear 01
flamear 01
flanquear 01
flaquear 01
flechar 01
fletar 01
fletarse 01
flexibilizar 16
flexionar 01
flexionarse 01
flipar 01
flirtear 01
flocular 01
flojear 01
florar 01
flordelisar 01
florear 01
florecer 45
florecerse 45
floretear 01
flotar 01
fluctuar 09
fluidificar 13
fluir 52
focalizar 16
foguear 01
foguearse 01
foliar 08
fomentar 01
fondear 01
fondearse 01
forcejear 01
forestar 01
forjar 01
forjarse 01
formalizar 16
formar 01
formarse 01
formatear 01
formular 01
fornicar 13

forrajear 01
forrar 01
forrarse 01
fortalecer 45
fortalecerse 45
fortificar 13
fortificarse 13
forzar 33
forzarse 33
fosar 01
fosfatar 01
fosforescer 45
fosilizarse 16
fotocomponer 69
fotocopiar 08
fotograbar 01
fotografiar 07
fotolitografiar 07
foulear 01
fracasar 01
fraccionar 01
fracturar 01
fracturarse 01
fragmentar 01
fragmentarse 01
fraguar 11
fraguarse 11
franjar 01
franjear 01
franquear 01
franquearse 01
franquiciar 08
frasear 01
fraternizar 16
frecuentar 01
fregar 24
fregotear 01
freír 42
freírse 42
frenar 01
frenarse 01

fresar 01
frezar 16
fricar 13
friccionar 01
frigorizar 16
frisar 01
fritar 01
frotar 01
frotarse 01
fructificar 13
fruncir 15
frustrar 01
frustrarse 01
fucilar 01
fugarse 19
fulgir 18
fulgurar 01
fullear 01
fulminar 01
fumar 01
fumarse 01
fumetear 01
fumigar 19
funcar 13
funcionar 01
fundamentar 01
fundar 01
fundir 03
fundirse 03
fungir 18
fusilar 01
fusionar 01
fusionarse 01
fustigar 19

G

gafar 01
gaguear 01
galantear 01
galardonar 01
galguear 01

libar 01
llardear 01
llear 01
llofear 01
lonear 01
lopar 01
lopear 01
lvanizar 16
mbetear 01
nar 01
narse 01
ndulear 01
ngosear 01
ngrenarse 01
nguear 01
nsear 01
ñir 03
rabatear 01
rantir 79
rantizar 16
rapiñar 01
rbear 01
rbearse 01
rbillar 01
rfear 01
rgajear 01
rgantear 01
rgarizar 16
rlar 01
rpar 01
rrafiñar 01
rrapatear 01
rrapiñar 01
rapiñar 01
rrar 01
rrear 01
rrochear 01
rronear 01
ruar 09
sear 01
sificar 13

gastar 01
gastarse 01
gatear 01
gayar 01
gelificar 13
gemir 39
generalizar 16
generalizarse 16
generar 01
geometrizar 16
gerenciar 08
germanizar 16
germinar 01
gestar 01
gestarse 01
gestear 01
gesticular 01
gestionar 01
gibar 01
gimotear 01
girar 01
girarse 01
gitanear 01
glasear 01
globalizar 16
gloriar 08
glorificar 13
glosar 01
glotonear 01
gluglutear 01
gobernar 22
gobernarse 22
gofrar 01
golear 01
golfear 01
golletear 01
golosear 01
golosinar 01
golosinear 01
golpear 01
golpearse 01

golpetear 01
gongorizar 16
gorgojarse 01
gorgojearse 01
gorgoritear 01
gorgotear 01
gorjear 01
gorrear 01
gorronear 01
gotear 01
gozar 16
grabar 01
gracejar 01
gradar 01
graduar 09
graduarse 09
grafilar 01
grajear 01
granar 01
granear 01
granizar 16
granjear 01
granjearse 01
granular 01
granularse 01
grapar 01
gratar 01
gratificar 13
gratinar 01
gravar 01
gravitar 01
graznar 01
grillarse 01
grisear 01
gritar 01
gruir 52
grujir 03
gruñir 03
guachapear 01
guadañar 01
gualdrapear 01

guantear 01
guapear 01
guaquear 01
guarachar 01
guarachear 01
guardar 01
guardarse 01
guarecer 45
guarecerse 45
guarnecer 45
guarnicionar 01
guarnir 79
guarrear 01
guasearse 01
guatear 01
guayabear 01
guayar 01
guayarse 01
guerrear 01
guerrillear 01
guiar 07
guiarse 07
guillarse 01
guillotinar 01
guinchar 01
guindar 01
guindarse 01
guiñar 01
guiñarse 01
guipar 01
guisar 01
guisarse 01
guisotear 01
guitar 01
guitarrear 01
guitonear 01
gulusmear 01
gusanear 01
gustar 01
gustarse 01

H

haber 76
habérse 76
habilitar 01
habitar 01
habituar 09
habituarse 09
hablar 01
hablarse 01
hacendar 22
hacendarse 22
hacer 68
hacerse 68
hachar 01
hachear 01
hacinar 01
hacinarse 01
halagar 19
halar 01
hallar 01
hallarse 01
hamacar 13
hamacarse 13
hambrear 01
haraganear 01
harmonizar 16
haronear 01
hartar 01
hartarse 01
hastiar 07
hatajar 01
hatear 01
hebraizar 16
hechizar 16
heder 26
helar 22
helarse 22
helenizar 16
helenizarse 16
helitransportar 01
henchir 39

hender 26
hendir 03
henificar 13
heñir 39
herbajar 01
herbar 22
herbecer 45
herborizar 16
heredar 01
herir 55
herirse 55
hermanar 01
hermanarse 01
hermosear 01
herniarse 08
heroificar 13
herrar 22
herretear 01
herrumbrar 01
herrumbrarse 01
hervir 55
hesitar 01
hibernar 01
hibridar 01
hibridarse 01
hidratar 01
hidrogenar 01
hidrolizar 16
higienizar 16
higienizarse 16
hijear 01
hilar 01
hilvanar 01
himplar 01
hincar 13
hincarse 13
hinchar 01
hincharse 01
hipar 01
hipertrofiar 08
hiperventilar 01

inventar 01
inventarse 01
inventariar 07
invernar 22
invertir 55
invertirse 55
investigar 19
investir 39
inveterarse 01
invitar 01
invocar 13
involucionar 01
involucrar 01
involucrarse 01
inyectar 01
inyectarse 01
ionizar 16
ir 77
irse 77
irisar 01
ironizar 16
irradiar 08
irreverenciar 08
irrigar 19
irritar 01
irritarse 01
irrogar 19
irrumpir 03
islamizar 16
islamizarse 16
italianizar 16
italianizarse 16
itemizar 16
iterar 01
izar 16
izquierdear 01

J

jabalconar 01
jabardear 01
jabonar 01

jabonarse 01
jacalear 01
jacarear 13
jactarse 01
jadear 01
jaezar 16
jaharrar 01
jalar 01
jalarse 01
jalbegar 19
jalear 01
jalonar 01
jalonear 01
jamar 01
jamarse 01
jambar 01
jaquear 01
jaranear 01
jarciar 08
jaropear 01
jarrear 01
jaspear 01
jemiquear 01
jaremiquear 01
jerarquizar 16
jeremiquear 01
jeringar 19
jeringuear 01
jeringarse 19
jeringuearse 01
jesusear 01
jinetear 01
jipar 01
jipiar 08
joderse 02
jonronear 01
jorrar 01
jubilar 01
jubilarse 01
judaizar 16
juerguearse 01

jugar 34
jugarse 34
juguetear 01
julepear 01
jumarse 01
junar 01
juntar 01
juntarse 01
juramentar 01
juramentarse 01
jurar 01
jurarse 01
jurgar 19
justar 01
justificar 13
justificarse 13
justipreciar 08
juzgar 19

K

kilometrar 01

L

labializar 16
laborar 01
laborear 01
labrar 01
labrarse 01
laburar 01
lacar 13
lacear 01
lacerar 01
lacrar 01
lactar 01
ladear 01
ladearse 01
ladrar 01
ladrillar 01
ladronear 01
lagartear 01
lagotear 01

lagrimar 01
lagrimear 01
laicalizar 16
laicizar 16
lamber 02
lambetear 01
lambisconear 01
lambisquear 01
lamentar 01
lamentarse 01
lamer 02
lamerse 02
lametear 01
laminar 01
lamiscar 13
lampacear 01
lampar 01
lampear 01
lamprear 01
lancear 01
lancinar 01
languidecer 45
lanzar 16
lanzarse 16
lañar 01
lapidar 01
lapidificar 13
laquear 01
lardar 01
lardear 01
largar 19
largarse 19
lascar 13
lastimar 01
lastimarse 01
lastrar 01
latear 01
latiguear 01
latinear 01
latinizar 16
latinizarse 16

latir 03
laudar 01
laurear 01
lavar 01
lavarse 01
lavotear 01
lavotearse 01
laxar 01
layar 01
lazar 16
lechar 01
lechucear 01
leer 12
legajar 01
legalizar 16
legar 19
legislar 01
legitimar 01
legrar 01
lengüetear 01
lenificar 13
lentificar 13
lerdear 01
lesionar 01
lesionarse 01
leudar 01
leudarse 01
levantar 01
levantarse 01
levar 01
levigar 19
levitar 01
lexicalizar 16
lexicalizarse 16
liar 07
liarse 07
libar 01
libelar 01
liberalizar 16
liberalizarse 16
liberar 01

liberarse 01
libertar 01
librar 01
librarse 01
licenciar 08
licenciarse 08
licitar 01
licuar 10
liderar 01
lidiar 08
liftar 01
ligar 19
ligarse 19
lignificarse 13
lijar 01
limar 01
limitar 01
limosnear 01
limpiar 08
limpiarse 08
linchar 01
linear 01
liofilizar 16
liquidar 01
liquidarse 01
lisiar 08
lisiarse 08
lisonjear 01
listar 01
listear 01
listonar 01
litar 01
litigar 19
litofotografiar 07
litografiar 07
lividecer 45
lixiviar 08
llagar 19
llagarse 19
llamar 01
llamarse 01

llamear 01
llanear 01
llegar 19
llenar 01
llenarse 01
lleudar 01
llevar 01
llevarse 01
llorar 01
lloriquear 01
llover 35
lloviznar 01
loar 01
lobreguecer 45
localizar 16
lograr 01
lograrse 01
logrear 01
lomear 01
lonchar 01
loquear 01
losar 01
lotear 01
lotificar 13
lubricar 13
lubrificar 13
luchar 01
lucir 47
lucirse 47
lucrar 01
lucrarse 01
lucubrar 01
ludir 03
lujuriar 08
lustrar 01
lustrarse 01
luxarse 01

M

macanear 01
macaquear 01

macarse 13
macear 01
macerar 01
macerarse 01
machacar 13
machacarse 13
machar 01
machear 01
machetear 01
machihembrar 01
machucar 13
macizar 16
macollar 01
macular 01
madrear 01
madrugar 19
madurar 01
maestralizar 16
maestrear 01
magnetizar 16
magnificar 13
magostar 01
magrear 01
magrearse 01
magullar 01
magullarse 01
majadear 01
majaderear 01
majar 01
malacostumbrar 01
malaxar 01
malbaratar 01
malcasar 01
malcasarse 01
malcomer 02
malcriar 07
maldecir 74
maleabilizar 16
malear 01
malearse 01
maleficiar 08

malenseñar 01
malentender 26
malgastar 01
malherir 55
malhumorar 01
maliciar 08
maliciarse 08
malinformar 01
malinterpretar 01
mallar 01
malmeter 02
malograr 01
malograrse 01
malparar 01
malparir 03
malpasar 01
malquerer 70
malquistar 01
malquistarse 01
maltear 01
maltraer 60
maltratar 01
malvender 02
malversar 01
malvivir 03
mamar 01
mamarse 01
mampostear 01
mampresar 01
mamullar 01
manar 01
mancar 13
mancarse 13
manchar 01
mancharse 01
mancillar 01
mancomunar 01
mancomunarse 01
mancornar 28
mandar 01
mandarse 01

mandrilar 01
manducar 13
manducarse 13
manear 01
manejar 01
manejarse 01
manganear 01
mangar 19
mangonear 01
manguear 01
manguerear 01
maniatar 01
manifestar 22
manifestarse 22
manijear 01
maniobrar 01
manipular 01
manir 79
manosear 01
manosearse 01
manotear 01
mantear 01
mantener 72
mantenerse 72
manufacturar 01
manumitir 03
manuscribir 03
manutener 72
manyar 01
mañanear 01
mañear 01
mañosear 01
mapear 01
maquear 01
maquearse 01
maquetar 01
maquilar 01
maquillar 01
maquillarse 01
maquinar 01
maquinizar 16

maravillar 01
maravillarse 01
marcar 13
marcarse 13
marchamar 01
marchar 01
marcharse 01
marchitar 01
marchitarse 01
marear 01
marearse 01
margar 19
marginalizar 16
marginar 01
marginarse 01
mariconear 01
maridar 01
marinar 01
marinear 01
mariposear 01
mariscar 13
maromear 01
marrar 01
martajar 01
martillar 01
martillear 01
martirizar 16
marujear 01
masacrar 01
masajear 01
mascar 13
mascarse 13
mascujar 01
masculinizar 16
mascullar 01
masificar 13
masificarse 13
masticar 13
masturbar 01
masturbarse 01
mataperrear 01

matar 01
matarse 01
matear 01
materializar 16
matizar 16
matonear 01
matraquear 01
matricular 01
matricularse 01
matrimoniar 08
matutear 01
maulear 01
maullar 05
maximizar 16
mayar 01
mazar 16
maznar 01
mear 01
mecanizar 16
mecanografiar 07
mecer 14
mecerse 14
mechar 01
mediar 08
mediatizar 16
medicalizar 16
medicamentar 01
medicamentarse 01
medicar 13
medicinar 01
medicinarse 01
medir 39
medirse 39
meditar 01
medrar 01
mejorar 01
mejorarse 01
melancolizar 16
melar 22
melificar 13
melindrear 01

mellar 01
mellarse 01
memorar 01
memorizar 16
mencionar 01
mendigar 19
menear 01
menearse 01
menguar 11
menoscabar 01
menospreciar 08
menstruar 09
mensualizar 16
mensurar 01
mentalizar 16
mentalizarse 16
mentar 22
mentir 55
menudear 01
merar 01
mercadear 01
mercantilizar 16
mercar 13
mercerizar 16
merecer 45
merecerse 45
merendar 22
merendarse 22
merengar 19
mermar 01
merodear 01
mesar 01
mesarse 01
mestizar 16
mesurar 01
mesurarse 01
metabolizar 16
metaforizar 16
metalizar 16
metalizarse 16
metamorfosear 01

metamorfosearse 01
meteorizar 16
meter 02
meterse 02
metodizar 16
metrificar 13
mezclar 01
mezclarse 01
mezquinar 01
microfilmar 01
migar 19
migrar 01
militarizar 16
milonguear 01
milpear 01
mimar 01
mimbrear 01
mimeografiar 07
mimetizar 16
mimetizarse 16
minar 01
mineralizar 16
mineralizarse 16
miniar 08
miniaturizar 16
minimizar 16
minorar 01
minusvalorar 01
minutar 01
mirar 01
mirarse 01
miserear 01
mistar 01
mistificar 13
mitificar 13
mitigar 19
mitotear 01
mitridatizar 16
mixtificar 13
mixturar 01
moblar 28

mocar 13
mocarse 13
mocear 01
mocionar 01
modelar 01
moderar 01
moderarse 01
modernizar 16
modernizarse 16
modificar 13
modorrar 01
modorrarse 01
modular 01
mofar 01
mohatrar 01
mohecer 45
mojar 01
mojarse 01
mojonar 01
molar 01
molcajetear 01
moldar 01
moldear 01
moldearse 01
moldurar 01
moler 35
molestar 01
molestarse 01
moletear 01
molificar 13
molliznar 01
molliznear 01
molturar 01
momear 01
momificar 13
momificarse 13
mondar 01
monear 01
monedar 01
monedear 01
monetarizar 16

monetizar 16
monitorear 01
monitorizar 16
monologar 19
monopolizar 16
montar 01
montarse 01
montear 01
moquear 01
moquetear 01
moralizar 16
morar 01
mordentar 01
morder 35
morderse 35
mordicar 13
mordiscar 13
mordisquear 01
morfar 01
morigerar 01
morigerarse 01
morir 57
morirse 57
morrear 01
morrearse 01
mortificar 13
mortificarse 13
moscardear 01
mosconear 01
mosquear 01
mosquearse 01
mostrar 28
mostrarse 28
motear 01
motejar 01
motivar 01
motivarse 01
motorizar 16
motorizarse 16
mover 35
moverse 35

movilizar 16
movilizarse 16
muchachear 01
mudar 01
mudarse 01
mufarse 01
mugir 18
muletear 01
mullir 03
multar 01
multicopiar 08
multiplicar 13
multiplicarse 13
mundanear 01
mundializar 16
municipalizar 16
murar 01
murmurar 01
muscular 01
muscularse 01
musicalizar 16
musicar 13
musitar 01
mustiar 08
mustiarse 08
mutar 01
mutilar 01

N

nacarar 01
nacer 44
nacionalizar 16
nacionalizarse 16
nadar 01
najarse 01
narcotizar 16
narrar 01
nasalizar 16
naturalizar 16
naturalizarse 16
naufragar 19

navegar 19
neblinear 01
necear 01
necesitar 01
negar 24
negarse 24
negociar 08
negrear 01
nesgar 19
neurotizar 16
neurotizarse 16
neutralizar 16
neutralizarse 16
nevar 22
neviscar 13
nidificar 13
nielar 01
nimbar 01
ningunear 01
niñear 01
niquelar 01
nitratar 01
nitrificar 13
nivelar 01
nivelarse 01
nombrar 01
nominar 01
noquear 01
normalizar 16
normalizarse 16
normar 01
nortear 01
notar 01
notarse 01
noticiar 08
notificar 13
novar 01
novelar 01
novelizar 16
nublar 01
nublarse 01

nuclear 01
nuclearse 01
nuclearizar 16
numerar 01
nutrir 03
nutrirse 03

O

obcecar 13
obcecarse 13
obedecer 45
objetar 01
objetivar 01
objetivizar 16
objetualizar 16
oblar 01
oblicuar 10
obligar 19
obliterar 01
obnubilar 01
obnubilarse 01
obrar 01
obsequiar 08
observar 01
obsesionar 01
obstaculizar 16
obstar 01
obstinarse 01
obstruir 52
obstruirse 52
obtemperar 01
obtener 72
obturar 01
obviar 08
ocasionar 01
occidentalizar 16
occidentalizarse 16
ocluir 52
ocluirse 52
octavar 01
ocultar 01

ocultarse 01
ocupar 01
ocuparse 01
ocurrir 03
ocurrirse 03
odiar 08
ofender 02
ofenderse 02
ofertar 01
oficializar 16
oficiar 08
ofrecer 45
ofrecerse 45
ofrendar 01
ofuscar 13
ofuscarse 13
oír 58
ojear 01
ojetear 01
okupar 01
olear 01
oler 37
olerse 37
oletear 01
olfatear 01
oliscar 13
olisquear 01
olivar 01
olorizar 16
olvidar 01
olvidarse 01
omitir 03
ondear 01
ondular 01
opacar 13
opalizar 16
opar 01
operar 01
operarse 01
opilarse 01
opinar 01

oponer 69
oponerse 69
opositar 01
oprimir 03
oprobiar 08
optar 01
optimalizar 16
optimar 01
optimizar 16
opugnar 01
orar 01
orbitar 01
ordenar 01
ordenarse 01
ordeñar 01
orear 01
orearse 01
orejear 01
organizar 16
organizarse 16
orientalizar 16
orientar 01
orientarse 01
orificar 13
originar 01
originarse 01
orillar 01
orillarse 01
orinar 01
orinarse 01
orlar 01
ornamentar 01
ornar 01
orquestar 01
ortografiar 07
orvallar 01
orzar 16
osar 01
oscilar 01
oscurecer 45
oscurecerse 45

osificar 13
osificarse 13
ostentar 01
otear 01
otoñar 01
otoñarse 01
otorgar 19
ovacionar 01
ovalar 01
ovalizar 16
ovar 01
ovillar 01
ovillarse 01
ovular 01
oxidar 01
oxidarse 01
oxigenar 01
oxigenarse 01
ozonizar 16

P

pacer 44
pachanguear 01
pacificar 13
pacificarse 13
pactar 01
padecer 45
padrotear 01
paganizar 16
pagar 19
pagarse 19
paginar 01
pairar 01
pajarear 01
pajear 01
pajearse 01
palabrear 01
paladear 01
palanganear 01
palanquear 01
palatalizar 16

palear 01
paletear 01
paletizar 16
paliar 08
palidecer 45
paliquear 01
pallar 01
palmar 01
palmear 01
palmotear 01
palotear 01
palpar 01
palpitar 01
pandear 01
pandearse 01
panderetear 01
panegirizar 16
panificar 13
papachar 01
papar 01
papear 01
papelear 01
papelonear 01
paquear 01
paquetear 01
parabolizar 16
parafinar 01
parafrasear 01
parahusar 05
paralizar 16
paralogizar 16
paramentar 01
parametrizar 16
parangonar 01
parapetar 01
parapetarse 01
parar 01
pararse 01
parcelar 01
parchar 01
parchear 01

pardear 01
parear 01
parecer 45
parecerse 45
parir 03
parlamentar 01
parlar 01
parlotear 01
parodiar 08
parpadear 01
parpar 01
parquear 01
parrafear 01
parrandear 01
partear 01
participar 01
particularizar 16
particularizarse 16
partir 03
partirse 03
pasamanar 01
pasaportar 01
pasar 01
pasarse 01
pasear 01
pasearse 01
pasmar 01
pasmarse 01
pasparse 01
pasquinar 01
pastar 01
pastear 01
pastelear 01
pasterizar 16
pasteurizar 16
pastorear 01
patalear 01
patear 01
patearse 01
patentar 01
patentizar 16

patinar 01
patiquebrar 01
patrimonializar 16
patrocinar 01
patronear 01
patrullar 01
patullar 01
paular 01
pausar 01
pautar 01
pavear 01
pavimentar 01
pavonar 01
pavonear 01
pavonearse 01
payar 01
payasear 01
pealar 01
pecar 13
pechar 01
pedalear 01
pedantear 01
pedir 39
pedirse 39
peer 02
peerse 02
pegar 19
pegarse 19
pegotear 01
pegotearse 01
peguntar 01
peinar 01
peinarse 01
pelambrar 01
pelar 01
pelarse 01
pelear 01
pelearse 01
pelechar 01
peligrar 01
pellizcar 13

pelotear 01
pelotudear 01
peluquearse 01
penalizar 16
penar 01
pencar 13
pendejear 01
pendenciar 08
pender 02
pendonear 01
penetrar 01
penitenciar 08
pensar 22
pensarse 22
pensionar 01
pepenar 01
peraltar 01
percatarse 01
perchar 01
percibir 03
percudir 03
percutir 03
perder 26
perderse 26
perdonar 01
perdurar 01
perecer 45
peregrinar 01
perfeccionar 01
perfilar 01
perfilarse 01
perforar 01
perforarse 01
perfumar 01
perfumarse 01
pergeñar 01
periclitar 01
perifrasear 01
peritar 01
perjudicar 13
perjurar 01

perlongar 19
permanecer 45
permitir 03
permitirse 03
permutar 01
pernear 01
perniquebrar 22
perniquebrarse 22
pernoctar 01
perorar 01
peroxidar 01
perpetrar 01
perpetuar 09
perpetuarse 09
perquirir 38
perseguir 41
perseverar 01
persignar 01
persignarse 01
persistir 03
personalizar 16
personarse 01
personificar 13
persuadir 03
persuadirse 03
pertrechar 01
pertrecharse 01
perturbar 01
pervertir 55
pervertirse 55
pervivir 03
pesar 01
pesarse 01
pescar 13
pespuntar 01
pespuntear 01
pesquisar 01
pestañear 01
petardear 01
petatearse 01
peticionar 01

petrificar 13
petrificarse 13
petrolear 01
piafar 01
pialar 01
piar 07
picanear 01
picar 13
picarse 13
picardear 01
picardearse 01
pichear 01
pichicatear 01
pichicatearse 01
pichulear 01
picotear 01
pifiar 08
pigmentar 01
pignorar 01
pijotear 01
pilar 01
pillar 01
pillarse 01
pillear 01
pilotar 01
pilotear 01
pimentar 01
pimplar 01
pimplarse 01
pincelar 01
pinchar 01
pincharse 01
pindonguear 01
pingonear 01
pintar 01
pintarse 01
pintarrajar 01
pintarrajear 01
pintear 01
pintiparar 01
pintonear 01

pintorrear 01
piñonear 01
piolar 01
pipiar 07
pirar 01
pirarse 01
piratear 01
pirograbar 01
piropear 01
pirrar 01
piruetear 01
pisar 01
piscar 13
pisonear 01
pisotear 01
pispar 01
pistear 01
pitar 01
pitorrearse 01
piular 01
pivotar 01
pizcar 13
placar 13
placear 01
placer 61
plagar 19
plagiar 08
planchar 01
planear 01
planificar 13
plantar 01
plantarse 01
plantear 01
plantearse 01
plantificar 13
plantificarse 13
plañir 03
plasmar 01
plasmarse 01
plastificar 13
platear 01

platicar 13
platinar 01
plebiscitar 01
plegar 24
pleitear 01
plisar 01
plomar 01
plomear 01
plumear 01
pluralizar 16
poblar 28
poblarse 28
podar 01
poder 71
podrir 43
poetizar 16
polarizar 16
polarizarse 16
polemizar 16
polentear 01
polimerizar 16
polinizar 16
politiquear 01
politizar 16
politizarse 16
pollear 01
pololear 01
poltronear 01
polucionar 01
polvorear 01
pompearse 01
pomponearse 01
ponchar 01
poncharse 01
ponderar 01
poner 69
ponerse 69
pontear 01
pontificar 13
popularizar 16
popularizarse 16

pordiosear 01
porfiar 07
porfirizar 16
pormenorizar 16
portar 01
portarse 01
portear 01
posar 01
posarse 01
poseer 12
poseerse 12
posesionar 01
posibilitar 01
posicionarse 01
positivar 01
posponer 69
postergar 19
postinear 01
postrar 01
postrarse 01
postsincronizar 16
postular 01
potabilizar 16
potar 01
potenciar 08
potrear 01
practicar 13
prebendar 01
precalentar 22
precaucionarse 01
precautelar 01
precaver 02
precaverse 02
preceder 02
preceptuar 09
preciar 08
precintar 01
precipitar 01
precipitarse 01
precisar 01
preconcebir 39

preconizar 16
preconocer 46
predecir 74
predestinar 01
predeterminar 01
predicar 13
predisponer 69
predominar 01
preelegir 40
preestablecer 45
preestrenar 01
preexistir 03
prefabricar 13
preferir 55
prefigurar 01
prefijar 01
prefinir 03
preformar 01
pregonar 01
pregrabar 01
preguntar 01
preguntarse 01
prejubilar 01
prejubilarse 01
prejuzgar 19
preludiar 08
premeditar 01
premiar 08
premorir 57
prender 02
prenderse 02
prensar 01
prenunciar 08
preñar 01
preocupar 01
preocuparse 01
preparar 01
prepararse 01
preponderar 01
preponer 69
presagiar 08

prescribir 03
preseleccionar 01
presenciar 08
presentar 01
presentarse 01
presentir 55
preservar 01
presidir 03
presionar 01
prestar 01
prestigiar 08
presumir 03
presuponer 69
presupuestar 01
presurizar 16
pretender 02
pretensar 01
preterir 79
pretextar 01
prevalecer 45
prevaler 62
prevaricar 13
prevenir 73
prever 75
primar 01
primorear 01
principiar 08
pringar 19
pringarse 19
priorizar 16
privar 01
privatizar 16
privilegiar 08
probar 28
probarse 28
proceder 02
procesar 01
proclamar 01
proclamarse 01
procrear 01
procurar 01

procurarse 01
prodigar 19
prodigarse 19
producir 59
producirse 59
profanar 01
proferir 55
profesar 01
profesionalizar 16
profesionalizarse 16
profetizar 16
profundizar 16
programar 01
progresar 01
prohibir 03
prohijar 04
proletarizar 16
proliferar 01
prologar 19
prolongar 19
prolongarse 19
promediar 08
prometer 02
prometerse 02
promiscuar 10
promocionar 01
promocionarse 01
promover 35
promulgar 19
pronosticar 13
prontuariar 08
pronunciar 08
pronunciarse 08
propagar 19
propagarse 19
propalar 01
propasar 01
propasarse 01
propiciar 08
propinar 01
proponer 69

proponerse 69
proporcionar 01
propugnar 01
propulsar 01
prorratear 01
prorrogar 19
prorrumpir 03
proscribir 03
proseguir 41
prosificar 13
prospectar 01
prosperar 01
prosternarse 01
prostituir 52
prostituirse 52
protagonizar 16
proteger 17
protegerse 17
protestar 01
protocolar 01
protocolizar 16
proveer 12
providenciar 08
provocar 13
proyectar 01
proyectarse 01
prudenciarse 08
psicoanalizar 16
psicoanalizarse 16
publicar 13
publicarse 13
pudelar 01
pudrir 43
pudrirse 43
pujar 01
pulimentar 01
pulir 03
pulirse 03
pulsar 01
pulsear 01
pulular 01

pulverizar 16
puncionar 01
pungir 18
punir 03
puntear 01
puntualizar 16
puntuar 09
punzar 16
purgar 19
purgarse 19
purificar 13
purificarse 13
purpurar 01
purpurear 01
putear 01
puyar 01

Q

quebrajar 01
quebrantar 01
quebrantarse 01
quebrar 22
quebrarse 22
quedar 01
quedarse 01
quejarse 01
quemar 01
quemarse 01
queratinizarse 16
querellarse 01
querenciarse 08
querer 70
quererse 70
querochar 01
quimbar 01
quintaesenciar 08
quintar 01
quintuplicar 13
quintuplicarse 13
quitar 01
quitarse 01

bozar 16
bozarse 16
brincar 13
brotar 01
budiar 08
bufar 01
bujar 01
bujarse 01
bullir 03
bullirse 03
burujar 01
buscar 13
buznar 01
cabar 01
caer 49
calar 01
calcar 13
calcarse 13
calcitrar 01
calentar 22
calentarse 22
calificar 13
calzar 16
camar 01
cambiar 08
capacitar 01
capitular 01
cargar 19
catar 01
catarse 01
cauchutar 01
caudar 01
cebar 01
celar 01
centar 22
centarse 22
cepcionar 01
cetar 01
chazar 16
chiflar 01
chiflarse 01

rechinar 01
rechinarse 01
rechistar 01
recibir 03
recibirse 03
reciclar 01
recidivar 01
reciprocarse 13
recitar 01
reclamar 01
reclinar 01
reclinarse 01
recluir 52
recluirse 52
reclutar 01
recobrar 01
recobrarse 01
recocer 36
recocerse 36
recodar 01
recodarse 01
recoger 17
recogerse 17
recolar 28
recolectar 01
recolocar 13
recomendar 22
recomenzar 23
recomerse 02
recompensar 01
recomponer 69
recomprar 01
reconcentrar 01
reconcentrarse 01
reconciliar 08
reconciliarse 08
reconcomer 02
recondenar 01
reconducir 59
reconfigurar 01
reconfortar 01

reconocer 46
reconocerse 46
reconquistar 01
reconsiderar 01
reconstituir 52
reconstruir 52
recontar 28
reconvalecer 45
reconvenir 73
reconvertir 55
reconvertirse 55
recopilar 01
recordar 28
recordarse 28
recorrer 02
recortar 01
recortarse 01
recoser 02
recostar 28
recostarse 28
recovar 01
recrear 01
recrearse 01
recrecer 45
recrecerse 45
recriar 07
recriminar 01
recriminarse 01
recrudecer 45
rectificar 13
recuadrar 01
recubrir 03
recular 01
recuñar 01
recuperar 01
recuperarse 01
recurrir 03
recusar 01
redactar 01
redar 01
redargüir 53

renvalsar 01
reñir 39
reobrar 01
reordenar 01
reorganizar 16
reorientar 01
reorientarse 01
repacer 14
repagar 19
repampinflársela 01
repanchigarse 19
repanchingarse 19
repantigarse 19
repantingarse 19
repapilarse 01
reparar 01
repartir 03
repartirse 03
repasar 01
repatear 01
repatriar 07
repatriarse 07
repechar 01
repeinar 01
repelar 01
repeler 02
repelerse 02
repellar 01
repensar 22
repentizar 16
repercutir 03
repesar 01
repescar 13
repetir 39
repetirse 39
repicar 13
repintar 01
repintarse 01
repiquetear 01
replantar 01
replantear 01

replantearse 01
replegar 24
replegarse 24
replicar 13
replicarse 13
repoblar 28
repodar 01
repollar 01
reponer 69
reponerse 69
reportar 01
reportarse 01
reportear 01
reposar 01
repostar 01
reprender 02
represaliar 08
represar 01
representar 01
reprimir 03
reprimirse 03
reprivatizar 16
reprobar 28
reprochar 01
reprocharse 01
reproducir 59
reproducirse 59
reprogramar 01
reptar 01
republicanizar 16
republicanizarse 16
repudiar 08
repudrir 43
repudrirse 43
repugnar 01
repujar 01
repulgar 19
repulir 03
repulirse 03
repulsar 01
repuntar 01

repuntarse 01
repurgar 19
reputar 01
requebrar 22
requemar 01
requemarse 01
requerir 55
requerirse 55
requintar 01
requisar 01
resabiar 08
resabiarse 08
resacar 13
resalir 65
resallar 01
resaltar 01
resanar 01
resarcir 15
resbalar 01
resbalarse 01
rescaldar 01
rescatar 01
rescindir 03
resecar 13
resecarse 13
resellar 01
resembrar 22
resentirse 55
reseñar 01
reservar 01
reservarse 01
resfriar 07
resfriarse 07
resguardar 01
resguardarse 01
residenciar 08
residir 03
resignar 01
resignarse 01
resinar 01
resistir 03

revirarse 01
revisar 01
revistar 01
revitalizar 16
revivificar 13
revivir 03
revocar 13
revolcar 29
revolcarse 29
revolear 01
revolotear 01
revolucionar 01
revolver 35
revolverse 35
rezagar 19
rezagarse 19
rezar 16
rezongar 19
rezumar 01
ribetear 01
ridiculizar 16
rielar 01
rifar 01
rifarse 01
rilar 01
rimar 01
ripiar 08
ritmar 01
rizar 16
rizarse 16
robar 01
roblar 01
roblonar 01
robotizar 16
robustecer 45
robustecerse 45
rociar 07
rodar 28
rodear 01
rodearse 01
rodrigar 19

roer 50
roerse 50
rogar 30
rojear 01
rolar 01
romancear 01
romanizar 16
romper 02
romperse 02
roncar 13
roncear 01
rondar 01
ronear 01
ronquear 01
ronronear 01
ronzar 16
roscar 13
rostizar 16
rotar 01
rotarse 01
rotular 01
roturar 01
rozar 16
rozarse 16
rubificar 13
ruborizar 16
ruborizarse 16
rubricar 13
rufianear 01
rugir 18
rular 01
ruletear 01
rumbear 01
rumiar 08
rumorear 01
rumorearse 01
runrunearse 01
ruñar 01
ruralizar 16
ruralizarse 16
rusificar 13

rutilar 01

S

sabanear 01
saber 67
saberse 67
sablear 01
saborear 01
sabotear 01
sacar 13
sacarse 13
sacarificar 13
sachar 01
saciar 08
saciarse 08
sacralizar 16
sacramentar 01
sacrificar 13
sacrificarse 13
sacudir 03
sacudirse 03
saetear 01
sahornarse 01
sahumar 05
sahumarse 05
sainar 04
sainetear 01
sajar 01
salar 01
salariar 08
salcochar 01
saldar 01
salgar 19
salificar 13
salinizar 16
salinizarse 16
salir 65
salirse 65
salivar 01
salmear 01
salmodiar 08

singar 19
singlar 01
singularizar 16
sintetizar 16
sintonizar 16
sirgar 19
sirlar 01
sisar 01
sisear 01
sistematizar 16
sitiar 08
situar 09
situarse 09
soasar 01
sobajar 01
sobajear 01
sobar 01
soberanear 01
sobetear 01
sobornar 01
sobrar 01
sobrarse 01
sobrasar 01
sobreabundar 01
sobreactuar 09
sobrealimentar 01
sobrealimentarse 01
sobrealzar 16
sobreañadir 03
sobreasar 01
sobrecalentar 22
sobrecargar 19
sobrecargarse 19
sobrecoger 17
sobrecogerse 17
sobrecomprimir 03
sobrecurar 01
sobredimensionar 01
sobredorar 01
sobreedificar 13
sobreentender 26

sobrentender 26
sobreentenderse 26
sobrentenderse 26
sobreentrenar 01
sobreexceder 02
sobreexcitar 01
sobreexplotar 01
sobreexponer 69
sobregirar 01
sobrehilar 04
sobreimprimir 03
sobrellenar 01
sobrellevar 01
sobrenadar 01
sobrepasar 01
sobrepasarse 01
sobreponer 69
sobreponerse 69
sobreproteger 17
sobrepujar 01
sobresalir 65
sobresaltar 01
sobresaltarse 01
sobresanar 01
sobresaturar 01
sobrescribir 03
sobreseer 12
sobresellar 01
sobresembrar 22
sobresolar 28
sobreestimar 01
sobrestimar 01
sobrevalorar 01
sobrevenir 73
sobreverterse 26
sobrevestir 39
sobrevirar 01
sobrevivir 03
sobrevolar 28
sobrexceder 02
sobrexcitar 01

sobrexcitarse 01
socaliñar 01
socalzar 16
socarrar 01
socavar 01
socializar 16
socorrer 02
sodomizar 16
sofaldar 01
sofisticar 13
sofisticarse 13
soflamar 01
soflamarse 01
sofocar 13
sofocarse 13
sofreír 42
sofrenar 01
soguear 01
sojuzgar 19
solapar 01
solar 01
solazar 16
solazarse 16
soldar 28
soldarse 28
solear 01
solemnizar 16
soler 82
solevantar 01
solfear 01
solicitar 01
solidar 01
solidarizar 16
solidarizarse 16
solidificar 13
solidificarse 13
soliloquiar 08
soliviantar 01
soliviantarse 01
soliviar 08
sollamar 01

ollozar 16	sorber 02	subsidiar 08
oltar 28	sorberse 02	subsistir 03
oltarse 28	sorocharse 01	substanciar 08
olubilizar 16	sorprender 02	substantivar 01
olucionar 01	sorprenderse 02	substituir 52
olucionarse 01	sortear 01	substraer 60
olventar 01	sortearse 01	substraerse 60
omatizar 16	sosegar 24	subtender 26
ombrar 01	sosegarse 24	subtitular 01
ombrear 01	soslayar 01	subvalorar 01
ometer 02	sospechar 01	subvalorarse 01
ometerse 02	sostener 72	subvencionar 01
omorgujar 01	sostenerse 72	subvenir 73
omorgujarse 01	sotaventarse 01	subvertir 55
omormujar 01	soterrar 22	subyacer 48
omormujarse 01	sovietizar 16	subyugar 19
onar 28	sprintar 01	succionar 01
onarse 28	suavizar 16	suceder 02
ondar 01	suavizarse 16	sucumbir 03
onorizar 16	subalimentar 01	sudar 01
onreír 42	subalquilar 01	sufragar 19
onreírse 42	subarrendar 22	sufrir 03
onrojar 01	subastar 01	sugerir 55
onrojarse 01	subcontratar 01	sugestionar 01
onrosar 01	subdelegar 19	sugestionarse 01
onrosarse 01	subdividir 03	suicidarse 01
onrosear 01	subemplear 01	sujetar 01
onrosearse 01	subestimar 01	sujetarse 01
onsacar 13	subestimarse 01	sulfatar 01
onsear 01	subexponer 69	sulfatarse 01
oñar 28	subintrar 01	sulfurar 01
opapear 01	subir 03	sulfurarse 01
opar 01	subirse 03	sulfurizar 16
opear 01	sublevar 01	sumar 01
opesar 01	sublevarse 01	sumarse 01
opetear 01	sublimar 01	sumariar 08
oplar 01	subordinar 01	sumergir 18
oplarse 01	subrayar 01	sumergirse 18
oplonear 01	subrogar 19	suministrar 01
oportar 01	subsanar 01	sumir 03
oportarse 01	subseguir 41	supeditar 01

supeditarse 01
superabundar 01
superalimentar 01
superar 01
superarse 01
superoxidar 01
superponer 69
superponerse 69
supersaturar 01
supervalorar 01
supervenir 73
supervisar 01
supervivir 03
suplantar 01
suplicar 13
suplir 03
suponer 69
suponerse 69
suprimir 03
supurar 01
suputar 01
surcar 13
surfear 01
surgir 18
surtir 03
surtirse 03
suscitar 01
suscribir 03
suscribirse 03
suspender 02
suspirar 01
sustanciar 08
sustantivar 01
sustentar 01
sustentarse 01
sustituir 52
sustraer 60
susurrar 01
sutilizar 16
suturar 01

T

tabalear 01
tabalearse 01
tabellar 01
tabicar 13
tabicarse 13
tablear 01
tabletear 01
tabular 01
tacañear 01
tachar 01
tachonar 01
taconear 01
tafiletear 01
tajar 01
tajarse 01
taladrar 01
talar 01
tallar 01
tallecer 45
talonar 01
talonear 01
tambalear 01
tambalearse 01
tamborear 01
tamborilear 01
tamizar 16
tangar 19
tanguear 01
tantear 01
tañer 02
tapar 01
taparse 01
tapear 01
tapiar 08
tapiscar 13
tapizar 16
taponar 01
taquear 01
taquigrafiar 07
taracear 01

tarar 01
tararear 01
tarascar 13
tardar 01
tardecer 45
tarifar 01
tarificar 13
tarjar 01
tartajear 01
tartamudear 01
tasar 01
tascar 13
tasquear 01
tatuar 09
teatralizar 16
techar 01
teclear 01
tecnificar 13
tecnocratizar 16
tediar 08
tejar 01
tejer 02
teledirigir 18
telefonear 01
telegrafiar 07
teleguiar 07
teleprocesar 01
teletrabajar 01
teletransportar 01
televisar 01
temblar 22
temblequear 01
temer 02
temerse 02
temperar 01
temperarse 01
templar 01
templarse 01
temporalizar 16
temporizar 16
tender 26

transbordar 01	trasbordar 01	traspirar 01
transcender 02	trascender 26	trasplantar 01
transcodificar 13	trascodificar 13	trasponer 69
transcribir 03	trascolar 28	trasponerse 69
transcurrir 03	trasconejarse 01	trasportar 01
transferir 55	trascordarse 28	trasportarse 01
transfigurar 01	trascribir 03	trasquilar 01
transfigurarse 01	trascurrir 03	trastabillar 01
transformar 01	trasdosear 01	trastabillear 01
transformarse 01	trasegar 24	trastear 01
transfundir 03	trasferir 55	trastejar 01
transfundirse 03	trasfigurar 01	trastocar 13
transgredir 79	trasfigurarse 01	trastocarse 13
transigir 18	trasformar 01	trastornar 01
transistorizar 16	trasfundir 03	trastornarse 01
transitar 01	trasfundirse 03	trastrocar 29
translimitar 01	trasgredir 03	trasudar 01
transliterar 01	trasguear 01	trasuntar 01
translucir 47	trashumar 01	trasvasar 01
translucirse 47	trasladar 01	trasvasar 01
transmigrar 01	trasladarse 01	trasvenarse 01
transmitir 03	traslapar 01	trasver 75
transmitirse 03	traslucir 47	trasverberar 01
transmudar 01	traslucirse 47	trasverter 26
transmutar 01	traslumbrar 01	trasvinarse 01
transparentar 01	trasmigrar 01	trasvolar 28
transparentarse 01	trasminar 01	tratar 01
transpirar 01	trasmitir 03	tratarse 01
transponer 69	trasmontar 01	traumatizar 16
transponerse 69	trasmudar 01	traumatizarse 16
transportar 01	trasmutar 01	travesear 01
transportarse 01	trasnombrar 01	travestir 39
transvasar 01	trasoñar 28	travestirse 39
transverberar 01	traspalar 01	trazar 16
tranzar 16	traspalear 01	trazumar 01
trapacear 01	traspapelar 01	trechear 01
trapalear 01	traspapelarse 01	trefilar 01
trapear 01	trasparentar 01	tremolar 01
trapichear 01	trasparentarse 01	trencillar 01
trapisondear 01	traspasar 01	trenzar 16
traquetear 01	traspintarse 01	trenzarse 16

repanar 01
repar 01
repidar 01
resdoblar 01
riangular 01
riar 07
riarse 07
ributar 01
ricotar 01
rifurcarse 13
rillar 01
rinar 01
rincar 13
rincarse 13
rinchar 01
ripartir 03
ripear 01
riplicar 13
riplicarse 13
riptongar 19
ripular 01
risar 01
riscar 13
risecar 13
riturar 01
riunfar 01
rivializar 16
rizar 16
rocar 29
rocarse 29
rocear 01
rompear 01
rompearse 01
rompetear 01
rompicar 13
ronar 28
roncar 13
ronchar 01
roncharse 01
ronzar 16
ropezar 23

tropezarse 23
troquelar 01
trotar 01
trovar 01
trozar 16
trucar 13
trucidar 01
trufar 01
truhanear 01
truncar 13
truncarse 13
tuberculinizar 16
tuberculizar 16
tullir 03
tullirse 03
tumbar 01
tumbarse 01
tunantear 01
tunar 01
tundir 03
tunear 01
tupir 03
tupirse 03
turbar 01
turbarse 01
turboalimentar 01
turificar 13
turistear 01
turnar 01
turnarse 01
turrar 01
tusar 01
tutear 01
tutearse 01

U

ubicar 13
ubicarse 13
ufanarse 01
ulcerar 01
ultimar 01

ultrajar 01
ultrapasar 01
ulular 01
uncir 15
undular 01
ungir 18
unificar 13
uniformar 01
uniformizar 16
unir 03
unirse 03
unisonar 01
universalizar 16
untar 01
untarse 01
upar 01
uperisar 01
uperizar 16
urbanizar 16
urdir 03
urgir 18
usar 01
usarse 01
usucapir 03
usufructuar 09
usurpar 01
utilizar 16

V

vacacionar 01
vacar 13
vaciar 07
vaciarse 07
vacilar 01
vacunar 01
vacunarse 01
vadear 01
vagabundear 01
vagar 19
vaguear 01
vahear 01

valer 62
valerse 62
validar 01
vallar 01
valorar 01
valorizar 16
valorizarse 16
valsar 01
valuar 09
vaporizar 16
vaporizarse 16
vapulear 01
varar 01
vararse 01
varear 01
variar 07
vascularizar 16
vaticinar 01
vedar 01
vegetar 01
vejar 01
velar 01
velarse 01
velicar 13
vencer 14
vencerse 14
vendar 01
vendarse 01
vender 02
venderse 02
vendimiar 08
venerar 01
vengar 19
vengarse 19
venir 73
venirse 73
ventear 01
ventearse 01
ventilar 01
ventilarse 01
ventiscar 13

ventisquear 01
ventosear 01
ver 75
verse 75
veranear 01
verbalizar 16
verbalizarse 16
verdear 01
verdecer 45
verguear 01
verificar 13
verificarse 13
verilear 01
verraquear 01
versar 01
versificar 13
versionar 01
versionear 01
vertebrar 01
verter 26
vestir 39
vestirse 39
vetar 01
vetear 01
viabilizar 16
viajar 01
viaticar 13
viborear 01
vibrar 01
viciar 08
viciarse 08
victimar 01
victimizar 16
vidriar 08
vidriarse 08
vigilar 01
vigorar 01
vigorizar 16
vigorizarse 16
vilipendiar 08
vincular 01

vincularse 01
vindicar 13
vinificar 13
violar 01
violentar 01
violentarse 01
virar 01
virilizar 16
visar 01
visionar 01
visitar 01
visitarse 01
vislumbrar 01
vislumbrarse 01
visualizar 16
vitalizar 16
vitorear 01
vitrificar 13
vitrificarse 13
vitriolar 01
vituallar 01
vituperar 01
vivaquear 01
vivar 01
vivificar 13
vivir 03
viviseccionar 01
vocalizar 16
vocalizarse 16
vocear 01
vociferar 01
volar 28
volarse 28
volatilizar 16
volatilizarse 16
volcar 29
volcarse 29
volear 01
volitar 01
voltear 01
voltearse 01

Achevé d'imprimer par Mame Imprimeur à Tours
n° 07032016 - Dépôt légal Avril 2007